# THE
# PIN-UP
# GIRLS
# ★ OF ★
# WORLD WAR II

## BRETT KISER

Published in the USA by:
BearManor Media
PO Box 1129
Duncan, Oklahoma 73534-1129
*www.bearmanormedia.com*

ISBN 978-1-59393-274-9

Printed in the United States of America.
Book design by Brian Pearce | Red Jacket Press.

# TABLE of CONTENTS

*For my parents William and Barbara Kiser*
*And paternal grandparents James and Dolly Kiser*

# ACKNOWLEDGEMENTS

Thanks should initially be given to the folks at BearManor Media: Ben Ohmart, Sandy, and especially Michelle, for their guidance and helpful recommendations. I must also thank my uncle Harold Weislocher, a Navy veteran of World War II, for his "soft-serve ice cream story" found within these pages. I extend thanks to Sarah Reese — who, as a child, was introduced to pin-up girls who tenanted cigar boxes — for her assistance in locating a portraitist. Although no portraits were used in this work, I appreciate your effort nonetheless.

# PROLOGUE

Throughout time, man has been a great admirer of beauty. Admiration is also lavished upon those selfless individuals who make sacrifices for their country in time of need. In the annals of history, there has perhaps never been a more perfect combination of these two qualities that elicit admiration than the conception of pin-up art during World War II. The ladies who posed for the photographs made for the ideal model of physical assemblage, while the same ladies, in many cases, were also lauded for their character and national pride. Not only did they pose for photographs in bathing suits and short skirts but they also sold war bonds, entertained troops, and lifted the morale of a worried and weary world.

Societies often find it necessary to erect a form of remembrance to its many heroes, but such lasting veneration, for whatever reason, has failed to find the war-era pin-up girl. Our libraries and bookstores are not populated with the stories of World War II era pin-up girls, yet extensive ink has been used to retell nearly every facet of the Great War. We read biographies of famous generals and the battles they fought, and peruse detailed accounts of the engagements waged in the many volumes that cover the war, yet the pin-up girls, up until now, have been an aspect of war that historians and authors of America neglected. But the role of a pin-up girl was of no small importance, and it is my hope that this book will give the pin-up girl the respect she is due.

When I first decided to research this topic, I found a handful of books dedicated to war-era pin-up art, but not a single volume dedicated to the women who posed. The famous artists, like Vargas and Petty, can have their life story and art collections purchased in book format, but those ladies who inspired them were neglected by the author's pen. The war-era pin-up girl not only inspired the artist who captured her likeness but also the throngs of men in the armed forces — as well as civilians — who were in need of beautiful images capable of creating that needed escape from a world at war. Although such famous film actresses as Jean Harlow and Elizabeth Allan had posed for cameramen before the war, the celebrities who had their likeness photographed during the war years did so in order to uplift national morale. Despite their selfless actions, the pin-up girls received few accolades and fewer awards for their admirable deeds. It is the goal of this author to remedy the apathy directed toward the war-era pin-up girl.

My admiration for bygone beauty, coupled with my appreciation for those persons devoted to their country during World War II, served as the catalyst that led to this book's creation. Beauty is saluted within these pages, but more important is the salute given each respective lady for her selfless actions during a time of war. From Ramsay Ames to Marie Wilson, the lovely ladies detailed herein are worthy of a grand ovation. They were idols of countless soldiers stationed stateside and overseas, and they were kept within the breasts of American fighting men who coveted awareness of decency and beauty. The concept of pin-up art has evolved over the years, but during its widespread inception at the start of World War II, the glorification of the female form took a backseat to building morale among Uncle Sam's combat troops. This little book serves as my tribute to the celebrity women, those enchanting pin-up girls worthy of national adulation.

# INTRODUCTION

Every branch of the American military, from the Army to the Marines, adopted pin-up girls as a symbol of unification during World War II. The pin-up girl was not simply an object of lust, to be admired wantonly — even though such veneration was indeed lavished upon her — for she symbolized more than the embodiment of female perfection; she was the supreme unifier who served as a tie that bound troops together. As the supreme unifier she did more than corral platoons, for her role was wide-ranging, servicing each soldier on an individual basis. She may have been an actress or a model by vocation, but as a pin-up girl she was much more: she was the personification of all nature's beauty, represented in one single photograph. She was the lover left behind, the dream girl one desired to cradle, the mother who offered a tender embrace, and the sister whose pen kept their world alive; this lone vision of beauty was all the goodness that had vanished. The world was a realm of despair for the men in the armed forces, where all that was innocent, all that was agreeable, had been replaced by darkness. But by securing the image of a pin-up girl to their barracks wall, they reassured themselves that beauty still existed.

To claim that the pin-up girl craze that swept the nation during World War II was uncouth, decadent, and demeaned women would be a false assertion of the practice. Women were, most certainly, objectified by the practice — for only ladies of exceptional appeal were engaged as pin-up girls — with focus clearly on her physical assets. They were leggy, they were busty, they possessed the physical attributes men sought, and the stills that populated military bases proudly displayed the female image that soldiers found ideal. However, the photographs served not as images that elicited unbridled passion, where tethers that held men to the angels of better reason were severed, but served a nobler cause as representations of decency. The world, to the soldier engaged in combat, was a place devoid of benevolence, where countenances bore that sinister stare of the adversary. He needed a symbol that could vanquish evil — something decent, something beautiful. That image was found in the pin-up girl. The pin-up girl occupation was a noble one; no woman was demeaned and no entrance to wickedness or a diversion from morality was presented. The sounds of battle, the clamor of war, were absent when the pin-up girl was present.

While reading this book, one will be taken back in time to an era in American history regarded by many as more patriotic — more selfless. This analysis is not without merit, for young men enlisted in the military during World War II at a rate never seen before or since. They were devoted to their country, and they would often depart high school before a diploma was acquired in order to defend the shores of their beloved homeland. The welfare of the nation came before their individual pursuits. America in the 1940s may have been a simpler age, where electronics and technology were crude, but that sense of national pride was refined. They adored the Stars and Stripes, and employed her as an emblem of majesty and fought for her honor. America during the 1940s was a simpler age, but not an age of simple-mindedness. This book will honor those women who served as the image of hope during this tumultuous period, who didn't view their work as pin-up girls as tasteless and obscene, but as inspirational. These ladies are all worthy of our admiration for their support of the men who kept the flag flying while enemy nations longed to destroy it. Although gazed upon wantonly, and regarded as ideal physical specimens, the ladies detailed herein were worthy of an all-encompassing admiration for their role during a time of war.

# CHAPTER ONE

# THE ORIGIN
## ★ OF THE ★
# PIN-UP GIRL

To claim that the female influence in battle was first adopted during World War II would be erroneous; women have played a role in battle for centuries. Granted, they did not typically take up arms — although there are some rare occasions when they were engaged in war — but their role was one of support, which elevated the morale of the fighting man. This method of lending support reached its high point during the Second World War when beautiful women, typically actresses and models, lent their image to the boys in service. Servicemen would purchase such publications as *Yank* — the soldier's magazine — which proudly displayed centerfolds of lovely young women in seductive poses, typically adorned in bathing suits, which the boys would "pin-up" on their barracks walls. However, prior to World War II and before the age of the photographic lens, soldiers and fighting men didn't possess the luxury of hording an eight-by-ten image of their idol.

Before the advent of the photograph, a retentive mind was needed to summon up the portrait of a beauty from one's past. The picture is a constant reminder of that which has been separated from us, but before the picture, all the soldier had was his ability to conjure up the image of his heart's desire. Whether that desire was a woman from his homeland or any woman in general, the soldier had to rely on constructing the image of her, since the lens to capture her likeness had yet to be invented. This little foray that stimulated the imagination by conjuring up an image was not an endeavor that soldiers during World War II were forced to under-take. They could, thanks to the photographic lens, secure on their person any number of pictures of ladies loved and ladies pined for. They could locate a pin-up picture of a favored actress or pack the captured likeness of their high school sweetheart, and they could tote the image of their heart's desire on all their military travails. The photograph enabled men to envision their loved ones with greater ease than the ancient warrior who was forced to rely solely on his capacity to retain an image within his memory bank.

Securing photographs of women in seductive poses to pin-up on barracks walls may have been a unique practice during World War II, but the practice of employing the female figure as a source of battlefield inspiration was a time-honored concept. The study of ancient literature informs us that women have played a pivotal role in war. Ladies populated the famous tale from Homer, *The Iliad*, despite the fairer sex's absence from combat and the taking up of arms. In more of an auxiliary, inspirational capacity, women in *The Iliad* were lauded for their beauty, and those men of renowned fighting prowess could secure a beautiful woman through his battlefield accomplishments. Homer depicts women during this ancient period, as they were often viewed, as nothing more than war prizes — booty to be claimed by the victorious aggregation. Battles were staged, even amongst allies, for the hand of a lady. For confederates Achilles and Agamemnon quarreled over the beautiful Briseis, war prize of the legendary warrior Achilles, who had her removed from his chamber and placed in the quarters of his battlefield ally. The quarrel over a female war prize led to Achilles's refusal to participate in the Battle of Troy. The legendary warrior spurned his associate-in-arms for the wrong done to him — the removal of a female from his bed who he claimed during war.

Euripides gave the annals of literature its most famous play to detail the plight of women at war, with his epic piece, *Trojan Women*. The elderly feared enslavement while the youthful feared the violent, amorous clutches of victorious enemy soldiers. To be young and beautiful in this ancient era, as a maiden of a defeated nation, was to be subjected to the role of a concubine. They were forced to share a bed with a strange man from a strange land, whose views towards her people were hostile and whose views towards her were not the tender sentiments harbored by a lover, but the vehemence cradled by an adversary. She was a war prize — booty to be collected by the victorious party, and nothing more. The ladies in the play bemoaned their existence, for they knew what fate was soon to produce. Their homeland had fallen to the enemy and a grim existence awaited them all.

The history of women's role in war has taken many detours from the days of Homer to the modern era of women in fatigues who serve side-by-side their male compatriots. Once women were regarded as unfit for military service but now their gender populates the rank of many units in the United States armed forces. Well before women were allowed to join the major branches of the military their role was supportive, and most women served as bystanders who awaited the outcome of man's violent endeavors. But the outcome was not always ideal for the women. In the instance of Homer's *Iliad*, ladies were treated like possessions to be removed from their conquered homeland and displayed in the bedchambers of soldiers who comprised the victorious party. The fate of women by the men in service was not a concept that was lost on them — they understood fully the plight that awaited their wives, sisters, and daughters should they be defeated. The knowledge that a woman who captured your heart could soon be the bedmate of an enemy soldier was oftentimes all the inspiration a fighting man needed to subdue his adversary. But his adversary also possessed this knowledge, for the fate of his nation's women was much the same, and so he sought to keep his female loved ones pure from the tainted grasp of a hostile troop.

Women, as viewed by the Roman historian Tacitus, were eager to preserve in their fighting man's mind the image of what they fought to defend. While he studied the German people, Tacitus was impressed by the German women's wherewithal to inspire their fighting men, both before they marched off to war and when inspiration for a further assault was needed. In the same fashion that American soldiers were informed that they fought for American womanhood during WWII, the German women were informed, in fewer words but with no lesser imagery, that German womanhood was worth fighting to uphold. As the German battalions prepared to march to meet their enemy on the battlefield, the maidens would congregate and encourage their soldiers to perform at their uppermost, lest they should become prizes for the enemy. Their methods were simple, much like the methods employed by pin-up artists during World War II. Tacitus explained their inspirational technique when he wrote, "Tradition says that armies already wavering and giving way have been rallied by women who, with earnest entreaties and bosoms laid bare, have vividly represented the horrors of captivity, which the Germans fear with such extreme dread on behalf of their women, that the strongest tie by which a state can be bound is the being required to give, among the number of hostages, maidens of noble birth."

Perhaps the German ladies referenced in Tacitus's work, who inspired soldiers by the revelation of their bare breasts, were history's first pin-up girls, but the title would have to be loosely applied, for there was nothing for soldiers to *pin up*. Their methods were performed in haste, and if done premeditatedly, their actions were made of the same inspirational stuff as the pin-up girls of World War II. The ladies who posed for cheesecake pictures during the Second World War did so with the purpose of building morale among the fighting forces — the same motive employed by the breast-baring ancient Germans. However, the brief exhibition of an uncovered female torso, enchanting as it may be, was not a lasting image that the German soldiers could carry with them in a physical manifestation, for the image was retained in the mind and was minus a corporeal flavor. The inspiration the German soldiers felt, courtesy of the breast-revealing of their maidens, served simply as motivation for the present, while the soldiers of later generations, capable of carrying a photographed likeness of beauty, were able to review this likeness, thus garnering motivation for future forays. As the sands in the hourglass slowly sift to the bottom, with the grains delve the mind's capacity to retain fleeting images; for that which is witnessed is not always easily evoked.

In order for there to be a pin-up girl, there must first be a method to capture the likeness of the girl on some portable medium, whether it is a canvas, tablet, or photographic paper. Man has engaged himself in numerous artistic pursuits wherein he can laud the female image, from etchings on cave walls to the painting of cathedrals. However, for the concept of pin-up artwork, there must be a living model, a method to capture her likeness, and — of the uppermost importance — a manner in which that likeness can be transportable. In theory, pin-up pictures could have existed in ancient times, for soldiers had the means at their disposal to draw the image of a fair maiden on some article — perhaps a shield — that could have been situated in an elevated position for personal admiration. However, the pin-up girl — in the sense she has come to be known — was a woman who posed for a photograph or an artist's painting with the purpose of mass distributorship in mind, and she earned payment for her time, thus negating the role of a soldier's lover during ancient times as a professional pin-up girl. Her likeness was meant for the adulation of one man — not to be distributed in bulk to his comrades.

The two commonly accepted modes of capturing a pin-up girl's likeness are via the camera's lens and the artist's brush. The first person to create a photographic image is generally accepted to be Joseph Nicephore Niepce, who performed the feat in 1827. Artists had painted for hundreds of years prior to Niepce's invention, therefore rendering the medium of art a more obvious selection for giving history its first pin-up girl. However, the pin-up girl is not simply a model who poses for a painting — Mona

Lisa would never be considered among the rank of pin-up girls — but one who poses with the purpose of having her likeness circulated among an array of admirers, most notably soldiers in the armed forces. A painting that goes unduplicated does not serve a pin-up's function, for it remains nothing more than a piece of artwork to be displayed at one locale at a time. Only through duplication and mass distribution can a painter's work be regarded as pin-up art.

When a historian, professional or amateur, claims that pin-up artwork was first brought into being during World War II, their claim is made by disregarding the possibility of the practice during the First World War. The concept of securing photographs of lovely ladies on walls may have reached its crescendo during the 1940s when the Second World War was underway, but during the 1910s — the decade of the First World War — soldiers had the means at their disposal for this amusement as well. Before Alberto Vargas and George Petty enchanted men of the World War II era with their paintings of scantily-clad women with awe-inspiring anatomical construction, there was a painter by the name of Raphael Kirchner who performed the same trick for men of World War I. Kirchner's paintings were reproduced, although his works were paintings of beautiful ladies who he captured in postcard format. The Austrian artist painted portraits of women in provocative poses, typically dressed in undergarments, as they dressed in their chambers or brushed their hair in front of mirrors. These postcards were often found in the trenches of British and French soldiers during World War I, oftentimes secured in a soldier's pocket. But the ability to display them openly, like a pin-up photograph, was at their disposal, thus making the postcards of Kirchner widely regarded as the first legitimate display of pin-up artwork.

The first notable pin-up artists were Charles Dana Gibson and Kirchner, who, during their day, produced stills of lovely ladies for a wide audience. What restricted previous generations from engaging in the mass production of pin-up artwork was the simple concept of limited technology. Items were not reproduced on the scale they are today, for the crude instruments of bygone eras were not suitable for mass distributorship of many items. Only when man developed the wherewithal to produce artwork, literature, and other modes of written and drawn artistic works, could the pin-up industry truly thrive and reach its pinnacle and proper purpose. With the limited means to duplicate their paintings and postcards, both Gibson and Kirchner had their work exposed but only on a modest level. Only in later years — those prior to the Second World War — when magazines like *Esquire* were in circulation, could artists reach a mass audience. The legendary George Petty achieved his fame first as a pin-up artist under contract to *Esquire*, while Vargas and other artists followed his lead. Oftentimes Petty is credited with leading the rise of American pin-up artwork during the years before and during the war.

The pin-up phase reached its high-water mark during the war years, and the term "pin-up" is credited to have been first used during the Second World War. The practice of securing photographs to barracks walls and the inside of lockers was a habit that soldiers in the military engaged in, which enabled the term "pin-up" to be coined. From training camps to ships serving in hostile waters, troops under the employ of Uncle Sam secured photographs of lovely ladies wherever a thumbtack could be pushed through a surface. The practice was not a common one during previous wars; its eruption clearly originated during the period of World War II. C.E. Chidester claimed, "We don't remember that the pin-up girls figured much in World War I. Soldiers, of course, carried their pictures in their wallets, or Bibles or kits. Certainly historians have not recorded anything about pin-ups in the Civil or Revolutionary Wars. The fad seems, therefore, to be an exclusive product of World War II." Previous wars had their inspirational figures. Items found on the person of dead soldiers during the Civil War prove that many fought with loved ones on their mind — whether the proof was evident by crude photography or a soldier's journal — but photography was relatively in its infancy, therefore limiting the possibility for folks to be photographed, and thus limiting the soldier's ability to engage in the pin-up practice of securing his heart's desire in an open display.

Although the pin-up practice is widely regarded to have begun during World War II, the concept of photographing ladies in provocative poses originated much earlier. Before there was Hollywood, where motion pictures are churned out at an exceptional rate year after year, America's most notable form of gaudy entertainment was vaudeville. Vaudeville was a popular source of amusement before the age of motion pictures, and the industry was populated with performers of various backgrounds. Typically in skit format, performers on the vaudeville circuit would appear on stage and perform juggling acts, slapstick skits, impersonations, and song-and-dance routines. A very popular medium, many athletes, even the manager of the New York Giants, John McGraw — who was known for his serious, hot-headed demeanor on the ball diamond — would participate in vaudeville after the close of the baseball season. McGraw lost perhaps his finest position player to vaudeville; Mike Donlin — known as "Turkey Mike" because of the arrogant manner in which he strutted when he walked — found his calling with vaudeville actress Mabel Hite (later his wife.) Many ladies in the vaudeville circuit were regarded not as ladies at all but women of loose moral character. This stance didn't change over time as vaudeville had its stranglehold on entertainment usurped by motion pictures, which led many vaudeville performers toward the arena of burlesque.

If vaudeville was regarded as cheap and showy, than burlesque was a new detour towards decadence that the entertainment industry charted. Burlesque was the offshoot of vaudeville: it took the concept of vaudeville — skits acted out on stage — and added ribald comedy, excessive dancing, and the exhibition of nudity. Many of the legitimate actresses on vaudeville tried their hand at motion pictures — to include Hite, who went California way with her husband Donlin — while others, who possessed less acting talent but were no less physically appealing, steered a course toward burlesque. A great number of the prewar burlesque stars adopted the pin-up concept of World War I artist Raphael Kirchner, and they had photographs of themselves displayed on small postcards — like the images the Austrian artist was famous for painting a few decades prior. The leading burlesque stars like Gypsy Rose Lee would hand out these provocative postcards that displayed their scantily-clad images to patrons and would-be patrons. Burlesque stripteasers during the war, like Ann Corio and Sherry Britton, adopted Lee's provocatively-posed business cards and often sent hand signed cards to soldiers who pinned the five-by-sevens on walls at their installations.

Burlesque didn't have the market cornered on racy photography, for film studios in Hollywood followed the ways of the stage dames, and they lined up photo shoots for their new contract players prior to the war. The difference between the burlesque stills and the studio shots were a matter of distribution and attire. While the ladies who were employed in burlesque were willing and able to hand out professional postcards of themselves wearing next to nothing, censorship, which held a looser reign on burlesque than the film industry, kept the motion picture bigwigs from distributing their cheesecake stills of actresses. The well-fed studio executives often lined up bathing-suit shots of their actresses for no other purpose than to acquire a clearer image of the lady in question's structure. Such star actresses like Maureen O'Hara despised the practice and would not engage in such photography, but newcomers were forced to oblige lest they should lose their status as a contract player. Some of the young actresses who posed for these pointless cheesecake photos felt that it served little to no purpose. One such aspiring starlet was Lynn Bari. A writer, Wood Soanes, expressed her concern when he penned, "Little Miss Bari said she was willing to play ball with the publicity department at 20th-Fox but it seemed to her that the more leg art she posed for, the fewer good acting breaks she got." Shortly after Soanes's story hit, Lynn informed her studio that she would no longer pose for the bathing suit cheesecake photos, but once the war hit, and the pin-up craze

*Veronica Lake.* COURTESY OF MOVIEMARKET.COM

was underway, Miss Bari relaxed her stance — the photos finally had a purpose — and she became a top pin-up girl.

To claim that film studios prior to the war were sexist would not be an inaccurate estimation. When a newfound beauty was discovered, who had aspirations of a career in acting, her studio would parade her in front of a camera — for still photography — and photograph the young darling from every angle and in clothing that ranged from puffy period-piece costumes to form-fitting suits that women typically swam in. But not all men in Hollywood found the bathing-suit stills necessary. The legendary filmmaker Cecil B. DeMille never asked his actresses to pose for purposeless leg art. DeMille even went out of his way to make certain that his newfound talent would not be exploited by the typical Hollywood shark. When he signed the lovely Evelyn Keyes to a contract, DeMille trained her as an actress and forbid photographers to exploit her ingénue status by informing her that leg art photography was common practice in Hollywood. Although DeMille was protective of his young actresses, the studios were a male dominated workplace, and executives typically took advantage of a young aspiring starlet by thrusting her toward arenas whose paths were of no necessity for a career in acting.

Another favorite practice of studios was the arrangement of dates for new actresses. In order to promote a newly discovered beauty, studios would line up dates for their contract players with popular men, film stars, directors, and producers, so the lady could be spotted in public. When the wolf with a new lamb chop in his mitts was viewed out on the town, tabloid writers would inquire as to the new love interest's name. If dates weren't arranged, the studios suggested — in a less than coy fashion — that the newly signed actress might haunt the Hollywood night spots for publicity's sake. This endeavor erected the careers of sexpots Lana Turner and Ava Gardner, who seemed designed specifically to attend night clubs, while other studio players like Veronica Lake deplored the tactic. When Miss Lake was a fresh face in Hollywood, the married mother was pressured to frequent Hollywood dives, but the outspoken, opinionated blonde bomber wasn't keen on the notion of having wolves howl at her figure. She said, "I'm not going to go out and run around to a lot of nightclubs and other party places with a bunch of visiting firemen — just because some studio executive may think that's good business." Alexis Smith echoed her sentiments when she said, "I always figured that a reputation for hard work around the studio would be worth a hundred 'how-do-you-dos' in a night club." Miss Lake was adamant in her refusal to play social butterfly, and Alexis viewed dedication to her craft as more important, while the glitzy Hollywood nightlife defined the lifestyle of starlets like Turner and Gardner.

When photographers delved into the arena of cheesecake art at the outset of the war, they needed models to represent American beauty. The dames who populated burlesque were ready and eager to lend their forms to the shutterbugs, but those stripteasers who basked in the glitter and feather boas of the ecdysiast trade, appealing as they were, were little known to the world at large. They represented not the girls who soldiers left behind but the racy, sensuous broads who steamed the surroundings for a lone night. Soldiers enjoyed the provocative stills of the lightly clad burlesque strip artists, but what they really craved was photographs of lovely ladies who exuded a girl-next-door charm that the sexy thread-peelers of burlesque lacked. Women capable of representing these pined-for ladies populated the profession of acting. A good actress could depict the image of the girl who waits, even if her constitution was minus the pages of monogamy, for the trade of acting requires that the actress portray various characters — to include ladies of lust as well as ladies of trust.

Although the profession of acting was the occupational pursuit of many individuals from different backgrounds, the world at large typically viewed ladies with show business aspirations as women of loose moral fiber. Many parents didn't want their daughters to earn a living based on how sharp they looked while scantily clad, for the outlet of show business is one of exhibition, and this exhibition, when young ladies are the focus, often calls for the display of the figure. The array of origins in the acting profession allowed for women who looked less the part of the sultry stripteaser of burlesque and more the role of an ideal American lady, but the show business trade, whether it was stage work or film work, was viewed as an improper occupation for a respectable young woman. Audrey Totter, the great bad girl of film noir, told of how she had fallen in the favor of an old woman she visited while selling floor wax, when she informed the elderly lady of her aspirations for a career in acting. Miss Totter said about her encounter with the lady, "The old gal told me that I didn't look like a wicked woman, but she allowed as how you never can tell." Engaged as a door-to-door salesperson before her big break in acting, Audrey Totter put heels to the pavement to sell merchandise, but her ambition for a career in show business was off-putting to many persons, like the old lady who showed Audrey her door, who thought such dames were wicked.

The ideal pin-up girl was one who looked physically appealing while also exuding an allure that remained elevated from the cheap and tawdry.

This presented quite a problem, for women who were regarded as respectable by the populace did not pose for portraits wearing limited attire and glorifying their assemblage. The stripteasers of burlesque were regarded as lewd; therefore their ability to project that girl-next-door image was limited. Burlesque ladies were ill-equipped to represent the loves soldiers had waiting for them back home; film actresses were better suited for the part. Even if they were lewd and tawdry in person they could employ their acting faculties and depict a woman capable of transcending the cheap and vulgar. Many young actresses were eager to lend support to the troops, which mirrored their eagerness to gain a foothold in the film industry and, in turn, made them ideal candidates for cheesecake models.

One of the primary stereotypes of actresses, which instilled the lewd reputation of the profession, was that actresses would do anything to further their career. The dominant view of an actress was that of a woman hampered by an uncontrolled avarice, and who disregarded her principles for the stardom that Hollywood provided. However, many young women with show business aspirations were not the wicked dames who many in the public imagined; this sentiment was driven by tabloid writers who detailed the amorous escapades of such female stars as Lana Turner, Ava Gardner, and model Chili Williams — but they were simply ladies looking to satiate their drive for creativity. Many young ladies who entered the arena of show business understood the stigma that surrounded the profession — given the tell-all exploits of such dames as Turner and Company — and kept their desires a secret. When pretty and proper Constance Dowling decided to embark on a career in show business, the lovely blonde landed a gig as a chorus girl at the swinging Paradise Night Club in New York. Young Constance knew that her folks would disapprove of the endeavor, so she informed her mother that she had gained employment as a telephone operator. The aspiring young actress kept up the charade as long as she could, which led to her discovery by studio talent scouts.

Actresses were branded with unfair stereotypes. Not every young female film player was willing to cavort her way to a lead movie role. But if the gals were hampered by unfair stereotypes, the industry of show business was more heavily marked by negative sentiments than any actor who ever earned a dime. Wolves populated show business and often took advantage of young aspiring actors and actresses looking for their big break. The needless scantily-clad photo shoots that studios arranged for their young female players have been well documented. They were not manufactured for the sake of building morale in fighting men but simply to massage the curiosity that executives harbored for the shape of their lovely contracted actresses. But the film industry was not alone in this regard. When Joan Caulfield first embarked on her acting career, she landed a role in a university play that called for minimal attire. Joan had grown up as a modest girl in East Orange whose naiveté was exploited by theater hound dogs. In her first play, Joan's wardrobe consisted of a skimpy black bra and panties ensemble, which the wide-eyed beauty donned for the sake of another's art. With her mother in attendance, Joan felt uncomfortable but acted in the undergarments throughout the play regardless. About her first brush with acting, Miss Caulfield said, "My mother all but fainted. Then she practically fainted again when I started my lines. They were decidedly off-color. And believe me, I was partly confused myself. Even I didn't know what some of them meant. I was so dumb, in fact, that the stage manager gave me a large key to keep for him and said it was the key to the curtain and I believed him."

Proper ladies like Miss Dowling and Caulfield became popular actresses, transcending their origins in show business as nothing more than alluring images for the eye. But as images for the eye, actresses became the favorite subject for pin-up art by both the photographers taking the pictures and the soldiers pinning them up. The outset of America's involvement during World War II coincided with pin-up artwork's firm establishment. What enabled pin-up art to flourish wasn't simply the knack soldiers had for admiring beauty by thumb-tacking photographs to walls but by the role actresses played in popularizing the practice. No longer was the realm of posing seductively for cheesecake stills resigned solely for the pocket of burlesque, whose stars went unseen by most Americans. It became a pastime that ensnared actresses of the film industry whose talents were known across the world via the medium of motion pictures. By employing ladies who audiences were familiar with, rather than the dames who populated the narrow world of burlesque, the practice of pin-up photography exploded as gents were able to spy their favorite film darlings in seductive poses. No longer were the pin-up beauties nameless dames with well-constructed contours, they were stars of the screen. That stardom gave rise to pin-up artwork and laid the foundation for its role as an American institution.

# CHAPTER TWO

# THE RISE
## ★ OF THE ★
# PIN-UP GIRL

Soldiers of earlier generations, before the era of World War II, were no less admirers of beauty than the troops who engaged in the practice of pinning up cheesecake photographs during the 1940s. The fighting men prior to the Second World War, if they possessed a photograph, typically carried images of loved ones rather than popular actresses of the time. The perfected mode of relaying images via the motion picture camera was absent in the decades that preceded WWII. Only when cheesecake photography broadened — or was allowed to broaden by the censors — did the pin-up girl craze fully envelope American popular culture. Photographs of famed film starlets became easily acquired, as the racy swimsuit pictures were no longer resigned for the well-fed studio executives to stew over. The rise of pin-up photography was due in large part to the expansion that led to film actresses providing the cheesecake. And with the rise of pin-up artwork came the rise of the pin-up girl.

With a world at war, many citizens who had occupied themselves up until the fighting with common trades had become soldiers to defend their country and way of life. The man who delivered milk to your doorstep yesterday could very well depart for basic training the following morning. Occupational certainty had become a thing of the past; for those persons not engaged in employment crucial to the war effort were targets for the draft. However, the draft may have called numerous men and ushered them into the military ranks, but many men of the 1940s were more fit for the title of "man," and waited not for the come hither sign from Uncle Sam's draft boards, but enlisted in their preferred branch of the service. They understood that should they leave the safety of their country to a small population of professional soldiers, the concept of security — whether it be occupational or otherwise — would be nonexistent. So the lives they had led before the fighting as milkmen, firemen, grocery store clerks, farmers, etc. were willfully abandoned for the assignment of defending their country. The men who entered service removed themselves from the common routines of mankind and entered an arena where they were able to answer the harms perpetrated on their homeland.

There was nothing typical about the soldier of World War II. When a man attended basic training to become a soldier, he was introduced to fellows of various walks of life and from a broad age range. The eighteen-year-old recent high school graduate could train alongside a twenty-seven-year-old former garbage man, or, in more newsworthy cases, a young baseball phenom like Bob Feller or Ted Williams. The life of a young American man was anything but stable during the war years, for today's pursuit and tomorrow's goals could be altered by a simple draft notice or by the answering of that keen sense of national duty many men of the time possessed. They knew that, at any moment, their country could employ their service and that their world of order and routine would be lost for the duration, substituted by an alternate reality where war was the day's chief pursuit. This shake-up of reality enabled the pin-up girl craze to sweep the nation, for soldiers who had departed their usual surroundings and cloaked themselves in military customs found it easy, removed from the typical, to accept unattainable beauty as symbols of their heart's longing. Enemy forces had replaced peacetime activities as the mind's focus, and those common aspects of life, those things attained before the war, seemed almost lusterless in this new alternate reality where bullets flew and tanks traversed. The war enabled men, who sojourned through military avenues under a certain haze of unreality, the wherewithal to view pin-up girls as not dream girls but the image of the gal they would pursue upon their homeward journey.

Given that the men in service came from many diverse backgrounds, with a bulk of the servicemen drafted into service, Americans took a keen interest in the daily life of the soldiers. No longer were the armed forces populated with men whose occupational pursuit was strictly military; after the bombing on Pearl Harbor, brothers, cousins, neighbors, and friends were now dressed in the uniforms of Uncle Sam's fighting forces. These men were not career soldiers who enlisted in the armed forces with the focus of soldiering but were a collection of fellows who, although from different backgrounds with various prewar occupations, were made of the same patriotic stuff needed for the defense of a nation. These selfless men became national heroes — men worthy of admiration — and every American worthy of the title of *American* sought to support them any way they could. This support came in many forms ranging from businesses offering military discounts to entertainment shows headlined by celebrities. But those shapely ladies of the screen found a way to lend support that stimulated the aesthetic-response mechanisms in man.

The pin-up craze was promoted by the soldiers. They admired the girls who lent their figures to the cameras and allowed their shapely shapes preserved by the shutterbugs, and those photographs were then distributed to their ardent admirers. Soldiers did not let their admiration go unnoticed. A common practice among men in the air forces was the artistic pursuit which became known as "nose art." This little hobby had nothing to do whatsoever with extolling a pin-up girl's nasal instrument: the nose in question was found on the servicemen's aircraft. Men in uniform who possessed a talent for painting would decorate the headmost portion of their airliner by frescoing a portrait of a pin-up girl on its surface. It was not uncommon during the war to see a plane with a seductively posed Betty Grable likeness cruising through the air alongside another aircraft boasting an effigy of the busty Jane Russell as nose art. These paintings served as rallying symbols which kept the gents in the armed forces ever mindful of the beauty left behind who they swore to protect.

Pin-up girls were exhibited in many modes during the early part of the war. Soldiers painted a pin-up girl's likeness wherever anything large enough to serve as a canvas was spotted. They christened their planes after pin-ups by plastering a seductively posed portrait of the plane's namesake upon the craft's nose. The popularity of the pin-up girls, however, expanded beyond the fenced-in installations of Uncle Sam's fighting forces and flooded American popular culture. Many of the day's magazines printed pin-up pictures while numerous businesses, adhering to social trends, employed pin-up girls as spokespersons to interest patrons. Such lovely pin-up girls as Paulette Goddard and Linda Darnell were seen in printed advertisements for the popular soft drink Royal Crown Cola. The beverage company produced many ads in newspapers with various photographs of featured pin-ups, tilting back a bottle of Royal Crown with servicemen at their canteens. It seemed that a person couldn't unfold the daily ink without spotting a pin-up girl smiling at him in the pages, promoting some item to be purchased. Although pin-up girls were quick to populate the American scene, many accepted the girls because most Americans were eager to lend support to the troops. The pretty, shapely actress and model could show her support simply by exuding a fetching appearance.

Hollywood escalated the rise of the pin-up girl; the film industry was overflowing with pulchritude, which made the field a perfect supplier of cheesecake models. The film industry showed their support for the troops by producing war-themed films that glorified the heroism of soldiers, while also employing their pretty starlets as pin-up models. In stark contrast to modern day Hollywood, 1940s Tinseltown was a staunch supporter of the war effort. Studios produced patriotic films on a regular basis, sent their leading stars out to entertain troops, and — perhaps most importantly to the men serving overseas — lined up photo shoots for their female stars so the troops away from home could marvel at an American beauty, even if the object of affection was simply a photographic image.

The war shook up the film industry as stars like Laurence Olivier and his bride Vivien Leigh, star of the classic *Gone With the Wind*, left Hollywood and returned to London to offer morale support. Leigh's costar in the epic flick, Clark Gable, surrendered his cushy Tinseltown trappings for the life of a soldier. The master of the macabre, Vincent Price, who was rejected for military service on medical grounds, nevertheless donated blood to be shipped overseas because he wanted a little part of himself engaged in the war effort. Hollywood was well represented in the military ranks with such stars and future stars as Ernest Borgnine, Audie Murphy, George C. Scott, and Jimmy Stewart in the armed forces, to name but a few. And the ladies, those lovely gals who posed before the camera, both for motion pictures and cheesecake purposes, did their bit for the country. Such ladies as Sheila Ryan, Carole Landis, and Myrna Loy assisted in the war effort under auxiliary roles. Ryan and Loy taught first aid classes while Landis was employed for a time as a finger printer for the FBI. Due to the supporting roles the pin-up girls of Hollywood were engaged in, the American populace embraced them despite the stigma of lewdness that surrounded scantily clad photography.

Censorship at the time of the war kept America under an umbrella of decency. Burlesque may have thrived on the east coast, but across the American expanse many folks were unaware of the decadence that surrounded the trade. Motion pictures were perused by censors before distribution, which meant that the most shocking elements that were passed via the film medium were courtesy of the lips and manners of Mae West and the double meaning of the Marx Brothers' speech. Audiences laughed as Harpo Marx chased girls and posted pin-ups of full-figured majorettes, but the antics were simply those that massaged the funny bone and ventured softly through the realm of bad taste. It took a world at war for censors to soften their stance on what was socially acceptable. Soldiers were informed that they were fighting for American womanhood but were restricted from seeing that which they took up arms to defend. Pin-up photography served as a catalyst to lessen those restrictions.

The censors — namely the Hays Office, which established a moral code that Hollywood studios had to adhere to — came under pressure during the early part of the war years. American soldiers stationed stateside and overseas had adopted the practice of pinning up photographs of women on their bunk walls as their favorite military pastime. These photographs, cheesecake by nature, displayed pin-up girls in provocative poses and limited attire, which made folks engaged in the profession of censorship take exception to the practice. What was deemed a sexist enterprise by some was seen as a way for American troops to rekindle that flame for the American girl who went unattended to while he was in the military. No one at the time of the war — including the Hays Office — wanted to be seen as an agent of restriction for the troops, so the guidelines of decency began to waver. The boys could have their pin-ups, but the movies still had to be monitored. But folks in the film industry, like comedic starlet Marie Wilson, championed looser restrictions on films when she famously asked, "Our boys are fighting for American womanhood — why can't they see what they're fighting for?"

The most famous case study of censorship during the war was a film endeavor from the legendary Howard Hughes. The lead female starlet for his western *The Outlaw* was the brunette beauty Jane Russell, who when described physically is often chronicled under the heading of full-busted actresses. An unknown to filmgoers, Jane's popularity was nearly unrivalled among the servicemen who devoured her racy pin-up photographs. Miss Russell's physical appeal was unquestioned but her acting ability remained unascertained. Her first feature film, *The Outlaw*, had run into a snag with the Hays Office on account of Jane's wardrobe. Her revealing threads were approved for the pin-up photographs popular among the fighting men but not for the American masses. She exuded a voluptuous, lusty image in her pin-ups, and admirers were eager to learn whether that translated to the screen. Russell's debut film was held up for several years, but the busty brunette was nevertheless catapulted into stardom due to the media frenzy that followed Hughes's issues with the Hays Office. By shelving the film, the Hays Office was instrumental in the ascension of pin-up photography, for the servicemen's favorite busty pin-up was prohibited from acting due to clothes that displayed plenty of cleavage. Interest arose among the average American regarding Jane

Russell, the pin-up girl of the haystacks, whose trials with the censors were well documented — she became the face and figure for a relaxation of moral codes.

There was no extra ingredient needed for pin-up picture's acceptance among the servicemen — the image was all they needed. Cheesecake stills were popular among the servicemen who found in the photographs symbols of Americana worth fighting for. But the average American, the civilian, and the female who posed not for pin-up purposes, needed a little assistance in order to accept the pin-up practice. The gals were admired by the men in the armed forces simply for their allure, but the pin-up girls had to expand their arsenal of appeal to corral those individuals who were not impressed with cheesecake photography. To their credit, they did just that by exuding an admirable level of patriotism. The ladies became vocal supporters of the war by headlining war-bond rallies, entertaining troops at their bases, and lending their time to Uncle Sam in various capacities. The majority of the pin-up girls had a sense of duty that wasn't dwarfed by the men in the armed forces, despite their inability to fight alongside them. This sense of duty endeared them to the American public.

Shortly after America's involvement in the war, many celebrities found that they could support the war effort by raising funds for the war department. A number of male leads ventured off to the military ranks, which left Hollywood hampered by a loss of male stars, but those unable to serve or not yet drafted found they could be of assistance by selling war bonds. Studios would line up war-bond rallies, oftentimes at the behest of a film player who desired to headline the rally. Several of the top female stars in Hollywood became war bond sensations, and they raised sizable amounts of money to be used by the military to thwart the nefarious plans of the Axis. Recognizable glamorous pin-up girls such as Marlene Dietrich, Paulette Goddard, and Dorothy Lamour saw their names reach the papers because scribes of the daily ink lauded their fundraising actions for the war effort. Dietrich was awarded a citation from the treasury department as the nation's leading seller of war bonds in 1942, while Dottie Lamour raised over $52 million in war bonds during one northeastern tour. Due to Lamour's success as a seller of war bonds, the town of Portsmouth, New Hampshire, set up a "Dorothy Lamour Day" in the fall of 1942, where money spent in Portsmouth stores went to war bonds.

There were many critics of pin-up girls — those who viewed the ladies who posed for the cheesecake stills as indecent, shameless dames — but that criticism began to wear off thanks in large part to the pin-up girl's dedication to the troops and the country. When they made headlines for their war bond success, the many models and actresses, envied by countless women for their fame and figures, suddenly became accepted courtesy of their patriotism. By traveling the nation and selling war bonds to gatherings both large and small, the girls who posed provocatively for the admiration of soldiers suddenly lost the lewdness label and became symbols of American womanhood. Such a lady was Paulette Goddard (best known as Charlie Chaplin's wife at the time) whose star status had yet to be secured before the war. Miss Goddard gained respect by devoting her time to war-bond rallies early in the war effort. In a war-bond tour through Delaware County, Pennsylvania, Paulette raised over $750,000. Not only did the lovely pin-up girl sell war bonds, but she met with the people, the war plant workers, and handed out miniature flags to workers at the Sun Shipbuilding and Dry Dock Company as appreciation for their patriotism.

America's Sweetheart, Ginger Rogers — the leggy blonde famous for her song-and-dance numbers opposite Fred Astaire — joined the war-bond circuit and gave the rallies she attended a little Ginger twist. The dancing darling was not content by merely selling bonds: she wanted to make her stops memorable. In selfless fashion, the film starlet would often load her trunk with various personal articles that she would auction off at rallies. Although she would put forth her own possessions, such as dancing shoes, bracelets, gloves, and earrings, no money found her pocket: the funds were instead donated to the war department through bonds. At a war-bond rally in Tucson, Arizona, Ginger auctioned off a kiss for a $1,000 bond. Fellow fair-haired film starlet Greer Garson used the war-bond rally as a stage to offer patriotic speeches, which detailed the sacrifices needed to ensure victory. During a war-bond rally held at Laidley Field, Greer informed the attendees that "There is no one who can't help in some way. The harder we all give, the quicker it will be over." Miss Garson headlined her own war-bond tour titled "The Greer Garson Victory Bond Rally," and gave her patriotic speeches under the auspices of "The War Bond Cavalcade," which teamed her with other celebrities like Lucille Ball, James Cagney, Judy Garland, and Harpo Marx.

When a pin-up girl was a relative unknown to the public, a way she could build name recognition was to join a known star who headlined a war-bond rally. Many ladies traveled with the tireless Bob Hope in order for exposure, to both entertain crowds and further their acting career. The soldiers who stared at their curvaceous contours while pinned up in their bunks knew their names, but since many were ingénues in Hollywood and were not yet established stars, these unknown beauties sought exposure they couldn't get via the cheesecake route. One such aspiring actress was Frances Gifford, a hit among the servicemen for her pin-up pictures, but an unknown to the film-going public. When the opportunity to travel with film star Martha O'Driscoll was presented, Miss Gifford leapt at the chance. Spotted by film producer Samuel Goldwyn in a chance encounter the day before she was set to start her collegiate career, Frances instead signed a studio contract. Although Goldwyn knew who she was, her beginner status in Hollywood during the war kept her name in the obscure ranks until she ventured out on the war-bond circuit with Miss O'Driscoll. When war bond gatherers spotted the stunning dark-haired beauty, they understood the fuss soldiers made in regard to one of their favorite cheesecake girls. After the rally, Frances landed a film role and gained respect as an actress with her role in the western, *American Empire*.

War-bond rallies were an easy way for pin-up girls to display a level of patriotism. They would travel to various parts of the United States and give the assembled gathering the war department sales pitch. Exceptional salespersons, the glamorous gals were ideal for the task — to refuse a lovely lady was a struggle for many men. Millions of dollars were acquired by pin-up girls for the war effort, and when the American citizens saw the staggering sums they accumulated, the ladies gained a level of respect not given cheesecake models of other generations. The pin-up girls were known to plant kisses on the cheeks of males who bought sizable war bonds, and many, like Ginger Rogers, would playfully auction off a kiss to the highest bidder. Studios often urged their new contract players to attend war-bond rallies in order for American audiences to spot a new beauty they might desire to watch onscreen. The rise of the pin-up girl meant that many studios were busy signing up pretty young girls in order to supply the servicemen with new slices of cheesecake. Dee Lowrance wrote, "Never before have attractive young misses — with or without movie experience — found themselves so much in demand. Every studio is stocking up on them." And when the studios stockpiled lovely ladies, the promotion of their new finds during time of war was an easier task than at peacetime. All a studio had to do was urge their new ingénue toward a war-bond tour and watch as her star started to shine.

All avenues of popular culture eventually become trampled under the feet of countless followers, and a shift is soon in the making. The pin-up girls received plenty of accolades for their war-bond rallies — newspapermen lauded their fundraising capabilities and desire to entertain crowds — but many of the beauties wanted to separate themselves from the common flow of selling bonds. The war-bond rallies became passé, for it seemed that every entertainer had been on a rally or twenty. The cheesecake darlings sought to show their support for both the troops and their country in many forms. Many pin-up girls wanted to prove that posing before a camera and raising funds for the war department was not the extent of their capabilities. When Jinx Falkenburg, the top cover girl among American models, heard a plea via the airwaves from the War Manpower Commission for tomato pickers to harvest the southern California crop, she and chum Evelyn Keyes — fellow pin-up girl and up-and-coming actress — assisted in order to save the crop. The stunning pair used their star status the following day to appeal for 500 more pickers. The two ladies painted their thumbs green for a few days to keep the tomato crop from spoiling on the vine.

The pin-up girls' elevation in social status coincided with their wartime endeavors. Many of the girls were not content to act and model during the war years, for the world had entered a harsh reality where the occupation of playacting seemed mundane. Men and women were being killed by the thousands in Europe thus rendering the pursuit of entering a false world of make-believe an endeavor best suited for little minds. Many of the pin-up girls, the most popular among the American populace, were the lovely ladies seen on the screen, but during the war years these ladies didn't idle away their time with parties and paparazzi-dodging. Such established stars like Joan Bennett and Hedy Lamarr volunteered many hours at Hollywood Canteens — places where servicemen could unwind after training and dance with a girl or two. Joan Bennett, she of unrivalled grace and elegance, took it upon herself to furnish many canteens on the west coast with funds straight from her pocket. Miss Bennett not only furnished canteens but she was also a fixture at the handful of soldier-spots she helped develop. A tireless, grounded woman, despite her status as a leading film star, Joan Bennett would divide her time between acting, entertaining troops, and raising a teenage daughter. Not the type to erect a pedestal for herself, Joan didn't shirk wartime chores as tasks beneath a glamorous actress, which was evident by her many appearances in canteen kitchens washing dishes.

While Joan Bennett was busy washing dishes and maintaining west coast canteens, other actresses and models kept busy in their *off hours* by assisting in occupational capacities. Carole Landis, whose body was the envy of every woman in Filmdom, possessed enough glamour for eight women, but that didn't stop the shapely blonde from helping in the war effort. Early in the war, before she made headlines with her trips to the fighting lines, Miss Landis joined the Aerial Nurse Corps of America. Her duties with the Nurse Corps entailed the instruction of nursing students on the proper technique of folding and applying bandages. Like Joan Bennett, Carole was also a regular face at the west coast canteens, but the girl who would become known as "The Morale Builder" accepted an assignment from the FBI to fingerprint individuals working at various airplane factories. Security of the nation was of utmost importance and the lovely Miss Landis helped in this regard by assisting in the background checks of war plant workers. Espionage was a common fear among plant managers, and Carole's fingerprinting assignment served to deter terrorists from attacking through the channels of construction.

While Carole Landis was fingerprinting war plant workers, dark-haired model Eve Whitney, whose pin-up pictures were some of the most provocative, kept busy while removed from the shutterbugs by driving an air raid ambulance. Actress Vera Zorina, whose streamlined figure earned her the nickname "Vera of the Long Legs," was employed by the American Theater Wing War Production, which kept her busy operating an elevator when she wasn't acting. Sheila Ryan and the star Myrna Loy, who gained fame for her role in *The Thin Man*, held down pivotal roles in the Red Cross as instructors of first aid classes. The women of the motion picture industry, as well as those lovely gals of the modeling profession, made headlines in the nation's papers for devoting their time to the war effort. Although they were recipients of envy for their uncommon pulchritude, these ladies gained a level of respect based not off their looks but on their merits and selfless actions. Pin-up artistry became tolerated by many who viewed the practice as obscene, based largely on the patriotic actions of the aforementioned women.

During the Second World War, it was common practice among Americans to place the best interests of the country above personal pursuits. Many individuals placed their dreams and desires on hold in order to topple the evil that had diseased the world at this time. What was best for the person was of little importance when it came to the welfare of the country. The pin-up girls conveyed this message in a number of ways. Granted, the pulchritudinous dames were restricted from many military activities, which hindered their wherewithal to defend liberty, but their tasks were of no minor importance. They could display, by a number of methods, their support for the country and did so to show their fellow countrymen they were more than just appealing bodies. Actress Olivia De Havilland, who was born overseas in Tokyo, stated that she hoped her birthplace would be bombed as retaliation for the attack on Pearl Harbor. Newspaperman William C. Payette interviewed Miss De Havilland when she made the statement, and he titled the article, "Olivia De Havilland

Wants Her Hometown Bombed." Such a headline would seem shocking, but the foreign-born De Havilland proved her devotion to her country with the suggestion of Tokyo as a target for allied bombs.

Sacrifices were made daily during the war years. While men left behind families and jobs to defend the country, the women — who were forced to live on tighter incomes since their husbands earned smaller wages from Uncle Sam — had to manage budgets with a nod to frugality. It was uncouth for a woman to spend excessively on gaudy clothing and flashy accessories because Uncle Sam required many materials to construct items for the war effort. The lady prudent with her purse strings was more admired than the society dame who flaunted her wealth. Actress Vivian Austin showed ladies how they could make new dresses for themselves in the rationing days of World War II. Miss Austin altered her husband's old suits, and transformed the threads her spouse no longer wore into outfits for herself. Vivian even wore a few of these tailored ensembles in a couple of her films. Film star Michèle Morgan — a relocated actress born in Europe — wanted to impress her soldier husband with her skills in economic planning while he was away. She said, "I'm trying to do everything economically and I want to finish the house on a budget and then show my husband. With this war that we have to win — I want him to be proud of me as a planner."

Women left behind were expected to manage the household, but when it came to beautiful pin-up girls, expectations weren't as clearly defined. Their task was to look appealing for the boys in service — their management of affairs was of lesser importance to the servicemen who delighted in their photographs. Despite their hazy expectations, many pin-up girls were just as sacrificial as the gents who surrendered their prewar lifestyle for the chores of a soldier. Australian actress Betty Bryant, one of the top pin-up girls from Down Under, quit acting during the war to devote her time to the entertainment of troops at military bases. Perhaps the most impressive display of sacrifice made by the ladies of the film industry were the actions of bedroom-eyed Ann Dvorak. While stars such as Marlene Dietrich and Carole Landis were near the frontlines entertaining troops, Miss Dvorak worked in war-ravaged Britain as an ambulance driver and volunteer for the Women's Land Army. The American-born actress, married to a British film director, performed skits and acted in plays with little more than rubble serving as stage props. Ann carried a gas mask to and from the bombed-out Denham Studio where she acted in plays for the enjoyment of the Blitz-ravaged British. After three years in a foreign land — her husband's home country — Miss Dvorak was set to return stateside, but when she was informed that the Army production of *The Eve of St. Mark* — put on free of charge for the benefit of the troops — was due to be disbanded because the lead actress was ill, Ann changed her itinerary and single-handedly saved one of the few plays British troops could view. Had she not agreed to perform in the play it would have been dropped for the duration.

The greatest sacrifice an American individual can make during a time of war is the separation from family to defend the American way of life. The son, the husband, the father, all were needed during the Second World War to defeat the Axis, while the ones they held dear waited for their return back home. Pin-up girls were the ideal figures to represent American womanhood; they were women of uncommon beauty but were, nonetheless, women with common tribulations and struggles that the average woman could identify with. A number of the popular pin-up girls had husbands, and like the average young American wife, had to bid adieu to her betrothed once he was ushered into the armed forces.

When the popularity of pin-up art approached its zenith, studios took full advantage of its general esteem. Promotional posters would often-times flaunt the figure of a pin-up girl in the cast rather than detail the plot summary of the motion picture in question. A great number of films produced during the war years were made for the purpose of exhibiting a favored pin-up girl of the armed forces. Betty Grable starred in the vehicle *Pin-up Girl* that milked her status as one of the world's premier cheesecake girls. Although studios would boast that they employed the talents of the soldier's favorite pin-up girl — lauding any number of women with the title — there was no clear cut pin-up girl to wear the crown. Photographer Frank Powolny's famous still of Miss Grable in a bathing suit, twisting her enviable contours so that her backside as well as her spritely countenance was displayed, was generally regarded as the preeminent pin-up photograph, but that didn't stop studios from proclaiming other female stars as the top pin-up girl. The leg art of Betty Grable became, over the years, synonymous with the phrase "pin-up," thanks solely to the photography of Powolny. Whenever a Grable film was promoted during the war years, her studio often displayed a full body shot of Betty upon the film poster to lure patrons, with an emphasis on her extraordinary gams.

While pin-up photography gained momentum in popular American culture, studios didn't refrain from the practice of setting up cheesecake photo shoots for their female players. Some stars like Maureen O'Hara refused to be photographed in bathing suits, but almost every female star of the time posed for cheesecake stills. A soldier could pin up a photo-graph of racy tabloid divas like Lana Turner and Ava Gardner, whose amorous escapades were common newspaper fodder, but if he cared not for the decadent dames, girl-next-door actresses like Jeanne Crain and Deanna Durbin also posed for pin-up art. The momentum of the prac-tice of pin-up photography charted an upward course because actresses

*Deanna Durbin.* COURTESY OF MOVIEMARKET.COM

of every genre and typecast — not just the lusty dames — posed for the cameras. Pin-up photography had a sense of diversity during the war years, since ladies who weren't made of the burlesque ingredients felt it their duty to pose as well. Deanna Durbin's prim and proper screen image did not tarnish when she showed off a bit of leg, because she posed for the benefit of troops and not for the issuance of catcalls and amorous applause. Due to her pin-up work, a soldier sent Deanna a picture of his jeep, which he named after her as appreciation for her cheesecake output.

The film industry changed greatly during this time of war. Producers churned out one war film after another as American audiences craved films that showed their boys in heroic struggles. Whereas the war genre became popular, the lavish period-piece films that had been devoured just years prior were often viewed as excessive. The days where Vivien Leigh and Olivia De Havilland peacocked about in sumptuous gowns onscreen seemed numbered, for many filmgoers, pressed into rationing, found the extravagant attire in bad taste. Hence, movies like *Gone With the Wind*, where the wardrobe department spared no expense, were looked upon as bygone films and were replaced with motion pictures like *So Proudly We Hail*, which donned its glamorous stars Claudette Colbert, Paulette Goddard, and Veronica Lake in Army nurse's garb. Actresses were asked to do things in films beyond looking pretty, such as the case of Goddard and Company playing war nurses in *So Proudly We Hail*. The scribe Erskine Johnson mused comically on the diverse roles for females after he viewed Paulette's performance in the war-themed epic. He wrote, "Beautiful ladies of the screen were doing nothing more energetic than lifting Martini glasses. They were heroines in dream worlds, running the gamut if falseness and folly. They were clothes-horses and social butterflies."

The film industry's twist to depict war-era life, highlighting the struggle of modern man, was not wholly accepted by film critics. Many critics felt that movies were one of the few ways that citizens had to escape the madness of reality, and viewed the trajectory of realism in films as a downward spiral that failed to fulfill film's responsibility to the public. When starlets like Paulette Goddard surrendered their evening dresses for blood-spattered nurse uniforms, critics of Hollywood's entrance into realism became vociferous. One of the more vocal critics of the realism campaign was scribe Jimmie Fidler, who voiced his displeasure when the film industry adopted what was coined the "Down to Earth Movement." The movement employed motion pictures as a method to champion the mundane chores of the average person, with glamour toned down and sizzling starlets donned in typical attire. Fidler felt the campaign was ridiculous, and he chastised the movement when he wrote, "The average male doesn't care to picture Lana Turner in a $1.98 house dress, sans makeup, brewing coffee. He wants to see [her] in cloud-like dancing frocks, or in sophisticated, beauty-revealing bathing suits. He expects the movies to provide the glamor [sic] that he otherwise would never find."

When Hollywood adopted the "Down to Earth Movement," not all producers supported the campaign either. The Joel McCrea/Veronica Lake film *Sullivan's Travels* poked fun at the film industry's obsession with realism. McCrea's character Sullivan, a hot-shot film producer, was possessed with a desire to make a film that depicted the struggle of life, complete with every blemish proudly displayed. Sullivan traversed the American expanse on railcars with the stunning Miss Lake at his side, and he researched the true-to-life toil that average Americans faced. When he reached the bottom of the social ladder, he found that those people who struggled to survive looked to the motion picture industry for solace and sanctuary. Only through the medium of film could they exit their mundane existence, and Sullivan, after his return to Hollywood, decided to produce a lighthearted comedy instead.

Whereas the motion picture industry had a responsibility to the public, which was defined differently by various critics, the players in the industry used the system to their advantage when able. At the height of World War II, with the pin-up girl craze in full swing, many sexy young ingénues found the gates to Hollywood more easily breached. Marie McDonald shifted from hand modeling to full-figure modeling and then to acting during the war years. Her talent as a thespian surprised many critics who felt she was employed by the motion picture industry as window-dressing and nothing more. Like McDonald, pin-up girl Martha Holliday changed her occupation courtesy of her work as a pin-up. She originally went to Hollywood with designs as an actress but instead accepted employment with Warner Studios as a dance director. But after her pin-up pictures were circulated among the troops, she signed an acting contract with Warner's rival RKO Studios. Careers were built due in large part to cheesecake modeling, and this concept was lampooned in a pin-up picture of up-and-coming starlet Lorraine Miller, who had a cheesecake still circulated of her seated on a rafter, hammering nails into boards. Many people failed to understand the joke she and the photographer made, as the pin-up of lovely Lorraine, constructing a building while wearing the briefest of short pants, struggled to convey the statement that Miss Miller was in the midst of building her acting career.

Pin-up artwork's ascension in popular culture had plenty to do with the girl's devotion to their country and the men who served, but the basis for its popularity was unquestionably the appeal of the female figure. When censorship loosened its grip on the moral code handbook and allowed the binding to be bent a little, stills and photographs of scantily-clad ladies circulated military bases as well as pockets of male-populated industries. The girls were applauded for their patriotic acts, but the rise in pin-up artwork is attributed to the ability to exhibit the female form. Although the practice was sexist, and viewed as crude and tasteless by many critics, pin-up art exploded during the war years. Pin-up girls were seen everywhere, from the bunks of servicemen to pages of leading newspapers. American beauty was no longer to be hidden under layers of clothing and forced into a state of modesty, it was to be flaunted as a method to rally soldiers around a symbol worth fighting for. Soldiers fought for Dorothy Lamour's bright smile, Betty Grable's long legs, Jane Russell's exceptional torso, and Annie Miller's dancing feet. It was beauty on parade during the war years, and the merriment was open to all.

When the doors that censorship had barred were cracked, beauty was exhibited and envy became rampant. It seemed that every soldier toted a pin-up photograph of some starlet, which made the average American girl green with envy. To compete with the heavenly contours of Carole Landis or the ethereal beauty of Gene Tierney seemed too insurmountable for the typical gal, which gave voice to a large pocket of pin-up disparagers. They found fault in the pin-up practice and chastised the artwork as a mind-altering substance that imbued in men a false image of American womanhood. Despite their jeers, the practice continued and gained steam until the nay-saying of critics was muzzled to a point of low volume. Writer E.V. Durling supported the practice of pinning up cheesecake photographs, and had a bit of advice for gals who felt that their men obsessed over film starlets. In order to combat envy, Durling urged women to enter the pin-up practice themselves. He wrote, "So, young woman, if you are worried by the rivalry of the pin-up girl perhaps you had better arrange to have your picture taken in provocative poses and rush same to your husband overseas."

The exhibition of the female body was the primary concept of pin-up pictures. What made pin-up artwork acceptable during the war years was the patriotic theme that enveloped the practice. In both previous and later generations, when the country was not at war, photographing scantily-clad women and posting the images in well-traveled avenues where the public eye could view them, was regarded as tasteless and sexist. There was, however, even with regards to the patriotism, a level of sexism that permeated the pin-up industry during WWII. When beauty Virginia Cruzon was named "The Pin-up With the Most Beautiful Eyes," by the Armed Forces Photographers, a photograph of the sexy brunette in a barely-there black dress circulated, which emphasized her sizable bust more so than her optical orbs. Critics cried about the accepted sexism, but the girls who posed for the pictures typically had few reservations. They posed for the boys in service, and they showed the fighting man that the most mesmerizing piece of Americana was left behind.

Cameramen trained their lenses on legs, backsides, and busts in order to capture the angles of American women who they knew fighting men longed to leer at. When pin-up pictures first gained acceptance they were often referred to as "leg art," since leggy lasses donned bathing suits so as to keep not an inch of their landing gear concealed. The boys whistled at the leg art, admiring such leggy starlets as Anne Gwynne, Ginger Rogers, and Betty Grable, but film star Marlene Dietrich felt the emphasis on legs was of little importance. To Miss Dietrich, it was beauty more than bare legs that the men craved. She said, "A girl's legs don't matter. I think if a man's in love, he doesn't care what the girl's legs look like." This sentiment was shared by a few, but the cameramen seemed to focus on the uncovered stems of the posing girls. Photographer Hal McAlpin enjoyed focusing on legs, which he did when he photographed the lovely blonde starlet Constance Dowling. The shutterbug marveled at Constance's underpinning and proclaimed that she had "the most beautiful showgirl legs" he had ever seen. But it was the complete package of beauty rather than an isolated piece of the anatomy that made the pin-up girl. When Constance Dowling's film *Up in Arms* was promoted, it wasn't her legs alone that the press agents lauded. To lure viewers to the theater, her studio promoted the picture by claiming, "Constance Dowling can't hide her feminine charms 'neath GI fatigues!"

Feminine charms were the central point of focus for the photographer's lens when it came to pin-up photography. A woman's beauty was a symbol, both provocative and wholesome, which American soldiers could rally behind. For the appeal of a nation's fairer sex, and the security thereof, have been of uppermost importance to fighting men throughout history. The pin-up girls, those paragons of the female frame, whose peerless images serve as the idealized models of beauty, were agents of ascension who offered tips to American gals on how best to acquire that pin-up-type figure. Evelyn Keyes detailed an exercise that women could employ to enhance their bust, while Evelyn Ankers regaled the readers of women's health pages with her method of maintaining her delicate skin: rolling around naked in the early morning dew. Men needed nothing more but the pleasing image to accept pin-up artistry, while the gals, not over-impressed with the practice, began to accept pin-up girls when they shared their beauty secrets. The rise of the pin-up girl was escorted along by the gals who longed to look like them, for men could not pressure the practice of pin-up photography upon the public without help from the ladies. Ladies came on board and accepted the pin-up girls for their patriotism, advice, and beauty secrets, and this was the moment that pin-up artwork reached its height. The war may have asked Americans to ration many materials, but there was to be no rationing of glamour.

# CHAPTER THREE

# THE ROLE
## ★ OF THE ★
# PIN-UP GIRL

Occupational duties tend to be concise — firemen fight fires and surgeons perform surgeries — but the role of pin-up girls during World War II saw an expansion to the function that cheesecake models served. With the world engaged in an epic battle, even the dolls who posed for cheesecake purposes were expected to broaden their vocational duties. To their credit, the majority of the models were not content simply to serve as stimulation for the senses, pleasing the eye with their physical dimensions, so they sought out avenues where they could better support the troops and assist their country. The role of the pin-up girl may have been, initially, to please the troops by striking seductive poses, but their duties progressed over time. Their primary function was to look appealing for photography's sake, but as the war escalated, such an exercise became insufficient; they could do plenty more. Pin-up girls proved this point by performing a multitude of tasks ranging from selling war bonds to visiting military bases on entertainment junkets.

In order to build morale among the fighting forces, pin-up photographs were accepted as the paramount symbol for the task. To adopt a single symbol as a rallying device is a difficult endeavor, for what stimulates one individual may turn off another. But when it came to the troops — an aggregation of young, healthy men — the symbol to heighten unit morale was easily ascertained in the female form. Actresses and models, positioned in striking poses and adorned in bathing suits and short skirts, were ideal fodder for morale-boosting in the trenches, foxholes, and cockpits. So, photographs of the flame-haired beauty Rhonda Fleming were pinned up in bunkhouses, and, if the soldier was unimpressed with redheads, he could pin-up blondes like June Vincent and Jane Randolph, or brunettes like Rochelle Hudson and Gale Storm. Morale was heightened courtesy of the exhibition of the female form, but it was up to the individual soldier to choose which form he desired most.

How pin-up pictures became the primary mode of building morale among soldiers took little insight to understand. Men who had worked in the civilian labor force up until the war had abandoned their normal existence for the life of a soldier — whether their departure was courtesy of the draft or enlistment. No longer were their days centered on work and leisure pursuits, for they traded the office and time clocks for the bugle call of the fighting man. Chief among the leisure pursuits of young men was the chasing of women, and when they joined the armed forces, the boulevards of beauties had been sealed off by roadblocks. Their hours were consumed with military training, for the time they spent in pursuit of dames after work hours was now spent under the watchful eye of Uncle Sam. Despite their removal from avenues that led to ladies, it was ladies who were foremost on many soldiers' minds. Pin-up photography showed the boys what they longed for — what had become a limited commodity in the ranks of the military — which gave rise to the popularity of cheesecake stills. It was the cheesecake model, the stunning pin-up girl, and the shutterbug who took her picture that kept the image of American womanhood fresh in the fighting man's mind. Thanks to pin-up art, soldiers saw — even those struggling with debt and absent the finer aspects of life — something worthwhile to come home to.

The pin-up model served as an emblem of future bliss — a representation of a physical treasure who could be obtained once the war concluded. When soldiers spend years overseas, engaged in hostile war zones, it is not beauty that occupies their surroundings but a canvas of despair, populated with images of horror and dread. War does not offer a picturesque tableau of striking sublimity but a collection of elements that tend to incline the fighting man to yearn for absent beauty. Removed from surroundings where beauty inhabits, the soldier has only the power to desire for that which is no longer presented, and his desire was often personified by the image of pin-up girls. The pin-up girl's role was not strictly to strike a comely pose. For the pose, seductive as it may have been, served not as one singular function but was the catalyst to higher aspirations on the troop's part. Simply by allowing herself to be photographed for the benefit of the troops, the pin-up girl was employed by the soldier as a force capable of illuminating Cimmerian caverns. She offered proof that darkness was not perpetual and the entrance into war was simply a sojourn where darkness was temporary and resplendence was the order for future days.

One of the main attractions to pin-up pictures, aside from the obvious aesthetic lure, was the symbolism they possessed. The pin-up girl was more than an alluring figure — loveliness to be pined for — for she also served as a symbolic representation of home. While troops were engaged in wartime missions, their homeland — whether it was a country farm in Nebraska or an apartment complex in Yonkers — was ill-represented in foreign lands. His tie to home was courtesy of the letters he received from loved ones and photographs that depicted the American way of life. The beauty of his homeland was best represented by the ladies of America who posed for cheesecake stills, which offered boys in the military a fetching glimpse of the nation's capital attraction. Servicemen used the pin-up practice as a way to connect with their homeland. One such case concerned a homesick soldier named Harry Yazzi, whose story was told in the *Gallup Independent*. Yazzi, a member of the Navajo tribe who was stationed in New Guinea, wrote a letter home that detailed his remorse for his inability to attend the Inter-Tribal Indian Ceremony held in Gallup, New Mexico. He nevertheless had a recommendation for the Ceremonial Association: Yazzi wanted the council to select a native pin-up girl at the ceremony and send him a picture of the crowned beauty.

By associating the pin-up girl with home, soldiers were able to combat the crippling ailment of homesickness by lavishing attention on a still photograph. To many, the ideal pin-up girl was an unattainable beauty, the Gene Tierneys of Hollywood whose elegance and winsomeness seemed beyond the boundaries of reality. But to others, the ideal pin-up girl was a beauty from their past — a better representation of home, for she was ideally back home and waiting for her fighting man to return. A number of married soldiers would employ photographs of their wives as cheesecake models. Staff Sergeant Allen Blake of Defiance, Ohio, had a photograph of his altered leather jacket reach the American newspaper wires during the war. Daily papers across the country showed Blake modeling his leather jacket in the European Theatre of Operations, which displayed a pin-up image of his wife, who he called "Flossie," upon the backside of the leather integument. Blake chose not the popular actresses of Tinseltown to adorn his jacket, but the shapely bride he had tucked away back home in Defiance.

A means to tie units together was often a role for pin-up girls. If a unit failed to name a pin-up girl as their official mascot of pulchritude, then they seemed behind the times — too archaic to remain under the supervision of Uncle Sam's many fighting units of pin-up admirers. The morale of the men was of uppermost importance, and by creating a unit-wide vote to establish a unit pin-up girl, military outfits kept morale sharp. The men would often devise a list of popular pin-up girls and distribute ballots among their unit in order to discover the company's most sought-after piece of cheesecake. Many times, the girl was named strictly on her pulchritude, but in other instances the unit named a pin-up girl as their official pin-up based on background and character. Lynne Baggett was named "The Star Spangle Girl" by a unit based at Kelly Field, Texas, because she was a native Texan. Jane Randolph, she of *Cat People* fame, was adopted by troops at Randolph Airfield as their official pin-up based on her surname as well as her first-rate feminine charms. By adopting an official pin-up girl, military aggregations built a community where the residents participated in the democratic voting process and established a symbol that represented womanhood, beauty, and, most importantly, home.

Although pin-up girls had numerous roles, the advent of the pin-up practice was devised solely to please soldiers who were removed from feminine company. Whenever possible, pin-up girls showed their appreciation to the men in the armed forces for their admiration and, in many cases, for boosting their stagnant careers. The girls were grateful and many would haunt the west-coast canteens to dance and chat with servicemen. A great number of the California canteens were created by actress Joan Bennett who saw to the furnishing of many of the establishments herself. Not only did the elegant and stately Miss Bennett break ground on a number of canteens, but she was also a common face at the lively spots, washing dishes, dancing with soldiers, and treating the gents like royalty. Soldiers clamored to the west-coast canteens because they knew there was a solid chance that a comely actress was jitterbugging on the prancing platform. Deanna Durbin, that spritely beauty of the silver screen, spent many hours at the Hollywood Canteen where she served as hostess and dance partner. She described the hectic scene inside the canteen, saying, "I wish I could say that I danced at the Canteen, but you could never call it dancing. I am yanked from one pair of arms to another and the orchestra is very loud and I try so hard to have conversations — and then someone else cuts in and you begin all over again."

Canteens weren't relegated to the west coast, although since Hollywood was the film industry headquarters, the gents on the west coast were treated to more recognizable pin-up girls. While Joan Bennett made headlines by erecting canteens on the west coast, troops on the east coast were just as eager to establish a few of the lively joints as well. When the Park Avenue Canteen was opened in 1942, the New Yorkers made the grand opening a spectacle worthy of the pomp of Broadway. Starlet Marjorie Woodworth, who reminded many studio executives of the legendary Jean Harlow, was asked to lead the ceremonies. Miss Woodworth, who had twirled a baton at USC, led an Army band down Park Avenue and raised a boisterous, yet harmonious, clatter towards the front entrance of the new canteen. A grand show was made of the Park Avenue Canteen's opening, for the boys in service deserved a dwelling where they could unwind and caper with a pretty girl or two.

To dance and make breezy dialogue with the fellows at the Canteen was a pin-up role that many girls accepted, but the gals were more than prattle horses and perform-the-steps partners. The boys liked to hold the gals on the dance floor and speak easy into their delicate ears, while the girls, willing to be admired in such a fashion, did more for the troops than serve as swell-time companions. Established stars such as Myrna Loy and Ida Lupino would hand out sandwiches to soldiers on blackout assignments. Penny Singleton, the pin-up girl of the Marine Corps — she was married to a Marine captain — established an alterations and repair community for the servicemen, which she called the "Sew and Sew Club." The fair-haired actress, best known as the lead in the many *Blondie* pictures, enlisted a number of Hollywood personalities to assist her in this free-for-the-troops endeavor.

Where there were troops, there was a collection of men eager for the visit of a pin-up girl. A number of lovely ladies decided it was a role of pin-up girls to meet with the troops at various installations — even hazardous duty assignments. Such alluring cheesecake models as Marlene Dietrich, Jinx Falkenburg, Candy Jones, and Carole Landis entertained troops in foreign settings, and the troops were eternally grateful for their sacrifice. Little meant more to the American fighting man than to know that the ladies had them uppermost on their minds. To be greeted by a pin-up girl and given a fond farewell by her, before departure into war, was a gesture of profound magnitude. Marlene Dietrich, the most hated thespian of the Nazi regime — for she was a German national who aligned herself with the Allies — traveled to war zones and endeared herself to the troops by sharing in their horrific experiences. She did her part to limit the horror by serving as the image of mercy and tenderness, for Miss Dietrich would plant a farewell kiss upon the face of each soldier she knew was due to enter battle. Her kiss did not signal a final farewell, such as that issued to soldiers who enter a hopeless setting where death is inevitable, but a warm salute that promised the recipient that the current hardship would soon subside and rapture, in time, would take its place.

An easier role for pin-up girls, rather than enter war zones and issue farewell kisses, was to serve as the welcoming committee when troops returned from war. The cacophony of battle lent itself to Marlene Dietrich's ear, but it was an assault on the nerves not suitable for all; Miss Dietrich and those few like her were made of indomitable stuff — the constitution possessed by the admirable, zealous patriot. Other pin-up girls, admirable as well, chose instead to greet returned heroes rather than avoid hostile forces on their homeland. The gorgeous Martha O'Driscoll, who had a brush with the enemy on the Aleutian Islands, knew that the soldiers — especially those wounded in battle — needed the sight of a beautiful American girl upon their return home to lift their spirits. When the injured veterans of the Texas 36th Division returned home, Miss O'Driscoll welcomed their convoy. They had been engaged in heavy battle in the Anzio Beachhead Operation, where many of the unit were wounded in battle, and Martha showed her appreciation for their selfless sacrifice by greeting the injured boys as they set foot back on American soil. Unsure of themselves and their future, for the war had physically impaired many of them, Miss O'Driscoll restored their resolve by presiding over their homecoming ceremony.

The common method pin-up girls had for entering war zones was via the radio. A number of pin-up girls — such as Yvonne De Carlo and Rochelle Hudson — would give special radio broadcasts for the benefit of the troops. Carole Landis, that husky-voiced sensation of sultriness and a delight of servicemen all over the globe, was asked by troops to sigh over the airwaves, and the ever-obliging doll did just that. In her film *Four Jills in a Jeep*, Carole is introduced in the motion picture by loosening from her lips that same seductive sigh she issued for the benefit of the troops on the radio. Whereas De Carlo, Hudson, and Landis sojourned on the radio waves, two lovely lasses who became top-notch pin-up girls courtesy of their devotion to the troops, Betty Rhodes and Ginny Simms, entertained troops throughout the war by headlining their very own radio programs. Miss Rhodes was the voice on *Everything for the Boys*, a radio program that held two-way conversations with servicemen overseas. Ginny Simms, one of the top female recording artists of the war years, hosted the radio program *Johnny Presents*.

Among the leading songbirds in the United States, Ginny Simms's work for the soldiers was unrivalled. The honey-voiced crooner would regale soldiers with love songs and patriotic ballads that were written for the enjoyment and morale-boosting of the armed forces. Her songs endeared her to the servicemen but her devotion to the troops elevated her status among the men in the armed forces. Ginny was lifted above the status of morale-builder and placed in a region where few other ladies resided. Her radio program, *Johnny Presents*, was not only popular among the servicemen but the average American civilian also tuned into the program. Miss Simms would never hesitate to assist a soldier in need, and when a Marine's fiancée contacted Ginny, with the hope that in some way she could help her reconnect with her wounded husband, Ginny, through *Johnny Presents*, reunited the injured battle veteran with his worried fiancée. Ginny Simms was able to locate the wounded Marine, stationed at a military hospital, and welcomed him on her show so that his fiancée and mother could hear his voice and know that he was alright. The Marine, Edward J. Stanton, was severely wounded at Guadalcanal, and through Ginny Simms was he able to put the troubled minds of his future bride and mother at ease.

It would be erroneous to claim that the pin-up girl's role was resigned for the men in service, for they catered to the needs of the country as much as the needs of the servicemen. The cheesecake models adopted the war-bond drive as a way to assist in the war effort, since the ranks of the armed forces were, for the most part, closed to them. Many of the girls took it upon themselves to join war bond parties that traveled the nation, while others were pushed toward the war-bond circuit by their studio. The Hollywood Victory Committee sent dozens of stars on the road to give the bond sales pitch, to include a number of favorite pin-up girls. Actress Lynne Carver aligned herself with the "$15,000,000,000 Third War Loan Drive", and America's top cover-girl, the stunning Jinx Falkenburg, accepted an assignment with a unique war bond campaign called "Lips For Liberty." Under the auspices of "Lips For Liberty," Miss Falkenburg and her fellow lovelies planted kisses on gents who bought war bonds. A photograph of Jinx, engaged in the smooching crusade, hit the nation's papers and showed the breathtaking beauty sharing a kiss with a sallow looking, yet over-anxious kissing companion.

By selling war bonds, female celebrities could engage themselves in the war effort, for Hollywood sought to secure victory and supported the armed forces. Stars such as Clark Gable — perhaps the most recognizable film star of the war era — ventured off to the military, but female thespians were limited to certain specialized military occupations and didn't serve beside the fighting men. So the ladies of Hollywood took up not arms but the role of the salesperson, and they put the pitch on the

American civilian. Dorothy Lamour and Marlene Dietrich earned early plaudits for their sizable war-bond sales and many actresses mirrored the endeavors of the two leading ladies. Barbara Stanwyck, the legendary actress of film and television fame, showed remarkable character upon completion of a motion picture in 1942. It was typical behavior for actors to go on vacation after completing a film, but Miss Stanwyck put country first and declined a leisurely few weeks in the sun for a war bond trip.

Cities that excelled in gathering an ample amount of funds for the war effort, via the purchase of bonds, were often celebrated with a pin-up girl to entertain locals. To show appreciation for the hamlet's patriotism, Hollywood would send out a star or two to serve as master of ceremonies for a celebratory bash. When Howard County, Texas, reached the one million dollar mark in the purchase of war bonds, sexy starlet Cindy Garner and a troupe of entertainers headlined by Big Boy Williams entertained the locals with a series of shows. But, entertainment wasn't the prevailing ingredient at war-bond rallies: the pin-up girls took them seriously. Gale Storm was a common face on the war bond circuit, not as a means to elevate her status in Hollywood, but as a way to support her soldier husband. Miss Storm, whose real name was Josephine Cottle (she won the stage name Gale Storm in a radio contest titled *Gateway to Hollywood*) would often take the floor at war-bond rallies and give the audience a patriotic sales pitch. While she headlined a war-bond rally at Galveston, Texas, Gale told the gathering, "My husband is in the Coast Guard; I know what a gun means to him. If I can put that gun in his hands, then I've helped a little bit in doing America's big job."

The war-bond circuit aided a number of aspiring actresses, but the campaign meant more to the selfless individual than simply a method to gain name recognition. War-bond rallies were a patriotic assembly of like-minded persons who were all eager to assist in the war effort, and the stunning cheesecake models who entertained the crowds made certain that those who came out to support the country were well taken care of. Ellen Drew, film starlet and pin-up girl whose husband served as a bomber pilot in England, traveled to Britain early in the war effort to be near her husband. Once she returned home, Ellen accepted the role of war bond promoter, but her experiences in England — she assisted the British in cleaning up their war ravaged streets — spurred her to lessen the showbiz quality of the war-bond drive and focus on the heroes who served. Miss Drew traveled with returned war heroes and POWs on her bond selling campaign, and when she was slated to headline a rally at Syracuse, rather than invite another film star to attend the rally with her, Ellen extended an invite to the Bataan Relief Organization, which was comprised of female relatives of soldiers captured at the infamous peninsula.

Studios held signed contracts on many pin-up girls, for the bulk of the cheesecake models were either professional models or actresses. Executives in charge of studios saw their contracted players as persons at

*Gale Storm.* COURTESY OF MOVIEMARKET.COM

their disposal, and when the war was in full swing they suggested many of their contracted talent get out and support the war effort. A number of the roles that pin-up girls adopted during the war years were suggested by the studio executives who oversaw their careers. They knew that via patriotic routes, a newly-signed beauty could easily gain name recognition and thus become a force in the film industry. It was good for business when a contracted player became an overnight hit, and given the popularity of pin-up photography, sexy ingénues were enlisted by studios at a record clip. When former beauty pageant winner Jeanne Crain entered the realm of filmmaking, the gorgeous brunette established herself as a pin-up girl first and as a quality actress second. Due to her newfound fame, fan mail poured into the studio, and her representatives joked that they had to hire new mail sorters to keep up with the requests for Miss Crain's autograph.

The war years were a time of unmatched patriotism in the annals of American history, and Hollywood studios — quite vocal in the opposition of military conflicts in decades following the Second World War — were staunch supporters of the war and the troops in the 1940s. Whenever their male film stars joined the service, studios applauded their nationalist mindsets — putting the country first, above their careers — even though the box office proceeds might take a hit. Imagine — for it would take quite a creative mind to conjure — the box office stars of today leaving Hollywood to join the military. What effect would it have on theater-going should big names like Johnny Depp and Brad Pitt enlist in the armed forces? Such things happened during World War II when Clark Gable was joined by a steady stream of actors in the armed forces. The singing cowboy, Gene Autry, served the duration of the war, and Richard Boone held a post in the Navy. Jackie Coogan and Charles Durning — who recently gained notoriety for his hilarious portrayal in the Coen Brothers' masterpiece *Oh Brother Where Art Thou?* — served in the military. Glenn Ford of *The Big Heat* and his costar in that classic film noir, Lee Marvin, both served — Marvin was wounded in combat. Steve McQueen and George C. Scott were both Marines, Tyrone Power was a pilot and Ronald Reagan, who later became president of the United States, was an officer in the Air Corps. Legends of westerns, Audie Murphy and Jimmy Stewart, were decorated war heroes and Donald Pleasence, best known for his recurring role as Dr. Loomis in the *Halloween* franchise, underwent horrific experiences as a prisoner of war. They are but of a few stars of the film industry who fought evil during World War II.

Whereas the actors were able to slide into military fatigues and enter into combat, the actresses were forced to show their support in less demanding roles. Although the foxholes and bullets were not presented to them — although some, like Marlene Dietrich and Carole Landis, sought foxholes out — the pin-up girls held positions of no little importance during the war years. The studios, for the most part, obliged the ladies in whichever endeavor their starlets chose to display their patriotism. Studios encouraged their actresses to participate in war-bond drives, USO tours, and public appearances. Many executives encouraged their starlets to be creative and to devise unique ways to entertain troops and show support for the war effort. When Anne Baxter was slated to go on a film promotion tour, the little starlet chose to alter the traditional promotional voyage where stars visited theaters, and suggested that she should instead champion her latest film at military hospitals. Because of the national pride many stars held, scribe Melrose Gower penned, "Hollywood is proud of the countless thousands of miles its famous stars have traveled to carry pleasure and entertainment to soldiers and sailors in camps and on distant fighting fronts."

Film studios championed the role of the pin-up girl and often created images of the actresses under contract. Some lovely actresses, like Ingrid Bergman, Jeanne Crain, and Rochelle Hudson owned a countenance that lent itself to the typecast of a devoted woman, and studios encouraged these typecasts because soldiers wanted to know that their wives remained faithful while they served overseas. The proper girl-next-door image was right for some actresses but was unwisely thrust upon others. Scandals, of which Hollywood has always had many, were no less prevalent in the 1940s than they are today. Although studios were apt to cover up scandals in the past, they couldn't bury all the vicious gossip and unwanted truths that circulated about their stars. Ingrid Bergman's career spiraled downward in the latter stages of the war when her many infidelities went public concerning her amorous liaisons with men while engaged on a USO tour. Married at the time, Ingrid was depicted as the ideal woman — not just by her studio but by all the leading newspapermen. She was perceived to be a woman of unmatched character who could be counted on to remain strong in the presence of a smooth-talking lothario looking to add another notch to his bedpost. However, in the case of Bergman, the reverse was true. Even though she despised the girl-next-door image that Hollywood had created for her, she knew it didn't fit.

As long as Hollywood has been operational, the film-going public has, for whatever reason, been enamored with the private lives of the film stars. Today, one can purchase any number of gossip magazines that litter the shelves at grocery stores, as they are conveniently positioned near the check-out aisles serving as impulse buys. Before the age of gossip magazines, newspapers kept tabs on the shady doings of the Hollywood crowd when the film star's studio failed to sweep their transgressions under the carpet. Since the film stars were public figures, many served as role models and characters to be copied by an enamored public. Their status meant that it was in the best interest for publicity departments to sugarcoat the star's misdeeds. During the war, America needed role models, and many stars served this purpose by entering the service or entertaining the troops, but other celebrities, to include pin-up girls, had their dark secrets exposed. The sensual blonde Lila Leeds was arrested for the possession of marijuana while she escorted a famous leading man. Chili Williams, the wanton Conover model who popularized the polka-dot bikini, had her name reach the scandal sheets when the wife of photographer Earl

Moran filed for divorce from her husband. Mrs. Moran claimed to have surprised her spouse at his studio only to find him sharing an intimate moment with a nude Miss Williams. Despite the actions of Leeds and Williams, many studios during the war years took their star's public image quite seriously; the nation needed individuals to look up to, so the studios tried to keep negative press from being exposed.

The images that studios created could be useful, and a number of ladies used their screen personas as a way to show support for the war effort. Two such ladies were Penny Singleton and Ann Sothern. Both Miss Singleton and Miss Sothern were quality actresses during the war years whose popularity had been achieved thanks to recurring roles. Penny Singleton, that beautiful, slender blonde, gained fame in filmdom for her many portrayals of the title character in the *Blondie* series — based off the famous comic strip. Ann Sothern was known to Americans as Maisie, the displaced former big city showgirl. Both leading ladies made ten or more films playing their signature role and, to go along with their personal patriotic feelings, employed their characters as supporters of the war. Penny Singleton made radio appearances as Blondie to assist in the war effort, and the motion picture *Blondie For Victory* debuted the first year of America's involvement in the war. Ann Sothern's famous character accepted a war plant job in the installment, *Swing Shift Maisie*, produced the year after Blondie sought victory. Offscreen, Penny Singleton was a Marine Corps wife and devoted to the troops: She created "The Sew and Sew Club" that altered soldier's uniforms, and Ann Sothern was famous for visiting troops at their bases. One photograph of Ann circulated the country that showed her preparing milkshakes for troops at the Salt Lake Army Airbase.

Some critics might claim that pin-up girls had limited roles for their respective studios, and were, despite their status as symbols of Americana, little more than utensils to be deployed by studio executives. The girls had minds of their own but they were, given their status as contract players, possessions of studios. If a studio wanted to send a certain starlet out on a film promotional tour, they expected the gal to capitulate given that she signed a contract to be a member of a studio's system. But, during the war years, ladies under contract to film studios knew that much was demanded of every American, and even fabulous divas like the eccentric Marlene Dietrich showed remarkable selflessness by putting country first. There were some pin-up girls whose role for the studio was different than others. Lenore Aubert, an Austrian actress who ventured to America to escape the Nazis, was used by Samuel Goldwyn — her studio's president — to promote anti-Nazi sentiment. The beautiful European actress had been driven out of her homeland due to her role in a number of anti-Nazi activities. She relocated to America, was discovered by Goldwyn, and was employed as a symbol to overthrow the Nazi party. When interviewed by writer Louella Parsons, Lenore said about her trying experiences, "I felt if I could only reach the United States and get a job I could erase from my mind the horrors that beset my beautiful Vienna and the land that we loved so much before Hitler tried to conquer us."

Most pin-up roles weren't as demanding as Lenore Aubert's, who was forced to retell her story of escaping Hitler's forces numerous times. Whereas Aubert had to regale the public with her trying evacuation from war-torn Europe, other pin-up girls had the simpler task of pleasing the male eye. Studios, whose eye always follows the roller coaster of public appeal, witnessed the arrival and burgeoning popularity of pin-up artwork, and they quickly sought out dames with the ideal pin-up physique to employ in their features. Pulchritude was all the rage, while a lady's acting ability seemed of lesser importance. With the emphasis on oomph, studios signed up sexy women like the Caribbean Cyclone, Maria Montez, and placed her in films, despite her lack of acting ability, simply based on the image she projected in revealing costumes. Due to her lack of acting skill, Miss Montez, a flamboyant self-promoter if ever there was one, was often cast in cheesy fantasy films like *Arabian Nights* and *Cobra Woman* which allowed her to wear skimpy costumes. Although the wildly self-absorbed actress understood the studio's thinking, her healthy self-image led her to believe that she was a sensational actress and not just the window-dressing her studio, and most of the film-going public, thought her to be. Maria once complained about her sexy roles to a writer, telling the scribe, "I take dramatic lessons two hours a day for a year and a half. I study Shakespeare and read the great plays of history. I knock myself out to become a great lady of drama — and what happens? I get nothing but uncover parts!"

Throughout the history of playacting, female actresses are expected to exhibit their frame — unless they are master thespians or aged. What made actresses and models ideal pin-up girls is that a lack of inhibition was already theirs, for they needed little coaxing to flaunt their figures: it came naturally, thanks to their profession. With that beauty-on-parade mentality that show business has always projected, girls who entered the realm of cheesecake modeling knew that the emphasis of the photographs would be on their physical assembly. With that knowledge going into the side occupation, the gals assumed the role of objects of lust, whose purpose was the uplifting of morale among Uncle Sam's fighting forces. Whereas many critics would call the enterprise of scantily-clad photography sexist, it was, as far as the ladies were concerned, a simple way to show their support for the troops. About serving as a lusty pin-up girl, the legendary Jane Russell said, "A pin-up reputation is a very flattering thing, and I am happy if some of my pictures have helped brighten a few moments for our boys overseas." To feel desirable, to have plaudits attained based on your image and comportment is a natural want, and to have that admiration, to feel it lavished upon you by men who selflessly defend the liberty of a nation's populace, is not a base proclivity for self-admiration but a noble pursuit that salutes the troops.

To pose before a camera, one would imagine, would be a simple assignment for an actress or model. Their vocation is populated with cameras and the men who operate them, for the female thespians always have a camera trained upon them on a film set and models are desired targets for the shutterbug's utensil. Despite the constant affiliation with cameras, many pin-up girls struggled to master the cheesecake image. Actresses, when in the presence of a camera, typically were on a film set and had entered that realm of make-believe where the story and the character's background is fictitious. When it came to posing for pin-up purposes, the lady being photographed was the lady in question — not a character on paper she brought to life through playacting. It was a chore for some actresses to appear natural in front of a still photographer's lens, such as the stunning brunette Paulette Goddard, who felt that the falsity of acting might shine through her pin-up photographs. Miss Goddard said, "When there are pictures to be taken, I try to do it as naturally as possible. If you aren't careful, you get a false smile. You have to think twice to look natural."

To project a natural image while posing for cheesecake pictures proved a difficult task for a number of ladies. The attire they adorned for the pictures was typically not their usual getup, for photographers would outfit the women in skimpy ensembles and ask them to wear high-heeled shoes while they sported bathing suits. A natural image of a woman on the beach is not one gallivanting about in her most lavish high-heeled footwear, but nautical settings seemed the most popular surroundings for pin-up photographs. Whether a lady felt comfortable adorned in a bathing suit or not meant little to the photographer, so long as she could convey a comfortable image. Posing in swimming suits was a more natural assignment for stars like Vivian Austin and Esther Williams who were champion swimmers in their youth, but a number of the pin-up girls felt more comfortable in tight-fitting sweaters or low-cut evening dresses.

Typically, the attire a woman felt more comfortable in allowed her to exhibit a level of poise that was absent when dressed in more foreign attire. Hence, Esther Williams — the nautical sensation of World War II — looked more fashionable in bathing suits than the popular sweater girls of the era.

Like a criminal operating under a plethora of aliases, pin-up pictures were often referred to by a number of names. One of the more common terms for pin-up artwork was "leg art," as the bulk of the photographs soldiers pinned to their bunk walls displayed comely lasses displaying plenty of bare leg. It seemed that a primary assignment for a pin-up model was to show off her lower structure, and those revealing bathing suits were more than adequate for the task. Thanks to the popularity of leg art, women's legs began to suffer from the over application of aliases as well. Soldiers often gushed about how they admired a woman's "landing gear," and "underpinning." They were enamored with Betty Grable's "gams" and Ginger Rogers's "stems." Even the term "pin-up" was played with, for *pin* was given a double-meaning; it could mean the tacks soldiers used to secure photographs to the wall, or the set of slender legs on a sexy cheesecake model. A soldier from Monett, Missouri, kidded when he stated that "being a pin-up girl is no secret — you just have to have nice pins."

Because the pin-up girls possessed the full physical arsenal that men craved, from legs to comely coiffures, American girls sought to mimic the stunning dames their male chums adored. The pin-up girl had her role for the men — pleasing them via seductive posture — but they too had a role for the women. Women wanted to know just how Veronica Lake managed to make her hair fall in that peek-a-boo fashion, and how Betty Grable maintained the most famous pair of legs in the world. The pin-up girls, eager to be accepted by the gals, were quick to offer a beauty tip here and there, and found the proper channel for their inside dope via the newspapers. Within many of the nation's leading papers there was a women's section that would typically employ a writer to pick the brain of a leading pin-up girl. The beauty tip experts pressed the cheesecake goddesses, those ladies who the soldiers designated as bunkhouse sentries from the Norfolk Naval Station to the island of Tinian, for tricks of the pulchritude trade. The gals offered tips ranging from maintaining healthy skin tone to enhancing the size of the bust. Evelyn Ankers, the famous scream queen who played opposite Lon Chaney Jr. in a number of his fright flicks, was noted for being loosed-lipped when it came to detailing both Hollywood and personal beauty tips. The best bit of beauty advice

Miss Ankers offered the American girl was a little strategy she learned while living in Chile: something she called a "dew bath." She informed gals that she maintained her beauty by rolling about, bare as the day she was born, in the backyard of her California home in the pre-dusk dew that covered the grass. The more modest the gal, the less likely she was to mimic Evelyn's early morning routine.

The bulk of the beauty tips that stars offered weren't as revealing as Evelyn Ankers's dismantled morning exercises. Pin-up girls were usually asked to detail their use of cosmetics, their hairstyling secrets, what clothes to wear, and other fashion tips that could turn Peggy Paducah into a stunning socialite, quick to acquire the approving whistle of every man in a gathering. When the pin-up girls weren't regaling the gals with tips in the newspapers, they were offering some advice on the big screen. Film star Olivia De Havilland informed gals to watch her film, *Government Girl,* and mimic the way her character dressed because all the outfits she wore in that feature were easily acquired on minimal budgets. Shapely blonde knockout Jane Randolph was employed by beauty writer Lois Leeds to detail the proper technique of applying face cream; a series of pictures showed Miss Randolph rubbing lotion on her face. Lois Leeds stressed that one shouldn't use the back of the hand to apply face cream — the reverse side of the paw, she reasoned, was too harsh for molding the contour. Since pin-up girls were quick to offer inside beauty tips, their role as a passer-on of pulchritude endeared them to many young ladies in the United States.

Whereas pin-up girls showed women how to look their best, they also showed women, by a variety of methods, that they too could assist in the war effort; there wasn't any one person in the country who couldn't do a little to secure liberty. The wearing of uniforms was typically a man's domain, and many dames felt that wearing company-issued regimentals wouldn't flatter their appearance. Pin-up girls were used in a campaign to get girls out and enroll in nursing courses and auxiliary roles in the military. In order to make the nurse's outfit and the military threads appear appealing, such stunning pin-up girls like Pat Clark, Jane Greer, and Martha Vickers were engaged to model the livery. Since the three lovely dolls could look swell in any getup, they were ideal models to pass along the concept that uniforms would not turn a pretty darling into an unattractive hag. Pictures of Pat, Jane, and Martha modeling nurse's uniforms urged gals to pursue the profession, while model Selene Mahri served the same capacity to get girls to enlist in the Women Accepted for Volunteer Emergency Service (WAVES). Miss Mahri became the face and figure of the WAVES, for she was the model used on the majority of the recruitment posters WAVES distributed.

Due to the unquestioned appeal of the pin-up girl, the gals who posed were often asked to assist the country in passing along information. Whereas cheesecake models like Jane Greer were seen in the newspapers fashion-modeling occupational uniforms, other gals had the glamorous task of serving as the face and figure for a war-themed campaign. Since many Americans had loved ones serving overseas during the war, folks needed to know when they could ship a care package to their soldier so he could acquire the mail by a certain date. When Christmas rolled around in 1944, pin-up girl Angela Greene was adopted as the spokesperson for the postal service — although her figure did all the talking. Her task was to inform the populace on when to ship out their packages so Uncle Sam's troops would receive them before the yuletide cheer. Since Miss Greene was a former Powers Model and a stunning pin-up girl, the advertisements the postal service used showcased plenty of Angela's assemblage, while also displaying the best dates to ship out packages. A pin-up poster of Angela seated on a swing, holding a placard with the dates September 15th to October 15th, circulated the nation, which informed civilians when they could send out their holiday parcels.

Some of the campaigns that pin-up girls found themselves attached to didn't seem to require the presence of a sexy girl leading a crusade. Perhaps the oddest use of a pin-up girl in this fashion was the spritely sexpot Elaine Riley, who despite her slender, streamlined physique was employed as the figure for kitchen fats. A gorgeous brunette of exceptional sex appeal, Miss Riley left her job as a personnel manager at a New York radio station to try her luck in the modeling and acting professions. She quickly became, courtesy of the war department, a figure of no unimportant clout when she was engaged as the pin-up girl to urge folks to store away kitchen fats to later donate to the service. Kitchen fats were used to manufacture several goods, one of which was the production of plastic bullets that troops used when they fired weapons during training exercises. For a publicity ad, Elaine was positioned behind an anti-aircraft gun, wearing the typical minimal attire of a cheesecake gal, to urge women to save those kitchen fats for the production of plastic bullets. There were a number of Elaine Riley pin-up photographs that the leading newspapers distributed in order for the accumulation of kitchen fats. One month, Miss Riley was photographed in her bathing suit, holding a chart that recommended the amount of fat a family of four should save. While a later image of Elaine showed the stunning beauty building a pyramid made from cans stored with kitchen fats. It seems odd that the face and figure of fat should be a thin, striking beauty like Elaine Riley.

Representing campaigns and spearheading social causes were roles many pin-up girls chose to support. While Elaine Riley asked Americans to retain their kitchen fat, other pin-up girls took up social causes when the cause met with their approval. Thanks to pin-up artwork, many individuals felt that the country's moral compass no longer pointed in the direction of good taste but adopted decadence as its course to steer. When the police chief of Decatur, Illinois, tried to implement a ban on the wearing of shorts in public, pin-up girls Barbara Bates and Jean Trent traveled to the Midwestern hamlet to boycott the chief's proposal. Their boycott was a playful jest, even though the leggy ladies were serious about uplifting the absurd ban — they just showed, by their presence, how foolish the chief's prevention of short pants was. Other pin-up girls took up more serious social causes, like Penny Edwards who, in order to show her support for the United National Clothing Drive, donned a barrel over her bathing suit while she toted a sign that read, "I did my bit, did you?" Dolores Moran, the blonde beauty who starred opposite Bogart and Bacall in the classic *To Have and Have Not*, did her bit for the Clothing Drive by modeling, believe it or not, a dress made of paper. Since rationing threw into question what fabrics women could acquire to make clothing, that ever-ready commodity of paper was experimented with; Miss Moran's dress was fastened with Scotch tape and cost all of fifty cents.

Although pin-up girls had their many roles, some viewed their presence as damaging and purposeless. The girls who posed for pin-up art were often depicted as loose women whom you hoped your daughter would not emulate. They had their role as sex goddesses, for soldiers stewed over their racy stills, and could not live down their elevated status as ideal physical figures. When pin-up girl Maris Wrixon landed a modeling gig for her newborn baby — the child was to be photographed for the cover of *Liberty Magazine* — the publication's editor hired another model to hold the infant for the photograph because, as Miss Wrixon was informed, her pin-up appearance didn't possess that motherly image. Rather than have the child's real mother portray the mother on the magazine's cover, a lady who appeared more motherly was hired to sit in for her.

One of the more vocal voices of pin-up opposition was actor-turned-serviceman Louis Hayward. Married to film star Ida Lupino, Hayward was appalled by the attention his battle buddies lavished on photographs of stunning women who worked in his peacetime profession. He found the pin-up hobby not a simple diversion but a destructive influence that hindered servicemen from being the best soldiers they could be. Hayward felt that the attention that gents directed upon pin-up girls could be diverted to more meaningful and constructive pursuits. Hayward explained his stance to a writer when he asked, "Why don't men pin-up blueprints showing them how to construct a motor? They could get much more profit from them because they would be learning a post-war trade." Perhaps Hayward's dislike for the pin-up practice stemmed from seeing a photograph or two of his wife secured in a battle buddy's bunk. Although Ida Lupino wasn't of the sweater-girl crowd, she was a popular actress with a throng of fans, thus allowing for the possibility of Louis Hayward spying his better half's image near the sleeping quarters of a chum in his platoon. Admiring beauty is not destructive, as Hayward suggested, but in his defense, the practice consumes time that could be employed elsewhere.

While there were pockets of individuals who demurred the pin-up practice with unchecked antipathy, the girls went about their business, posing for photographs and supporting the troops. The Red Cross was a favored outlet for many pin-up girls, and they would gladly accept assignments from the organization. Lovely screen star Joan Leslie agreed to star in a motion picture titled *This Is the Army*, produced by The Emergency Relief Fund, which detailed the life of servicemen. The role did nothing to line the pocketbook of Miss Leslie, but she accepted the role out of sense of duty to her country and not a commitment to her bank account. All proceeds for the film were donated to the Red Cross to provide aid for servicemen and their families. Other pin-up girls had more hands-on roles with the Red Cross, such as Evelyn Keyes who devoted plenty of her time to the organization. Under the auspices of the Red Cross, Miss Keyes toured military installations, and said of her work, "The Red Cross is such a far-reaching organization and does such wonderful work, that I am only too happy to do anything I can to help in this drive."

Touring military installations, whether under the umbrella of the Red Cross or as a member of a USO troupe, was a way for many pin-up girls to show their appreciation for the troops. Ladies would visit troops at their encampments, eat at the mess hall, watch training exercises, and sign autographs for the boys in service. They traveled wherever Uncle Sam sent the troops, from stateside camps to overseas areas of hazardous duty. Hardships were experienced by many of the girls, such as Conover model Candy Jones, who visited troops in the Pacific Theater where she contracted eczema. Martha O'Driscoll performed during an air raid siren on the Aleutian Islands, Carole Landis claimed to have had all of two hot baths her entire trip to Africa, and Marlene Dietrich hunkered in fighting positions to avoid enemy bullets. But the girls knew how important their role of morale-builder was to the men, and the USO enabled them to best serve this purpose by placing them where the gents were. Betty Hutton, America's number one jitterbug, said about her military entertainment tour, "There's more satisfaction in one USO appearance than a dozen Hollywood pictures." Her sentiment was shared by many pin-up girls who braved hostile conditions to show their appreciation for the boys in service, even though many individuals back home felt that pin-up girls served little importance.

Whether you disfavor pin-up artwork or are a supporter thereof, the devotion the girls showed for their country and the troops during World War II cannot be denied. The pin-up girls' paramount role was to build morale among the men in the fighting forces. Photographs of them in skimpy swimwear, tight fitting sweaters, and revealing skirts were distributed for the admiration and stimulation of the armed forces, which, given their representation of American womanhood, made the cheesecake stills ideal for the task. The gals that represented American womanhood in pin-up photographs did not project the image of the idle, self-absorbed beauty, but, like Linda Darnell, displayed a level of patriotism admirable by any estimation. Miss Darnell, although a stunning pin-up girl whose beauty was out-of-this-world, enlisted in the Women's Ambulance and Defense Corps of America and even took lessons on motor vehicle repair in her spare time. The pin-up girls of World War II were not useless layabouts, sustaining their merry existence by paychecks earned courtesy of their unrivalled pulchritude, but ladies of action who were eager to lend a hand to secure victory for the country. Their role as morale-builders are worthy of ten thousand salutes.

# CHAPTER FOUR

# THE SOLDIERS
## ★ AND THE ★
# PIN-UP GIRL

In the previous chapter, the roles that pin-up girls played were detailed but their primary role was the building of morale among the fighting men in Uncle Sam's military. This task was not a difficult assignment for the stunning gals, for their appearance, and not some mastery of a trade or possession of some useful knowledge, was the catalyst for them acquiring this unique responsibility. Men in the service grew weary of the ceaseless training, for even though victory was foremost on their minds, one item's monopoly on the senses tends to fatigue a person's mental faculties. In order to function soundly, there must be reprieve and outlets of diversion from that which is presented continuously. When the primary influence in question is an action as powerfully brutal as war, the outlets of diversion must possess a quality capable of diminishing the commanding brutality of the battle stage. Where there is war there are repellent surroundings, and these uncomely environs can only be brightened by the introduction of a foreign beauty. The men in service adopted cheesecake pictures, which depicted the loveliest actresses and models in sensuous settings, as their needed symbols of beauty.

Those who have neither experienced the departure for the military, nor bid farewell to a loved one who departed for the armed forces, can truly grasp the sundry emotions that grasp the psyche while goodbyes are said. Once the departure is final, even if it is merely a sojourn of a year or two, the knowledge that those held dear will not serve as accompaniment on the journey offers dispiriting sensations. Love is beautiful, even if the image loved bears not the striking resemblance of the popular pin-up girl: the emotional link that is shared with a cherished person cannot be substituted. Although they could not be substituted for, memories of loved ones offered sanctuary during trying times while something else — something capable of offering a removal from a harsh, war-themed reality — was needed. With reality an exhibition of horror, a fictitious center one could escape to was a desired locale for those admirable gents who fought for liberty. There, they could sit beside Barbara Stanwyck, they could chat with Dorothy Lamour, and dance the night away with Ginger Rogers. This land may have been a counterfeit setting where dreams excelled at the expense of fact, but the pin-up girls were an outlet for escape, not replacements for those whose heart had connections.

Much was written about soldiers' obsession with pin-up pictures during World War II, as every social analyst and crackerjack psychologist questioned the effect the photographs would have on soldiers once they returned from battle. Employing a narrow critique of the pin-up practice, many felt that Uncle Sam's fighting men were engaged in a tragic disservice by entertaining themselves with images of unattainable beauty. The voices that opposed the pin-up practice — supposedly learned and capable of thought beyond the common scope — simply espoused the concerns of those absent from the struggle who didn't understand the soldier's entrance into a land of fantasy in order to escape his tumultuous reality. Dorothy Dix was a staunch critic of pin-up photography, who felt that servicemen's delight in cheesecake art was detrimental to their well-being. Miss Dix said, "G.I.'s have lost their realistic snapshot of things and people as they are and they see them only through the rosy picture their fancies paint. Thus, every man's wife or girl he left behind becomes as pulchritudinous as the pin-up girls upon whom he daily feasts his eyes, and who establish his ideal of what a woman should really look like." What Dix failed to understand is that the "realistic snapshot of things," for the troops during the war, was a scene so horrific that an exit, one only attained through fancy, was the lone means at their disposal for sanctuary. Once the snapshot no longer bore the countenance of the enemy, soldiers would accept reality and live accordingly, harboring not those battlefield dreams of entertaining Carole Landis in amorous settings but returning home where a girl awaited his arrival. The soldiers painted so few pictures in battle, to deny them their "rosy pictures, their fancies painted" would have crippled, if not completely obliterated, their capacity to achieve victory.

Whereas Dorothy Dix chastised soldiers for escaping the horrors of war through the fanciful, aesthetically pleasing exercise of pin-up photography, girls who read Dix's work developed a sense of inferiority. Dorothy

Dix worried American girls into thinking that since every soldier overseas was admiring pin-up girls with otherworldly figures, the girls of
modest structure would fail to attract the attention of returning heroes.
Young ladies read Dix's column and imagined sailors and soldiers stepping off their ships and planes only to start beating feet to Hollywood
or Broadway where they could converse cutely with Marie McDonald
or follow the high heels of Rhonda Fleming. Those who accepted the
poisonous ink of Dix's pen became a dejected lot of worrisome lasses,
imagining that girls with shapes like Audrey Totter, of which there were
few, would be the target of the recently discharged servicemen. Although
Dix saw to making her feminine readership morose, other writers reassured gals that returning servicemen would not cast them a cold shoulder.
Ernie Pyle offered his analysis when critics like Dix surmised that pin-
ups hindered the prospects of girls back home. Pyle wrote, "Personally I
don't see that there's much conflict. I've never heard of a soldier writing
to his real girl to break off the engagement because he had fallen in love
with a picture." Since Pyle served in Italy with the troops, his take on
the situation soothed the gals who Dix, and those like her, had worried.

The pin-up girls were not designed to be symbols of virtue or the
perfect representation of the ideal bride but as objects of lust capable of
spurring the troops toward victory. Their presence could be worrisome
to the average bachelorette, for images of stunning starlets entertaining
throngs of troops populated the nation's newspapers. To the American
readership, servicemen seemed to create a massive line, stretching from
their installation to the entrance of the Hollywood Canteen, simply to
catch a glimpse of — or ideally dance a step or two with — a sexy actress.
The anxiety on the part of single women seemed grounded, but for every
popular pin-up girl there were countless soldiers; pin-up girls could not
be duplicated — only their image. So the disquieting dreams that girls
harbored of their sought-after beau cupiding in their khaki uniform with
the latest pulchritudinous film starlet was baseless and nonsensical. The
men in service may have held dreams of holding hands with a famous
starlet when she visited the troops, but his dreams, such as the dreams
of the worrisome girl, were entirely absurd. Falling in love with a pin-up
girl only happened when the mind entered a state of juvenile fancy, which
was removed from the grounded factuality that they were objects to build
morale: not individuals the average Joe would recite nuptial vows with.

When it came to their interaction with the troops, the pin-up girls
played up the image of the gay and spritely dreamgirl, and they would
chat coyly with the troops while they visited their camps or entertained

at canteens. The most popular hangout for troops on the west coast was undoubtedly the Hollywood Canteen. Canteens were clubs that soldiers could visit on their off-time, where they could unwind, have a drink, listen to some music, and dance with any girl in attendance. When it came to the Hollywood Canteen, there were typically actresses — many well-known — serving as hostesses and dance partners. Such beautiful young film stars like Joan Leslie would spend hours at the canteen after shooting films. Miss Leslie juggled her time between acting, college preparation studies, and entertaining troops. The lovely young starlet possessed an admirable sense of duty: Joan understood what she meant to the troops. When Joan received a flattering letter from a wounded soldier in Europe, who informed her that her songs in the film *Rhapsody in Blue* helped him convalesce, Miss Leslie agreed to give the sergeant a private solo at the Hollywood Bowl. When the sergeant returned stateside, Joan proved that her promise wasn't an idle boast.

On the west coast, soldiers were treated to more starlets at their canteens than any other location. Troops based in the midwest would have to be content with an isolated visit or two from some known film star, but the fortunate gents stationed near the hub of the film industry could be introduced to a different star every night. Joan Bennett — the legendary star of several Fritz Lang features and later the matriarch of the successful gothic soap opera *Dark Shadows* — saw to the furnishing of many canteens. Early in the war effort, she saw the need soldiers had for leisure spots and took it upon herself to erect and furnish a number of military canteens. Oftentimes the stately beauty could be seen at one of her canteens, handing out meals, dancing with troops, and engaging in the less glamorous task of washing dishes. By contrast, stunning starlet Anne Gwynne put the emphasis on glamour when she visited the Hollywood Canteen. Miss Gwynne adopted the unique assignment of a personal pin-up girl. Many nights, Anne would show up at the canteen, wearing a bathing suit and toting a camera, and allow soldiers in attendance to take their very own, personalized pin-up photo of her. Perhaps the variety of Anne Gwynne pin-up pictures was unrivaled among pin-up girls given that she posed for countless photographers — professional as well as amateur.

Sailors aboard ships were typically denied visits from pin-up girls, lest their ship should dock at a navy base where a USO show was underway. Gents in the Navy, who served in foreign waters, had not the Hollywood Canteen to haunt, where pretty gals with their dainty, dancing feet could be met, which meant the pin-up pictures were usually their lone outlet for the admiration of pulchritude. In order to see a stunning pin-up girl in action, sailors aboard ships in foreign waters were reliant on motion pictures. They could not make with the wolfish dialogue in a dame's ear, for that ear was not given them in person, only in reproduction via the film reel. So in order to see a pin-up girl in motion, the medium of movies was their primary outlet. When sailors desired a certain movie that featured a star of their liking, if the film wasn't in the ship's motion picture coffers, they were forced to trade with other ships to acquire the film they wanted. Some ships had enticing trading chips, like the vessel that Seaman Harold Weislocher served on, which housed one of the few soft-serve ice cream machines found in the Pacific waters. Whenever sailors aboard another ship would balk when discussing a trade for a film, the sailors aboard Weislocher's vessel turned to their secret weapon that dispensed the tasty, cold confection, and would typically acquire the film they desired. The girls they admired on their bunk walls could finally come to life when the film reel began to churn.

The soldiers were grateful for the cheesecake pictures the gals posed for, and in order to convey their gratitude, troops adopted a number of methods to show their appreciation. One of the most common methods servicemen adopted was the christening of military vehicles in the honor of pin-up girls. Aircraft, ships, and jeeps were handed aliases by servicemen who christened their conveyances in order to honor their preferred pulchritudinous pin-up girl. Oftentimes a pin-up girl would receive notification in the mail from a soldier, who spoke on behalf of his outfit, which informed the comely lass of his unit's decision to honor her support for the troops by naming a vehicle after her. Rita Hayworth was named an honorary MP by the military lawmen at Camp Bowie in 1942, and while there she christened a tank. Photographs of Miss Hayworth placed in the turret of the "Rita Hayworth Tank" circulated the nation's papers. Ginny Simms, the patriotic doll of the airwaves, received the same treatment when she had a flying fortress named in her honor — the first flying fortress so christened. Because the soldiers had a penchant for pinning monikers on their transports, such bulky war machines bore titles better suited for pretty girls.

When flyers adopted the habit of appellation, the skies were suddenly littered with aircraft that had been christened for pin-up girls. To the men in the skies, Jane Russell could mean the bosomy actress under contract to Howard Hughes or an aircraft fluttering through the great blue expanse. Many of these so named aircraft boasted pictures of their namesake, serving as "nose art" to beautify the metallic structure. Starlet

Brenda Joyce received a letter from an Australian flying cadet in 1942. Miss Joyce was informed that she had been chosen as their unit's mascot. Her image was duplicated on a bomber, and the flyer, James MacDougall, wrote, "The boys are more cautious about landings. They don't want any ground loops to ruin such a lovely picture." But the christening of aircraft could confound the boys in the tower, as in the case of brunette beauty Marguerite Chapman. Miss Chapman and her stand-in Mary Ann Featherstone toured military bases in 1943 and were ferried to and from installations via aircraft. On one such flight, the commanding officer of a base phoned the next stop on their junket, and informed them that he would be flying in Marguerite Chapman and Mary Ann Featherstone, to which his conversation partner replied, "More new ships! Which kind are these?"

The servicemen enjoyed naming their vehicles after pin-up girls, but some troops exceeded the labeling of wheeled and winged transports. One searchlight battery based out of Albuquerque, New Mexico, were so impressed with the support that dancing film star Ann Miller showed the troops that they dubbed their entire outfit the "Annie Millers." The dark-haired dancing actress was a staunch supporter of the men in the armed forces, who was known to visit military bases and show the boys her prowess with a firearm at the rifle range. Miss Miller would gleefully state that she hit more than one bullseye. However, the sharpshooting pin-up girl was devastated when she learned that her military namesake, those searchlight gents from New Mexico, had been taken prisoner at Bataan. Devoted to the boys who were devoted to her, Annie tried in vain to ship personalized cheesecake stills to the captured soldiers, but feared that the Japanese wouldn't allow the pictures to reach the fellows.

There were military units known as the "Annie Millers" and the "Russell's Raiders," for servicemen enjoyed to honor pin-up girls by naming them their unit's mascot. When troops adopted a gal as their unit's preferred pin-up girl, they would often lavish a nickname upon the dame that typically began with "The Girl We'd..."

*Soldiers at Riggs Field named Ingrid Bergman "The Girl We'd Most Like to Share Oxygen With."*

*Anne Gwynne was "The Girl We'd Most Like to Corral" for the Fort Riley cavalry.*

*Betty Hutton was "The Girl We'd Most Like to Meet on a Blind Date."*

*The sarong goddess Dorothy Lamour was dubbed "The Girl We'd Most Like to Go Down in a Submarine With" from the crew of the USS Gudgeon.*

*The sexy blonde Veronica Lake was given the title "The Girl We'd Like in the Back Seat of a Tank."*

*The doe-eyed Deanna Durbin earned the nickname of "The Girl We'd Like to Come Home To."*

*Swimming sensation Esther Williams was referred to as "The Girl We Most Want to Spend a Minute Underwater With" by a group of sailors.*

*Ginny Simms was named "The Girl We'd Most Like to go Over the Hill With" by Marines on Guadalcanal.*

*Gents in the Coast Guard named Barbara Hale "The Girl We'd Most Like to Look Out For."*

*Margaret Landry received the nickname "The Girl We'd Like Most to Tidy up Our Foxholes."*

*London air raid wardens named the voluptuous Carole Landis "The Girl We Would Like to Put Out a Fire Bomb Together With."*

The soldiers weren't alone in concocting absurd little "Girl We'd…" and "Girl Who…" monikers for film starlets, for their studios saw the impact the handles had on the public and began to devise a few for their contracted players. The scribe Dee Lowrance found the little diversion amusing at first but it wore on the writer, and Lowrance wrote a column with the hope that the fad would soon pass. Lowrance's piece was titled *Leave Us Phrase It*, as Dee claimed that the "Girl Who…" snowball that began as lighthearted fun with a moniker bestowed upon Jane Russell, had become an exercise bordering on the mundane. Every stunning young starlet soon had a catchy alias, and Lowrance urged both the studios and the soldiers to cease the practice. Dee wrote, "Let's have no more "the girl who…" stories in the newspapers, no more titles handed about freely, bestowed by publicity departments and/or members of the armed forces. It is now just about time to call 'Stop!'" Dee Lowrance failed to make a convincing argument for the cessation of such nicknames, which made the scribe's article more of a rant than an appeal for the complete withdrawal of the practice.

The boys enjoyed lavishing the starlets with nicknames, and the pin-up girls were flattered that servicemen thought enough of them to get creative by supplying them with snappy aliases. Not all the nicknames began with "The Girl We'd…" as the Wilde Twins, Lee and Lyn, were named the "Barrage Girls" by the 341st Engineers, and Lynne Baggett was dubbed "The AAA Girl" by the 144th Gun Battalion based at Camp Haan, which meant that Lynne was "adorable, amiable and amorous." When pin-up girls learned of these aliases, they typically obliged the outfit that concocted the nickname with a special cheesecake photograph. When man-eater Ava Gardner was named the official pin-up girl by a Navy outfit, Miss Gardner set up a photo shoot designed specifically for the sailors. She donned the standard Navy uniform but gave the livery that pin-up twist, substituting slacks for a miniskirt. Helen Talbot, likewise, sported an MP's brassard on a skimpy outfit that no military policeman would be caught dead in. Model Daun Kennedy's personalized pin-up picture may have been the most unusual, for the pretty lady was photographed seated on a block of ice. Troops in the northern reaches named Daun "The Girl We Would Like to Warm Our Iceberg," and Miss Kennedy was inspired to perch on a mini glacier for those frozen gents stationed in the cold tundra.

The walls of a soldier or sailor's bunk could be littered with pictures of the gent's favorite pin-up girls, but when it came to community exhibition, many outfits felt that one pin-up girl could serve as the unit's symbol of womanhood. Betty Rhodes was a famous radio personality during the war, who, like Ginny Simms, was a singer and host of her own show. Betty's radio broadcast was titled *Everything For the Boys*, which, as its title suggests, held interviews with men in the armed forces. Due to the popularity of Miss Rhodes's radio show, the men in the Fourth Naval Construction Battalion named Betty their unit pin-up girl and adorned the walls of their mess hall with her cheesecake stills. The nautical assemblers spent their banqueting hours devouring Betty's beauty while they soothed their ears with her sweet serenading and radio broadcast. At Fort Osborne, one troop's barracks that scribe Clare Wagner visited had a lone pin-up of Marjorie Woodworth secured to a door. About the Fort Osborne pin-up sentinel, Wagner wrote, "Marjorie sweetly keeps an eye on all her menfolk, day in and day out."

Where there were units engaged in the practice of pinning up cheesecake stills, one could typically find shrines dedicated to the girls who saw to the soldier's morale. Betty Rhodes had her mess hall shrine, and individual bunks served as mini-shrines that servicemen dedicated to the ladies they admired. But scribe Ernie Pyle, who served with the fighting men in Italy, witnessed a shrine that dwarfed all others. An American bomber squadron based in Italy employed a crew of mechanics who so admired pin-up artwork that they littered, from floor to ceiling, their break room with cheesecake stills; they left not a single square inch devoid of the pinch of pulchritude. When Pyle gazed upon the mechanic's cheesecake chamber, the writer was impressed with their unique sense of décor, and he felt that the art, like ancient paintings and sculptures, deserved a place in Italian history. Pyle penned, "I think the pin-ups should be left there and the room roped off by the Italian government as a monument to the American occupation. I'll bet the piece, if given a few centuries time, would become as historic as Pompeii." Perhaps Pyle would elicit a smile, knowing that such beautiful pin-up girls as Julie Ege, Christine Kaufmann, Olivia Hussey, and Madeline Smith all starred in films based on the history of Pompeii, even if sculpted busts of ancient Romans are deemed a higher form of art than a photograph emphasizing the ample bust of *Up Pompeii's* beautiful starlet Madeline Smith.

If individual pin-up pictures were a gift from the girls to the boys, they were gifts that oftentimes acquired for the gals a reciprocal present from the servicemen. Whereas the pin-up girls lavished upon the fighting men photographs of them in comely poses, the boys, even with modest means to acquire pretty trinkets, found items they felt obliged to send back to pin-up girls. The actresses and models who posed for cheesecake photos typically found identification tags, unit insignias, or flier's wings in letters from servicemen — whatever the admiring troops could find and slide in an envelope. Cover girl Jinx Falkenberg was known to wear the identification tag of a deceased pilot wherever she went, while model Elaine Shepard was often seen sporting pilot's wings above her heart. Veronica Lake acquired over fifty sets of wings from cadets on one junket, as admiring gents surely wanted to pin their brass wings on the stunning Miss Lake's dress. The wearing of military paraphernalia by pin-up girls became a common practice, for the gals showed the men in the armed forces that their simple little admiring gifts did not go unnoticed or unappreciated.

Although the primary gifts that pin-up girls received were items that soldiers typically affixed to their uniforms, many troops got creative with the presents they bestowed upon their preferred pin-up girl. When a set of wings or a unit patch seemed too ordinary to the soldier, he sought to wow the object of his veneration with a gift that few other pin-up girls received. Identification tags seemed to be worn by every pin-up girl, so troops adhered to their inner creative voice to impress the gal of their dreams. Gene Tierney, the dark-haired goddess of *Laura* fame, was flattered when she received correspondence from a flier based in England who had written a number of plays with her in mind as the lead. Pretty blonde Elyse Knox was mailed a hula skirt from sailors based on the Solomon Islands, but the present came with a catch: they wanted cheesecake pictures of her wearing the skirt. Perhaps the most interesting gift a pin-up received during the war was the one Anne Jeffreys found in her mailbox. A soldier stationed in Burma shipped Anne a pair of cobra skins, showing a creative flare for the practice of gift-giving soldiers had undertaken. But when it came to creativity, Miss Jeffreys had the upper hand on her serviceman admirer. She took the two cobra skins, sewed them together, and created what she termed a "co-bra" out of the skins — a bikini top that made for unique swimwear on any beach.

The greatest gift that soldiers gave pin-up girls was nothing tangible but something altogether more useful, especially in their line of work: attention. There have been countless pretty gals, over the years, to have ventured out Hollywood way with visions of success on the silver screen foremost on their minds. Many fail to achieve success, not because they aren't appealing enough but because their ability to captivate the public is uncertain. There were many such gals during World War II, who set the boys to whistle when they walked by but whose ability to appease a film-going populace was too vague for producers to take a chance on them. When it seemed a gal was destined to wait outside the doors of Hollywood, never to breach the gates, the soldiers assisted them, swung the doors wide, and saw to the elevation of numerous lovely ladies. The stunning brunette Linda Darnell was, perhaps, the most popular aspiring actress assisted in this regard. Early in her film career, when it seemed there were few roles for her, Linda, rather than sit in her apartment and bemoan her plight, traveled to military bases and entertained troops. Her patriotic actions endeared her to the servicemen, and the servicemen in turn took up pens, rather than arms, and assaulted her studio with fan letters. About Miss Darnell's newfound popularity, Dee Lowrance wrote, "Her camp shows gave her dividends in new fans among the men in service — they wrote letters about her to the studio."

The soldier's pen helped Linda Darnell achieve notoriety in Hollywood, for the film studios, knowledgeable in regard to her physical appeal, were besieged with soldiers testimonies that seconded their belief in her attractiveness. Two other such ladies benefitted by the servicemen were Yvonne De Carlo and Elyse Knox. An exotic beauty who oftentimes portrayed

Native American ladies in film, Miss De Carlo was a common face around Hollywood but little more. At the time of the war, Yvonne had worked in many films but never in roles of much substance — she was typically a pretty figure in the background. All that changed thanks to the admiring missives that troops sent off to Hollywood. Wood Soanes wrote, "Miss De Carlo received a long-term contract and starring role as a direct result of efforts made by men in the armed forces — a tribute to the value of cheesecake, otherwise known as leg-art." A crew of American bombers stationed in Africa gave Miss Knox the boost when they requested enough pin-ups of the blonde beauty to paper the inside of their bomber. A virtual unknown at the time, the former model landed film roles based principally on the letters she received from troops overseas. Studios took notice of the wants of soldiers, which enabled them to feel a level of confidence when they cast a pretty ingénue in a feature.

Pin-up girls, ingénues or established screen stars and models, felt a sense of duty for the servicemen, an obligation that bound them to the men who fought to uphold liberty and the American way of life. They signed no social contracts, but they allowed their conscience to be their guide and supported many endeavors that lent support to the troops. A number of causes and organizations sprung up during the war years that saw to the needs and desires of men in the armed forces. The gals, who graced the glossy cheesecake photographs that troops devoured, lent their names and figures to many such campaigns. Evelyn Keyes, who became a popular face in the film noir genre after the war, was one of the more vocal supporters of campaigns designed for the benefit of servicemen. Miss Keyes accepted the role as spokesperson for the "V for Victory Book Drive." In that capacity, Evelyn diligently promoted the campaign that collected reading material to be sent to troops both overseas and stateside. During the war years, Evelyn collected books, volunteered many spare hours with the Red Cross, and attended military camp tours as her methods of support for the men in the armed forces. So dedicated was Miss Keyes to every soldier, when she attended a Purple Heart ceremony to hand accolades to wounded soldiers, many troops were too disabled to attend the ceremony, so she personally drove out to Bushnell hospital and greeted each soldier too incapacitated to join the festivities. All the recipients of the Purple Heart of the heroic unit that Miss Keyes visited felt the tender touch of her extraordinary, patriotic compassion.

Dolores Moran, who sizzled on the screen opposite Humphrey Bogart in the classic film *To Have and Have Not*, agreed to spearhead a campaign designed to soothe the dejection of Uncle Sam's most homesick soldier.

Miss Moran was teamed with fellow pin-up girls Lynne Baggett and Joan Winfield, and the heavenly trio was tasked with a unique mission. Their assignment was to locate the loneliest soldier in the armed forces. This unusual mission led them to a young private named Robert Wilson from Titusville, Pennsylvania, who they deemed to be the most forlorn GI who Uncle Sam had to offer. Their initial mission was to locate the soldier, while the second mission, one of uppermost importance, was to charge the poor bloke's spirits by showing him a good time around Hollywood. With three comely dolls beautifying his surroundings, Private Wilson visited the hot spots in Hollywood, to include the Hollywood Canteen and the film studios. Miss Moran and Company escorted the Titusville Disconsolate around Tinseltown, where they danced with him at happening night spots and put him on speaking terms with such stars as Jack Benny, Humphrey Bogart, and Joan Leslie. After Private Wilson's jaunt with Dolores and the Gals, Uncle Sam's loneliest serviceman was henceforth regarded as Uncle Sam's luckiest serviceman.

When it came to building morale among a concentration of servicemen, pin-up girls had a leg up on the competition. Funnymen like Bob Hope and Joe E. Brown toured military installations to the uproarious applause of the boys in the armed forces, but the objects of pulchritude — those enticing girls in their bantam skirts — placed the boys in dizzy spells more commanding than any rhubarb or wisecrack the great comedians offered. When cheesecake sirens visited the troops at their training spots, servicemen took delight in sharing their experiences — even regarding the drills that prepped them for war — with the dames they desired. The more daring of the pin-up girls would don a military helmet and enter an exercise or two simply to jolt the servicemen's spirits. The spritely Joan Blondell, who seemed a ball of energy in many of her flicks, would often run the obstacle course with the boys when she visited training installations. Evelyn Keyes participated in gas mask training with troops, and Rita Hayworth, the smoldering sensation of the silver screen, showed the gents at Camp Bowie her prowess with a bayonet. Although Miss Hayworth apologized for interrupting their training, the men found her interruption an interlude more than agreeable.

To show support for the troops was to laud the merits of the men who abandoned their civilian lives to defend the American way of life from foreign evils that threatened to destroy it. The lovely ladies of the entertainment industry were unable to take up arms and fight the enemy on their soil, so they did what they could under the circumstances. Whether they posed for the shutterbugs in leggy outfits, sold war bonds, or visited the servicemen at their bases, the ladies of the pin-up trade displayed a level of patriotism no less important than the men in uniform. The cheesecake poses and the installation tours were for the benefit of the troops, not the nation as a whole, but to attend to the servicemen was for the betterment of the nation. The fighting men sacrificed their lives so that not only Americans but also those individuals under the heavy foot of tyranny could breathe the air of freedom without inhaling the choking granules of oppression. To assist those admirable men whose mission it was to defend liberty was to add to the resolve of the only force capable of delivering the world from the doorstep of torment. The actions of those persons in a supporting role were praiseworthy, for the troops task at hand was of profound significance, and for them to know that their fellow Americans stood behind them and waved the flag they took an oath to defend, served as spiritual reinforcement.

The pin-up girls did more for the troops than flash a leggy pose for their enjoyment. Although their primary function was to build morale via an appeal to the aesthetic sense, those cheesecake cuties who went beyond the photographer's studio found that their show of support was not lost on the men in uniform. Soldiers cherished the pin-up girls who visited them at their bases and danced with them at canteens — they held dear those ladies who placed the needs of servicemen above their own. Joan Blondell delved into her own bank account in order to meet the demand of fan mail she received from soldiers who requested an autographed photo. The screen starlet didn't hesitate to honor the requests of troops even though by mailing photographs to servicemen across the globe, Joan forfeited close to one hundred dollars a week. Ann Sothern, best known for her screen alter-ego of Maisie, enjoyed visiting servicemen at their bases and dining in their crude mess halls, opting to eat with the grunts rather than ply a good knife and fork at an upscale eatery. She would even take dessert with the boys afterwards and prepare malts for their after dinner enjoyment.

The gals that posed for pin-up pictures were typically ladies who earned their bread courtesy of show business, and they were often found standing on stages or basking in the invisible spotlight created by rapt male attention. The business of show is to cast personal inhibitions aside, where restrictions are leveled for the sake of merriment and the joy of the spectacle. Times are merry when glasses overflow with spirits, and floors are littered with the bustle of dancing feet. Such were not the times during World War II, but the lovely ladies who posed for pin-up pictures created a pocket of felicity where soldiers could escape from their military endeavors. The photographs served this purpose, but the dolls, when in the flesh, were capable of combating the despair that many fighting men felt simply by presenting a pleasing image and flashy an inviting smile. When pin-up girls attended a gathering at a base — such as when Martha O'Driscoll graced the cadets at Minter Field during their graduation — they created that needed outlet of escape by dancing and chatting with the troops. The Minter Field cadets, who had spent months training and had been deprived of the intoxicating aura of female glamour, were offered a release from their typical surroundings courtesy of the selfless action of Miss O'Driscoll attending their graduation ceremony. Their companion, at least for a time, no longer was the bugle's call presented during military instruction, but the delicate hand and light feet of a stunning dancing partner in the lovely Martha O'Driscoll.

When the ladies of show business took the show to the boys, and incorporated them in their expositions, the servicemen proved both a rapt audience and a game straight man. Song numbers were extremely popular among the troops, as many songbirds would take the stage and dedicate their ditties to the men in the armed forces. Actress Dale Evans was one songstress who liked to incorporate uniformed men in her shows. Wherever her travails took her, Miss Evans typically reserved a love ballad for her final performance, at which time she would invite a lucky soldier from the crowd to assist her. The serviceman's task was simply to stand on the stage beside Dale as she crooned a ballad she wrote specifically for the soldiers, titled *Won't You Marry Me, Mister Laramie?* The lovely crooner would latch onto the lucky gent and proposition the fellow with a tuneful marriage request, all done to the thunderous amusement of the troops in attendance. After Dale's show at the Marana Airfield, the commander of the airfield's basic training school said, "These men are deeply appreciative. I watched them and it is a treat to see their faces light up. This was their first big show."

When troupes of entertainers traveled to military bases their roster often consisted of the show's headliner (Bob Hope, for example), a few showmen such as magicians and gagmen, a handful of pretty gals, and persons capable of crooning. The soldiers found plenty amusement when the pretty gals were capable of showmen antics or had a knack for trilling. "Let there be song!" and "Let there be girls" were exclamations from the boys that the entertainers desired to accommodate and to interlace when possible. Gale Robbins, the gorgeous honey-haired entertainer, was one such lady capable of blending beauty with vocals. Miss Robbins, who toured with the legendary Mr. Hope during the war, was a sexy singing sensation that her studio, 20th Century Fox, felt would replace Betty Grable as their leading pin-up girl when Betty became pregnant. The servicemen voiced their opinion when they littered her studio with fan mail after taking in her USO show. In their best starry-eyed, vapid teen-age girl impersonation, a group of soldiers mimicked the sweater girl fad of overzealously praising singers by going gaga over Gale. She received a letter from a unit of troops that viewed her USO show, which read, "We unanimously nominate you the Female Sinatra — we'll scream for you any time."

The pretty songbirds understood the therapeutic value that their charms had on soldiers, and would soothe the serviceman engaged in military endeavors via the radio. However, many of the gals would not hesitate to ply the medicinal ingredients their voice and beauty bestowed to the boys in the flesh. When men returned home from their wartime stint overseas they had a need for relaxation and an escape from the horrors that previously gripped them. Those fighting men in greater need for the healing charms of females were those wounded in battle. Pin-up girl Shirley Ross was noted for visiting wounded soldier hospitals and singing songs to injured troops in the infirmary. Due to her laudable reputation, when Miss Ross left photographs of her sons under her pillow during a USO tour at Clovis Army Airfield, the commander of the airfield instructed a pilot to retrieve Shirley's coveted pictures and deliver them to her. Since she spent countless hours uplifting the spirits of men who had been devastated, both physically and mentally by the war, the commander at Clovis felt that Uncle Sam could spend a little fuel returning the tokens that Miss Ross used to remember her children.

Before television sets populated every American home, the primary mode for entertainment was the radio. Folks were kept amused with musical numbers and radio serials such as the postwar laugh-a-minute comedy *The Bickersons* with Don Ameche and Frances Langford. The comely Ginny Simms hosted the popular program *Johnny Presents*, and she regaled throngs of supporters with her sweet singing voice. When it came to singing love ballads that soothed the overseas serviceman, Ginny Simms was the undisputed queen. It was the radio that kept folks aware of the day's struggles and the military's actions, and it was the radio that alleviated the burden of anxiety that came with a world at war. The pin-up girls even took time out from posing for the shutterbugs to offer their voice for the amusement of troops and the average Joe. Rochelle Hudson, the portrait of natural beauty, agreed to serve as guest host of the game show *Noah Webster Says*. When she headlined the program, only soldiers were allowed to participate in the show, and the serviceman who accumulated the highest score was awarded with a date with the beautiful Miss Hudson.

The soldier's primary mode for entertainment was the radio as well, but when the USO shuttled out celebrities to meet, greet, and entertain the troops, the radios were merely an afterthought. Servicemen would rather see the striking beauty of Rochelle Hudson in person than hear her fetching voice courtesy of the radio waves. Whether fighting men were encamped on the Aleutian Islands off Alaska or engaged in training exercises at Indiantown Gap, the USO saw to their needs and tried to boost their morale by depositing an entertainer for a day. Many of the day's leading stars headlined USO tours — stateside as well as overseas — to spread a little uplifting spirit to the troops under Uncle Sam's employ. Actress Ann Sheridan was a popular USO attraction before her stock as an entertainer dropped courtesy of her abrupt cancelation of an overseas tour. Ann felt that the USO was an organization that actors should support. When she returned from a warzone tour, Ann said, "Every actor and actress should visit our boys on the fighting fronts. We don't have to put on a great big show, just so we give them something to make them laugh. They need to see a friendly face from home to know we're with them." Many pin-up girls shared Miss Sheridan's sentiments and took to the USO circuit as an alternate method to boost morale.

USO shows were for the boys, and they could at times get a tad racy. The pin-up photographs were hot commodities among the men in the armed forces, and entertainers tried to appeal to the servicemen's wants and desires by displaying a package of pulchritude or two. Given cheesecake photography's popularity, folks on the troop entertainment ticket attempted to duplicate the pin-up's extreme appeal. Pin-ups ranged from poses of women in short skirts flaunting their legs to dolls sporting sweaters that accentuated their bosoms. The bulk of the pin-up pictures found in the employ of the servicemen were stills of dames exhibiting plenty of skin. So, if the boys wanted skin, skin is what the entertainers sought to give them.

Joan Blondell and Marie Wilson were two of the top accommodators of flesh exhibition on military tours. Noted more for their roles in comedy, the duo gained notoriety for their risqué routines for the boys. Joan and Marie would give impromptu striptease acts to the servicemen, although their acts would be deemed modest by today's standards. Neither woman completely peeled down for the servicemen's amusement, but when they did peel, it was done with a nod towards comedy.

Miss Blondell would inform the gents in attendance that she harbored a desire to be a stripteaser, and she would then begin her peel-down bit but would apply the brakes on her routine when she would simulate the zipper of her dress getting stuck. When she asked the audience for assistance, servicemen would try to outstrip the wind getting to Joan's pesky zipper. Marie Wilson, best known for her role as the airhead in the *My Friend Irma* series, gave a dismantling act a tad more exhilarating than Joan Blondell. Miss Wilson toured with Ken Murray's *Blackouts*, and she was a shapely blonde who cast the mold that subsequent actresses like Suzanne Somers and Loni Anderson were formed from. Marie would perform a striptease act emceed by Murray who would inform Wilson that her clothes had to be rationed: her wool skirt for Army uniforms, her silk blouse for parachutes, and her shoes for Russian relief. At the end of each *Blackouts* routine, Murray would call Marie back out on the stage for a final bow, and the full-breasted Marie would wear a low-cut blouse that nearly failed in its task of concealing her charms. Marie would take numerous bows to the applause of servicemen, with every pair of eyes on her ample chest, waiting for the blouse to give: it never did.

The men in the armed forces appreciated the hours that celebrities put in on the entertainment circuit, but it was the ladies who came to them when they were enmeshed in battle that they truly adored. Such stunning screen stars as Ellen Drew and Ann Dvorak left Hollywood to travel with their husbands when they were shipped overseas. Ellen and Ann were not absentee war brides, pining at home while their husbands fought in lands on distant shores, but women of extreme character who assisted the residents of the war-ravaged regions their spouses were deployed to. Both Drew and Dvorak were engaged in admirable, selfless actions to assist persons in England who had their homeland leveled by the Axis. Ann Dvorak drove an ambulance in England and served in the Women's Land Army where she helped plow and irrigate fields, while Ellen Drew gave up her status as a war bond seller to help reconstruct Bermondsey — an area of England devastated by the Axis. Both women were ladies of remarkable character, but their selfless actions of building morale among the English prohibited them from entertaining on the foxhole circuit. That circuit, where many an entertainer dared not set foot, was traveled by only a few patriotic women.

To venture off and visit lands where battles rage and security is absent elicits little temptation for the average entertainer. Where bullets fly and soldiers engage in battle is not an arena suited for the spectacle of show, for death has not cosigned its lease on the battlefield with glamour.

However, there are persons of glamour whose hearts are heavy with the patriotic stuff found in the frame of fighting men, and these persons, entertainers by trade, feel compelled by love of country — by devotion to soldiers fighting for liberty — to visit servicemen and bring cheer to their hearts. A select few pin-up girls possessed the indomitable inner drive needed to make such a journey. To leave the safety of Hollywood, where producers and directors serve as the rank and file, tempted few dames. They knew that by stepping out from the enclosed studio with the security it provided and entering battle zones, the script was not one completed by the hand of a screenwriter but an unfinished text whose pages could provide doom more easily than laughter. Not many pin-up girls made the rounds on the foxhole circuit, but the few that did should have earned a place in American history on equal footing with the greatest of all statesmen.

Many a soldier was left astonished when a jeep escorting a beautiful pin-up girl parked in an area near the frontline. Such occurrences were seldom, but pin-up girls like models Jinx Falkenburg and Candy Jones, and actresses such as Marlene Dietrich and Carole Landis, brought their pulchritude to the fighting lines. Miss Landis toured war areas with funny gal Martha Raye and entertainers Kay Francis and Mitzi Mayfair. When Carole returned home, she wrote a book about her war area experiences titled *Four Jills in a Jeep*, which was turned into a motion picture that starred three of the four gals. Jinx Falkenburg toured the CBI Theater and returned to the States with a shorter haircut, since she gave away locks of her tresses to admiring soldiers. The voluptuous Candy Jones, one of the elite Conover models, visited the Pacific Theater under the auspices of the "Cover Girls Abroad" tour, where she spent Christmas singing yuletide tunes to homesick troops. All these women braved hazards, but Marlene Dietrich, who was a German national aligned with the Allies, was a target of the Nazis who brazenly set foot on her fatherland and supported the actions of the American military. Before men would travel to the frontlines, La Dietrich would plant a parting kiss on the serviceman's lips, offering her own version of morale building. She was said to be a prime target of Hitler's.

Those pin-up girls who departed the photographer's studio and journeyed to lands where battles raged, were the premier boosters of morale. Marlene Dietrich was an established screen star and Carole Landis was perhaps Hollywood's most shapely oomph girl, but the two blondes, dedicated to their country and its servicemen, bid adieu to the lights and camera's lens in order to entertain soldiers in regions beset with war. Marlene visited such locales as Iceland, France, Luxembourg, Belgium, and Czechoslovakia on her war tour, and she spread patriotic cheer to the men determined to topple the Axis. Remembered more today for her fashion sense, Marlene enjoyed wearing military fatigues on her tour, and she made close friends of such American heroes as General Patton. Carole Landis, the blonde torpedo with the enviable figure, entertained troops stationed in the European Theater as well as northern Africa. An absolute treat for the servicemen, the beautiful Miss Landis took her meals in the mess hall with the boys, and the Hollywood glamour girl expected no preferential treatment simply because she was a rising screen star. But as a screen star, Carole was the target for many servicemen autograph seekers who, with little on their person to sign, would offer Miss Landis a dollar bill to inscribe. Once, after she had returned home from an overseas tour, a soldier handed Carole a dollar bill to autograph, shortly after she exited her plane. Miss Landis flashed the gent a smile, pulled foreign paper currency from her purse, and said, "Look what I have — Eisenhower!"

Carole Landis and her fellow "Jills" initially entertained troops in England and Ireland, but the quartet begged for an assignment to tour northern Africa to give the soldiers there a morale boost. Military life, especially in battle regions, was a hardship for all involved: mess halls, bedding quarters, and bathrooms were crude by civilized standards. Regardless of the primitive conditions, Carole and her three chums soldiered through the less-than-ideal setting of minimal amenities, for they felt that since the troops experienced few pleasantries in battle that those pleasantries should be foreign to them as well. Miss Landis claimed that the entire time she spent in northern Africa, she was able to manage only two hot baths. On soldiering through the poor conditions in Africa, Carole said, "We wore turbans and snoods and tried to camouflage the whole affair of knowing how filthy we were — but it was pretty uncomfortable." The conditions were uncomfortable for all involved, but Carole and her companion's presence allowed for a slight brush of comfort, which the servicemen sorely needed. Overseas in battle regions during Christmas of 1942, Carole spent the holiday season among the troops. During Christmas, Carole said that the men didn't want her to talk about Hollywood or the glamorous life of motion picture celebrities — what they wanted was the spiritual warmth the holiday season could provide. Miss Landis gave them that warmth, for she sang *White Christmas* countless times to homesick soldiers.

By volunteering to entertain troops in hostile regions, pin-up girls willfully entered arenas paved with the inimical terrain of antagonistic agents. Sanctuaries were abandoned by these admirable ladies who sought to elevate the morale of troops engaged in war. They served as symbols of justice, dedication, and duty: women who braved combative locales in order to show the servicemen that America was behind them. Carole Landis took cover more than once during an enemy raid, and Marlene Dietrich sought refuge from the Axis in military fighting positions. Martha O'Driscoll spat in the eye of villainy when she entertained troops at Attu. While she sang a number on stage for the troop's enjoyment, Japanese planes circled overhead while the air-raid siren disturbed the jovial atmosphere of Martha's show. Martha remained on stage, however, where she completed her ditty. She consequently earned the nickname of "Miss Fearless," given her by the troops in attendance. An awestruck soldier said, "Martha didn't even flinch. She didn't even look afraid!"

Pin-up girls served the soldiers a number of purposes, roles commendable and praiseworthy, but none were more admirable than tending to the wounded and impaired. Although cheesecake gals like Carole Landis visited the frontlines, such danger-traipsing wasn't in store for all pin-up girls. It took an intrepid constitution to brave the possibility of an enemy attack, but to console those men left disabled by the war took a constitution replete with nurturing qualities. Pin-up girl Lois Collier, a warm-hearted woman, volunteered her time to entertain a group of combat veterans left blind by their battlefield injuries. The servicemen who had recently been left sightless were unsure of themselves, for they were forced to transition into a world more foreign to them than any hostile enemy land. However, once Miss Collier began with the festivities, her caring demeanor eased the pain and confusion of the soldiers, and they were, for a moment, able to put aside their grief and despair and enjoy the presence of a dear woman.

A number of pin-up girls visited wounded soldier hospitals to cheer up troops who'd returned home, unfit for military duty. Their purpose was to show wounded veterans that their sacrifice did not go unnoticed or unappreciated, and that Americans would be forever grateful for their heroics. It was a mighty assignment for the sharp-looking cheesecake gals, for the men they visited in such a setting were no longer sound of body, and many of them felt that they were no longer appealing to the opposite sex. With limbs removed, sight impaired, and crutches supporting maimed appendages, the wounded viewed themselves not as prime specimens of masculinity as they had before but damaged bodies that the prettiest of American girls would pass over when selecting a mate. But the pin-up girls, those ideal images of American womanhood, put such morose sentiments to rest when they embraced the wounded gents as they convalesced in military infirmaries. Spirits that had once been dejected were jostled back into liveliness as stunning women like Bonita Granville flashed the boys a smile and offered a warm figure to embrace. But the assignment could be hazardous to the visiting pin-up girl's health, as Miss Granville found out when she contracted German measles on a tour at Ashburn General Hospital. The gal who came out to uplift the troops found herself a sickbed, and was tended to, hand and foot, by military personnel who appreciated her selfless visit.

Once the battlefield is abandoned and the war song's pages are turned to more lilting, peaceful lullabies, those heroes which combat has left physically impaired feel forgotten amongst a world of celebrating citizens. Unable to dance with a pretty girl at a night spot, for legs have been discharged courtesy of the enemy's attack, the celebration for wounded veterans presents not the full merriment experienced by those returned physically fit. Although the nation is grateful for their sacrifice, no level of accolades, no number of medals, can replace that which was lost. But while many celebrate, there are persons, sound of body, who feel that the celebration should be taken to the injured warriors who are unable to enter social settings and participate in the revelry. Singer Ginny Simms was one such person who kept the sacrifice of wounded soldiers at the forefront of the nation's mind when she formed the "Lest We Forget" organization, which provided entertainment for hospitalized war casualties. Another such entertainer was Rhonda Fleming, the titian-haired goddess whose film career had just begun during the war years, who entertained wounded veterans the first Christmas after the war had ended at Bushnell General Hospital. Ginny and Rhonda's actions, as well as others with like constitutions, showed the servicemen that although the fighting had ended, their heroics would not be forgotten.

For the soldiers, pin-up girls represented the ideal American woman — ladies who admired their dedication to the country, who offered a body to dance with, who warmed the still and frigid nights in foreign lands, and who served as symbols of love and tenderness. There were those pin-up girls who visited troops on the frontlines, and who toured infirmaries to rebuild a wounded soldier's crippled morale, but it was the image, the pin-up picture, that was constantly at hand. When Rhonda Fleming left the hospital or when Carole Landis journeyed to another post, the photograph remained — serving as a reminder that womanhood, that love, could be attained after the war's end. Soldiers were excited when news circulated that pin-up girl June Vincent had taken a flyer for a husband — a man she met while he served — for these symbols of beauty, these exceptional American ladies, were eager to wed heroes. Whether the woman wed was a sexy pin-up girl like Miss Vincent or a pretty gal from one's hometown meant little to the soldier overseas, for tenderness in the form of a female was his desire. His world was one of war, but knowledge that all wars conclude, that the final bomb, the final bullet, would someday be sent, and that love would replace hostility, kept the serviceman dedicated to his nation's cause of ending the horror.

Many soldiers were married — had wives and children waiting at home — and had their own pockets of love and warmth to return to. To a great number of wed servicemen, their pin-up girls were their wives, not Jane Russell and Betty Grable. The commander of the Fifth Army, General Mark W. Clark, kept common correspondence with his wife and would send her an occasional gift from overseas. Once, General Clark shipped a pair of triple pendant earrings to his wife, which aroused in Mrs. Clark the pin-up spirit, so she had photographs taken of her wearing the jewelry. She told a reporter, "I've never worn pendant earrings before and I want him to see these pictures. I'm my husband's pin-up girl and I expect my pictures to cover the walls of his truck completely."

Whereas there were a number of married soldiers who had already reeled in a spouse of their own, single troops peered at their pin-up photographs of celebrities and hoped that when the war ended, single gals would be aplenty. They had read that sexy blonde pin-up girl June Vincent had married a pilot and that *The Outlaw's* mysterious, buxom star Jane Russell was an Army bride, which kept those passionate fires ablaze within their chests. Yet, some of the pin-up girl love-scoops were fictitious, such as the case of Rochelle Hudson. Not made of the social butterfly stuff that comprised the constitutions of such a glamorous actress as Lana Turner, Hudson was more retiring, and her private life more obscure. When rumors circled that Miss Hudson was engaged to marry a lieutenant in the Navy, the lovely brunette simply rolled her eyes, for she understood the intention of writers: to show soldiers that pin-up girls were pining for them. The truth was, Rochelle was married to a lieutenant commander and the two were engaged in serious espionage work for the United States government south of the border (more on this interesting tale can be found in Rochelle Hudson's section in the biographical chapter). If the false scoop kept soldiers' hearts alert, Rochelle saw little harm in it, for she and her husband knew the market for her hand was one already settled.

What the men needed was not false scoops by writers, offering inside dope that held no water, but reprinted statements made by pin-up girls who described the need for their presence. Soldiers wanted to return home to American girls, but many of them harbored the fear that the best gals the country had to offer were already taken by men whose draft status kept them from military service. Many servicemen overseas were haunted by dreams of 3-A draft classification hound dogs, who corralled all the eligible dolls while they were off fighting for good ol' Uncle Sam. To put the servicemen overseas at ease, many pin-up girls and agencies eager to assist the troops informed the fighting men that ladies were patiently waiting their return. The beautiful Rita Daigle became the image of the "waiting" crusade when she was voted "Miss Stardust 1944," which meant that she won a contest as the prettiest serviceman's girl back home. Miss Daigle's popularity soared, and the stunning fair-haired girl from Lowell, Massachusetts, parlayed her "Miss Stardust" fame into a modeling contract. As the face of the servicemen's sweetheart, Rita's lovely features were reprinted on many of the nation's leading magazines — she was enlisted by *Newsweek* as the pin-up girl for their "Battle Baby" edition of 1945.

While Rita Daigle gained her fifteen minutes of fame, film studios lent encouragement to the lovelorn soldiers who were bereft of girlfriends and gals to chase. When a man serves his country overseas, the most common occurrence that disheartens the soldier is the knowledge that the girl he left back home has failed to wait for his return. The act of infidelity on a girlfriend or wife's part is more scandalous when her loved one is a serviceman fighting for liberty on foreign, hostile lands. The man has taken a vow to safeguard the nation, while his philandering inamorata seeks only to fulfill her selfish, carnal desires. During World War II, when American society was more supportive of soldiers, celebrities lent a supportive hand in order to help a dejected serviceman. Blonde pin-up girl Janet Blair informed her studio that she would like to support troops who had been so treated by their wayward paramours, and the executives devised what they termed "the love insurance policy." Janet had just completed the film *Two Yanks From Trinidad*, and the publicity department at her studio concocted the insurance policy as a method to draw interest to the film. The policy used Miss Blair as premium. If a soldier took out the policy because he lost his girl, then he could take Janet Blair out on a date. The struggle to come to grips with an unfaithful lover, the studio felt, would be easier to digest should a soldier be allowed to insure his relationship, and be rewarded by a date with a stunning actress like the lovely Miss Blair.

Other actresses supported men overseas, albeit in methods less creative than Janet Blair. Two of the more vocal supporters of waiting for serviceman's return were Evelyn Keyes and Martha O'Driscoll. These two remarkable women knew the right words to offer servicemen who envisioned the pool of pretty prospective brides to be dried up upon their stateside return. Martha O'Driscoll made her rounds on the USO circuit, with stops in Alaska and the nearby Aleutian Islands, where she would entertain and chat with servicemen from the various states. Whenever she would come across a chap who was homesick for a pretty girl or a soldier worried that girls were cupiding about with civilians that avoided the military, Martha would give their spirits a jolt. About uplifting love-sick soldiers, Miss O'Driscoll said, "They seemed to like to feel that it was a bit of a man-less world back home, that the fact they were away had made a great difference — as indeed it has. Who would want to tell them otherwise?"

When Evelyn Keyes received a letter from a sergeant who served overseas at Saipan, which was co-signed by members of his bomber squadron, she sprang into action. The letter Miss Keyes received from Sergeant Charles Kausel voiced the concern that many deployed soldiers felt over the availability of pretty American girls. Evelyn was known to be one of the staunchest supporters of troops in Hollywood for her many base tours and Red Cross volunteer work, which made her an ideal correspondence partner for Sergeant Kausel in regard to the worry that many servicemen harbored. Miss Keyes took up pen and paper and wrote the serviceman in Saipan a reassuring letter. Evelyn penned, "I think many other girls have the same idea I do. We know that many of the best catches are still overseas, and don't think the girls have forgotten." By reassuring the servicemen that girls would wait, that they desired to wed heroes who were the best the nation had to offer, both Evelyn Keyes and Martha O'Driscoll performed a service for the troops that proved quite therapeutic in regard to addressing their fear of limited female partners to choose from after the war.

Female celebrities were lauded for their desire to encourage soldiers both overseas and stateside. Whereas Martha O'Driscoll and Evelyn Keyes assured them that many desirable American girls would be available upon their return, other celebrities like the legendary Barbara Stanwyck — married to a serviceman herself — cheered the boys up by cheering herself up. Like many war brides, Barbara was lonesome and eager to share her life with a husband removed, but she found solace in visiting wounded servicemen in hospitals and corresponding with many fighting men via the mail. In order to cure the dejection she felt in regards to her loneliness, Miss Stanwyck met with a group of wounded soldiers and left with a spiritual awakening that showed her that she was not alone. Barbara

Stanwyck said, "When Bob left for the service, a great loneliness engulfed me. True, I had my son and my work, but a great void was there. I had only to visit the men in hospitals and hear their stories of longing for loved ones, to make me forget my martyrdom." Whereas the servicemen needed reassurance that ladies would wait for their return, war brides like Miss Stanwyck needed reassurance that their personal struggles were struggles experienced collectively, thus alleviating the magnitude of her burden. She found refuge also in the pen, and scribe Lois Leeds claimed that Miss Stanwyck had a roster of just over one hundred soldiers who she kept regular correspondence with.

Women like Barbara Stanwyck, Martha O'Driscoll, and other glamorous celebrity pin-ups were not prospective brides for the servicemen, but images of American womanhood. They were hearts pulsating with nurturing qualities, like Miss Stanwyck whose letters to servicemen were deeply cherished. They were voices of dedication, like Evelyn Keyes, who informed the boys that American gals were desirous of heroes and would wait for the ships to come in before choosing a husband. They were symbols of liberty, like Carole Landis, who braved hostile regions in order to spread not only cheer but something more profound, more ardent, which stoked the fires of courage in every soldier's heart. To the servicemen, the pin-up girls were not simply intoxicating figures to be admired, women who represented the ideal female assemblage, but the personification of decency — all worth fighting for. As Miss Landis so eloquently put it, "While you stand up there entertaining that most of the time you're not you, Carole Landis, but a symbol to the boys around — a bit of a wife, a sweetheart, a sister, a mother. You're just an American girl to an American boy, lonely for the feel of home." Home is what the pin-up girls represented: nothing sexist, nothing crude or base, but everything flattering. For home is that desirable sanctuary, that land free from war's contamination, and to represent that bodily is to debase not the female gender but to honor it in a way that few things have ever been honored before.

# CHAPTER FIVE

# THE HEIGHT
### ★ OF THE ★
# PIN-UP GIRL

The war years were made a tad more bearable for the men in service, as pin-up photography went mainstream. What was once a practice resigned for folks in the show business industry, who horded still pictures of comely actresses in various stages of dress and undress, became a phenomenon accepted by popular American culture. Actresses no longer posed for the benefit of studio executives alone — who arranged scantily-clad photo shoots mainly for their leisure and personal enjoyment, rather than images that would make up an actress's portfolio. These stills became images that instilled morale in the breasts of servicemen across the globe. The girls who posed for these photographs became symbols of American womanhood to many a weary soldier placed in a hostile setting. Due to the nationalistic tribute that cheesecake art paid America during the war years, the practice was widely accepted, which enabled pin-up art to reach its zenith near its moment of advent. The cheesecake stills encapsulated memories to the servicemen overseas, so those that they pinned up served as representations of that which they longed to be reunited with.

It took a war for pin-up art to reach its height, for many men who would have been home, thus able to pursue a gal of their liking, were engaged in battle maneuvers that removed them from the possibility of amorous pursuits. To appease their need for physical stimulation, the men in the armed forces turned to cheesecake art. They found photographic representation of those sought-after gals in the form of pin-up stills. For soliders on the frontlines, their only method of being visited by a lovely American woman was via the cheesecake picture. So, the pin-up practice mushroomed and created an interesting episode in history that saw the glorification of the female form go mainstream. Given that most Americans personally knew a man in the armed forces, the average United States citizen raised little fuss in regards to an act viewed as crude by a large pocket of the populace. If the soldiers desired images of female beauty to lift their morale during time of war, the bulk of Americans would not refuse their simple desire.

The soldiers were responsible for pin-up photography's inception in mainstream culture, yet once the fad caught on, civilians gave the practice a boost. Pin-up pictures of comely dames littered military quarters, bunks, and the inside of vehicles, but those same images later began to populate company break rooms, twenty-four-hour garages, and the inside of schoolboy's lockers. If Little Johnny were stopped in the halls en route to his algebra class and his textbook given a cursory examination, a photograph of Ava Gardner seated on the beach might be pasted on the book's inside cover. The mailroom workers for RKO film studios were placed in hot water when an executive visited their break room and found pin-up pictures of Lizabeth Scott on the wall — who just so happened to be a contract player of rival Paramount. The RKO postal sorters minor act of treason made for an amusing snippet in the newspapers, even if their bosses would prefer if they rifled through their studio's roster for their official pin-up girl. It seemed everywhere a photograph could be secured, whether it be the inside of a school locker or an empty space on the company wall, there was pinned a slice of cheesecake.

American culture embraced the pin-up practice, from the buck private just out of boot camp to the pretty coed that peregrinated from classroom to classroom on her college campus. Beauty was on parade during the war years and the ladies were eager to enlist their faces and figures as part of the pin-up campaign. To claim that the bulk of women found the pin-up practice sexist would be an erroneous assumption, for young ladies across the United States willingly enrolled themselves in pin-up contests. From Bangor, Maine, to Coos Bay, Oregon, American cities and towns have enjoyed the jubilation of summertime activity, with county fairs and township festivals the setting for revelry. Typically, in these settings, beauty pageants can be found. During the war years, the term "beauty pageant" went on hiatus and was replaced with the handle "pin-up contest." Crude or not, many young beauties gladly enrolled themselves in their local pin-up contests. Factories would even hold their own pin-up contests with the prettiest gals on the company payroll participating in the competition. To win was to be flattered: not to feel objectified for your good looks.

Today, the beauty pageant seems a staple of American culture — like baseball and apple pie — which leads one to imagine that an impromptu pageant was arranged for the gals who stepped off the *Mayflower*. Kidding aside, the beauty pageant circuit has served as a springboard to modeling and acting for numerous young ladies, including pin-up girl Jeanne Crain; she won a handful of beauty pageant titles early in the war effort.

*Lizabeth Scott.* COURTESY OF MOVIEMARKET.COM

During the war years, county fairs and war plants held their own pin-up girl contests, but not all organizations were eager to name an official pin-up girl. An article in the *Troy Record* placed a spotlight on one outfit that refused to participate in the pin-up practice: the Hoboes of America. During their 37th Annual Convention, the Hoboes, spoken for by Jeff Davis — the unofficial "King of the Hoboes" — informed guests at the gathering that they wanted no part in pin-up contests. Davis said, "We don't go for women hoboes. In 1932, the box cars were full of women hoboes — some with babies in their arms and that was bad. So we aim to map a campaign to get rid of the boxcar pin-up." If beauty pageants fail to fit into the category of American staples with baseball and apple pie, then perhaps organizing campaigns to draw awareness to a cause, no matter how miniscule or mundane, would make for an adequate substitute.

The Hoboes of America may have turned away from the pin-up concept, but America in general was pin-up mad. Striking poses of stunning beauties could be found everywhere during the war, from roadside billboards to the pages of the local newspaper. Every industry seemed to engage a popular pin-up girl as their spokesperson, with such beautiful gals as Paulette Goddard employed as pitchmen for everything from cosmetics to soft drinks. Step out in public in the mid-1940s and there would be leg art posted on shop walls and portraits of pretty, zestful gals urging young ladies to join the WAVES. Pin-up pictures were displayed out in the open, not tucked away in machine shops or shunned to a dark corner in the basement above father's workbench, for beauty was something to be admired — a rallying symbol — that gave Americans a collective aesthetic identity. The calendar manufacturer Brown & Bigelow — the top producer of calendars in the United States during the war years — was besieged with requests for pin-up calendars. No other theme was in greater demand than cheesecake. Brown & Bigelow churned out more pin-up calendars than any other theme during the height of the fighting.

People during the war years could purchase pin-up calendars, cheesecake photographs of their favorite female celebrity, and paintings created by legendary artists such as George Petty. The medium of cheesecake art was not hindered by a narrow focus, because actresses, models, and singers could supplement their income by posing for photographers and artists. Their images were used to promote goods as well as build morale for the men in the armed forces. The total number of pin-up images produced during the war years was a figure not easily ascertained. Ramsay Ames claimed that she sat for just under 1,000 pin-up stills, and for her many sittings, numerous prints were duplicated for mass distribution. Thousands upon thousands of pin-up pictures were distributed in many forms, and these images were shipped to lands overseas as well as for use stateside. Jane Russell, photographed no end during the war years, said, "Someone once said that if all the pictures taken of Jane Russell were laid out end to end, they'd reach around the world. I wouldn't doubt it." When American troops invaded the Nazi area of Aachen, they found a pin-up photograph of Miss Russell secured to the wall in the commanding officer's den; Jane's many pin-up pictures certainly were found across the globe.

The popularity of the pin-up practice attracted many Americans, as the bulk of Hollywood's top-flight female stars agreed to pose for cheesecake stills. Leg art helped many aspiring actresses land a studio contract, but those beautiful ladies already under the employ of a film studio were not hesitant to pose for the shutterbugs either. These women were the American trendsetters: the objects of beauty that girls desired to mimic. From their fashion to their poise their allure was established by an American audience that marveled at their appeal. Girls of the war years patterned their hairstyles after Veronica Lake and her famous peek-a-boo waves, and the glamorous coiffures of Carole Landis, to name but two. Ladies like Miss Lake and Miss Landis were respected for their beauty, but their actions as pin-up girls and morale boosters endeared them to film audiences that had previously displayed meager levels of interest. Their fan base soared courtesy of their work as pin-up girls, and the devotion they showed their country and the gents in the armed forces. Film starlets became idols of thousands.

The selfless actions of many pin-up girls allowed for the overall acceptance of the cheesecake trade. The ladies who posed were glamorous and sexy, but with the world at war, their desire to pose for cheesecake stills seemed less a self-aggrandized display of pulchritude and more an act of national pride. Many of the ladies went above and beyond what was expected of them, from Susan Hayward who volunteered to assist a shipyard in the collection of metal to Irene Manning, who took servicemen's children out caroling during Christmas time. The fact that these women, ladies of enviable beauty and status, devoted many hours to causes for their country, meant a lot to average Americans. If the glamorous, delicate beauty that was Susan Hayward was willing to get her hands dirty collecting scrap metal for the war effort, than any other American should roll up his or her sleeves and get dirty right along with her.

At the height of pin-up popularity, many pin-up girls were used as lures by folks in the media and organizers of events. The gals made headlines early in the war effort with their war-bond tours, and given the success of those events with the impressive turnouts, pin-up girls were aggressively petitioned to lend their name and figures to social functions. In Portsmouth, New Hampshire, the city leaders adopted a "Dorothy Lamour Day," where money spent in the local stores was donated to the war effort. Rita Hayworth was used in a similar fashion when her film *You Were Never Lovelier* was screened at the Onondaga Hotel in Syracuse. Although Rita was not present at the screening, patrons who purchased war bonds and stamps were given an autographed photo of the stunning actress. Folks in decision-making positions understood the powerful influence pin-up girls had on the public, and they opted to entice persons to desired locales and events by promising some cheesecake-themed tantalization.

The public's obsession with pin-up girls was noted by business executives in the field of promotion, but there was another pocket of persons who took an even greater advantage of the practice's fame: aspiring actresses. The most difficult aspect of making it in show business is to get discovered in the first place. Before the pin-up craze, a gal had to either rely on luck — with the hope that a talent scout would stumble upon her — or work tirelessly by attending one audition after another. During the war years, pretty girls who possessed dreams that were populated with stars, glitz, and the fame of the film industry, had pin-up photography as a means to enter the trade they so dearly coveted. All they had to do was to slide into a short skirt or slip on a bathing suit, stand on their tiptoes, and flash a big smile. Less work was needed to pose than was required at drama classes. Cheesecake art was an instant form of exposure.

The lack of exposure kept many young actresses from achieving star billing in pictures, so those ladies already in the film industry, yet slaving in background, unaccredited roles, turned to cheesecake art as means for name recognition. Lynn Bari had worked in Hollywood for many years with minor, nonspeaking roles throughout the mid to late 1930s. Late in the 1930s she began to land roles of more substance, but only a handful of filmgoers could spot her in a motion picture and correctly offer her name. All that changed during the war years when Miss Bari became a pin-up hit. Regarded as "a B actress" by many studio professionals, Lynn's popularity soared courtesy of her sexy pin-up photos, and she was thus able to land roles in films of higher budget. Today, she is best known for her work in the solid *The Bridge of San Luis Rey* and the psychological thriller *Shock*, opposite the great Vincent Price. Yvonne De Carlo's career followed much the same path. She toiled throughout the early part of the 1940s with minor roles as secretaries and students, yet when her pin-up pictures sizzled the military camps, soldiers demanded that Yvonne receive her just desserts with meatier roles. Late in the war effort — and with thanks to the power of the soldier's pen — she was able to leave minor roles behind and bask in Hollywood's spotlight with roles in *Salome Where She Danced* and *The Desert Hawk*, before she achieved her place in show business immortality with her signature role of Lily Munster.

Before they became pin-up girls, beauties Audrey Totter and Nan Wynn were known chiefly for their voice work. Although many filmgoers had heard Nan Wynn's exceptional singing voice, few ever saw her in person on the screen because she was employed as a voice over for such stars as Rita Hayworth. However, when Miss Wynn began to pose for cheesecake stills, the realization that Rita Hayworth's voice was a beauty as well spurred many to request her studio to place her in front of a camera. Audrey Totter, on the other hand, wasn't employed as the tuneful voice others would lip-sync to but as a radio personality of terrific comedic appeal. Noted for her brilliant impersonations of Ingrid Bergman on the airwaves, Miss Totter was such a hit on the New York radio circuit that Hollywood hotshots traveled east to lure her to the opposite coast. When those Hollywood birddogs got a look at the ravishing blonde, they felt America would like a dose of her as well, and lined up pin-up shots to help build her acting career. With her unique sex appeal, Audrey Totter eventually became one of the greatest film noir femme fatales, with notable work in such unforgettable fare as *Lady in the Lake, The Unsuspected,* and her most notorious portrayal in the underappreciated noir classic *Tension,* opposite Richard Basehart.

Whereas ladies like Bari and Wynn, who toiled in the industry with little fanfare, achieved that fanfare courtesy of their sexy pin-up pictures, other ladies outside the film industry, but desirous of crashing the gates, found their means of entrance into Hollywood via cheesecake stills. The roll call of such ladies was extensive during the 1940s. Blonde bombshell Marilyn Maxwell toured with Spencer Tracy in Alaska under the auspices of the USO, and when the boys in service spotted her curvaceous structure, they felt the arena of motion pictures would benefit greatly from her whistle-worthy presence. The shapely Linda Christian, widely regarded as the first "Bond Girl" (she starred in the 1954 television adaptation of *Casino Royale*) broke through in Hollywood courtesy of her racy pin-up stills. Her cheesecake work caught the eye of every man still amongst the living: including film heartthrob Tyrone Power, who made the curvy pin-up his bride. A young Dorothy Malone used the pin-up medium as means to gain a foothold in Hollywood. It worked for the willowy wonder who sizzled the screen opposite Humphrey Bogart in a cameo as a sultry bookstore clerk in the classic *The Big Sleep*.

Although many aspiring actresses achieved their big break courtesy of the pin-up route, perhaps it was Jane Nigh who garnered the most publicity in her efforts as a pin-up girl eager to make it in motion pictures. Conflicting reports say how Miss Nigh was discovered, ranging from her being spotted at Fort MacArthur during a camp tour to attracting a talent scout's eye while she worked in a war factory, but how she was able to gain success in Hollywood was widely publicized. In order to start Jane's acting career, her studio lined up a cheesecake photo shoot on a beach. Stills of her looking stunning in a bathing suit were distributed to the nation's newspapers, with her studio offering the caption the gents of the folded paper were to use: "Jane Nigh: Nobody's Pin-up Girl." The photograph showed a lonesome Jane seated on the beach, as if to claim that she was waiting, longingly, for someone to claim her as their own. The ploy worked. Jane's studio was besieged with pin-up picture and autograph requests, a gasoline detail on a destroyer stationed in the Pacific named her their "100 Octane Girl," troops in England painted a picture of her on their landing craft, and a soldier based in New Guinea wrote Jane, stating "It's beautiful women like you who make fighting worthwhile." Miss Nigh made her film debut in 1944 with a small role in the classic Dana Andrews/ Gene Tierney flick *Laura*. Two years later, she would have a larger part in another Gene Tierney film, *Dragonwyck*.

Studios were adept at building an actress's career during the war years. Jane "Nobody's Pin-up Girl" Nigh's unveiling was broadly targeted, but many ladies had designated targets that their studios aimed at. The stunning Jane Randolph was an obvious target for the airmen at Randolph Field, Texas. To further endear her to airmen, her studio distributed a background story which mentioned that Jane's father was a pilot who liked to take Jane in the air with him when she was a girl. Her mother forbade the practice, but as she reached adulthood, Miss Randolph longed to return to the sky and sought a civilian pilot's license — which she had to put off during the war years courtesy of the grounding of civilian planes on the west coast. It was even rumored that Jane took the stage name of Randolph as tribute to the Texas airfield. Donna Reed, likewise, had a targeted audience given her farm girl origins. The bulk of her pin-ups took advantage of her rural upbringing, as Donna was often photographed in farm settings, operating a plow, reclining on a fence, and milking cows, all the while wearing outfits that displayed her legs.

Those stunning young ladies, who were unknown to many Americans prior to their leg art work, became recognizable figures thanks to the popularity of pin-up art. There were a number of ladies the public had seen, in various capacities, but whose names rested not on the tip of many tongues. Ramsay Ames was a popular rhumba band singer who had to change vocation when the men in her band joined the armed forces during the war. Miss Ames had a few hundred cheesecake pictures taken — she claimed that she sat for 958 photos — which helped ease her way into the motion picture industry, but other dolls already had the habit of posing for pictures. During the height of pin-up art, the names of those beautiful gals who graced the cover of fashion magazines became known to the public. No longer were they nameless symbols of American beauty but stellar pin-up girls who populated the nation's catalogs and publications. In time, the stable of the elite Powers Models and the infamous Conover Girls, who all seemed to go by unusual nicknames like "Dusty," "Candy," and "Chili," were known to Americans who kept their eye on social events. As the two most popular model agencies in America, Powers Models and Conover Girls became fixtures in the arena of pin-up artwork.

With exposure came the ill-effects of celebrity, as many of the Conover Girls were enmeshed in scandals during the war years. Hollywood had a tendency to keep a lid on the nefarious doings of many of its elite players, but those sexy girls whose occupation was to look good had no such security. As the head of the Conover Modeling Agency, the shady Harry Conover assembled a stock of sexy young ladies to serve as his professional posers. The most vocal voice against what he liked to call "matchstick models," Conover typically signed women with healthy curves, and he had a strict aversion for gaunt, unhealthily thin models. Conover was no stranger to scandal, for he left his wife of many years (Gloria Dalton) for the cream of his curvy model crop: the shapely Candy Jones. The Conover Agency was either disinclined to cover up their scandals, or secretly enjoyed the publicity their tabloid exploits brought the agency. The stunning Chili Williams, who made the polka-dot bikini an American beach staple, was said to have a revolving bedroom door. During one photo shoot, the shutterbug's wife visited his studio unannounced, only to find her betrothed dressed down to his undershorts with a nude Chili Williams brightening the scenery. A much publicized divorce scandal made constant reference to the polka dot girl. More scandalous was the story of a Conover Girl named Dusty Anderson, who used her new-found pin-up fame to leave her Marine Corps captain husband, while he was away in service, and settle in the arms of filmmaker Jean Negulesco. The Conover Girls, although easy to remember, came with a decadent tag.

Sometimes studios found scandals impossible to cover up, even for the big names in Hollywood. Although her pin-up output was miniscule, slender model-turned-actress Lauren Bacall became a favorite sex symbol of wartime America with her sultry work in the underappreciated classic *To Have and Have Not* — her first picture. While on set, she and married star Humphrey Bogart fell in love, and their romance quickly became a favorite topic for the gossip columnists. Although Miss Bacall was a fixture in the newspapers, the stories concerning her were never in the same vein as patriotic pin-up girls like Martha O'Driscoll and Joan Leslie. At the height of pin-up's popularity, beautiful girls whose occupations fell under the umbrella of celebrity, were targets for tabloid writers eager to relay their transgressions to a populace equally eager to read about them.

Although pin-up girls made headlines for the occasional scandal, they were typically depicted in the papers in a favorable light. American boys had war heroes to look up to, but the American girl needed admirable role models as well. Girls could look to the newspaper with fascination as photographs of Carole Landis entertaining troops near the frontlines were distributed. They could read about the hours Evelyn Keyes spent working for the Red Cross, and the first aid instruction classes Sheila Ryan and Myrna Loy taught. They saw photographs of Lynn Merrick holding a V-shaped potato she dug up from her "victory garden," and gaped in astonishment at the alarming total of money Dorothy Lamour raised on her war bond circuit. Girls accepted Joan Bennett as a role model for her tireless work managing servicemen's canteens, and applauded young film stars like Peggy Knudson who frequented the Hollywood Canteen in order to cheer up the servicemen with a spritely step or two. Pin-up girls were the ideal image of female beauty during the war years, and many of the ladies saw to that image extending beyond the physical by displaying exemplary characters.

The gents in the armed forces were often credited with giving a pin-up girl an occupational boost. Oftentimes a flattering handle they bestowed upon their preferred piece of pulchritude, served as the catalyst to fame. Units would adopt a certain lady as their official pin-up girl and christen her with a pet moniker, such as the one given Veronica Lake by the 4th Armored Division: "The Girl We'd Like in the Back Seat of a Tank." When lesser-known actresses were so dubbed, and the newspapers mentioned her name and catchy alias, the film-going public's interest was aroused and they sought out films the girl in question appeared in. It leads one to imagine how actresses of postwar decades would have benefitted had the practice continued. Would Denise Galik be better known today had a military unit named her "The Girl We'd Most Like to Keep Us Warm During the Cold War?" Had the alias "The Girl We'd Like to Disassemble a MK-19 With" been a boon for Melanie Smith's career? If Zoe Trilling were dubbed "The Girl We'd Like to Fire Patriot Missiles With," by an outfit during the Gulf War, would her career have benefitted greatly like the ladies during the Second World War? The three actresses were solid thespians and possessed the requisite pulchritude of the most gorgeous pin-up, but the practice of military unit's naming an official pin-up girl was no longer in affect when Miss Galik, Smith, and Trilling toiled in Hollywood.

Thanks to the height of pin-up's popularity, girls of uncommon beauty whose names had been unknown to the American public became stars overnight. When a stunning girl posed for cheesecake art, and her image was duplicated and distributed, an admiring citizenship would seek to learn more about her background and keep a watchful eye on the trajectory of her career. Many ladies with show business aspirations posed for cheesecake stills simply to get their name, and more importantly their image, out there. The industrious and well-formed Lucille Bremer used her exceptional pulchritude to further her career in this way. She was a member of the famous *Rockettes*, but she had her eye set on the film industry and found the pin-up outlet an easy way to slide her delicate foot under Hollywood's door. Long-legged Lucille became a pin-up sensation, and the exposure allowed her to enter a higher level of show business. Work as a pin-up girl paid off — Miss Bremer costarred with Judy Garland in the lighthearted wartime musical *Meet Me in St. Louis*.

Actress Lizabeth Scott, a dead ringer for Lauren Bacall, was a tireless worker devoted to acting. She put in hours as an understudy on Broadway, toured with the show *Hellzapoppin'*, and accepted hard work as her calling card, which she imagined would lead her to Hollywood. Her drive and ambition were commendable, but she learned, via the pin-up practice, that another ingredient might be more important when one's focus is on setting up shop in the film industry. After photographs of her circulated, she found that interest on behalf of Hollywood's talent scouts had been piqued. Miss Scott put in countless hours on the boards, where she studied theater and honed her craft as an actress, but it was glamour that got her a trial in the film industry. About her break in Hollywood, Lizabeth said, "What puzzles me is the way I got to Hollywood. I worked hard for recognition on the stage and never got a peep from a talent scout. But the minute my picture got in a magazine, I started to get telegrams. Well, that's Hollywood, I guess."

Many young gals sought the pin-up circuit as a means to further their career, and when the method worked for one comely gal, others tried to mirror her success. When young ladies like Hazel Brooks found fame courtesy of pin-up art, other girls sought to mimic Hazel's actions and thus garner the same outcome. When famed pin-up artist Alberto Vargas claimed that Miss Brooks "possessed the most beautiful legs in Hollywood," pretty girls felt that by exhibiting their legs, à la Hazel Brooks, they too could sign a seven-year studio contract — which Hazel was awarded by MGM simply based on Vargas's proclamation. So, girls with Hollywood dreams posed for leg art and expected dividends to be paid in Hazel Brooks-like fashion. For Lorraine Miller, the set-up was conceived but the follow-through proved faulty. When Lorraine's coming-out pin-up picture was distributed, soldiers whistled to beat the band, but the name captioned on the stunning image was not Lorraine's. Since the distributors of the photograph erroneously listed the pin-up under another woman's name, Lorraine sued the outfit for $50,000.

Lorraine Miller's entrance into the public did not go as planned, but the hullabaloo surrounding her first pin-up image allowed her fifteen minutes of fame. Lorraine was able to parlay her fame miscue into a brief acting career with roles in forgettable flicks like *Men in Her Diary*. The fifteen minutes of fame experienced by other minor celebrities-turned-pin-up-girls didn't allow for a lengthy Hollywood stay either. Cute little Gloria Nord, the lead roller skater in Harold Steinman's *Skating Vanities*, appeared in Betty Grable's film *Pin-Up Girl* with a brief on-her-skates cameo. Burlesque queen Ann Corio, a pin-up sensation for the boys in the armed forces, found herself in demand during the war years and traveled to Los Angeles to try her luck in motion pictures. A classic entertainer who wowed audiences in The Big Apple with her striptease act, Miss Corio found that acting on the silver screen wasn't one of her talents. She starred in war-era films like *Swamp Woman* and *Sarong Girl* that milked her burlesque background, but she never settled into the film industry and opted to return to the east coast. A rather humble woman, despite her decadent profession, Ann thought of herself as a miserable actress, but she understood that sex sold during those tumultuous years. The gal the newspapermen referred to as the "Epic Epidermis" said, "So who cares if I can't act? I make money, the producers make money, the fans write letters praising my acting and everybody is happy."

When an unknown beauty became a hit on the foxhole circuit, with her image warming the hearts of cold soldiers in their chilly fighting positions, studio executives were presented with an unusual dilemma. Many gals were discovered during the war years via the pin-up practice, and soldiers were eager to see more of the ladies who captured their fancy. Eager to appease the men in uniform, film studios contracted pretty ingénues based simply on how sharp they appeared in their cheesecake stills, unaware as to how well they could act. Studios signed pretty figures with the purpose of using them in minor, window-dressing roles such as pretty coeds, sexy secretaries, and nurses who could spike a man's blood pressure. However, at times, studio executives would come across a pin-up girl capable of sharing the spotlight with established actresses. One such dame was Marie "The Body" McDonald. As sensuous as they come, The Body surprised critics with her work in the Anne Baxter flick *Guest in the House*. A newspaperman for the *Laredo Times* penned an approving critique of her acting, which read, "For a Miss Cheesecake who has been allowed to display only her legs and other charms, it was all pretty nice."

When other ladies who possessed acting talent were in preparation for their public unveiling, studios of the 1940s used the pin-up platform as a way to reveal their latest find. Gloria Grahame was made known to the public in such a fashion, and showed her range as an actress with a flighty role in the noir classic *The Big Heat*, as well as sensuous portrayals in flicks like *Human Desire*. The slender beauty was a top end-of-the-war find whose family background had that hint of celebrity. As the granddaughter of famous English artist Reginald Hallward, Gloria was arranged to pose for a pin-up photographer with a special nod to her lineage. One of Gloria's initial studio stills displayed her in a two-piece bathing suit, standing before an easel while she painted on a canvas. Barbara Hale, by contrast, had a special unveiling which stirred in the frame of many an American girl that green, malevolent feeling of envy. Miss Hale was touted, in her pre-stardom pin-ups, as Frank Sinatra's heart interest in her first major picture. Many a young American girl swooned for the legendary crooner, and when an unknown like Barbara Hale landed the role as his onscreen sweetheart, resentful eyes positioned themselves on Barbara's wonderful frame.

While studios adopted the technique of presenting to the film-going public their latest pretty find via the pin-up route, the girls so unveiled oftentimes felt that interest in them was simply physical. Throughout the history of film, producers have populated their motion pictures with appealing persons, for the fact that beauty sells has never been lost on

Hollywood. It seems that beauty, rather than acting skill, has allowed for more careers in the field of acting. During the war years, the popularity of leg art enabled gals with enviable figures a direct route into the realm of show business. One such leggy performer was pretty blonde Adele Jergens, who worked as a showgirl on Broadway prior to her contract with 20th Century Fox. Lauded for her legs, many film critics thought it a great sin when Fox cast Adele in a Civil War era picture; the wardrobe for the film didn't allow for the revealing skirts and bathing suits popular during the Second World War. Although leg art served as Miss Jergens's path to Hollywood, she was excited that focus, for once, would be redirected from her legs and placed on her skill as an actress. Adele said, "When they cover up my legs, that gives me more of an opportunity to concentrate on pure acting." To be admired for physical beauty is flattering, but to ladies like Adele Jergens, flattery was best accepted when those qualities that elicited admiration on the part of others was created by skill honed via hard work, and not the natural gift of beauty.

The beauty parade during the war years was as clamorous as it had ever been, and much of that had to do with the height of the pin-up industry. Pretty girls were flashing their comely smiles and striking come-hither poses on billboards, magazine covers, and newspaper advertisements across the nation. Although beauty tended to detract from the appreciation of an actress's talent as a thespian, beauty often served as the catalyst to her career in show business. To champion a woman's beauty, even those established actresses in Hollywood, was a common practice thanks to the rampant glorification of the female form that pin-up photography instilled. Although ladies like Barbara Stanwyck and Joan Bennett were well-respected, dignified ladies of the screen, they too were beautiful, and their beauty, like the young ingénue, was a point of focus during the war years. So companies would engage known actresses like Paulette Goddard to serve as their pretty spokesperson, while also extending a hand to a young sexy gal eager to gain a foothold in show business.

In order for pretty young ladies to garner that sought-after name recognition, they would pose for the still cameras. Girls would lend their amazing figures to advertisements, cheesecake photographs, and social causes. Americans were expected to do what was best for the country during that tumultuous period, and pin-up girls were often employed to pass along a certain message that the war department or the government felt necessary to translate to the people. The stunning Elaine Riley, whose nymph-like beauty could tame the wildest of hearts, was employed as the figure to inform Americans to save their kitchen fats. Used kitchen fats were needed to make many items, one of which was rubber bullets used by the Army for training exercises. In order to get Americans to eat better, and save money by growing food themselves, pin-up girl Marjorie Riordan served as the figure of the "Victory Food" campaign. A pin-up photograph of Miss Riordan made the circles in the nation's leading papers, which showed the Hedy Lamarr clone standing beside a barrel full of potatoes, showing off a lot of leg, and promoting potatoes as a "victory food." Although the lovely Miss Riley and Miss Riordan were synonymous with food during the war years, their work as social messengers placed them in the public eye and enabled them to enter the acting profession.

To employ sexy women as the symbols of such campaigns as saving kitchen fat and growing potatoes may seem odd, but pin-up girls during the war years had grown accustomed to unusual photo shoots. No longer were photo shoots resigned to studios where the wardrobes were common and the climate controlled: ladies found themselves placed in some unusual settings. The bulk of the photographs produced by pin-up artists employed beaches and swimming pools — the primary setting one could find a bathing beauty — but the surroundings and attire were not fixed. One of America's top models, Madelon Mason, posed for a cheesecake still amongst a setting of ordnance. Anne Gwynne was photographed straddling a rocket while wearing skimpy red, white, and blue attire. Frances "The Shape" Vorne was photographed on a beach wearing a bikini made from a captured Nazi's parachute. Pin-up photographers even sexed up holidays, while newspaper editors littered their pages during the festive days with holiday-themed pin-up photographs. Actresses Joan Caulfield and Sheila Ryan — of Irish descent — were employed as St. Patrick's Day pin-ups, Gale Robbins and Rita Daigle were two pin-ups used to make Halloween more arousing, and Martha Vickers donned a sexy star-spangled bathing suit to give the Fourth of July a pulchritudinous flavor. All things during the war years were best presented with pin-up accompaniment.

Pin-up girls were wildly popular, and given their popularity, they were targets for amorous escapades of high-profile male celebrities. Before there were The Beatles and uninhibited rock stars of more modern times, the most recognizable names in the music industry were the big-band leaders. Given their status as famous celebrities, the gents who headlined massive orchestras thought themselves in great demand, and given the demand for their services, their demands for beautiful accessories were focused on the pulchritudinous girls of the pin-up industry. Although romances with big-band leaders typically were described as flings, a number of cheesecake girls found themselves wed to the wolves of the music industry. Perhaps the marriage of Betty Grable to Harry James was the most high profile of this sort, but big-band leaders were quick to tender decorated rings to pretty pin-up girls. Tommy Dorsey wed Patricia Dane, Artie Shaw walked down the aisle with sexpot Ava Gardner — shortly after her divorce from Mickey Rooney — and Rudy Vallee (the volatile "Vagabond Lover") got hitched to the lovely Jane Greer. Grable and James's union didn't pass the test of time, but at twenty-plus years it made for a lengthy wedded state in Tinseltown. Ava's union with Shaw lasted a year, and Greer's ill-advised marriage to Vallee didn't procure for the couple that one-year anniversary.

Celebrity status introduced ladies to a world of great flash, unrivalled pageantry, for the bright lights of Hollywood was the desired destination for many dames who posed for pin-up art. There they could dine with the boys the newspapermen kept tabs on, they could make chummy with film producers in order to land a part in a film, and, most importantly, they could set the gears in motion to see their names in print. Fame and fortune, that intoxicating lifestyle, lured many striking beauties to the photographer's studio, but even when a gal acquired fame, that name recognition couldn't open every door. Two European actresses who ventured to Hollywood for that covetable fame, June Duprez and Michèle Morgan, found that after they had established themselves in Hollywood, a world at war wasn't too impressed with their status. Miss Morgan ventured to Los Angeles prior to America's involvement in the war, as the French actress found it difficult, despite her status as a leading female star, to locate her parents during the war. Michele's letters home were returned to the States, undeliverable, so she tried desperately to locate her folks; she sought the help of officials at the London embassy. June Duprez, born in England during World War I, left her homeland for Hollywood early in the war effort. Despite her status as film starlet in both England and the States, June didn't receive word of her mother's death until two weeks after she had died — which she heard via the radio.

Film starlets of unquestioned trendiness, those of great beauty who worked diligently as well as those sexpots who married for status, were the reasons why the pin-up practice reached its zenith during World War II. Beauty is easy to admire, but what is more admirable than exuding a pleasing image is showing a selfless demeanor by supporting the troops who fight for liberty. The 1940s gals of Hollywood are a breed unmatched in the annals of Tinseltown. They were pin-up girls who stood for national pride, and not bodies to be admired with a crude exclamation of arousal. In the decades following, pin-up girls were not employed as symbols of American womanhood, ladies of patriotism who placed their best interest underneath the interests of the world, but as sex goddesses whose lone purpose was to stimulate the aesthetic and carnal capacities of male admirers. During the war years, pin-up art reached its most accepted state due to the patriotic theme that surrounded the practice, and when the war came to a close, so closed the doors on its widespread acceptance. War-era pin-up girls were not personifications of gaudiness, dames to direct one's lust towards, but the representation of future bliss, where battlefields were silenced and where enemies dare not tread. For within a pin-up girl's beauty rested solace — a sanctuary devoid of ugliness, vulgarities, and decay — where the future promised warmth, love, and a return to normalcy. They represented all that was worth returning to. They represented home.

# CHAPTER SIX

# THE EFFECT
## ★ OF THE ★
# PIN-UP GIRL

At the close of the war, critics wondered what was to become of pin-up art. Soldiers who had used pin-up pictures as means to retain their capacity to appreciate beauty were now discharged from the armed forces. Glossy photographs of stunning women, which had entertained soldiers in battle theaters and had served four or more years as mementos of American womanhood, once removed from the military occupation seemed wholly inadequate. A warm body, a possessor of a hand to hold, and a heart to connect with was the desire of the troops who had been absent such splendor. The sense of gratitude for pin-up girls was immense, for they kept those amorous feelings — both wanton lust and a craving for a companionship — within the breasts of servicemen. However, with the war over, those feelings sought to be projected upon a lovely woman of their choice. The still photograph served its purpose in the foxholes and the fighting positions, where life seemed abstract and existence trapped in a false reality awaiting its conclusion. The pin-up girl's function was to serve as spiritual convoy through this harsh realm whose span was not fixed, but an end was forthcoming, which would signal the return to prewar endeavors. When the war ended, a chaperone was no longer needed; companionship for the present was foremost on the discharged soldier's mind.

When the soldiers returned home, the thought was that pin-up art would subside, if not die altogether. Still images of beautiful women were in demand during the war years, but when the boys returned from the battlefields and foreign waters, ladies stationary were replaced with ladies live. And the ladies, those gals eager to romance a returned hero, were thought to be instrumental in the expiration of pin-up art, for it was their arms, their embrace, which would make cheesecake photography obsolete. It was reasoned that young American women would serve as substitutes for the cheesecake photographs that saw soldiers through the war. Many critics of pin-up art envisioned wives and girlfriends gathering their mate's pin-up collection and setting it out for the garbage man to dispose of. But such a critique was offered in haste with a blatant disregard for the impact that pin-up art had on popular American culture. What served as inspiration for troops in the armed forces was adopted by men as the pinnacle of art.

Portraits of landscapes that depicted a snowy winter evening, sculptures of marble and stone that populated an exhibit, and paintings by a master artisan were displays of art placed on diminished pedestals near the lofty perch where pin-up art resided during World War II. Masterworks of da Vinci, Canaletto, and Vermeer were inferior works when judged against a striking pose issued by Betty Grable, or a sultry Ava Gardner leer, captured by a photographer. The men in the armed forces wanted stills of shapely ladies, for reprints of the *Mona Lisa* made poor bedfellows in a sailor's bunk beside the likes of a bikini clad Martha O'Driscoll. Although museums would prefer to erect a painting from the brush of Paul Cezanne over a seductive portrait of Dolores Moran reclining on a diving board, men during the war years had a preference in contrast to the modern day institution of fine art. Dorothy Kilgallen, the eccentric tabloid writer for the *Lowell Sun*, created her own fictitious museum of World War II mementos that housed "Fred Astaire's dancing shoes, Frank Sinatra's draft card and a time table autographed by Mrs. Roosevelt." She had a place for the pin-ups too, for she understood that cheesecake art was tops during the war years. Kilgallen wrote, "I have life-sized statues of Carole Landis in one of 'those' dresses, Marie MacDonald in a bathing suit, Sherry Britton in her Leon & Eddie's costume (!) and Betty Grable in shorts." Although her museum was one of whimsy, the artwork therein was one best representative of the times.

Soldiers were warned by many writers to leave their pin-up collection overseas — let the foxholes dispense them as they saw fit. A writer for the *Hutchinson News Herald*, known to his readership simply as "Elm," informed soldiers that their wives and girlfriends would not appreciate a duffel bag full of Jane Russell and Gene Tierney stills. But Elm wasn't like other writers who informed the boys to toss the cheesecake aside — he understood the impact pin-up girls had on the war and felt history should not deny the artwork its rightful place in the war annals. Elm wrote, "Maps and communiqués may be important to war historians but the pin-up girl has her place in posterity, too. Let us not permit the pin-up girl not to be in our postwar plans. If we build memorial stadiums as postwar projects let us plan a display place for the pin-up girls, perhaps large murals." Scribe Ruth Millett echoed Elm's sentiments, albeit in a more subdued manner, when she penned, "The part that women have played in past wars has a real place in history. So what about the pin-up girl of World War II? She deserves a better fate than to be discarded and forgotten when the men come marching home."

The words written by Elm and Millett seemed as if the death knell for the pin-up girl was eminent, but although the Second World War had heard the funeral toll, pin-up art would prove quite resilient. Cheesecake stills may have been a fad adopted by American culture circa World War II, but the critics who envisioned the fad's demise were soothsayers of an inferior stock. In favor of pin-up survival, foremost, was the interest men had in the artwork. Also, posing for such pictures opened doors to women that proved difficult to breach. So, men and women alike had reasons to see to pin-up art's continuance — men for the enjoyment it elicited and women for the occupational doors it opened.

One after another, beautiful girls flocked to the photographer's studio in order to achieve the fame of the brightest stars in the pin-up-girl galaxy. They had read stories in the papers about some unknown beauty who had crashed Hollywood based solely on her comely cheesecake stills. Socialite Mary Ann Hyde, who caroused with noted ladies' man Errol Flynn, gained fame outside the big city nightclub scene when she flashed her shapely legs for the shutterbugs. Yvonne De Carlo was able to land meaty roles in movies based on her stunning pin-up work — even though previously she'd spent several years toiling in the film industry with numerous unaccredited roles. Girls of unrivaled appeal found themselves in demand from the film industry who sought to populate their motion pictures with comely dolls the servicemen had pinned up on their barracks walls all across the world. The girls were not ignorant to the fact that cheesecake art paved an avenue towards fame: one that never would have been constructed had the servicemen not found the artwork to their liking. So they posed. And their work posing enabled them to secure occupations in those covetable fields that lead to motion picture stardom.

Although the effect of posing for cheesecake stills allowed for a studio contract, it did not lead to substantial roles in movies on every occasion. Studio executives understood that gents wanted to see those stunning beauties that littered the walls on their bases, yet they didn't want to place before a motion picture camera some young, naïve, pretty figure incapable of acting. So they became hat check girls, waitresses, dancers, and background beauties — issuing no lines but looking grand besides. Many of the girls were happy enough to have their image captured onscreen, but others felt that their beauty had positioned an obstacle in the middle of their road to fame. Granted, their beauty allowed for their entrance into filmdom, but their status as cheesecake girls didn't propel them into the ranks of the Stanwycks, Bennetts, and Colberts of Hollywood. The pin-up girls, those unproven as actresses before they struck a pose for the shutterbugs, were typically viewed as pretty faces and pretty shapes — not thespians. This irked many aspiring actresses, such as Elyse Knox, who felt that cameras needn't be trained on her gorgeous gams but should focus instead on the talent she exuded. Miss Knox said, "That bathing suit stuff doesn't have anything to do with the kind of actress I want to be." The effect of serving as a pin-up girl did open doors in Hollywood, but they were typically doors ajar that had to be thrust open with the projection of acting skill on the beauty's part.

The beauty cavalcade that stormed through America during World War II, elevated the careers of many aspiring actresses, but by emphasizing female beauty, a woman's other attributes were shrouded in a haze of indifference. The merit of a woman rested not in her character or in her occupational duties, but in the physical image she projected. American girls longed to be held in such regard by the opposite sex, like the cheesecake starlets, so they mimicked the doings of the pin-up girls. When the popularity of pin-up art was in full bloom, thousands of girls wore their hair like Veronica Lake, flaunted the bathing suits Betty Grable made fashionable, and tried to mirror the sultry countenance of Jane Russell. The nation was glamour obsessed. If a girl wasn't glamorous, her value was second to the pretty vixens who posed for patriotic purposes. There were a number of critics who voiced their concern with the overvaluing of glamour, but popular culture — thanks in large part to pin-up art — was glamour mad, and entertainment outlets had to deliver what society called for.

A major concern for sociologists during the war years was the infringement on social standards of conduct. When pin-up art mushroomed into the big business it became, modesty was feared to be an endangered commodity. The fewer clothes a young woman wore, the more appealing she was to a populace that was obsessed with pin-up photography. Whereas some critics derided the pin-up practice, a few pin-up girls spoke on behalf of the issue of America's moral compass, which was newly trained toward decadence. The lovely Gene Tierney understood the impact pin-up art had on young women and warned them against adopting the mannerisms that pin-up girls projected. Miss Tierney said, "Don't be conspicuous. Conspicuous makeup, color, line, detail and combinations violate the rules of good taste. The well-dressed woman looks just right for the occasion — blends into the moment." To be larger than the moment, and to have focus trained on a gown too revealing or manners too loose was uncouth. And Gene Tierney, who was regarded as one of the loveliest women in Hollywood, stressed that the pin-up look had its place and there it should remain.

Despite warnings from such amazing beauties as Gene Tierney, there was a vocal pocket of Americans who felt that girls had lost their modesty, and had abandoned good taste for the allure and attention of the pin-up girl. Pin-up girls were provocative, they were fascinating, and they served a unique purpose as patriotic beauties during the war, but what pin-up art wasn't, what the practice didn't project, was a model of modesty. Even though well-respected actresses, whose characters were rarely questioned — like Joan Bennett, Rochelle Hudson, and Barbara Stanwyck — took part in the pin-up practice, voices of opposition still populated every corner. Ginger Rogers, the leggy dancing starlet of many musicals who was referred to during the war as "America's Sweetheart," was criticized by Mary Davis, a professional beauty dramatics coach, for swinging her hips too much when she walked. Despite the criticism, the voices of support were stronger. Pete Westmore, the head of Warner Brothers' makeup department, stood up for Miss Rogers, saying, "Show me a producer, or any man, that wouldn't willingly wait outside any window to catch a glimpse of Ginger 'swinging her hips.'" Although the support Westmore offered failed to champion good taste, the pin-up girls had a roster of supporters more vast than the collection of persons who rejected pin-up art.

The pin-up practice may have led to a more sexual female population, but in regards to burlesque, which flourished well before World War II, pin-up art depicted more modest images than the famous satellite of the entertainment industry. Whether a scantily-clad woman was an invitation to amorous behavior or not was an issue banded back and forth between social critics. Burlesque promoted a number of dames to the pin-up community, whose attire, or lack thereof, could make many of the day's leading film starlets blush. Bathing suit pictures were not adopted by all pin-up girls, for Hedy Lamarr was rarely photographed in swimwear, and streamlined stars like Ingrid Bergman and Lauren Bacall produced a limited amount of revealing cheesecake stills. Burlesque stars like Ann Corio and Sherry Britton produced some of the raciest pin-up pictures, for their occupational threads were constructed to cover their modesty by the scantest of margins. Actress Martha O'Driscoll, who posed for many bathing suit photos during the war, was nevertheless worried about the rising degree of sexuality in America. When she was interviewed by scribe Hedda Hopper, Miss Hopper relayed Martha's thoughts when she cited the pin-up girl by writing, "Miss O'Driscoll is convinced that wolves — or men, rather — accord a young lady exactly the degree of respect that her conduct merits. If masculine courtesy and consideration fail, if chivalry lapses, if romance turns somewhat excessively amorous, why: 'It's the girl's fault every time,' declares Miss O'Driscoll."

To Americans at war, the era of the maiden — that untouched beauty who served as the beacon of goodness for many heroes in early litera-ture — seemed an antiquated period of history. The proper maiden would not indulge the populace nor vaunt her beauty by displaying her form in revealing clothing. Pin-up girls were viewed, by a wide collection of Americans, as women seductive and sexy but not as ladies of virtue who served as respectable models for young American girls. Despite pin-up art's stigma for an aversion to basic decency, the girls who posed for the artwork could not be slotted into a collective bracket with a collective identity. Sexpots like Ava Gardner and Lana Turner, whose exploits made for preferred reading material in the papers, posed, but so did Carole Landis and Jinx Falkenburg, whose hearts were as vast as an open prairie and whose constitutions were possessed of admirable quali-ties. Miss Falkenburg would buy meals for hungry soldiers and opened her home to friends so they could be close to their servicemen loved ones. Carole Landis was the personification of American womanhood for countless soldiers overseas, thanks to her bravery and dedication, for she traveled to hazardous arenas where troops were stationed and entertained the boys with shows. To claim that the pin-up practice was entirely disreputable would be to overlook the commendable practices of ladies like Carole and Jinx, who were pin-up darlings to many soldiers, and who served, like the maidens of early literature, that pivotal role of symbols of goodness.

The critics of pin-up art had their voice, however, their concerted reproach of the practice was merely a murmur compared to the over-whelming influence cheesecake artwork had on popular culture. Pin-up girls were the fantasy of men, and ladies who were eager to impress the opposite sex adopted the methods and beauty tips passed on by the girls who posed. Although many Americans viewed pin-up girls as libidinous dames whose toes tickled not the floor of good taste, they were, regardless their sexpot image, models of attraction that girls copied. Ruth Millett tried to uplift the spirits of women who thought men would be pin-up girl hungry upon their stateside return, when she penned, "Did you ever see a picture of a pin-up girl in any outfit fashion writers could describe as having 'the new look of elegance?'" The look of pin-up art concerned itself not with elegance, even if elegant women posed for the cameras, for its primary function was to distribute a pleasing image of physical beauty. Given that many soldiers had spent three to four years in the armed forces, women wanted to appeal to the returned servicemen by projecting a pleasing image rather than turn them off with the unattainable aura that comes with refinement.

The pin-up girl image caught on in America, as girls fashioned their looks after the stunning beauties men had pinned up on walls. High heels gave girls that leggier image and made them step out with the bounce and confidence of a Ginger Rogers. The sweater-girl fad caught on, as young ladies slid their frames in tight-fitting sweaters to give their chests that healthy, full Jane Russell appearance. However, mimicking the fashion of pin-up girls was a fad not resigned for the American girl alone. New York socialite Lilly Dache, who constantly bemoaned the influence pin-up art had on women's fashion, visited her native Paris shortly after the close of the war and was irked by the mode of fashion French girls adopted at the time: that of the pin-up girl. When she returned stateside, Miss Dache complained to a writer that French girls were "going in for the glamour bobs and the accentuated bosoms typified by the Hollywood pin-up girl." The Hollywood pin-up girl was the perfect representation of servicemen's postwar desire, and girls sought to emulate their appearance, bobs and bosoms alike.

Although pin-up art is commonly referred to as leg art, many cheesecake pictures trained their focus a little further north on the female anatomy. The girls who posed for cheesecake stills typically wore leg revealing outfits such as bathing suits and skirts, and they weren't all, as a collective body, necessarily buxom. Therefore, the term "leg art" stuck and became common nomenclature when cheesecake art was the focus. However, many of the popular pin-up girls possessed healthy curves, and weren't just an impressive set of legs. When an outfit began their search for the best representative for the postwar pin-up girl, they sought out a lady who possessed the physical traits men craved, and found her in Audrey Totter. Miss Totter, who would become a postwar sensation with her tough, sensuous roles as femme fatales in the film noir genre, was listed in an edition of the *Salt Lake Tribune* as "Postwar Pin-up Girl #1." Not constructed like the matchstick models the famous modeling magnate Harry Conover rejected, Audrey Totter possessed a voluptuous frame with an ample chest.

The legs of such pin-up girls as the legendary Betty Grable and Vera Zorina were still popular at the end of the war, but with gals like Jane Russell and Carole Landis, who enjoyed widespread attention as cheesecake models, it was reasoned that women with healthy chests better represented what returning soldiers desired. Suddenly, the Ingrid Bergmans and Katharine Hepburns were too willowy, too reed-like in appearance, and ladies like the curvaceous Audrey Totter were in demand. Studios in postwar America sought out aspiring actresses constructed in regards to the parlance of the times. Marie Wilson's career took off, and Jane Russell, who had been the greatest kept secret in Hollywood during the war years, was a hot commodity after the fighting. Peggie Castle, whose exceptional frame earned her the studio nickname "Miss Classy Chassis," became a popular postwar pin-up girl, who, like Audrey Totter, found success in the film noir and western genres with roles in *I, the Jury* and *The Lawman*. Although the leggy girls still did well at the box office, Jane Russell and her chesty compatriots brought that Midas touch, with less emphasis on legs and more on the chest.

America's obsession with glamour and beauty defined the film industry, for Hollywood talent scouts were quick to sign a beautiful girl with little regard to her ability as an actress. The pin-up girl craze lauded the physical appeal of females, and the artwork, despite the noble endeavors of many pin-up girls, further conveyed the notion that a woman's worth was based chiefly on her outward appearance. Society seemed to suggest to young women that to be beautiful was of greater importance than to be educated or to be proficient in a trade, and when Hollywood handed out contracts to pin-up girls, those pretty figures were rewarded rather than those who toiled in the theater. As Hollywood has evolved over the years, one looks back at old films and spots Jane Russell singing in *His Kind of Woman* and Lauren Bacall crooning in *To Have and Have Not*, and begins to wonder why the film industry no longer pursues actresses of multiple talents. Bette Midler and Beverly D'Angelo kept the old studio ways alive with their exceptional acting skill coupled with the aptitude for song, but they seem the last of the golden-era type. It is the physical appearance that Hollywood zeroes in on, and the pin-up girl craze served as a catalyst to this modus operandi.

Given the superficiality of the film industry, women with Hollywood on the mind could not be reprimanded for their belief that sexiness, and not talent, would enable them to enter the movie scene. Women tried for that out-of-this-world glamour look that such natural beauties as Gene Tierney and Paulette Goddard possessed. Feelings of inadequacy certainly gripped young women when they were unable to mirror the extraordinary

*Peggie Castle.* COURTESY OF MOVIEMARKET.COM

glamour of the select few women who tantalized Hollywood. Even pin-up girls felt inadequate and would adopt strange methods to further enhance their figures. Anne Baxter, the lovely actress of heightened talent but diminutive stature, tried to add a few inches to her height by dangling from the molding of her door. Evelyn Keyes, that chameleon actress capable of playing any role, wanted a bosom on par with the chesty stars of her day, and devised a stretching exercise to add mass to her breasts. Miss Keyes even described her exercise to women's health writer Alicia Hart, who relayed Evelyn's exercise to her readership. Hart quoted Evelyn as saying, "Stand erect, elbows at shoulder height, and fingertips of both hands touching. Now, press fingertips together hard — harder, HARDER. Relax and repeat several times." With popular pin-ups like Miss Baxter and Miss Keyes determined to change their physical structure, one could surmise that few women felt completely comfortable in their skin.

To seek perfection in the female form was not simply the proclivity recently discharged soldiers had when patrolling for a mate, for ladies wanted to possess that perfect figure as well. Many ladies felt that servicemen had spent their time in the armed forces fawning over their favorite pin-up pictures, and they would seek out a female companion that reminded them of their preferred pin-up girl. So, girls modeled their fashions after the leading pin-ups: they copied their style, their dress and their mannerisms. The desire was to be flawless, even if the human form was a flawed vessel, guaranteed to expire. Well before the days of widespread plastic surgery, only blonde actress Veda Ann Borg was known to have undergone radical reconstructive surgery. Veda had plastic surgery performed not because she felt inferior when gazing at her reflection but because her face was terribly lacerated in an automobile crash. Nowadays, the female cadre of the film industry seems to be steered toward the surgeon's office, perhaps as an after effect the pin-up craze had on American culture. When beauty is not beautiful enough, when age stretches its dire hands across the body, actions performed by the bearers of a saturnine constitution reek of despair, of hopelessness, which they imagine can only be combated by the renewal of youth and the onset of a reformed image.

After the war, many felt that the pin-up girl craze would come to a halt. It was reasoned that wives and girlfriends would not tolerate a photographic collection of scantily-clad women. The returned soldier would be forced to make the decision between a living, breathing mate and the reproduced image of a shapely gal deemed unattainable. The choice was simple for most men to make, but there was an unusual story printed in the *Oakland Tribune* regarding a soldier, his wife, and his obsession for pin-up girls. The husband, one Private Webster, belittled his wife so often that she filed for divorce. At divorce court, Mrs. Webster testified that her husband constantly reminded her "that (a) she didn't look like Betty Grable; (b) that her eyes weren't like Betty Grable's, and that (c) her hair wasn't blonde like Betty Grable's." Instances like the one shared by Mr. and Mrs. Webster, in which divorce by Betty Grable was filed, were uncommon yarns that amused readers of the daily ink. It was generally understood that most men would prefer a woman to a photograph.

When critics signaled the demise of the pin-up practice after the war, their words seemed credible. As former soldiers stepped off their ships and airplanes, newly returned to their beloved homeland, they sought to celebrate their victory with the companionship of close friends and comely girls. Cheesecake stills of Hollywood beauties saw them through the war, but after the final bomb was dropped and the troops made their return home, images on glossy photo paper no longer monopolized their desires. They sought girls removed from the picture that they could hold hands with. They wanted to feel the touch of a pretty girl's lips to theirs, for the pin-up image kept amorous desires within the breast but failed to bring such aspirations to fruition. So, the pin-up pictures, which served as reminders of beauty absent, were discarded for the partnership of a woman.

The postwar demise of pin-up art was evident to calendar publisher Brown & Bigelow. During the war years, when pin-up art was at its peak, Brown & Bigelow were besieged with requests for cheesecake calendars. The company saw a profitable haul courtesy of their distribution of pin-up calendars, but when the war ended, a change in the requests Americans sent the company intrigued their executives. Pin-up calendars, which had been their top-seller during the war years, had suddenly been driven from top rank. The soldiers now had girls in their arms, rather than a photo-graph to be pinned on a wall. This forced cheesecake calendars from the top spot on the Brown & Bigelow chart. The company held a survey in 1946 to find out what calendar theme would be the most popular in the postwar years. Their research concluded that Norman Rockwell's annual official Boy Scout calendar was in greater demand than their previous top-seller.

Although pin-up art had reached the apex of its popularity and had begun a slow descent in general esteem, the practice had, by no means, reached a state of demise. Pin-up art had simply reached its highest state of prevalence in its current form and had entered into a lull. There was to be a modification in pin-up art that would jumpstart the practice just a few years after the close of World War II. America entered another war shortly after WWII, the Korean War, and when the latter campaign was in its final stages, an entrepreneur named Hugh Hefner created a magazine that specialized in the glorification of the female form, à la pin-up art.

Hefner, a veteran of World War II, unveiled his creation — the magazine *Playboy* — near the end of the Korean War. To make certain his publication would be a success, Mr. Hefner secured nude photographs taken of starlet Marilyn Monroe for a 1949 calendar, and had the racy images published in his inaugural issue of *Playboy*. With America's top sexpot displayed as a centerfold in the initial issue of *Playboy*, Hefner had a huge success on his hands.

Publications like Hugh Hefner's *Playboy* took advantage of the popularity of pin-up art that had entranced the nation during the Second World War. In order to keep pin-up art from entering into another lull, the images were made more revealing, and cheesecake art of the post World War II decades adopted the exhibition of the nude female form. The pin-up photographs that soldiers had secured to their bunks during WWII served as a stepping stone to the nude centerfolds that magazines like *Playboy* displayed in their issues. Many social critics worried that the practice of pin-up photography would lead to a more sexual, less modest class of women, and when *Playboy* hit the stands, and the success of the magazine was evident, such cries of an absence of morals seemed legitimate. At the end of World War II, women's suffrage leader Alice Stone Blackwell was concerned with the rise of pin-up art and foretold of more decadent times in America's future. She said, "There will be a great tendency to obliterate moral standards. I can see young women doing things they never did before." Young women, like those who posed for cheesecake stills in bathing suits for the morale of troops during the war, were now, in postwar times, posing for photographs unclothed. Their desires were the same of those young, unknown cheesecake girls of WWII: to earn a little money and perhaps open up a door to Hollywood.

Just like the dames with stars in their eyes during World War II, for a nice payday, a pretty, shapely gal in postwar times could pose disrobed for a magazine and could gain name recognition, which could possibly lead to a job in the film industry. This route was taken by many film stars in the postwar decades, as such lovely women like Susanne Benton, Rosie Holotik, and Victoria Vetri parlayed a *Playboy* photo shoot into a career in film. More recently, centerfolds like Shannon Tweed and Kelly Monaco entered into acting courtesy of their photo shoots for the men's magazine. However, while America's pin-up art had evolved into the display of the naked female form, in England, during the time Benton and Holotik posed nude for *Playboy*, they still kept alive the tasteful, World War II era practice of pleasing, clothed cheesecake shots. Such beautiful British pin-ups like Veronica Carlson, Caroline Munro, Luan Peters, and the pinnacle of beauty Madeline Smith, posed for the admiration of men while remaining clothed for the bulk of their photo shoots. This practice had all but died out in the States. Although pin-ups like Farrah Fawcett and Lynda "Wonder Woman" Carter could still be seen pinned up to walls and posed in the fashion of those war years, the practice had entered into a crude state where the imagination was stunted by the onslaught of unrestricted images.

As time changes, so changes the structure of a culture. Women have always been regarded as the fairer sex, and fairness in regards to beauty gains appreciation based solely on the pleasure achieved through the aesthetic sense. The ladies who posed for pin-up pictures during the war years did so for the morale of a country, and they felt flattered by the attention and praise lavished upon them when the admiring eyes of men rested on their forms. In those war-torn times, women could feel obliged by a long, low appreciative whistle, yet to issue a wolfish whistle in a later decade, a man would feel the cold glare of hostility pierce his skin. Pin-up art has been labeled as crude, regarded in an air of bad taste, yet during those war years, when men fought for liberty and were absent beauty on any scale, those cheesecake images reminded them that beauty still existed. Those girls who posed for pin-up art during the war may have spawned the advent of the ostentatious, dissolute art of the bare centerfold, but the root should not be chastised for the ill fruit the plant bears. Pin-up art is, at its core, the glorification of beauty, and to commend that which is pleasing is an exercise never ending.

CHAPTER SEVEN

# THE TOP PIN-UP GIRLS
★ OF ★
# WORLD WAR II

# ★ RAMSAY AMES ★

Had it not been for the war, Ramsay Ames may never have started a career in acting. The New York native of Spanish/English descent had trained as a dancer with specialization in Latin-themed choreography. With an amazing voice as well, La Ames coupled her rhythmic oscilla-

*Ramsay Ames.*

tions with entrancing intonations. The dark-haired beauty was a classic entertainer who toured the night spots with her very own rhumba band, sang to crowds in smoky clubs, and gyrated on the stage to the beats that her band performed. But life 1940s style was tumultuous and Ramsay's band was broken up. The separation wasn't a conflict of artistic integrity, or the modern disruption of sojourns to rehab clinics, but the typical call young men received during the decade: that come-hither call from Uncle Sam.

When the members of Ramsay's band were called to service one at a time, the lovely Miss Ames found herself without trumpets and drums behind her. All of a sudden the rhumba had been removed from her life and Ramsay had to seek employ by other means. Fortunately for her, she was a knockout. Although her days performing at The Stork and La Conga in her home city had come to a close, Ames relied on her physical charms to remain in the entertainment business. She was introduced to famous photographer Ray Jones, who snapped a few photographs of her in 1943 — the height of the war. An unknown commodity outside of New York, Ramsay quickly became a sensation with the service boys when one of Jones's photographs was printed in a paper at the military installation of Fort Ord. The former songbird's lovely likeness was all the rage at the camp. Further accolades were presented Jones and Ramsay when film studio still photographers voted the Jones photo the best pinup picture of 1943.

The accolades from the still photographers may have gone to Jones, but the boys in the service were far less interested in the man behind the camera than the dame in front of it. Army men at the California encampment were upset that the photograph failed to display a caption, which would tell them the name of this wonderful, unknown goddess. To their dismay, as well as Ramsay's, the pin-up was displayed in the paper without mention to the pulchritudinous lady's handle. In order to place a name with their favored pin-up, the Fort Ord fighting men sent inquiries to the paper and begged the press boys to track down and slap a name on their intoxicating beauty. When the operatives of the ink hounded her handle, they passed it on to the boys in the barracks, and they, as Dee Lowrance put it, "swamped the studio with fan mail about her." Given the attention lavished upon her by the soldiers, Miss Ames landed a role in the film *Ali Baba and the Forty Thieves*.

Before the war, Ramsay was a songbird sensation with her rhumba band, but posing for cameras wasn't foreign to her. When fifteen, Miss Ames ran away from home and landed a contract with the elite Powers Modeling Agency. But with a lark in her throat and music in her knees, Ramsay gave up modeling to start a rhumba band. Thanks to Uncle Sam's need for her players, she returned to modeling and became a cheesecake siren which catapulted her to filmdom. The boys in khaki wanted to see more of Ramsay and the film studios heeded their demands. Miss Ames, talented as they come, had the Fort Ord servicemen to thank for her rising star. They sent letter after letter to studios, with petitions for them to place Ramsay Ames in motion pictures. A caption in the *Arizona Independent Republic* stated, "Ramsay Ames' picture caught the fancy of men at Fort Ord, and she became a starlet almost before the whistling had stopped." The whistles of servicemen helped the career of many a Hollywood actress, but in the case of Ramsay Ames, the catcalls were the cradle of her acting career.

A hypnotic beauty with dark hair and piercing eyes, La Ames was a rising star during the latter years of the war. Although more a "B" actress, Ramsay starred in several motion pictures, typically with roles as exotic beauties. Given her half Spanish ancestry, Ramsay's complexion was slightly darker than the average Caucasian American lady, so she was typecast as a foreign cutie. She played Middle Eastern dames in such films as the previously mentioned *Ali Baba and the Forty Thieves* as well as the horror flick *The Mummy's Ghost*, in which her part was central to the plot. Nicknamed "The Body Beautiful" by studio executives, the comely Miss Ames's star wasn't relegated to "B" films, where she played lasses from the land of sand. She starred in the war-era film *A Wave, a WAC and a Marine*, which gave the American populace the service-themed movies they craved during the Second World War.

The popularity of Ramsay Ames during the war wasn't typical of the modern "B" actress. Nowadays, only a select few, typically eclectic, audiences follow the career of "B" actresses, but before Barbara Crampton made a name for herself in the cheesy "B" films helmed by Stuart Gordon, the "B" list beauties enjoyed modest exposure. What helped Ramsay was her image. Born and raised in New York, the lovely Miss Ames had a worldly appearance but possessed attributes of the more modest lady. Scribe James Reid described Miss Ames when he penned, "She has a phosphorescent quality about her. Her hazel eyes seem to glow with banked fires. Her golden-brown hair seems to glint. Miss Ames is an odd combination of exclusive Long Island sophistication and down-to-earth Tin Pan alley forthrightness." She owned a remarkable beauty, one that effectively mixed an unattainable exoticness with the straight-shooting appeal of the common girl. It was this unique blend that allowed Ramsay to sit for, what she confessed to be, 958 photo shoots for pin-up purposes.

Like many actresses of the day, Miss Ames took time out from her schedule to entertain the troops. Since she had the boys in service to thank for her origin in Hollywood, she was eager to show her appreciation. The dark-haired beauty signed on with the Hollywood Victory Committee's "Bond Battalion" that toured America with the soldiers who adored her. She, as well as fellow Hollywood stars Edgar Kennedy and Gene Lockhart, toured with the "Bond Battalion," which consisted primarily of war heroes. With her rise in the film industry coupled with her work for the Victory Committee, Ramsay Ames became a hot commodity and thus attracted the attention of actor Jackie Coogan, who was serving in India when he took notice of her. After his initial whistle was issued, Coogan, who served as a glider pilot, wrote Miss Ames a letter requesting a date with her once he was discharged and back to his usual Hollywood haunts. Ramsay received Jackie's letter and responded: she agreed to a date, once his feet touched the soil of the USA.

Although Ramsay Ames seemed well on her way to stardom, it never really materialized for the New York native. She spent most of her acting career in lesser "B" pictures, but she soldiered through Hollywood for a couple decades, which proved that she was more than just a soldier's actress. When her career began to wind down, she married famous playwright Dale Wasserman and the couple relocated to Spain where she hosted a television program. A multitalented entertainer, Miss Ames had the beauty, the voice, the moves, and the thespian skill to excel in the business of show for several decades. She passed away in 1998 after a fight with cancer.

## ★ EVELYN ANKERS ★

When one thinks of the golden age of cinema, they typically conjure up images of lavish period-piece dramas or musicals taken from Broadway plays: Typically, a person in reverie doesn't recall films that gave the audience a jolt with monsters and creatures, ghosts, and the macabre. But Evelyn Ankers was a starlet during this fabled age of moviemaking, despite her failure to appear with Gable and Leigh in *Gone With the Wind*. Miss Ankers was Hollywood's top Scream Queen during the 1940s, exercising her lungs while a made-up Lon Chaney Jr. chased her through foggy surroundings. The best black and white fright films of the 1940s starred Evelyn as the damsel-in-distress. She screamed in *The Wolf Man* and protected her delicate neck in *Son of Dracula*, all to the amusement and fright of filmgoers.

Before the bombs rained down on Pearl Harbor, La Ankers had already established herself in the film industry as a leading lady in scare pictures. In 1941, *The Wolf Man* frightened audiences across the nation, but it was a fright of fantasy and not the ominous threat that blanketed the world courtesy of the Axis. America had yet to be attacked when Ankers's film hit the box office, but the presence of a global struggle was real — far more real than the werewolf that hounded Evelyn. Fear was made to order for the times and the horror genre became quite popular during the era thanks in part to stars like Ankers and producers such as Val Lewton, who breathed new life into the genre. Evelyn reveled in the chance to play the female lead, terrorized by some foul, sinister beast, as she served as the queen for all the film screamers. She said, "Something gruesome is always happening to me, and I do believe I have stretched the muscles around my mouth out of all proportion, screeching my terror for the cameras."

Well before Evelyn screeched her terror for the cameras, she was a little girl living in South America. Born to a British geologist who served as a mining engineer in Chile, the young Evelyn spent the bulk of her childhood south of the equator. Before her teen years, the family relocated to their native Britain, and little Miss Ankers found her calling in the field of acting. She began work in the business with bit parts in films and then moved across the pond and established residency in America with the intent of starting an acting career in Los Angeles. She worked her way up the ladder before she reached notoriety in the horror genre, where she played opposite Chaney in a number of fright flicks. But during the war years, Evelyn took time out from shrieking with fright in the presence of lumbering Lon to do her bit for the war effort, first as wife and secondly as starlet.

Married to "B" leading man Richard Denning, Evelyn was Mrs. Dick Denning in social circles. The actor left Hollywood after the bombing on Pearl Harbor to enlist in the Navy as a yeoman. The Hollywood couple lived comfortably in a ten-room house outside Tinseltown, but when Richard left for the service, Evelyn gave up the large estate and moved into a modest $40 apartment that was situated near her husband's Los Angeles military base. The relocation wasn't as difficult for Evelyn as it was for other stars — such as Jane Russell, who followed her husband to Georgia, and Ann Dvorak, who went to war-ravaged England to be near her betrothed. Since she was still in close proximity to Hollywood and the studios, Evelyn continued to act, but her household chores took top-billing in her life. Like most Americans, Evelyn made sacrifices and accepted the new roles that the hardship of war imposed. About being a military wife, Ankers said, "After Dick leaves I wash dishes, clean the apartment, wash and iron Dick's uniforms. Until now I never washed anything more than a pair of stockings in my life."

But it wasn't all Betty Homemaker chores for Evelyn during the war. She was a contract player who starred in many Universal Studios horror epics. Given the fame she achieved as the top Scream Queen in Hollywood, Miss Ankers was in the spotlight and thus constantly hounded by the writers of the folded page. Female newspaper scribes, whose occupation it was to offer beauty tips to the fair gender of America, often used Evelyn as a source for their bonny scoops. Who better to display the secrets of beauty, they imagined, than Miss Ankers, whose form was ideal. With legs so long they had their own detour signs, Hollywood's premier Scream Queen graced many a newspaper in the women's section, and she detailed the steps and methods she took to keep her body in peak condition. With an athletic, streamlined figure, Miss Ankers possessed the form that women wanted, prow to stern.

With her exceptional form and delicate beauty, La Ankers gave advice to women's health writers who in turn passed it along to their readership with the hope that their readers would administer Evelyn's techniques and thus adopt her stunning contours. Many of the tips Evelyn offered concerned exercise. The horror-icon detailed her workout routine for readers as part of the many duties the stunning Hollywood dames adopted during the war. While their husbands were off to war, women wanted desperately to do their bit, even those in Hollywood, and since they weren't allowed to fight on the frontlines, they stayed in the rear and did what they could. Starlets of Hollywood helped the morale of American women by offering them the top secret beauty tips that Hollywood horded for their dolls. Ankers was all too willing to help American girls achieve the figure they desired and had her physical fitness routine, complete with warm-up stretches, printed in the newspaper for all to see. She lifted the lid on the secrets of the silver-screen sirens, and gals across the States were grateful.

Although she passed along some common beauty tips, Evelyn had her own little secrets she felt necessary to share during the war-ravaged era. Athletics and calisthenics were ideal, but the Wolf Man's favorite dish also had a little extra advice absent other starlets. Many stressed the playing of tennis or swimming laps in the pool, but Evelyn, who championed these workouts as well, had other advice to offer. Movement of the limbs kept them from gaining access flab, but Evelyn also beat the drum for something a little more simple: sleep. La Ankers felt that a little respite from the daily grind did wonders for a woman's health. She said of getting a good night's rest, "sleep knits the reveled sleeves for care and also knits the body into shape." A firm disciple of beauty sleep, Miss Ankers knew that hours of leisure during the war were essential to maintain quality health — especially after the long hours worked by both men and women alike.

Beauty sleep wasn't Evelyn's idea and Evelyn's idea alone, but another beauty scoop she offered wasn't practiced by many dolls in the States. In fact, when she let the cat out of the bag concerning her top secret pulchritude pointer, she wasn't engaged in beauty secret chit-chat with a female writer, but a Hollywood beat writer who interviewed her for a film. When Robert Myers asked how she remained so beautiful and possessed her heavenly glow at such an early hour, Miss Ankers gave him quite a shock. She told the happy bloke that as a child in Chile, she and her mother were taught the secrets of what she called a "dew bath." She informed the scribe that a dew bath consisted of rolling around in the backyard of her house, before the sun ascended, in the fresh dew that coated the grass. Her attire for this pre-dusk ritual consisted of her birthday suit and nothing more. She assured Myers that her neighbors were never awake at five-thirty in the morning when the slender sylph was engaged in this odd south-of-the-equator exercise. Myers listened with rapt interest as Evelyn told him about her dew baths and ended his article by stating, "So I dragged myself away, telling Evelyn I hoped to see her again — say around 5:30 some morning. You can see I am a firm convert to the principle of dew baths."

Whether her dew baths had anything to do with her beauty or not is anyone's guess, but La Ankers was a pin-up girl extraordinaire during the war. She possessed an ethereal beauty with a modest charm that enabled her photographs to line more than one barracks wall. A delicate beauty, Evelyn looked exceptional in the bathing suits that she donned for cheesecake purposes, with her appeal residing chiefly in her charming facial features. Her lovely, dancing eyes sparkled with an enchantment that was resounding, which intoxicated many men who pinned up her photographs. Her beauty didn't seem to be that of she who sits in front of the makeup mirror for two hours, but more natural — more heaven sent — than the typical ravishing pin-up. When situated in front of bodies of water for cheesecake photos, the setting seemed right for Evelyn, who looked at home near pools of crystal, clear water. One of her more famous pin-up photos showed her seated on the dock at the edge of a lake, with her tantalizing beauty meshed well with the outdoor setting. She wasn't propped up on a swimming pool slide, or sunning at the beach, but placed in nature like the delicate sprite she appeared to be, extending her right leg towards the water while bending her left at the knee. The position of her legs, with her ankles extended and toes cast downward, gave her an ideal look of streamlined perfection. Yet her natural beauty and slightly tightened coiffure, made her pin-up appeal that of the elegant.

After the war, Miss Ankers continued in film for a few years until the horror genre began to dry up. American theatergoers began to crave the gritty noirs and Evelyn's screaming seemed dated to them. The conclusion of the war gave folks the knowledge that evil had a human's face, not that of a wolf or an undead creature, and they seemed to want films that were true to life: more easily accepted than vampires and werewolves. They had seen the evil of mankind and felt films should depict it more. When her meal ticket had fallen to more desired genres, she left acting and became a full-time mother. Unlike the typical Hollywood starlet, Evelyn was only married once. And unlike the typical Hollywood starlet, her only marriage was one that lasted. She and Richard Denning were happily married until her untimely death from cancer.

# ★ VIVIAN AUSTIN ★

Vivian Austin's star didn't shine quite as bright as many initially hoped. The dark-haired, pulchritudinous former beauty queen acted during the mid-1940s but health issues forced the stunning actress to cut her acting career short. With a debilitating eye condition that nearly left her blind, Vivian had to surrender her dream to address her weakening condition. Later in life, her eyesight was miraculously restored, but the miracle came twenty years after she shot her final picture. Although the lovely Miss Austin had to punch an early ticket out of Hollywood, she left behind a legacy of loveliness that reached its peak during World War II. A top cheesecake for the soldier boys, Vivian was often photographed in revealing western wear, when not in bathing suits, to take advantage of her status as a lady in gun-slinging westerns.

Like many beauty queens of the 1940s, Vivian parlayed her crowning into a career in show business. With the jeweled tiara of the vanity queen placed atop her head, Vivian's likeness was wanted to sell merchandise. Times haven't changed much; companies still hire beautiful models to help sell their wares, with the belief that an enticing dame flashing a smile and a bit more skin can sell whatever mundane article rests in their company coffers. Billboards across America were littered with pretty girls whose images were used to sell everything from toothpaste to auto parts. These overblown posters are how Vivian caught her break. A studio executive's jaw was set to drop when he got a glimpse of Vivian promoting some mundane piece of merchandise, planting an underwater kiss on some lucky bloke. The studio big-wig felt the lovely brunette on the poster should be in pictures, so he located her, gave her a screen test, and thus her acting career was set in motion.

Many young starlets tried to support themselves by acting in films or working in the field of modeling, but this was an avenue that Miss Austin didn't have to tread. Married to a wealthy businessman, Vivian could have relaxed in the lap of leisure, but the dark-haired beauty wanted to work in pictures. She spent some time as an extra in films before she caught her break in the western genre, where her finest performances can be found. But during the war, Vivian took time out from acting to engage herself in the bond-selling drive. She and her husband were huge supporters of bond rallies. Vivian took with her a $10,000 war bond of her husband's on each excursion. The promotion and sale of war bonds was a campaign that Hollywood got behind one hundred percent as they sent many of their

*Vivian Austin*

leading stars to towns and cities across America on drives. Vivian was one starlet who gladly went on the trips, where she would speak before large gatherings and explain the need to purchase bonds and stamps.

A beauty like Vivian could sell a fur coat to a bear, which gave credence to the enterprise of companies employing enchanting dames to hawk their wares. Even though pretty ladies make for solid salespersons, they were also used to build morale in Uncle Sam's fighting forces. Vivian, who was an exceptional swimmer in school, felt more comfortable in a bathing suit for cheesecake pictures than your average lass. Many models didn't feel too natural posing for cheesecake pictures in bathing suits, but Miss Austin, who put in many hours in soggy covers, felt right at home in them. All she had to learn was how to stand seductively in her bathing suits for the photos, which, it stands to reason, took little instruction for a stunning lady like La Austin. In fact, an Associated Press article used Vivian as a model when they described how a pin-up should position herself. A full-body photograph of Vivian was printed, and embedded in the picture were four captions that served as the four steps of achieving pin-up perfection. They were listed as: 1. Take a deep breath. 2. Pull tummy in. 3. Bend the knee nearest camera. 4. Rise up on your toes.

Being beautiful came naturally to Miss Austin, who won the title of "Miss Hollywood" early in the war — bestowed upon her by the Hollywood Chamber of Commerce. The comely brunette used her natural physical appeal as a film starlet and cheesecake model, but she endeared herself to the American people not by her beauty but by her more admirable qualities. The war was a hardship on most Americans. Many Americans had family members in the armed forces and also faced the rationing of essential supplies. Vivian informed ladies how they could add to their wardrobe on tight budgets. Whenever her husband wore out a suit, she would alter the male duds: cut and trim, pin and sew, to shape them into dresses that she could wear. Many American women weren't in the financial position that Miss Austin was in and had to be more fickle with their currency, but Vivian showed women how they could combat a tight budget, which allowed for limited clothes shopping, and still add to their wardrobe. Although the cloth of a man's suit may not have been the ideal fabric for a sundress, it gave women the opportunity to add additional dresses to their closet while not interfering with the widespread rationing of goods that the military needed to defeat the Axis.

Pin-ups were all the rage. They were popular among men for obvious reasons, and many women took a shine to them — after they pushed aside that useless feeling of envy — when they passed along beauty tips and advice to see them through the hardships of war. But, it was the fighting men who took the greatest shine to the pin-up girls. Units across America, and those fighting forces for the States overseas, named many a pin-up their unit's personal pet. They would also bestow upon their favored pulchritudinous pet unique nicknames, such as the one MPs at Fort Benning handed Vivian: "The Girl We'd Most Like to be Pinched By." A number of these "Girl Who" monikers were ridiculous, for units appeared to try and combat one another in the department of odd pet nicknames. But it was all done in good fun, and the girls liked it: it was an elevation of status. Studio executives would hear about these pet names that soldiers gave starlets and knew they had a hot commodity, so they'd offer the gals roles in films aware that the soldier boys would happily view a picture show starring their very own bonny lass. It was a win for everyone involved.

Pin-up girls could have their fun too. With every military unit announcing their personal pin-up, many war plants followed suit and did the same, and so cheesecake became quite popular. It seemed that every newspaper across the country printed at least one pin-up photo a day, which showcased an up-and-coming starlet or displayed an established star in swimming wear. But, the girls wanted some cake too. The pin-up girls of Hollywood hand-selected a soldier to be their very own pet pin-up and Vivian, with Evelyn Ankers, were photographed with Marine Sergeant James Marini — the "Pin-up Boy" of Hollywood pin-up girls. Marini was shown with Vivian on one arm and Evelyn on the other, as their photograph circulated the nation and was reproduced in nearly every major newspaper.

The Hollywood starlets selected their own pin-up boy, but with hundreds of military units all naming their special girl, there were far more pin-up girls than boys. The demand for cheesecake art was high, and Vivian, as a stunning, fresh-faced young starlet, was a hot commodity. Perhaps her most famous pin-ups were those that depicted her in western attire, given her background in Wild West films. The pin-ups were favorites of western viewers. One leggy pin-up photo showed Vivian wearing cowboy boots with some short, little hot-pants, which accentuated her magnificent legs. Her toes faced away from the camera but she was bent at the waist, and twisted at the hips, positioned as if she were firing a round or six at a cattle rustler. A six-shooter was in her glove-clad paw and her tiny midriff-bearing top was tied loosely on her streamlined back. Her curly brown hair cascaded under a cowboy hat, as the stunning western starlet flashed an amused grin, as if to claim that the six-shooter in her mitts spit pulchritude and not bullets.

On many photo shoots for cheesecake purposes, two pin-ups were thought better than one. The boys didn't mind at all: they received two dolls for the price of one. A pin-up famous among fishermen showed Vivian with Anne Gwynne as they traipsed in a creek with their mukluks, prepping for a little fly-fishing excursion. The two dames were dressed in sweaters — the popular, flattering attire of the times — with baskets lassoed around their torsos to store the fish they hooked. And, to keep within the pin-up motif, each brunette beauty was wearing the shortest of pants — although Anne's white shorts didn't quite show off as much leg as Vivian's ivory-colored skirt.

When the war ended, Vivian's health rapidly deteriorated and she was forced to quit acting in the late 1940s. The brunette beauty, whose eyesight was the primary concern of her physical plight, left the film industry and stayed with her husband until his death in the late 1960s. When her eyesight was restored, Vivian wed the doctor who brought life back into her eyes.

## ★ LUCILLE BALL ★

It may come as a shock to many that the oddball star of one of Hollywood's greatest sitcoms was a pin-up girl, but Lucille Ball was a ravishing, fair-haired starlet before she became that quirky dame we all know from her hit series *I Love Lucy*. Before the pratfalls and wide-eyed antics that made Lucy a television star, she was a film starlet and quite the box office success. Like the Dean Brothers, Miss Ball is best known as a bit dizzy and daffy, thanks to her television work, but World War II audiences found her enthralling and gorgeous. She was a top-flight showperson whose star took off during the war years with her breakout role in the flick *Du Barry Was a Lady*. A lavish movie with numerous musical numbers, the flashy film catapulted Lucille into stardom, but it was a rise long overdue.

Lucille wasn't an instant success story in Hollywood. Oftentimes folks expect the planted seed to bear fruit in short order, but it takes time for the seed to germinate. The daughter of a mining engineer who died before she was of school age, Lucille started at the lowest rung on the Tinseltown ladder and worked her way up. Miss Ball was an extra at the outset of her acting career, which kept her head from getting too swelled when she eventually rose to the top. Many stars who reach the top of the mole hill have a tendency to kick dirt upon those who linger beneath them, but Lucy was respected in the business as a performer who was on terrific terms with everyone. Due to her pedigree as a background performer, Lucille was known in the industry for her warmth and her genial character, which she gladly extended to stand-ins and extras on the shows she worked when a star.

When the war broke out, Lucille enjoyed a rise in Hollywood that lifted her to the regions of the film industry's top box-office draws. Box

*Lucille Ball.*

office success was hers, but her personal life during those turbulent times wasn't unlike many young American women who were missing their husbands in service. Madly in love, Miss Ball was married to Cuban-born film star Desi Arnaz, who, like many young American men, joined the armed forces to help knock off the Axis. After Desi enlisted in the Army, Lucille delved into her work to keep her mind preoccupied — she refused to obsess with worry for her betrothed. When her husband was on furlough, he visited Lucille on one of her movie sets and their departure spurred writer Dee Lowrance to use them as a model for the domestic struggles of war. Lowrance wrote, "Their quiet parting made one reflect on the way war touches the lives of everyone — from top-flight star to unknown extra. For it spares neither of them the heartache of saying goodby {sic}. Something in the way Desi paused by the door made his heartache very real."

The stable of married actresses with husbands in the service had limited vacancy, and the ladies tried to keep busy with their professional lives so as not to bemoan a personal life wrought with loss. Film industries were more than willing to see that their female commodities were kept busy, and they signed many actresses up for war-bond drives after they had finished on film sets. Miss Ball went on the war bond circuit and held rallies in numerous cities and towns across the wide American expanse. She was attached to the Fourth War Loan Drive that took her to such locales as the Sun Shipyard and Belmont Ironworks. An exceptional seller of war bonds, Lucille entertained crowds with skits at various war plants. She earned quite a solid reputation as a dynamite seller of war bonds.

It would stand to reason that many stars would be averse to entertaining crowds after shooting a film, but Lucille wasn't the typical vain actress. Having slummed her way through the life of a Hollywood extra, Lucille was agreeable and amiable with studios. A terrific work ethic carried her through Hollywood during those trying days as a player-in-the-shadows, and once she finally reached stardom, she wasn't about to discard the mentality that got her there. When she was asked how she felt about constantly working, acting in films, and entertaining crowds on war loan drives, Lucille showed the type of character that Americans from her generation harbored. She said, "In the ten years I've been working in Hollywood, I've never had a vacation. That's okay with me because I don't like to loaf. Just let me work and I'll gladly pay the taxes." Work meant a great deal to Miss Ball for it was her catalyst to stardom.

While she worked for Uncle Sam, Lucille lost her grandfather during the war. Notified of his death while on tour with the Fourth War Loan

Drive, Miss Ball said goodbye to the man who helped raise her. Having lost her father at an early age, Lucille was reared by her grandparents who instilled in her the work ethic that saw her through Hollywood. The death of one of the most important men in her life failed to subdue her resolve or discharge her from that admirable course she charted during the war effort. She simply worked harder. So well thought of was Miss Ball that she was asked to serve as master of ceremonies for the opening of a bowling alley at the Birmingham Hospital for Wounded Soldiers. Men who had fought for their country, and returned in poor condition due to battlefield injuries, were thankful that a star like Lucille took time out from her busy schedule to see that they were entertained. The grand opening of a bowling alley meant a lot to them, but perhaps not as much as welcoming Lucille to their area of recuperation.

Most folks know that a fine work ethic enables a person to excel, but Hollywood tends to place a greater emphasis on an individual's physical appeal. Although Lucille worked hard enough to put lumberjacks to blush, she was also a beautiful actress. Dee Lowrance wrote, "Nothing — and critics and press agents seem to agree on this point — can be lovelier than Lucille's peaches-and-cream complexion and tangerine hair on the screen in color." With a beauty classified as classic, Miss Ball and her fair features were found enticing to the boys in service. Often surrounded by red, Lucille's lips were typically painted a dark shade of the apple-skinned color, which accentuated her flame-colored tresses for her cheesecake stills. During the war, Royal Crown Cola employed — with a reckless abandon — pin-ups to sell their soft drink. They dolled Miss Ball up for a photo shoot and propped her on a rocking seahorse. They too used red to the hilt with Lucille — her lovely face seemingly burst off the page to entice you to buy their refreshing beverage. With her titian-hair and salutary epidermis, more than one sailor issued a grateful salute to Lucille for her pin-up pictures.

## ★ LYNN BARI ★

The stone-faced pin-up Lynn Bari seemed far more comfortable when she cast her piercing gaze away from the photographer's camera; her cheesecake-induced smiles appeared forced. Not every knockout can fake a smile, and Miss Bari's comfort seemed compromised when she painted on a false smile for the chaps behind the camera's lens. Not every pretty face can counterfeit a comely grin — to appear brummagem and gaudy for the sake of appealing images. Although an actress, and in the profession of exiting the self for art's sake, Lynn did not quite excel at tawdry ornamentation but made an appealing pin-up regardless. One needn't cast a cheap smile to pass herself off as enticing, and Lynn knew the boys would accept her pin-ups with or without the creases at the corner of her mouth.

Lynn Bari was known around Hollywood before the war years as an amiable actress who could be presented with scripts of varying degrees

*Lynn Bari.*

of worth. Whether it was done in a joking manner or not, Lynn was referred to around Tinseltown as "The Queen of the B Pictures." She was glad to work, and she often accepted roles that other actresses passed on — viewed by them as material unworthy of their valuable time. Time is a valuable commodity, but a person achieves value in show business by acting in pictures. Certainly, Lynn felt that by working around the clock she raised her value in the industry, but the critic would offer the old cliché that quality is better than quantity. Miss Bari rarely hurt for quantity — she often made a handful of movies in a single year — but the quality of her films were often suspect. However, her disposition endeared her to producers who knew that she would give their project serious consideration, and not belittle them with a rejection of their script. About her reputation as a B-actress, Miss Bari said, "I've been kidded about being Queen of the Bs and I've never minded. It is a living and I've been doing what I most want to do — act all the time."

At the outset of the war, Lynn was one of Hollywood's most tireless female thespians. However tireless her work ethic, she grew tired of some of the studio's publicity. Most actresses of the day, even before the cheesecake craze of World War II, were escorted to the photographer's studio to be shot in numerous wardrobe ensembles, which always led to the donning of bathing suits. Lynn wasn't the only actress who felt the photos unnecessary, and she was quite vocal about the pointless swimsuit stills that studios demanded from their lady actors. The leg-baring photos were for studio heads, and many in the industry felt they were taken strictly to massage the lustful curiosity of a predominately male aggregation. Just before America's involvement in the war effort, Miss Bari put an end to the studio-mandated cheesecake shots, saying "From now on the only time I'll wear a bathing suit is when I go in swimming." She told writer Wood Soanes that she was willing to play ball with her studio, but that the leg art didn't help advance her career. She put the kibosh on it, but the kibosh didn't take.

After Pearl Harbor was bombed, America entered the war effort, and Americans from Maine to Seattle were eager to help in any way possible. The boys in the armed forces were told, among other things, that they were fighting to safeguard American womanhood. Since soldiers fought for womanhood, what they fought for should be seen from all angles — hence the rise of the pin-up. Lynn, who had spoken out against the studios demand for needless cheesecake photos, now saw a need in the seductive stills. No longer were they reserved for the eyes of the wolfish studio magnates — they were widely disseminated to the fighting men of Uncle Sam. The building of morale in the nation's fighting men allowed

Lynn to relax her stance on the bathing suit photo shoots, and she became a pin-up favorite for the boys in service.

It took a war to get Miss Bari to take a rest. However, her rest, in regards to the production of motion pictures, was not a typical rest, for the hard-working actress merely redirected her work ethic to other avenues. Lynn would often make anywhere from five to six pictures a year, but in the war years of 1943 and 1945, she appeared in just one picture each year. She may have cut back on acting, but Lynn was exposed to more crowds during her hiatus from playacting. The stunning brunette simply shifted gears and entered into the assistance of the war effort. She became one of the first actresses to enter into the war bond circuit. In 1942, she teamed with actor Ronald Colman as they toured the nation in the "Salute Our Heroes" celebration. They entertained crowds and sold war bonds and stamps at such locales as Hutchinson, Kansas, where they attended the Kansas State Fair and held an after-barbecue show. They would sell war bonds and give patrons at their gatherings free autographs. In 1943, Lynn was asked by WAAC Commander Oveta Culp to attend a ceremony held in honor of the first anniversary of Canada's Women's Auxiliary Army Corps.

Miss Bari toured the nation to drum up business for the sale of war bonds, but the boys in the armed forces enjoyed the fact that her stance on cheesecake stills had relaxed. Although she was considered a "B" actress, Lynn was strictly A-list when it came to cheesecake. Scribe Dee Lowrance touted Lynn as the woman who possessed the "ideal American figure," and detailed her measurements in an article. Lowrance proudly boasted Bari's bust at 35 inches, her waist at 25 inches, and her hips at 35 ½ inches. With those dimensions positioned on her five-foot-six-inch frame, Lowrance felt that her contours were well equipped for the art of posing for cheesecake purposes. And the boys agreed. Pinned up every-where from pre-flight schools in Florida to the island of Tinian, Lynn Bari helped build the morale of many American fighting men.

Lynn's most famous pin-ups were of her decorated in a candy cane striped bikini on what was clearly a studio-built beach. Positioned on a stage littered with sand, Lynn struck a few poses that sailors, soldiers, and Marines took with them on their many excursions. The dark-haired beauty stood with her right foot resting on a beach ball for one shot, and for another she was seated on the sandy stage, cradling a leg that Dee Lowrance found ideal. The Queen of the Bs made the strategically placed beach a hot spot where boys longed to set up volleyball nets and impress the striking pin-up with their physical prowess. For there she was, wait-ing, with a cloudy backdrop behind her and with the hope that a sailor might dock on shore and offer her an umbrella for protection from the encroaching storm. It was stills like that, with a beauty such as Miss Bari, seated patiently on the beach and awaiting someone's arrival, which kept many a fighting man focused on the fight, eager to return home victorious and gather in their heroic arms a sharp-looking dame to celebrate with.

Even though Lynn decided to rethink her stance on cheesecake stills, she was forced to give up leg art for the boys. She had married notorious hothead Sidney Luft, an arrogant Hollywood producer who served as a test pilot during the war, and became pregnant during the latter stage of the war. Prepping for motherhood took most of Bari's time as the war-bond drives became a thing of the past. But perhaps her unrivalled drive and work ethic took its toll as Lynn gave birth to a daughter who failed to survive her initial day. When the war ended to the grandest of celebrations, one of the ladies who gave men across the world reason to cheer, found it difficult to cheer herself.

# ★ ANNE BAXTER ★

The vest-pocket pin-up, Anne Baxter was a petite beauty, who despite her obvious charms was quite insecure about her short body type. Not the tall, leggy stunner that other pin-up dolls were, Miss Baxter possessed not the on-stilts look that some of the top cheesecake models owned. The diminutive dame wanted desperately to grow — to cast a taller shadow than her mite-like frame created — so she adopted exercise techniques many might find odd today. In order to stretch out her frame, Anne would engage herself in stretching exercises designed to elongate her body. Like former Red Sox legend Smoky Joe Wood, who tried to cure his sore arm by hanging from the rafters in his barn, Anne tried to add a few inches to her height by dangling from the door molding in her house. She retained her usual five feet three inches despite her determination, but a true ailment, of which a short stature is not, found its way to Anne's body. Of her monkey-like dangling drills, Anne said, "I wrenched a shoulder and broke a few fingernails and door moldings."

Many people feel that the body reflected in the mirror has room for improvement, and Miss Baxter too shared this sentiment. Even though she found fault in her frame, many a fighting man in the armed forces found a frame devoid of fault. Short she may have been, but her frame was neither stocky nor compact: it was well-structured and toned, thanks, in part, to her adherence to unique exercise drills. Extremely pretty, with lively dancing eyes and a smile that could melt the polar ice caps, Anne's beauty was a charming elegance that endeared itself to men of many backgrounds. She possessed not that towering, leggy stature that made many pin-ups unattainable to the average Joe, but that girl-next-door sweetness, firm and ripe for the picking. Because of her frame, she was one of America's top sweethearts during the war, and not the too-small dame who she envisioned herself to be.

*Anne Baxter.* COURTESY OF MOVIEMARKET.COM

Anne was an early promoter of fitness. Her time was before stores that specialized in supplements littered every mall — before the vanity crowd was well-acquainted with metal structures that do as much for the body as sit-ups and pull-ups. Miss Baxter knew that to keep the firmness of youth, one had to work to retain that desirable structure. Although she was a self-professed lover of all cuisine, Anne worked out strenuously and kept the intake from expanding her frame. She said, "Anyone who doesn't have perfect proportions — and, I might put in, anyone who wants to keep them — is almost compelled to do special exercise." She stressed not only exercise but also stretches — even those that weren't designed to add an extra inch or two to your height. In order to keep the body limber — pin-ups had to twist and hold positions for an extended period of time — stretches were essential to keep the cameras clicking.

Despite her small standing in the realm of height, Anne was an opinionated woman who rarely held back her views. When asked what should be done with Japanese emperor Hirohito after the bombing on Hiroshima, Anne said, "We should let him stew in his own juice. He's got so much trouble over there he'll cook himself." But before she offered her viewpoints on postwar society, Miss Baxter had placed herself in good standing with the boys of the armed forces. One of Hollywood's single darlings during the war, Anne was considered a top catch in Hollywood circuits. Much was written about her personal life, and tabloid writers wanted desperately to know who Anne went out dancing with and what Hollywood heartthrob got her all a-flustered. Newspaper writers made a big to-do about Anne's standing in the lanes of romance, and made the soldiers across the nation feel like they had a shot at her too. When Anne planned a trip to New York, Dee Lowrance wrote, "Her main concern as she started off on her New York vacation was whether there would be any escorts out of the armed services to beau her around New York when she got there."

In the realm of motion pictures, where reality gets substituted for fantasy, reality has the greatest of all influence on the creative aspects of filmmaking. Movies are at their best when they offer an escape from reality, but when reality is too encompassing — when the realm of fantasy seems too juvenile, even for those folks in Hollywood — society expects the film industry to champion the noble aspects of life. During the war years, Hollywood made one battle-themed flick after another, and actresses had to adapt to a world where fighting was real. The make-believe setting of Hollywood was asked to depict the reality of war life. One famous war movie of the time was *The Fighting Sullivans*, which focused on a real American family who lost five boys in one attack. When the widow Katherine Leary Sullivan was asked who she wanted to play her in the film, she selected Anne Baxter. Little Miss Baxter accepted the daunting, heart-wrenching task of depicting a war widow in one of Hollywood's most astounding tearjerkers, as she played an All-American girl widowed at the age of twenty.

Anne endeared herself to soldiers and American audiences by playing the most dramatic role any actress was asked to play during the war. The role of the widow Sullivan catapulted an already up-and-coming young actress into the region of film stars. Whether a celebrity agrees to it or not, they are public figures, and as public figures they are viewed as models for the public. Many young women adopted Anne as their role model, and she made for a solid person to pattern one's self after during the war. She agreed to appear at war-bond rallies in between pictures to sell stamps and bonds at various locales. She once sold $7,775 worth of war bonds at a rally held at Germantown, where a picture of her planting a kiss on a star struck young man named Ben Carr circulated the nation's papers.

When the war entered its final stages, Anne became an even larger role model than before when she approached her studio with a request. During the 1940s, it was common studio practice for stars to be sent out to theaters across the country to promote their latest film. Anne wanted to shake things up a bit in 1945. When the war had ended, Anne asked General Omar Bradley if she could tour hospitals and visit with wounded soldiers. The general, of course, agreed, but this put her studio in a bind. They wanted Anne to travel around the country to promote her latest picture and felt that by sitting with wounded soldiers, the film would not receive the trumpet's blast of excellent publicity. They were wrong. Anne convinced the brass at her studio that she could promote her latest film effort just as easily at hospitals as she could at theaters. They relented and allowed their diminutive starlet to entertain the wounded troops. Had the studio executives not relented, the headstrong actress may have gone on with her tour anyway. Anne said, "I just get sick to my stomach every time I think of how the public fusses over the wounded during wartime and then forgets all about them the minute the shooting stops." Although she wasn't a singer, or much of a dancer, Anne entertained the troops simply by being Anne; she listened to the boys tell their war stories.

By touring the hospitals to lift the spirits of wounded soldiers, Anne said her thanks to the fighting men who endured the greatest strug-gle and sacrifice of war. The boys, in turn, were thankful for her selfless spirit. A girl who had been a stunning pin-up, captured in still-life by a photographer's lens, became a figure of strength who urged them to get well. Her many pin-ups, such as the famous Anne-on-a-swing shot, in which the short dress she wore showcased a lot of leg, inspired men to fight for several years, but her postwar inspiration was far greater. The warrior with postwar dreams, who had them dashed courtesy of the tumult of the battlefield, saw in himself not the man capable of reaching those dreams, but a man lessened by battle. His agony is a profound one, for it was introduced to him at a time of selfless sacrifice, serving his country to protect it from evil, yet his noble actions led him to the hospital beds and infirmaries. And there, healing his body and his mind, he finds Anne Baxter, who had chosen to visit him rather than the hearty, healthy filmgoer — and he is healed, if only for a day. To look upon the beauty of the pin-up captured in a photograph is to set a symbol to fight for, but to look upon the pin-up in the flesh, knowing she is here to see you — to thank you — is to know what true beauty is all about. Anne Baxter gave that to the wounded soldiers she visited, and for that, she deserves an overdue salute.

## ★ JOAN BENNETT ★

A woman of unrivalled class, Joan Bennett was the walking definition of dignity and grace. Limited have been the actresses in cinema history who have been able to stand beside Miss Bennett and feel her equal in the department of sophisticated deportment. She was a woman of exceptional poise, whose elegance was obvious to those who worked with her or viewed her from the screen. Although not the typical pin-up — she was not of the sweater-girl, swimsuit-clad ilk — Joan Bennett was nevertheless a favorite of servicemen who gladly pinned up her likeness as tribute to her good nature and patriotic endeavors. At a time when the nation was in flux, with many young men uprooted from their everyday lives and thrust in the role of soldier, Joan was a beacon of rightness and responsibility. She mirrored no person when she, at the outset of America's involvement in the war, took it upon herself to see that servicemen away from home were entertained and taken care of. A woman of exceptional character, Miss Bennett was responsible for the creation of many servicemen canteens where soldiers could unwind, have a bite to eat, and dance with ladies before shoving off to war.

Many pin-up girls were lovely young newcomers to Hollywood who gained name recognition thanks to their work as cheesecake models. There were also ladies like Joan Bennett, who had established themselves in the film industry many years ago, yet did their bit to assist in the morale of the servicemen. Joan, who came from a long line of stage actors, never intended to become an actress herself, but she had the role thrust upon her when she divorced her alcoholic husband and had to support their daughter. All throughout the rough 1930s, when America was in the midst of the Great Depression, Joan was a leading lady in Hollywood.

*Joan Bennett.* COURTESY OF MOVIEMARKET.COM

Miss Bennett had entered the industry she felt was right for her comely sisters but not her. Joan knew it was an industry obsessed with physical appeal, and she felt her sisters more beautiful than she. About her entry into show business, Joan said, "My sisters, Barbara and Connie, were the beautiful ones and everybody took it for granted they'd follow the Bennett tradition and go on the stage. But I developed a curve here and there, so I wound up as an actress." Miss Bennett had initially set out to be a dress designer, but with her beauty and elegance, she found entrance into the acting profession an easier task.

As an established Hollywood player at the time of war, Joan used her status as a top-flight thespian to help servicemen. When she made appeals to radio stations to be let on air in order to promote the fundraising of her canteens, she found the executives of radio stations agreeable, as they helped promote her patriotic plans. Most celebrities use their name to get pet projects started and then leave the dirty work to others, but Joan wasn't adverse to rolling up her sleeves and leading the charge. After she had established and furnished canteens, Joan would visit them after filming her current motion picture and dance with soldiers, as well as lend a hand in the kitchen washing dishes. Imagine today's leading vain starlet on a military installation, wearing those unsightly yellow plastic kitchen gloves, and scrubbing the plates that soldiers had just dined from. It seems too farfetched to even fathom, but Joan, a huge name during the war, did just that. About her work for the soldiers, Jimmie Fidler wrote, "Joan Bennett equipped her eleventh and twelfth canteens for men in nearby camps and bases. She has underwritten their maintenance for the duration."

When one understands the personal life of Joan Bennett, they acquire a better appreciation for what she did during the war. Still very much in box office demand, Joan went to work for studios in the morning where she shot films. After she put in a full day's work on a film set, she would leave the bright lights for one of the local canteens she established. While there, she would work even harder: taking care of kitchen chores, playing hostess to servicemen, and dancing with men from the armed forces when they requested it. Her chores still went undone after she departed the canteen, for Joan was also a devoted mother who made time for her daughters. With no disrespect to Lynda Carter, Joan was the ideal wonder woman for her ability to multitask, and to do so in a selfless fashion.

Perhaps no woman in the film industry has had the work ethic that Joan Bennett owned. Certainly, there have been actresses just as devoted to their craft, but one would be hard pressed to find an actress capable of excelling under Joan's mammoth workload. Studios asked many actresses to run across country and sell war bonds, but Joan wasn't the type to wait for others to line up her comings and goings; she was the table setter, the go-getter who showed others how things were done. Her self-imposed schedule was a maddening one that demanded all of her time, with no less than full dedication and exertion. However daunting her many tasks, Miss Bennett never allowed the fervor of too many pots boiling to get the better of her nerves. She was a woman under control. Systematic and thorough, Joan would have made for an ideal general in the military ranks. About controlling her day, Joan once said, "Since things must be done as when planned, punctuality is the soul of a system. To make sure I go places and do things on time, I have a clock and watch in the house set at a different time. Since I'm never sure what time it is, I always rush to meet my schedule and generally finish ahead of time."

Time is an aspect of life that few people can manage well, but Joan excelled at it during the war. Motherhood came first to Joan, and her acting profession received no little attention from the workaholic, but the war effort demanded so much time from so many people. Miss Bennett saw what the war meant to the country and sacrificed time she could have spent with her daughters, or perfecting a role in film, to make certain that the men in the armed forces felt comfortable and appreciated. Her work establishing canteens was greatly appreciated and she also made numerous appearances at military camps. She never shirked one chore at the expense of another, for Miss Bennett understood the importance of every activity she undertook. Not many people with her heavy workload would accept additional duties, but Joan, even with her canteen work, agreed to serve as recreation director for the California AWVS. Her selfless work during the war was nothing short of awe-inspiring.

Perhaps even more awe-inspiring is how Joan remained beautiful while operating on little rest. A highly-respected actress among men and women alike, Joan's classic beauty was the type many American women aspired to mirror. Miss Bennett understood her role as a celebrity and knew that women looked to her for beauty tips. She knew that a woman's beauty was not something that objectified her or demeaned her in any way but that beauty was a catalyst to healthy self-esteem. In between her many tasks, Joan found time to write a book which gave insight and pointers to women on how to look and feel beautiful during time of war. Role models lead, and role models urge us to aspire, and Joan Bennett, who gave her all to the war effort, made for the perfect role model for her generation and every generation that follows.

# ★ INGRID BERGMAN ★

To claim that Ingrid Bergman was the world's most popular actress during the war years would not be much of a stretch. The tall, beautiful Swedish native had plenty box office appeal, for she exuded elegance and seemed typecast for roles of noble women. Her appearance lent itself well for the typecast. Her beauty was not of the boisterous variety but of the sophisticated kind that seemed to never take a holiday, not even at the first blush of daylight. If you asked anyone around the days of war if there was a female celebrity who could look beautiful upon first rising from bed, who needed not an hour with the makeup brush, you would certainly hear the response of Ingrid Bergman over and over again.

Best known today for her classic role as the torn, war-ravaged bride of a resistance fighter in the Bogart epic *Casablanca*, Ingrid won legions of fans with her exceptional work in what might be Hollywood's greatest achievement. War can tear apart families and can ruin the bond of love, as husbands perish in battle and the women they left behind mourn their passing. Such was the fate of Bergman's character in *Casablanca* — or at least so she thought. Her husband was very much alive, yet when she thought him dead, she romanced Bogie until knowledge of her husband's whereabouts came to light. She returned to her first love and bid adieu to the budding romance. The story of *Casablanca* captured the hearts and minds of many a filmgoer, and Bergman's sympathetic portrayal earned her a place among the acting elite.

As one of the top female actors in the world, Ingrid's name was constantly in print. Women have a tendency to mimic the ways of silver screen lovelies, and when Bergman's star shined its brightest, many women began to pattern their looks after her. Across America, many young ladies patterned their coiffures after the Bergman model. Her tall, tenuous frame became the ideal physique for females, who tried to locate threads that gave their figure a Bergman-like thinness. Louella Parsons wrote, "Bergman is the popular type for 1943. Even the fashion magazines acknowledge that the Swedish star's cool, calm beauty is the most popular type style." The Bergman look became all the rage, as Ingrid was groomed by her studio to be the ideal woman — she who looks stellar in any dress, and she who possesses a collected beauty, which is designed for the adulation of all men but the possession of just one.

Her pin-up photo shoots were never of the gaudy type, for her studio refused to present her as a woman with loose morals but as a lady of

virtue. Although soldiers pinned up her pictures, they weren't as provocative as other pin-ups. Ingrid wasn't asked to don a bathing suit and
tilt her reedy frame to accent her backside and show off her legs. When
the magazine for soldiers, *Yank*, published a pin-up of Ingrid, it wasn't
your typical cheesecake still but a photo more conducive to the wholesome image her studio desired. She wasn't situated on a diving board or

*Ingrid Bergman.* COURTESY OF MOVIEMARKET.COM

leaning against a ladder, standing on her toes while wearing the briefest of skirts. No, she was dressed conservatively, in a button-down blouse, and resting on a stack of hay with her delicate left arm raised skyward, as if to say that she was waiting back on the farm to greet her heroic fighting man upon his triumphant return. It was a well-staged photo shoot and passed along the Bergman image of untainted virtue that her studio demanded. There was nothing loud about her pin-up, simply down-home wholesomeness.

Her studio took full advantage of her subdued beauty and promoted her as the ideal woman — one of grace, sophistication, and most importantly, staunch fidelity. Ingrid played the role for the cameras, but in secret she was furious about the image. The moguls of Hollywood placed upon her shoulders the blueprint of the loyal wife and Ingrid wasn't suited for the role in real life. Although married and a mother, Bergman's eye was one of the wandering persuasion, and scandal followed her during the war years. Many soldiers across the world pinned up her photographs on their barracks wall, with the belief that the willowy Miss Bergman personified female dignity. Named "The Girl We'd Most Like to Share Oxygen With" by soldiers at Riggs Field, many a fighting man saw in her the image of the girl they left at home, who waited patiently for their return. But Ingrid wasn't one to bide her time pining for a departed love.

Ingrid showed a selflessness when she requested to be sent overseas on a USO tour to entertain troops. Her studio depicted her as the shy, stay-at-home type, but that typecast was ruined during the war thanks to a torrid love affair Bergman had while on her USO tour. She met up with a flamboyant, egotistical war photographer by the name of Robert Capa, who sought to make Ingrid another of his many conquests. She proved an easy target for the lothario who seduced and won the heart of Bergman, but his heart was never one to be given away — at least for too long. The Swedish dame, undaunted by one failed affair, accepted the offer of another fling and left her young family for playboy filmmaker Roberto Rossellini. When news spread of Bergman's less-than-faithful ways, her status as a leading Hollywood star was tarnished. Many people who gladly purchased tickets to watch her films — thousands of Americans who waited for their loved ones to return from the greatest of all battles — lost interest in Ingrid and refused to watch her films, knowing that she was not the ideal image of female dignity. But to Bergman's credit, she never tried to live up to that image — she only played it well for the cameras.

# ★ JANET BLAIR ★

Songbirds didn't come any comelier than Janet Blair. Prior to the war, Miss Blair was a songstress with exceptional vocal dexterity, who wooed the night club crowd with her syrupy-sweet serenades. She lent her lullaby qualities to the big band circuit where she crooned for Hal Kemp. But the big band bonanza wasn't the end of the line for Janet. Off to Hollywood she went to star in pictures, and star she did, for the delicate darling didn't bide her time as a film extra learning her craft from the shadows, she was quickly thrust into the spotlight. In no time, Miss Blair was an up-and-coming talent in Hollywood. Although eye-candy roles were handed her, Janet was more than window dressing, for she received close to top-billing in her films and even played the title role in a war-era feature. A darling of war-era America, La Blair had a face the camera adored. Her intoxicating smile and bright, bouncing eyes made her a favorite of the pushpin crowd.

As a child, Janet was raised very much the belle, with dancing lessons and aspirations of a life in music. She developed an enviable voice, which enabled her to catch on with Hal Kemp's band, but after the band split due to death, Janet was without employ. Her spell among the unemployed was a span shortened courtesy of her talents. Many pin-ups got by on pulchritude alone, like the elite Conover Girls or the stunning Powers Models, but Blair had an ace up her sleeve. With a look that could have bought her way into any modeling agency, Janet relied more on her talents in show business to make her bread. When her band dispersed, Janet found employment in the burgeoning film industry, which pursued, in earnest, lovely women with numerous talents. They found in the lovely Miss Blair a woman in need of little training, for her big band background had exposed her to the large crowds and bright lights that would be her daily surroundings in the field of pictures. Many studios subjected their newly inked actresses to hours of singing lessons, but the lessons had already gained hold in regards to Janet Blair. Weeks and months of coaching weren't needed to make Janet a film industry songbird: she came equipped for the role.

At the time Janet had reached Hollywood, America had entered the war due to the bombing of Pearl Harbor. The American people needed symbols, and they searched in desperation for any item, any form, that could serve as a rallying figure. There was the Statue of Liberty of course, but her features were frozen, locked and cold, hardened not by disinterest but by her construction. The Statue of Liberty was not a living entity, and the symbol fighting men needed was a living, breathing form. This form was female. Janet Blair joined the growing ranks of pin-up girls early in the war. The role of a pin-up was good for professional exposure, for lesser known actresses and new-to-Hollywood thespians such as Janet, found the cheesecake photos an easy way to build a name in the cutthroat film industry. Further exposure could be had courtesy of the war bond circuit, which Janet pursued — it also took her to Mexico on a goodwill tour.

*Janet Blair.* COURTESY OF MOVIEMARKET.COM

New to Hollywood during the war, Janet found that men in the industry could salivate with the best of them. Many pin-ups had little concern
with posing for the soldiers, for that was an avenue of morale-building,
but posing for studio stills in bathing wear seemed a tad uncouth to
many actresses. Studio heads liked cheesecake as much as any man, but
their demands for the dessert were crude. What the soldiers asked for,
the big-wigs in Hollywood demanded. The war broadened the scope of
cheesecake photographs — widening the range of persons who could get
their mitts on the seductive stills. They had been for studio purposes and
studio purposes alone, which rubbed many actresses the wrong way, but
with a war on, the studios mass-produced the photographs and allowed
men in the service to acquire them. The hounds of Hollywood, who
loomed over actresses, intimidated many ladies in the industry — far more
than Army Joe serving his country in the South Pacific. Janet knew the
hounds of Hollywood well, and she had no intentions of pursuing one
of the wolfish crowd. Of the Tinseltown Toms, Janet said, "Hollywood
men are too easily distracted. Whenever a new girl comes to town, the
stag line starts jockeying for position."

Many Hollywood executives had a bit of the wolf in their blood, but
the fellows could also be cunning like the fox. Say what you will about
Hollywood, they went all-in during the war effort and helped the servicemen whenever they could. Many were the promotions that were held by
studios as a way to salute the boys in service. They often looked to their
contract players to assist in their wild publicity stunts to drum up patriotism. Janet Blair was worked into a gag concocted by her studio's publicity
department that used her as premium for an insurance policy soldiers
could purchase. In order to promote her film *Two Yanks from Trinidad*,
the minds of the publicity department created the "Love Insurance Policy,"
that could only be obtained by servicemen. An Army camp was informed
that the first troop to take out the policy because he lost his girl could be
escorted by Janet for an evening. With the beautiful starlet as premium,
the studio must have been besieged with applicants for the enticing policy.
Could there be a better way to soothe the pain of losing Miss Fanny
Footloose than cupiding a perky pin-up for a night?

Although the "Love Insurance Policy" was more of a gag than a promotion, Janet became a hit with the servicemen. Her lovely likeness graced
the pages of *Leatherneck*, a Marine Corps publication, and she was offi-
cially named the honorary pin-up girl of a Marine tank battalion. She
further endeared herself to Uncle Sam's fighting forces with her war-bond
rally work. Many stars spent weeks upon weeks on the road, travelling to

various cities to sell bonds. These junkets were an all-consuming venture, and stars like Janet put in eighteen-hour days, holding rallies in towns, making public appearances, and dancing with soldier boys. The heavy workload wasn't ideal for pulchritude, as the dainty dames had less than ample time to doll-up before the show. Pin-ups, whose job it was to look glamorous, often felt less than pulchritudinous on the war bond circuit. After a lengthy stay on the circuit, Janet said, "There was so little time to take proper care of my hair, it became dull and thin. I had only three weeks to do something about it before starting my new picture." Although La Blair felt that glamour had been sacrificed during the tour, the boys were eternally grateful for her patriotic showing and could, to ease the mind of their premier pin-up, accept a mane she viewed as unmanageable.

The war-bond tour allowed Janet to build upon her status as a rising star in the film industry, for Americans applauded the role of drum-beater for the war effort by their film players. The film players themselves often found the tours beneficial as well, in other avenues besides the name exposure. On one such tour, Janet was reunited with three high school chums who were members of the Army Air Force band. The comely crooner was able to catch up with the trio while out on the road selling war bonds for Uncle Sam.

The selling of war bonds was a noble cause for the pin-ups, but the pin-ups top priority, as far as their fans were concerned, was to look good. While shooting cheesecake pictures, Janet had little trouble with hair management, for she had a makeup crew to pamper her and wasn't left to prissy herself by her own hand. Beauty came naturally to Miss Blair, but she had a constant, nagging fear whenever she posed before the photographer's lens: squinting. She was worried that she would ruin many a shot by closing her eyes at an inopportune time, thus negating the flash of the bulb. Janet said, "It's the one thing I have to watch. If I don't my face looks like an old lemon." Possessing modesty in spades, many soldiers who pinned her bathing-suit-clad captures on their wall viewed her face as something bestowed with an ethereal quality, and not overripe produce kept at a fruit stand.

Even with her worries concerning squinting, Janet's background enabled her to feel relatively comfortable posing for cheesecake stills. About posing for pin-up photos, Miss Blair said, "I think it's easy for me because I've been dancing since I was seven. In that time, you acquire a certain poise. You learn the angles most favorable to you. Posture becomes second nature." Since she knew how to stand in a flattering position — or seat herself on a poolside in an ornamental pose — La Blair knew the right parts to push forward to make herself most appealing. However, many a soldier, staring at her pin-up while wearing Uncle Sam's khaki, couldn't see how the dainty darling could ever look less than fetching. She looked amazing seated on a beach, cradling a striped beach ball on her lap. She looked equally enchanting resting on a sofa in a negligee. And when soldiers worldwide got a glimpse of her black lace attire in a pin-up produced by *Yank*, they knew that every angle was an angle flattering to Janet Blair.

# ★ JOAN BLONDELL ★

With an exuberance and spunk that only those individuals with a zest for life possess, Joan Blondell endeared herself to filmgoers for several decades. In many pictures, she was typecast as a vociferous dame with a jaw set to wag and a mind and body in constant motion. Always outgoing, Joan was made-to-order for roles of wise-cracking twists, given her vocal dexterity and casual, breezy demeanor. Even when she was in a support role, Joan oftentimes stole the spotlight from the headliners with her eccentric performances. Used more as a comedic actress by the time of World War II, Joan had become one of Hollywood's elite support players. Films in which she appeared had that much needed addition of sprightliness Miss Blondell owned, which enlivened the motion picture with a frisky actress adept at caressing the funny bone. When watching Joan on film, you always knew that she was where she was meant to be.

Joan ventured to Hollywood well before the war effort to much fuss and fanfare. Like a prospect in pro sports who has received all the hoopla and buildup upon signing, Miss Blondell was expected to be a pivotal player in the film industry. While working on Broadway, Joan was engaged in a hit play that Warner Brothers studio decided to adapt into a motion picture with the two leads — Joan and James Cagney — reprising their Broadway roles. The two stars-of-the-boards were billed as Hollywood's newest dynamic duo, and their first feature, *Sinners' Holiday*, was a huge success. The film was released in 1930 and the two leads were deemed up-and-coming powers in the film industry. The prognosis was affirmative in the case of Jimmy Cagney, but Blondell, who had a solid career in film that lasted through the early 1980s, became more of a role player — typecast as a wisecracking dame who lent support to the top-billed star. Although Miss Blondell never became one of Hollywood's elite actresses, she worked without reprieve and made many an impressive picture.

By the time America had entered World War II, Joan was in her mid-thirties and was juggling a career as an actress with the duties of motherhood — both fulltime occupations. However, after Pearl Harbor was bombed, Miss Blondell entered the war effort with an abandon steeped in patriotism. Very few folks in the film industry did more to raise money for the war effort than Joan. As one of the first actresses to

*Joan Blondell.* COURTESY OF MOVIEMARKET.COM

engage herself in the Victory Caravan, which raised money by the sale of war bonds, Joan's help allowed the first Caravan to haul in a staggering $750 million. Under the umbrella of the First Victory Caravan, Joan traveled across the nation entertaining troops, leading war-bond rallies, and working hand-in-hand with the Red Cross. A hardworking actress, a dedicated mother, and a patriot, Joan became an even bigger hit with American audiences. They loved her wisecracking roles on the big screen, but found that their favorite little acid-tongued blonde was also a devoted American, which endeared her greatly to a land in the midst of turmoil.

Many actors have a screen persona in stark contrast to their away-from-the-camera demeanor. Joan, whose enthusiasm onscreen was ebullient, tapped her reserve of zeal kept for her screen characters to see her through the long hours she kept as war bond promoter. She entertained large crowds at rallies at the expense of earning a higher salary on film and spending time with her children. But America was a different land then, when Americans were dedicated to their country and sought to protect it from outside evils, and Joan personified this sacrifice as a celebrity who put her nation first. The wacky dame who audiences came to love had transformed into a symbol of national duty. More than one person saw the work that Joan Blondell had performed for the war effort, while also making time for her children and the occasional film, and thought her an ardent crusader for America's victory. She who made America laugh had become she who inspired a nation.

Due to her constant work on war-bond rallies, which took her to numerous military camps, Joan became a favorite of the boys in service. Miss Blondell wasn't the type of actress who entertained the boys simply for a show and then exited the stage for another stage in another town: she exited the stage and rubbed elbows with the soldiers. And the soldiers loved her for it. In 1943, Joan said that she received anywhere from 750 to 1,500 fan letters a day from men in service. The dear that she was, Joan, who wanted to help the fighting men in any way she could, sacrificed plenty of her own salary to see that the soldiers had a little bit of Americana in their duffle bags. When soldiers requested an autograph picture that they could pin-up on their barracks wall, Joan supplied the requested cheesecake and used funds from her pocket to mail the letters to the boys. Without batting an eyelash, Miss Blondell would shell out close to $100 per week, shipping autographed pin-ups to soldier boys at various military camps.

Joan didn't confine her patriotic enthusiasm to the shores of our great nation — she transplanted it overseas when she visited lands where soldiers had encamped. She toured overseas at such locales as Iceland and Greenland. But an occurrence during the war devastated Joan. On her trip overseas, she was ferried out to Newfoundland on a boat that had to travel via blackout in order to go undetected by the enemy. Enemy submarines were thought to be in the water, but her ship made it to Newfoundland and she gave a rousing performance for troops, building morale in the northern regions. After her tour, she flew home to the States but later received word that the boat which ferried her to Newfoundland, whose crewmen she had befriended, was torpedoed by the enemy and 165 people were drowned.

Entertaining the troops was a Blondell family tradition, one she embraced wholeheartedly. Her parents were also performers in the business of show during the First World War, as the younger Blondell was eager to carry on her parents' legacy. But sometimes the persons brought in to entertain the troops found the soldiers more eager to entertain them. The boys under the employ of Uncle Sam's fighting forces weren't in the field of entertainment, but that didn't stop them from putting on a show for their celebrity guests. Miss Blondell thought the world of the boys and was ever appreciative for everything they did. She said, "You'd kill yourself for them, they're so appreciative. They want to put on a good show for you so they take you for rides in jeeps. They let you fire guns. I think I've fired more guns than any soldier in the war. I've christened everything that could be christened and some that couldn't." Although it was the celebrity's job to build morale in the fighting forces, the men in uniform were grateful for the visit and gave the stars the treatment they deserved.

Joan Blondell was able to fire weapons on ranges and christen airplanes, but her favorite thing to do with the soldiers was run the obstacle course. A funny yarn circulated the country's papers which told of a soldier who thought himself mad when he spotted a bubbly blonde chasing after him on the obstacle course. When he completed, he asked a buddy whether he had spotted the dashing dame, hustling her frame through the treacherous avenues. His buddy thought him mad as well until Joan came jogging out the final path, flashing a salute to the awestruck boys as she finished her jaunt. Her screen persona as a fiery, excessively exuberant doll was carried along for the troops as she channeled her never-go-idle mindset into military training.

The guns were a blast to fire and the obstacle course teemed with adventure, but Joan understood that the primary function of a pin-up was to look appealing. She knew exactly what the boys wanted: pulchritude, and they wanted it in spades. After she returned home from an overseas camp tour, Joan went beyond her duty as a morale-building pin-up who let boys whistle and applaud her appearance, and became a carrier-pigeon who delivered care packages of pulchritude. If a soldier received a letter from Joan, there was typically a nugget of beauty, an individually wrapped piece of eye candy, tucked firmly in the bosom of the envelope. Upon her return from her overseas tour, Joan said, "When I got back I sent them all the pictures I could find of legs, arms and sweater art." It may seem more than a tad unusual for a woman's shopping list to have "legs of Ginger Rogers" and "sweater shots of Audrey Totter" upon it, but this was America World War II style, and Joan, like any decent red-blooded American determined to support the troops, adapted her daily routine to assist the boys in service.

The boys wanted beauty art, whether it be a pin-up photo of some leggy dame or the caricature of the ideal female form drawn in pencil. But the ideal was the real McCoy — beauty who lived and breathed. Pin-ups like Joan Blondell, who traveled all over the world to entertain the troops, offered exactly what the servicemen craved. She gave gifts to soldiers through the mail, sent photographs to fighting men, but the greatest gift she gave them was being amongst them. By being amongst the troops, she knew better than most pin-ups what the soldiers, sailors, and Marines desired. They wanted a living woman to look at, to spend time with, to talk to, and Joan lent them her time. She even devised her own routine overseas for her stage performance. Joan said, "I strip, but nothing really comes off. First I explain how I've always wanted to be a stripteaser. I take my jacket off, then a scarf. Then I pretend that the zipper of my dress gets stuck and I ask a soldier or sailor to volunteer to get it unstuck. You should see them race to the platform!"

Joan Blondell gave the boys what they wanted and they loved her for it. They applauded her work on stage, her rubbing elbows at every port of call, from the far-off regions of Iceland to the searing heat of a southern rifle range. Wherever the boys trained, Joan would visit them and give the troops that glimpse of American womanhood they yearned for. But it was more than beauty, something far more profound than appealing flesh, which endeared Miss Blondell to the men in the service. She knew their struggle. She was not an outsider, offering her pretty still photographs to be the only portion of herself in the war effort, but an insider who went with the boys, lent them her ear — her soul. She was, despite her celebrity status, a down-to-earth American girl who wasn't ignorant to the sacrifice that servicemen had thrust upon them. After visiting troops overseas, Miss Blondell said, "When I came back and stayed at a hotel in New York it seemed all wrong. Why should I have comfort and they so little of anything? Why should I eat meat and fruit when they can get so little? And then there are those people in night clubs who don't even know there's a war going on."

# ★ LESLIE BROOKS ★

The bad blonde was a staple of the film noir genre of the 1940s and 1950s, and Leslie Brooks often found herself cast in such unflattering roles. Rarely did she play the sweet and innocent doll who exuded a subdued charm. No, her characters were often rowdy dames, tawdry to the tenth power, who employed cunning, trickery, and manipulation to achieve their decadent desires. Leslie had fun with her villainous typecast because she toiled in the background for a number of years before catching her break. It seemed ideal to be known as a bad girl in films than to not be known to the film-going public at all. Her family and friends cracked wise about her onscreen persona, for they joshed her endlessly and referred to the film femme fatale as "Stinky Mae." But the talented honey-haired actress took the rib-poking in her stride. She could play the crass man-eater onscreen, but away from the bright lights and cameras, Miss Brooks was an All-American gal who achieved stardom despite her modest beginnings.

Born in the Midwest, Leslie was practically raised by her grandparents in their Nebraska hamlet of Crofton. The couple operated a hotel where the young Miss Brooks passed her early years. It was from this modest beginning that Hollywood gained the talents of a woman who would become one of film noir's finest dastardly dames. But the road from a Nebraska boardinghouse to Tinseltown wasn't a direct avenue to stardom. Leslie had to put in plenty of time as a background player in the film industry. The red carpet is rarely rolled out for a beginner in the business of show, and Leslie bade her time until the crimson rug was meant for her slippered feet.

At the outset of America's involvement in the war, Leslie Brooks was just another pretty, nameless figure in Hollywood. The slender beauty had worked in film, but she was never featured and hadn't garnered a speaking role. Essentially, the platinum-haired Nebraska native was employed as window-dressing by Hollywood studios. She was clearly pretty enough for pictures, but whether or not she could act had yet to be seen. Such an existence may seem to an actress a life confined to a pillory, where one always stood erect but was forbidden to cast the head about to spot that elusive direction to fame. Work had come her way, but it was work that left the muse ravenous. One doesn't go to Hollywood to stand in the background, sipping martinis where the cameraman pans but once, but yearns for the spotlight. The spotlight was soon to find La Brooks, but first she had to pay her dues.

*Leslie Brooks.*

Like many pretty darlings in Hollywood during the war, Leslie was sent out on the road to entertain the troops. Warner Brothers created a little traveling cheesecake troupe they dubbed "The Navy Blues," of which Leslie was a member, which would tour installations and offer their pulchritude to the boys in uniform. The Navy Blues were a group of stunning models and aspiring actresses who posed for numerous pin-up shots when they weren't out flaunting their frame for male-dominant crowds. While employed as a Navy Blue, Leslie earned her paycheck under her given name of Lorraine Gettman (her given name varies depending upon the source). This little endeavor allowed La Brooks to make contacts and establish herself as an up-and-coming beauty in the motion picture business. The project proved fruitful, for Leslie quickly became a player in the motion picture industry during the middle of the war.

The bad girl image seemed destined for Leslie from the start. The Navy Blues enabled Leslie to crash the gates of Hollywood, but she also gained some support from a fashion photographer who once took photos of Leslie's legs. Leslie dabbled in modeling before the war and was one of the top stocking models in America. For what it's worth, Leslie's legs were known commodities, for they graced many a catalog, but the blonde beauty wanted stardom as a thespian. Help came her way when a photographer named Hurrell claimed that she was "the ideal composite for glamour." After the flattering boast, people in the industry began calling Miss Brooks "The Hurrell Girl." Shortly thereafter, the former stocking model was a contract player and slated for roles of women from the seedy side of life.

Many actresses were asked to pose for cheesecake art that would be made available to the fighting men in the armed forces, but these very same actresses were also asked to stand in front of cameras for film still purposes. More than once, La Brooks heard the click of a camera while wearing a bathing suit, but she found studio publicity shots a tad more demanding. For pin-up pictures, all Leslie had to do was look enchanting — which came naturally to the cute Cornhusker — but for publicity stills, more was expected of her. To build upon her bad girl image as a film noir stick of female dynamite, her studio set up racy, and, more aptly put, dangerous photo shoots to appeal to the wickedness of her movie characters. One such photo shoot her studio cooked up was for the zoology inclined, as Leslie was placed in a cage full of lions. The beasts, thankfully, declined to dine on the stunning pin-up, as the magnified kittens enhanced the frosty, ice-in-the-veins persona her studio concocted for her. She survived her sojourn in the animal kingdom, but she found the setups for the soldiers far more ideal.

Her relationship with the servicemen wasn't all give and take. The boys certainly enjoyed her taking cheesecake photos and giving them away, but the fighting men also inspired the creative outlets that coursed through La Brooks. While visiting the boys at their military marching grounds, Leslie saw, in their attire, items useful for everyday living. She saw that soldiers seemingly had a pocket designed for every article issued them, and felt that she should be just as organized as the boys in service. When she returned home, Miss Brooks carried her apron to the sewing machine and promptly stitched a number of pockets upon the cover. After she had finished, Leslie modeled the modified apron for newspaper boys to show women that they too could be as placement-oriented as servicemen. Her final design looked something like a cross between a normal kitchen apron with an Army rucksack. About her new apron, Leslie said,

"I just borrowed an idea from the boys in uniform. It's a blessing to have everything in its place, and saves so much hunting-time."

Leslie used her Army-inspired apron to store tissues and makeup, but her beau Tony Shay filled his compartments with military issued materials. During the war, Leslie was cupiding with Shay, who served in the Marine Corps. After a tour in the South Pacific, the two were married. Shay returned home to a stunning blonde who was named "The Posture Queen of 1944" by the aptly titled Better Posture Committee. Her perfect posture was toted on airbases in America to Navy ships in foreign waters, via the pin-up images Uncle Sam's fighting men tucked in their rucksacks. Her most famous pin-up displayed why she had been chosen the top posture queen during the war, as she showcased her stunning contours while kneeled before a flowerbed for a cheesecake shot. With her knees resting on covered pavement, Leslie arched her back and placed her right hand on her waist and her left hand behind her head, to better showcase the shape her ideal posture could position. Perhaps the members of the eccentric committee had her pin-up posted on the wall where they held their vote.

## ★ MARGUERITE CHAPMAN ★

Modeling has always been an inroad to Hollywood, for film studios will never end their pursuit for fresh faces. Many lovely ladies have mimicked the mannequin for occupational pursuits, with the desire to eclipse looking pretty in clothes that belong to others, for a lifestyle which enables them to afford the clothes they sport in fashion magazines. Marguerite Chapman became a solid motion picture actress, complete with a star on the Walk of Fame, but she too had her origins in modeling. The ravishing brunette had worked in the stuffy realm of clerical cubicles and dumpy desks, but her extraordinary beauty enabled her to fasten her last paperclip to a stack of company papers. Before America's involvement in the war, Miss Chapman landed a job with the prestigious Powers Modeling Agency. This occupation opened up avenues she never dreamed of breaching as a typist. She would go on to make movies with such notables as Marilyn Monroe and appear in many of the leading television programs of the 1950s and 1960s.

Born in New York, Marguerite was raised very much the tomboy. With four siblings — all brothers — little Marguerite had nothing but roughhousers to her right and left. However, despite surroundings cluttered with boy things, Miss Chapman grew into a stunning young woman. She joined the workforce in the 1930s as a clerical typist but many of her friends felt that she had the right look for pictures. With a beauty akin to that of the ravishing Hedy Lamarr, the brunette bomber had little trouble getting discovered by the elite Powers Modeling Agency. In short time, Marguerite was one of America's most popular models. Given the exposure of modeling, for her face and figure were reproduced in many leading magazines, Miss Chapman caught the eyes of the heads in Hollywood. Warner Brothers was the studio that brought Marguerite

*Marguerite Chapman*

out west and quickly placed the doll in pictures. When America joined the war effort late in 1941, Warner Brothers placed Miss Chapman in the morale-building "Navy Blues Sextet" who toured military camps.

As a member of the sexy sextet, Marguerite received extra exposure. With her military tours, coupled with her rising quota of films, La Chapman was quickly becoming a recognizable name in the industry. Not only was she recognizable to folks in the film business, but her beauty garnered her plenty attention from other outlets. The soldiers, who gladly accepted her pin-up photos, nicknamed her "The Morale Builder" because she personally autographed her cheesecake stills for the fighting men. Committees that perused American pulchritude saw in Miss Chapman the same sensual sensation that the soldiers saw, and she was named "Miss Breathless of 1943." With as many lungs as she incapacitated, simply by looking as comely as a fence corner peach, one would imagine Miss Marguerite would have been brought up on charges for ending the intake of air of numerous men. But this was America World War II style, and rendering the opposite sex breathless, whether they are essential to the war effort or not, was something applauded by those who gasped. They wanted to look at a beauty capable of stifling oxygen and frowned not when they found her.

During the war, pretty pin-ups were sought not only by the fighting men for inspirational purposes, but by American women for tips on how to look like a pin-up. It wouldn't surprise many if the pin-ups were too vain to offer their secrets, for a unique beauty, one would imagine, would like to remain unique, but Marguerite was quick to pass along the inside dope to other ladies. Newspapers across the nation printed articles on female beauty tips that were given by dames in the film industry. Marguerite's most famous tip during the war was leg care. Everyone knew how important legs were to a model who posed for leg art, so when Miss Chapman's advice hit the ink, women took notice. Her leg maintenance tips were printed in an article published by the *Delta Democrat-Times*, which had Marguerite detail the best method to wax one's legs. She explained why waxing was better than shaving and flinched not when photographers for the paper took photos of her applying and removing wax strips. Since many a man carried a pin-up photo of La Chapman, complete with her streamlined pins, ladies accepted the advice of a flower who men longed to tend in their garden.

While pin-ups offered the occasional bug in the ear, their main chore was one that came natural to Miss Chapman: looking good. The dark-haired darling was a favorite of servicemen because she often entertained at military camps, and she was quick to cap off a pin-up with her signature.

Many gents in the armed forces liked to concoct catchy nicknames for their favorite piece of cheesecake. Units across the American armed forces would bestow upon their prime pin-up a flattering moniker, with the hope that the doll of their dreams would give them a good and hearty salute, pin-up style. The 541st Parachute Infantry regiment at Camp Mackall, North Carolina, tagged Marguerite with the alias, "The Girl We'd Most Like to Go 'Chuting With." Another favorite pastime among soldiers was to christen a plane or automobile after a pin-up, which led to a little confusion amongst the boys in service. When Miss Chapman and her stand-in Mary Ann Featherstone toured camps, they were escorted by air to their destinations. Once, on one of their ferries to an installation, the commanding officer phoned their next stop to give them advance notice of the two ladies arrival. The officer informed his receiving caller that he was flying in with Marguerite Chapman and Mary Ann Featherstone. Believing the two names relayed were craft christened by pin-ups, the other end responded curtly, "More new ships! What kind are these?"

Miss Breathless of 1943 was a top pin-up during the war years, for she owned a face the camera adored and a streamlined body that seemed designed specifically for cheesecake stills. Leg art was wildly popular among cheesecake photographers, and Marguerite's pins were so long and well-formed that she was often asked to sport short skirts to showcase her stilts. One of her more popular pin-ups was a unique shot that showed her lying down on the floor, wearing a short skirt with her slender legs crossed. With four brothers in the service, Marguerite was photographed for this cheesecake still writing her siblings letters while they served. Of course, that was the reason Marguerite had taken pen and paper, but photographers like to take pictures of dames in various positions, which inform the carrier of the cheesecake that a lady somewhere has you on her mind. Many a soldier could tack that pin-up of the letter-writing La Chapman on their barracks wall and imagine that the envelope by her side was addressed to him. It was an excellent way of building morale, and Marguerite's natural sensuality took morale to another level.

# ★ ANN CORIO ★

When one tries to rattle off the names of World War II era pin-up girls, they typically start with the ladies featured in films. The casual follower may name Betty Grable, Rita Hayworth, and Jane Russell as top pin-ups, but begin to sputter after listing the elite lady thespians of the time. But the pin-up girl craze wasn't resigned for Hollywood and Hollywood alone. No, it took the nation by storm, and pin-ups cropped up all over the country as if Johnny Appleseed had traded his bucket of seeds for a box of pin-ups. Hollywood's contender for pin-up hub of the world was hundreds of miles away, situated on the opposite coast: New York City. The babes of Broadway were just as well received by the pin-up purchasing public as the fair-featured dolls of the motion picture industry. But the girls on the

*Ann Corio.*

east coast had a leg-up on their west coast competition, for that alluringly decadent industry called burlesque had reached its height there. The dames of burlesque, known for their barely-there costumes and stripteaser artistry, produced the more risqué of the pin-up pictures during the time. As one of the top burlesque attractions, Ann Corio became an idol of servicemen.

Before the war, the name Gypsy Rose Lee was synonymous with the industry of burlesque. But around the time of World War II, a new bevy of beauties had begun to steal the spotlight from the reigning queen of burlesque. There was the shapely Sherry Britton, the blonde bombshell Dagmar, and the mesmerizing Marian Morgan. However, it was the daughter of an Italian immigrant, who passed away when his little girl was thirteen, who would become the brightest star of burlesque during the war years. Ann Corio, who had danced with Earl Carroll's Vanities before she became a peel-down artist, would be the dame to supplant the legendary Gypsy Rose. The stunning, dark-haired Corio, often donned in sequin outfits that accentuated her ample bust, set many a lips to whistle during her shows. Hollywood may have had the market cornered on mass-producing its stars via the big screen, but Broadway boasted the pulchritudinous talents of dames like Corio, who were able to show far more skin than was allowed by motion picture censors of the time.

The entertainer they dubbed "The Epic Epidermis" felt that she had a duty during time of war — one that more modest ladies would skirt as far too gaudy for their good behavior. Many felt the lifestyle of a burlesque entertainer too garish and tawdry — too scantily-clad for polite society — and looked upon the dolls in Ann's profession as Mae West-esque women of lose moral fiber. However, men who ran off to fight for their country were often told that one of the main symbols they were fighting for was American womanhood. Young men took up arms to fight not only for mother, sister, grandma, and aunt Myrtle but also for women who others deemed floozies. Whether burlesque queens were women of ill repute or not is a personal assumption, but they were women, American to the core, and thus under the umbrella of "American Womanhood." And Ann showed just how American she was by taking it off for the war effort.

Many celebrities toured the nation engaged in war-bond rallies, but Ann was engaged in a tour of a different feather. Feathers in her profession were used for concealment purposes — feathers or fans — and Miss Corio bundled her tiny outfits and loose ostrich plumage for a tour she dubbed "How to Undress with Finesse." The Broadway stripteaser felt it her wartime duty to offer tips to American women, eager to impress their fighting man, on how to unbutton in the most appealing manner.

The "How to Undress with Finesse Show" was a hit — male audiences, of course, found the theme to their liking as well, even though the show was more of an instructional performance for ladies with men in the armed forces. Thanks to Ann's work, burlesque, always fashionable in the Broadway circles, began to catch on across America. Many were the number of soldiers who toted pin-up photos of "The Epic Epidermis" while training for war. If America hadn't accepted the meretriciously flashy ambiance of burlesque during the war, it certainly loosened its feelings of wrathful regard to the gaudy profession, for ladies in Ann's profession mimicked her cry of "I'm prepared to go all out — maybe I should say, WITHOUT — for the war effort."

The war was a hardship on most Americans and peel-down artists like La Corio felt the wartime pinch as well. Rationing goods was the order for WWII and Americans either gave up many conveniences or cut back their consumption and use by an alarming degree. Stripteasers like Ann, who one would think would be used to less, found the ration order rough business. La Corio's compatriot Dagmar complained that she couldn't do her snake routine, which consisted of her slinking her lightly-clad frame down a rubber-coated staircase, because rubber had been removed from the stage. The blonde torpedo wasn't about to bruise her peaches-and-cream by attempting the routine on a hardwood surface. Ann was a little more comfortable than Dagmar, but the rationing hurt The Epic Epidermis as well. About rationing, La Corio said, "I can get along if I got my bobby pins and lipstick. If I can just have those, much of the rest doesn't matter. After all, I can slice a bit off a stage curtain, drape it around me and still go on with my act, can't I?"

The rise of burlesque during the war, thanks to soldiers and their affinity for scantily-clad dames, allowed Ann Corio to broaden her occupational endeavors. Many soldiers and sailors couldn't get to Broadway and watch Ann peel out of her clothes, so they pleaded with filmmakers to capture Ann's likeness on film. Eager to fulfill the request of servicemen, Ann ventured out to Los Angeles and sojourned in Hollywood for a few years. Making movies wasn't meant to be for Ann, who felt that she was a lousy actress. But she understood the method of the Hollywood machine, and knew just how the gears moved. Concerning her venture to the west coast, Miss Corio said, "So who cares if I can't act? I make money, the producers make money, the fans write letters praising my acting and everybody is happy."

Corio satisfied audiences across the globe during the war, initially with her burlesque show, then with her racy pin-ups, and lastly with roles in film. But, she would spurn Hollywood and return to Broadway, putting on shows — or, more aptly put, putting on *taking-off* shows — for burlesque audiences. Her popularity reached its height while the world was engaged in an epic battle, and the Epic Epidermis had her busty likeness printed by numerous outlets. The famous soldier magazine, *Yank*, appeased the boys by publishing a pin-up of Ann. Shown in her trademark bust-accentuating gown of sequins, fighting men across the globe gathered her sensual pose, which showed her seated with her legs crossed and her back arched to thrust her sequin-covered bosom to the fore. They fought for their country, they fought for liberty, and they fought for womanhood, and the fighting men were eternally grateful to La Corio for showing them a bit more womanhood than most women would allow.

## ★ JEANNE CRAIN ★

America is known for many things, ranging from Fourth of July celebrations to toys placed in a child's meal at eating stands. When people across the globe think of America, they think of apple pie, baseball, and the Statue of Liberty. Another staple of Americana is the gathering of beauty, for Americans have always enjoyed applauding a ravishing dame and examining her pulchritude in test-like surroundings. All across this great nation of ours there are young ladies engaged in the enterprise of beauty pageants, where dolls take the stage and attempt to sway judges, trying, with their good looks mostly, to be named queen of a beauty pageant. We, as Americans, enjoy the excitement of contest and do not flinch to measure ourselves to our neighbors. Jeanne Crain was such a girl, eager to climb the pedestal of American pulchritude during the early days of the war. One pageant after another, Miss Crain would be crowned as the comeliest among a crowd of comely cuties, and thus earned titles that many American lasses longed to have bestowed upon them.

When the United States took up arms after the bombing of Pearl Harbor, Jeanne Crain was just another lovely young woman on the North American shores. She had yet to be discovered by Hollywood, but beauty pageant judges had taken notice. With a face so fresh it seemed absent an expiration date, Miss Crain entered beauty pageants in her native California and quickly earned one title after another. When a group of amateur photographers from the Long Beach area spotted the ravishing Miss Crain, they bestowed upon her one of her first titles: "Miss Camera Queen of 1942." Cameras, as one knows, are designed to capture images, and the fellows who christened Jeanne with her stately alias certainly felt that a camera's highest purpose was capturing a beauty like hers. With a tag such as "Miss Camera Queen," Jeanne had a moniker aptly suited for the beauty circuit. She certainly wasn't surprised when she was named "Miss Long Beach of 1943" the following year.

Although Jeanne had won a bevy of beauty awards, the door to Hollywood had remained closed. Her eyes didn't glisten with the starlight of Tinseltown, even though her Long Beach home was in relatively

*Jeanne Crain.* COURTESY OF MOVIEMARKET.COM

close proximity to the land where stars walk the earth. She may have won beauty pageants after beauty pageants, but her image went undiscovered by the studio hound dogs assigned to sniff out the latest new talents and beauties. When Jeanne was finally discovered by Hollywood, the espial treatment given her came when she was least aware, for she wasn't approached after receiving a tiara or met before walking the stage at a pageant; she was taken off-guard by her exposure to Hollywood while attending a show. While viewing a play, a talent scout spotted Jeanne in the audience and felt she had the stuff for pictures. When the spotlight was removed from her, away from the stage where peaches were paraded in pageantry, was when the lovely Miss Crain caught the attention of Hollywood.

Hollywood saw in Jeanne a classy commodity it needed during time of war. Although she had won beauty pageants, Jeanne's beauty was unique — no mold was set that cast the visage and figure of Miss Crain. Her beauty was obvious, subdued, and modest, not bold, flashy, and showy. She had the perfect look for a certain war-era role that studios sought to fill. With the battles raging overseas, the film industry was in need of ladies like Jeanne Crain who could be promoted as symbols of American womanhood: women of virtue, dignity, and unquestionable appeal. Jeanne had the right look and the proper ingredients to play the all-American girl who waited patiently for her love to return from war. Her girl-next-door qualities forced her into an early typecast, for roles written for her typically were of military wives — ladies who soldiers had left behind and who they hoped pined for them while they fought on distant shores. Because of this typecast, coupled with her extraordinary beauty, Jeanne became a favorite pin-up of the men in the armed forces.

One of Jeanne's earliest film successes was the picture *In the Meantime, Darling*. Portraying an Army wife, Jeanne's typecast as the ideal soldier's bride endeared her to audiences — crowds of civilians and crowds of soldier filmgoers were all left enchanted and awed by her work. Back when Hollywood unquestionably supported the troops, roles were written that glorified the average American. This glorification wasn't resigned solely for the lad fighting overseas but also for the gal he had left behind. The darling Miss Crain, who typically played the virtuous girl a man could trust, saw her popularity soar during the war years. Movie patrons enjoyed watching heroic displays of the patriotic American, and Jeanne embodied the woman-of-sacrifice to a degree few actresses could match. When the studio introduced the logline for *In the Meantime, Darling*, the boast that the picture depicted "Army wives who wouldn't trade their memories of a second-rate hotel near camp for all the water in Niagara," seemed legitimate and not idle thanks to Jeanne headlining the cast.

As her popularity reached new heights during the war, Jeanne felt the impact of celebrity status. Gone were the days of simply exhibiting a fetching image in gowns, which was her task on the beauty pageant circuit, and in their place was the cyclic motion of studio exposure and publicity. Miss Crain's mailbox swelled with the onslaught of fan mail sent her by film audiences and gents in the armed forces. It was printed in the *Tipton Tribune* that her studio "had to add a girl to the staff of the fan mail department to handle the thousands of letters she is receiving." Fanmail had its perks, for the recipient was informed, simply by the excessive bulk of her stack of mail, that her star had caught on and she was now amongst the famous. Words of flattery typically find a star when they tear open fan mail, since those who take up pen in order to write a movie star, commonly massage their ego with sweet phrases and praise. But others are out to get something and hint not at their desires but boldly display them — no matter how crude or eccentric. One such letter Jeanne received during the war amused her. An awestruck gent penned Miss Crain a letter that read, "I love you very much. I dream about you. I'll even adore you, if you'll send me a carton of cigarettes."

Many letters addressed to the enchanting Miss Crain came from civilian filmgoers but the bulk had return addresses from far-flung locales where soldiers were stationed. They wanted to convey their gratitude for her morale-building roles, for her depiction of loyal, patient war brides helped many a fighting man endure those long hours abroad, where idleness ignites the mind and sets it to wander. Her roles helped ease the wandering mind and put it to rest, since a delicate beauty like Jeanne Crain could wait for her man, many soldiers felt comfortable that their war bride would act much the same. She had become, by design of her studio, a symbol of fidelity, and one much needed in an age of turmoil and strife. Her fair beauty seemed the proper visage for female duty during time of war. The duty of the American man was to defend its shores from foreign evils, while the fighting man with a love left behind hoped that his lady felt it her duty to remain loyal to her lost warrior. Jeanne Crain personified this duty.

Film studios all have publicity departments and they worked more diligently during World War II than ever before or than they have done since. It was their task to build the morale of a nation through moving pictures, but when the picture had been completed, there was still the need for drumbeating the cause of victory. In order to help win the war, studios sent out their stars on war-bond rallies, because they knew their top-flight talent could shepherd in large crowds. Jeanne Crain made a number of such morale-building junkets. She would travel to military bases and meet the soldiers, sign autographs, and lend support in a number of ways. With the blonde beauty June Haver, Jeanne attended a show for the troops at Camp Perry, Ohio, where the two Hollywood honeys drummed-up business for their picture while giving the boys a show. At Camp Perry, the two doves called T-5 John O. Gunn to the stage, where they planted a kiss on the lucky soldier's cheeks. The soldier magazine *Yank* proudly displayed a photograph of the comely cuties smooching the fortunate fighting man, as many a soldier and sailor hoped for the chance to change positions with T-5 Gunn.

Although Jeanne's studio built the image of her as the ideal war bride who remained faithful to her fighting man, they also promoted her sex appeal. An uncommon beauty, Jeanne's appeal could not be denied even under the veil of studio-concocted fidelity, and she was photographed for cheesecake purposes, which created many a stunning still. However, her cheesecake stills were never gaudy but well-staged. One of her more popular pin-ups showed her dressed in a native-patterned bikini that flattered her exquisite shape, but she was not standing erect, tiptoeing for the camera , and arching her back to further accentuate her bosom, but seated upon a lofty rock formation with the heavens creating a backdrop that highlighted her ethereal beauty. The shot was unquestionably leg art, for her fair pins were positioned in a manner of display, but the photograph reeked not of tawdriness but of an angelic nature that better suited her war-era image. To many a fighting man who toted her pin-up, the angels of heaven were second rate to the earthly morality that Jeanne Crain conveyed.

## ★ LINDA DARNELL ★

If an editor for a dictionary were searching for a female photograph to serve as the image for the definition of "sultry," he would be wise to position a pin-up of Linda Darnell beside the word's description. The dark-haired stunner was the ideal model of sultriness, even at an early age, which led to much trouble on the Darnell family's behalf. Their ravishing daughter, not quite legal to drive when she ventured out Hollywood way, had already developed her striking beauty and figure, which led many Tinseltown wolves to the assumption the lovely looker was of courting age. In order to get work in the industry, Linda used her mature appearance to her advantage and often claimed to be older than she was to land gigs. Few people knew that Hollywood's latest prospective sexpot was but a babe in her mid-teens. But Linda had a stable family environment that helped her navigate the hostile waters of the film industry. Her father, a postal clerk from Texas, uprooted the family and moved them to Los Angeles so his gorgeous daughter could pursue a career in acting.

*Linda Darnell.* COURTESY OF MOVIEMARKET.COM

Success wasn't immediate for the toast of Texas. Linda's striking beauty was evident from the time her streamlined legs hit the west coast soil, but acting in pictures, at that time, took a little more than just attractive ornamentation. Although her physical appeal was unquestioned, Miss Darnell had to hone her craft as an actress — learn the ways of the thespian — before stardom was hers. However, at the time Linda had made her way to Tinseltown, the world was in turmoil, and the pretty aspiring actress had more important things to do than read scripts and play make-believe. With the world engaged in war, the business of make-believe seemed shallow to many folks, and Linda, whose ambition was to be an actress, felt that a person's duty to their country was just as important as her occupation. Between acting classes and prepping for roles, Miss Darnell volunteered for war work. She was very active in the Hollywood Unit of the Women's Ambulance and Defense Corps of America. As a member of that organization, Linda took courses in motor vehicle repair.

It seems safe to say that Miss Darnell would have made for the sexiest grease monkey the world has ever known, but changing oil and rebuilding transmissions wasn't the occupational calling meant for Linda. She wanted to act, but early in the war, roles didn't come her way. Studio heads knew she was physically appealing and could put patrons in the seats at any movie house, but she had yet to establish herself as a legitimate actress. Many filmmakers opted to hand lead female roles to stars who audiences had accepted during the war, and chose not to hold the hand of a fresh-faced actress on set in order to coax a decent performance out of some comely ingénue. But Linda knew she had talent beyond the ornamental, so she decided to continue in her acting lessons and wait for her big break. However, the life of an idle stoic, patiently waiting for her elusive dream to become reality, was not an ideal setting for Miss Darnell. A woman of action, the southern stunner found little contentment twiddling her thumbs. She made the choice to venture out and attend war-bond rallies to elevate her status as a Hollywood player.

Miss Darnell had shown her patriotism early in the war effort by donning the coveralls of a mechanic, but she opted to surrender the Motor City tuxedo for the body-accentuating garb of the pulchritudinous morale-builder. She went on USO tours where she entertained crowds of troops and civilians, which enabled her to build a following of admirers. The heads of Hollywood all knew that Linda was a knockout, but they were unaware of just how much appeal she would have to film audiences. They soon found out. After her initial tour, Linda's representatives were besieged with letters, which implored them to make motion pictures that starred Miss Darnell, so they could gather a glance of her on the silver screen. Dee Lowrance wrote about Linda's plan to tour, stating, "The plan of action brought results. Her camp shows gave her dividends in new fans among the men in service — they wrote letters about her to the studio." When her studio's mailbox expanded — it strained to contain the awestruck epistles from servicemen — they finally came to the realization that Miss Darnell was a gold mine.

Linda had landed roles in entertaining films opposite heartthrob Tyrone Power in *Mask of Zorro* and *Blood and Sand*, which helped her gain a foothold in Hollywood, but the coveted roles failed to come Linda's way until her war bond shows. But the war-bond circuit started an inferno of support for the sexy Texan, which blazed all the way back to Hollywood. The dark-haired stunner became an instant hit and film-goers across America wanted Darnell, but quick. Still a youngster — not quite twenty years old — Linda found stardom, and that elusive dream of fame and fortune was hers. Hollywood was abuzz with the occupational and personal exploits of its newest star, who entranced audiences with her otherworldly appeal. Victor Gunson wrote, "A new heat wave has hit Hollywood. The reason for the sudden soaring temperature is Linda Darnell. For movie land has awakened with a start to the realization that luscious Linda has blossomed into a devastating young woman." Slightly shocked by the attention given her, Linda, although still a young lady, didn't allow the glitz to get to her head. Showing modesty beyond her years, Linda was more impressed with the beauty of Hedy Lamarr than her own. She said of the classic Miss Lamarr, "With a gorgeous face like that, she wouldn't have to know how to act a bit. It's a thrill just to look at her."

But fame and fortune isn't all flattery and fancy times, for the exposure of stardom also exposes a star to danger. When her star was at its brightest, Linda began to receive letters from a degenerate who demanded money from the starlet. If Linda failed to pay the skunk off, he claimed that he would cause bodily harm to her or a member of her family. During the time she received these letters, Linda was preparing for another war-bond tour, but her studio felt that she should remain in Los Angeles, in close proximity to her family and friends who could protect her. But Miss Darnell felt it her duty to entertain troops during time of war and wanted to travel the road despite the threats sent her via the mail. Her studio had lined up Constance Moore to replace her on the tour, but at the last minute Linda stepped back in and departed for the east coast to participate in her war bond engagement. Shortly thereafter, Linda was able to breathe a litter easier when she was informed that the FBI had nabbed seventeen-year-old Oren Haws, the author of the threats, and charged the nefarious teen with extortion.

The east coast welcomed the comely actress on her military camp tour, but when she returned home it was back to her usual routine. Today's star-lets may have plenty to do, but the dames of World War II had a schedule minus an idle hour. Their engagements were typically selfless, for they surrendered many hours to assist in the war effort. Servicemen's canteens sprouted up all over America and Linda was a fixture at the Hollywood Canteen. Her schedule revolved around her work as an actress, but when she was free from the set, Linda entertained troops by dancing with them at the Hollywood Canteen. Soldiers were always eager to attend the Hollywood Canteen and dance with stars like Annie Miller, Anne Gwynne, and Miss Darnell, but studios tried their damnedest to set-up their starlets on arranged dates with Hollywood wolves. Linda was once set-up with a Hollywood heavy-hitter who she found a loathsome brute. They bickered and disagreed on everything all evening, and when the chap felt he had delivered the final insult of the evening, Linda countered with "after all, you're not the only 4-F in town." Linda bid adieu to the draft-deferred snob and went back to the Canteen where she danced the night away with men grateful to be in her presence.

Although studios were notorious for fixing dates, starlets had little trouble attracting attention from men — they didn't need executives playing Cupid for them. Linda attracted the attention of playboy cameraman Peverell Marley, a much older man who she wed despite the protests from her family and friends. Marley already had two failed marriages under his belt and Linda had yet to reach her twentieth birthday, but the two became man and wife. Marley had joined the Army during the war and Linda, not quite out of her teens, became a war bride. But she had plenty things to keep her busy. She acted, she headlined war-bond rallies, danced at the Hollywood Canteen, but it was an endeavor that didn't require social exposure that Linda delved into during the war. A woman of multiple talents, La Darnell may have been a treat in a dress but she was also a wizard with the pencil. When Dr. Max Rubenstein searched for an artist to illustrate his medical textbook on endocrinology, Linda agreed to supply the artwork for his text.

Many fans of Linda Darnell may have surrendered their sanity if she hid herself away from the cameras and accepted the life of a sketch artist, but Linda remained in the film industry. Although she was no longer on the matrimonial market, Uncle Sam's fighting men gave her warm welcomes whenever she attended camp entertainment gigs. She was appreciative to the boys because, although she had starred with Tyrone Power before the war, it was the boys in uniform who catapulted her career. She knocked 'em dead at the airfield in Yuma, Arizona, where she headlined a soldier's show and gave a comedic reading of a letter she had in tow. Her brother was in the service and wrote her an amusing yarn about his adventures on KP duty, which she relayed to the servicemen at the airfield. The boys at Yuma were doubly entertained, for they were able to soak in an optical sensation like La Darnell, while also getting their funny bone massaged by her guffaw-inducing recitation of her brother's military yarn.

Entertaining the troops meant a great deal to Linda, but what also meant a lot to the Texas Tornado was stacking the dollar bills for the war effort. Miss Darnell was a war-bond circuit sensation who was proud of the work she performed as a seller of bonds. She was once greeted by over 7,000 patrons at a war-bond rally held at the Oakland Naval Supply Depot for their Independence Day Rally. At the rally, she emphasized the importance of paying for, through war bonds, the construction of an air transport Skymaster, which was valued at $400,000. She was given a grander welcome when she went home to Dallas on a war-bond tour, where she also promoted her latest picture. Her fellow Texans gave her a warm reception as they bought bonds and watched her act on the screen. Jack Rutledge, among others, felt that Linda's war bond success was due largely to her physical appeal, but Americans came out to attend her headlined tours whether to buy bonds or satiate their desire for eye candy. Rutledge said about Darnell's Dallas war-bond junket, "Linda helped sell bonds and if it hadn't been for her the bond sales might not have been so good." Perhaps, the directors of the war-bond circuit thought that just by the presentation of a pretty face, purse strings are loosened. But patriotism was in the hearts of most Americans and winning the war was the number one goal.

War-bond rallies were often headlined by entertainers, such as funnymen like Bob Hope and Joe E. Brown, or lovely ladies such as Dorothy Lamour or La Darnell, for the purpose of attracting crowds. The use of the pin-up was another ploy, and delicious cheesecake like Linda — who any man would like to long for — were ideal sellers of bonds as well. Beauty can attract a crowd, and Linda Darnell's beauty was of the sultry variety. Her studio used this to full effect and coupled it with her Texas roots for her pin-up pictures. Linda's most remembered pin-ups are not of her standing by a cement pond on her tiptoes but placed away from resting waters and among the grain of the Midwest. Many a provocative Darnell cheesecake lined barracks walls during the war, which showcased the ravishing beauty in a field of hay, wearing, in the loosest sense of the term, a blouse with only half its buttons employed. Her skirt was slit so high that a profile of her legs wasn't left for the imagination but emblazoned on the photo in all their glory. More than one soldier was forced to take a cold shower when under the blazing spell of her scorching, tattered-clothed pin-up pictures. To many soldier, sailor, and Marine, Linda Darnell was the ideal pin-up. She was the perfect picture of sexiness, who exuded sensuality as casually as a person lights a cigarette. We lost our pin-up sensation tragically when she was killed in a house fire while in her early forties.

# ★ YVONNE DE CARLO ★

Best known to modern audiences as the matriarch in the cult television series *The Munsters*, Yvonne was a ravishing pin-up well before she donned the horrifically streaked mane sported by her frightful small screen personality. Miss De Carlo was the sensuous type whose raven hair entranced many a fighting man during World War II. Leggy and exotic, the stunning starlet had an uphill climb in Hollywood. Her voyage to stardom charted a rocky terrain. She wasn't blessed with the easy route in life, but she was blessed with extraordinary physical charms, and these charms, fancied by the boys in service, enabled her to level the uneven terrain she had charted before the war and make the path smooth and navigable. The reason for the shift in terrain was courtesy of the fellows in the fighting ranks. Soldiers attended the shows Yvonne performed at various bases and, completely smitten, inquired with the bigwigs at Hollywood as to why the delicious dark-haired dame had yet to secure her star. Only after the soldiers pressed the film executives did Miss De Carlo attain her place among the stars.

Before the soldiers gave Miss De Carlo an occupational jolt, she was a hard-working lass eager to make the big time. She took her enticing charms to vaudeville where it was written that, as a teenager, she refereed a kangaroo boxing show. Fisticuffs among herbivorous marsupials may not have been an ideal gig, but a showperson must get her start some place, regardless of the eccentric ticket they officiate. The young beauty would eventually leave the glitz of the animal pugilism circuit behind and venture out Hollywood way to secure her star. Although she no longer had to contend with the dander and odor of Australian critters, she found life in the motion picture business no less hectic. Her work ethic, which was exemplary, allowed her to land a few gigs — superior in quality to officiating a kangaroo boxing match — but those assignments gave her about the same amount of exposure. When first she worked out California way, Yvonne was one of the many nameless aspiring actors stuck in the background, who chewed up scenery as an extra while others like Bette Davis and Claudette Colbert netted the enviable assignments.

As a youngster growing up in Canada, Yvonne was ever the entertainer and she had an agreeable mother who took her to California as a teen to pursue a career in acting. She initially failed and returned to Canada, but the undaunted Canadian cutie continued to work toward her goal. In 1941 she finally landed a part in a film and would, over the next three years, appear in a handful of movies, but never with a speaking part. Often unaccredited in her early Hollywood work, Miss De Carlo would typically play clerks or bathing beauties who made the background appealing but who never stepped into the spotlight. These roles enabled her to work in the industry, but it was unfit for a ravishing beauty with desires for stardom. With her minor, furniture-esque roles in films during the early

*Yvonne De Carlo.*

years of the war, Yvonne had plenty time on her hands and kept herself busy by entertaining the troops — her greatest career move.

While engaged in the preparations for war, soldiers receive little time to engage themselves in aesthetic pursuits. Their assignment is to train for battle, but man must, even when presented before a great struggle which requires all their dedication and gallantry, unwind lest they go mad. The members of the armed forces would take in motion picture shows, but their ideal form of entertainment were camp visits by celebrities. The Hollywood studios showed their support for the troops by sending out their contract players to visit camps, sign autographs, and rub elbows with the boys in khaki. When stars weren't at hand, studios would deliver a bit of pulchritude to the boys, for morale-building sake, who would sing and dance for the fighting men. Yvonne De Carlo, who was anything but a known commodity in Hollywood during the height of the war, was one such astonishing beauty who entertained troops at various camps. A gifted entertainer, the luscious Miss De Carlo would perform a song and dance number for the troops, serenade the boys with ditties she penned herself, while wearing dresses she designed herself. The boys loved it. They loved it so much they wanted more.

There were a number of rumors as to how Yvonne received her big break during the war, but all seemed to involve the armed forces in one way or another. It was printed that many soldiers, wowed by her performance, would take up pen and paper and write letters to Hollywood studios, clueless as to why the stunning Miss De Carlo had yet to secure her star. This assuredly happened, for Yvonne set many a fighting man to swoon, but the more widely accepted story of her chance at fame came courtesy of her cousin and the troops he was stationed with. As a member of the Canadian Air Force, her cousin was pressured by his fellow airmen to enter a photograph of his kin in the "Salome Sweepstakes." At the time, a film studio was in search of an unknown beauty to play the lead in an exotic fantasy feature titled *Salome*, and set-up a contest to find their desired commodity. They urged folks to send in pictures of beautiful girls, and when Yvonne's cousin sent in a photograph of her, at the behest of his battle buddies, her image was the one selected. Rosalind Shaffer wrote, "Her cousin and a group of bombardier students in the RCAF sent in a pin-up picture of her in the 'Salome' contest. It was a 2,000-to-1 chance, but she got the part."

Although *Salome* wasn't a well-received film, it was certainly a starmaker for Miss De Carlo. Gone were the days of sitting in the background, filing papers, or looking good in a bathing suit, and in their place were lead roles that showcased her multiple talents. Although she had been in Hollywood for a handful of years, and more than one producer caught a glimpse of her unquestionable physical appeal, it took cheesecake art to open doors for the ravishing beauty. Wood Soanes wrote, "Miss De Carlo is said to be the only girl in motion picture history to receive a long-term contract and starring role as a direct result of efforts made by men in the armed forces — a tribute to the value of cheesecake, otherwise known as leg-art." By entering the war effort in a supporting role, Yvonne De Carlo became an immediate sensation and the men in the armed forces rewarded her by requesting films for her to star in.

When folks in the film industry finally took notice of the ravishing actress, she was just an ordinary girl with an extraordinary appearance. She lived in modest quarters whose dimensions could be measured in short order. She rented out a room in a small auto court, but when she attained stardom with her lead performance in *Salome*, folks in the industry sought to better her surroundings. They felt such a mesmerizing beauty was ill-suited to live in such cramped quarters. Erskine Johnson wrote, "She is now a star and deserves something better than a building with a sign reading 'weekly rates' out front." Many view the life of a Hollywood star as a lavish one, ensconced in the comforts a bulky bank account allows, but Miss De Carlo had no such life during the war. Forced to live frugally during the war, Yvonne found reprieve from her auto-court quarters by hitting the road and entertaining troops at military bases. But when *Salome* secured her status as an up-and-coming movie star, she was able to ascend the social ladder and acquire a setting more befit a stunning starlet.

Having put in years as a nameless player in the industry, Yvonne, thanks to her cheesecake work, finally found her handle displayed on the screen. A credited actress after years of background work, Yvonne found fame to her liking, and she was a common name in the papers the final two years of the war. She palled around with Martha O'Driscoll and the two pin-ups, whose political affiliations were not identical, made a bet as to which politician would win a local vote. They agreed that whoever lost the bet would have to kiss the first fifty servicemen she met on Hollywood Boulevard. When Yvonne lost the bet, it stands to reason that uniformed fighting men clamored to the bustling boulevard to receive a smooch from the lovely actress.

Yvonne, who wasn't unaccustomed to hardship, used her new status as a Hollywood star to help those in need. As a child, her father deserted the family and she was raised by her mother and grandparents. When a neighborhood girl, whose father had been sent overseas and whose mother was recently invalided, had nowhere to go, Yvonne took the little girl into her home and looked after her until her father could return from the war. Miss De Carlo took special care of the five-year-old girl. She kept her occupied with an assignment on her film set as a stand-in for the child star in *Frontier Gal*. Taking care of others came natural to Yvonne. She felt it her duty, when an American sailor made a remark — printed in the *Stars and Stripes* — that British women made ideal wives because they were more natural. Yvonne defended women of North America when she responded to the sailor, saying, "One of Webster's definitions for 'natural' is a 'feeble-minded person.' Could this be what our sailor friend had in mind? Another definition is 'anything bound to succeed or prosper.' Have a good time, but put a zipper on your pocket."

Eager to make it in the film industry in a big way, Miss De Carlo posed for numerous cheesecake photos for circulation among servicemen. She knew that by getting her image out there, among a large populace of men who all America supported, she could get the exposure necessary to build a name in Hollywood. Some of her pin-up pictures were quite racy, as the well-put-together lady couldn't help but appear sultry before a camera. There exists a fine line between sultriness and decadence, and the Hays Office, responsible for censoring Hollywood, served as a moral compass during the war. The photographers who took pin-up pictures knew that the soldiers wanted to see womanhood, but censorship meant there were nooks and crannies of womanhood that had to be concealed. When Yvonne was late for an interview with scribe Wood Soanes, she informed the writer that she had to be dressed enough to appear undressed for her latest pin-up picture. Soanes wrote, "Undressing is a very peculiar chore in Hollywood because the Hays Office has an eagle eye, and it takes quite a time for the dressmakers to fix a model so that she'll look unclad for the pin-up pictures and still be wearing all that the law requires."

A top-flight pin-up, Yvonne De Carlo had cheesecake and the devourers thereof to thank for her rise in the film industry. With three years spent as a bit player who was used as extras in background scenes, she became a sensation thanks to the efforts of the soldiers who viewed her pin-ups. There was more than one ooh and ah issued from fighting personnel when her stunning figure was tacked to a military wall. She had the proper look for the pin-up: exotic beauty, streamlined legs, and enviable curves. The war presented many hardships to folks across the globe, but to others, like Yvonne De Carlo who allowed patriotism to elevate their position, it was the catalyst to greater things. The soldiers were grateful for her selfless service to them and they in turn rewarded her by bombarding Hollywood with requisitions to put her in pictures. Yvonne De Carlo became a star based largely on her wartime endeavors to build morale among the servicemen. Perhaps there was never a star more deserving of the fame she achieved.

# ★ GLORIA DE HAVEN ★

Some women are destined to become actresses. Gloria De Haven, whose father (Carter De Haven) was an actor/director and whose mother (Flora Parker-De Haven) was an actress, followed in the footsteps of her show business parents. More fortunate than most, Gloria was able to enter the film industry without the typical entrance of minimal exposure as an extra. As a child of established thespians, the acting gene was part of Gloria's makeup and needn't be introduced by outside influences. Before she was legal to drive, the blonde beauty worked in film opposite such heavy-hitters as Joan Crawford and Ann Rutherford. America was able to witness firsthand, via the movie ticket, young Gloria grow into a beautiful woman of delicate grace. Although in her mid-teens when America entered the war, Miss De Haven became a popular pin-up among the young fighting men who found in her a symbol of womanhood, who, like themselves, was coming of age in an era of turmoil.

*Gloria De Haven.*

A vest-pocket pin-up, Miss De Haven was a petite young woman who cast a miniscule shadow. Not of the tall, leggy variety, Gloria's popularity as a pin-up was due largely to her average stature, which gave her not that larger-than-life aura many stunning pin-ups possessed but more of an every-girl look. There was no denying her beauty and charms, but those charms were more akin to the girls who young soldiers grew up with, girls they loved back home, than the ravishing, unattainable beauty of Hollywood's sultry glamour girls. Gloria was, in her own right, a glamorous woman, but her appeal was not of the showy, gaudy fashion, but more tasteful, more pleasant, like the ideal girlfriend soldiers hoped to find after the war. She was the ideal cheesecake for the recently inducted soldier or sailor, who pined for a young doll he could hold in his arms and celebrate the end of the war with. Because of her appeal to young men in Uncle Sam's battle ranks, Jimmie Fidler claimed that Gloria was "the runner-up to Betty Grable for G.I. cheers."

During the war, Miss De Haven grew into a young woman of unquestioned beauty. As a child actress before the war, American filmgoers were able to grow up with Gloria — share in the experiences and rites of passage that make a person an adult. Young men and women of the war generation had to age quickly, for the nation needed not young individuals of selfish means but patriotic folks who put the betterment of the nation before their own personal dreams and desires. Many young men put on hold their dreams to enter the war and lick the enemy, and young women like Gloria, although forbidden from the frontlines where the infantry fight, were no less eager to lend a hand and vanquish foreign evils. While still a teenager, Gloria entered the military base tour scene and became wildly popular among the men in service due to her support for the troops. As an actress, her schedule was hectic, but the blonde beauty made the most of her spare time.

Many stars during the war could often be found at the Hollywood Canteen, where they entertained troops before they were shipped off. When not on set or off on a tour, Gloria was a fixture at the Canteen. Most celebrities would figure that washing dishes in a packed kitchen was a chore that was beneath them, but Miss De Haven volunteered her time in the Canteen's kitchen, performing such a mundane chore, so the soldiers could unwind before training or departing for foreign waters. But, it wasn't all soap suds and plastic gloves for Gloria at the Hollywood Canteen. No sir, the gents in the armed forces wanted to trip the light fantastic with the diminutive blonde. Gloria would dance with the boys, sing tunes on the stage and pass out sandwiches, all to the merriment and satisfaction of our soldier and sailor boys.

Movies may have been Gloria's primary medium, but the talented beauty also owned an enviable singing voice and would often serenade the troops, cutting records for their amusement and enjoyment. But the airwaves were not designed simply to transmit ballads — there were purposes of greater importance during the war. The radio was the primary source of information. Through the airwaves, intelligence could be disseminated from one source to another. Celebrities also used the airwaves to let the fighting forces know that they, and the American populace, were behind them all the way. Miss De Haven lent her voice to the War Department on numerous occasions. Jill Warren wrote, "She has made many appearances on the various war department broadcasts which are shortwaved to our fighting men overseas, and has recorded several albums of songs which are sent to every spot on the globe where our boys are stationed." The troops were grateful and appreciated the time stars like Gloria De Haven spent reiterating their unwavering support.

Besides posing for cheesecake stills, the way pin-ups built morale among the fighting forces was by attending military camps in person. Thanks to her work supporting the troops, Gloria's star brightened during the war years. She claimed that her mail box typically held in the excess of a thousand fan letters per week. While on tour, the box swelled, for the letters kept pouring in, but the boys were not amiss, because they would gladly trade a signed photograph of Miss De Haven for the chance to meet her face to face. The chances came quite often, for Gloria toured the country, entertaining troops at various bases as part of a troupe that consisted of radio queen Ginny Simms and Sergeant Gary Bell. Sergeant Bell was chosen to tour with the lovely ladies because he was fortunate enough to be the millionth man to have walked through the entrance at the Hollywood Canteen. With Simms and Bell, Gloria entertained troops in 1943, shortly before marrying actor John Payne.

Pin-ups had their obvious assignment for the troops, but they also were used tirelessly by female beauty writers who picked their brains for pulchritude tips. With a classy beauty reminiscent of the ideal girl-next-door, Miss De Haven was a favorite subject for newspaper writers who penned their articles in the women's health section. These beauty writers, who some found to be kibitzers of pulchritude, passed along advice on how to look fetching, using pin-ups as their models. They would show women the popular way to fix their hair, how to apply certain makeup, or wear stockings, and so on and so forth. One such writer even printed inside dope on how a buxom actress expanded her bust, but the proper Miss De Haven was used as a model for skincare. Jill Warren penned, "She has one of those peaches and cream complexions most girls dream about and keeps it by the simple old-fashioned method of using glycerin and rose-water." Due to the printing of such articles, young women knew the secrets — the tricks of the pin-up trade — and employed them at their leisure, with the hope that they could achieve that enviable glow of the glorious Gloria De Haven.

Whereas the women envied her "peaches and cream complexion," the soldiers were satisfied to simply gaze for an uninterrupted moment at her pin-up photographs. The bantam beauty was a favorite model for the editors at *Yank*, the servicemen's magazine that printed a pin-up photo in every issue. She wowed the boys in a provocative flower-print bikini in the pages of *Yank*; the published pin-up pic had her seated on a beach and smiling fetchingly at the camera. Her appeal often lent itself to a visual focus that was incapable of spying flaws in the photograph. When a pin-up circulated in *Yank* that showed Gloria fishing, the magazine received one letter from its vast readership concerning an error in the cheesecake picture. Jimmie Fidler detailed the reader's complaint, writing, "So pictorial is Miss De Haven's beauty that only one G.I. reader out of 2,000,000 noticed the error when *Yank* printed a picture of her deep-sea fishing — with a five ounce trout rod." Certainly the bulk of the readers excused the error, for deep-sea fishing, although interesting to some in its own right, failed to outshine the therapeutic charms of appreciating the beauty of a lovely woman like Gloria De Haven.

## ★ OLIVIA DE HAVILLAND ★

Olivia makes up half of perhaps the most famous sister pair in Hollywood history. The Bennetts are well known (Joan and her sisters), as are Natalie and her sister Lana Wood, but Olivia and her kid sister Joan Fontaine would be named as a favorite screen sibling duo by a great number of critics. The dark-haired De Havilland kept their father's last name, while Joan, who was but a mere babe when their old man fled the family, took the maiden name of their mother. Both women became stars on the silver screen with Joan gaining fame with roles in Hitchcockian thrillers and Olivia securing her place in film immortality for her brilliant work in the classic *Gone With the Wind*. Having starred with the likes of Clark Gable and Vivien Leigh before the war, Miss De Havilland was a known, popular commodity in the film industry at the war's outset. Although born in the land of America's enemy, Olivia proved to be a staunch patriot who visited troops in conditions ill-fit for the stereotypical pampered screen star. But

Olivia De Havilland was never one to fit into stereotypes — her roles in film varied — she showcased a talent too incredible to be typecast and a mentality well-suited for a world beset with hardship and battles.

Before her birth, Olivia's father accepted an assignment in an overseas office, a position that relocated the family to Japan. Due to her father's occupational duties, Olivia was born in the nation that bombed Pearl Harbor

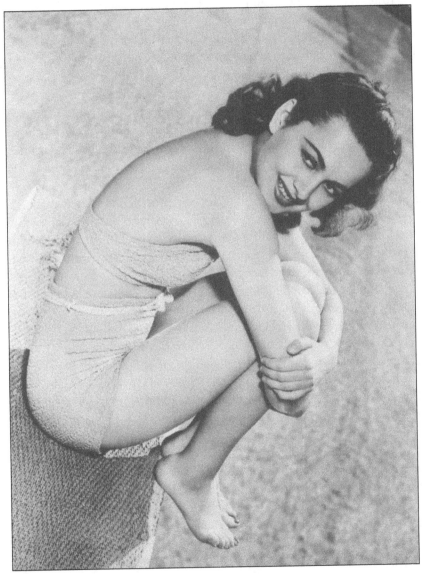

*Olivia De Havilland.* COURTESY OF MOVIEMARKET.COM

in 1941. Having been born in Tokyo, Japan, it would stand to reason that Miss De Havilland would harbor warm sentiments of the region, but when the Japanese became America's enemy during World War II, those sunny sentiments were dimmed. Interviewer William Payette asked Olivia how she felt about her hometown the year after Pearl Harbor was bombed. In his newspaper article, Payette headlined his De Havilland interview with the title: "Olivia De Havilland Wants Her Hometown Bombed!" Payette wrote, "Miss de Havilland hopes they bomb the blazes out of her old hometown. She thinks it would be nice if they used a de Havilland-made bomb to do it. A relative makes British bombers, [so] there will be a little spiritual satisfaction in having some kind of a de Havilland representative on the firing end." Many foreign-born Americans were eager to show their allegiance to their new homeland during the war, and those born in enemy lands were under greater scrutiny. De Havilland — not of Japanese ancestry but born in Japan — was under less scrutiny to prove herself patriotic, which she, nevertheless, did in spades.

Few stars in Hollywood were more accommodating to the troops than Miss De Havilland. Early during the war effort, Olivia was a constant hostess at the Hollywood Canteen, a place where soldiers could unwind and forget about the war for a few hours. They would dance the night away and dine with lovely ladies like Miss De Havilland, who showed admirable support for the troops by entertaining them after their work hours. But dancing, cooking, and chatting with the boys at the Hollywood Canteen, fulfilling as it was to many starlets, wasn't an ideal assignment for ladies like Olivia De Havilland. She wanted to get out on the road and visit troops outside California — those not fortunate enough to be stationed in close proximity to the alluring actresses of Tinseltown. When she decided to tour for entertainment purposes, Olivia asked chum Paul Stewart to write some routines that they could perform together for the troops. Her intentions were good, but when she read Stewart's material, she had little to do but look pretty. Stewart wrote all the good lines for himself and left Olivia with the assignment of decoration. Miss De Havilland was more than a woo-woo girl and scoffed at Stewart's skits — she wanted meaty material, not just pulchritude, to deliver to the boys.

Shortly after rejecting Paul Stewart's on-the-sidelines skits, Olivia opted to venture out and visit the boys in foreign settings. She packed her grip and went northward, up from California and along the western coast, and stopped along the Aleutian Islands in the vicinity of Alaska. A number of American troops were stationed in the frigid regions, and they hadn't spotted a swell-looking dame in months, but that all changed when Olivia graced them with her presence. To Miss De Havilland, entertaining the troops was a broader assignment than simply standing on a stage and reciting lines from a script. She felt that the proper way to regale the men in the fighting forces was to be amongst them — share in their experiences and listen to their tales. Despite her desire to offer the boys plenty of disport, she knew the primary role of a pulchritudinous pin-up was to look appealing. She said, "I wore my beaver coat over one of my best and most expensive dresses, and a hat with a veil. I felt the boys wanted me to look my prettiest and I tried to please them."

The Aleutian Islands received a heavy dose of glamour courtesy of the visit of Miss De Havilland early in the war effort. The troops were grateful: they cheered Olivia on and applauded her sacrifice. Her trip to the islands wasn't a slight sojourn, traipsing among the boys in flimsy dresses and giggling like a silly coquette, but was a trip that lasted close to two months, with plenty chores beyond casting a pretty reflection. She forfeited the opportunity to make films in Hollywood, surrendering a healthy lifestyle for the hardship of a serviceman in an uncompromising locale. But, ever the trooper, Olivia never complained and felt that by choosing to be amongst the servicemen, she made the right decision. Her outlook was noble, for she had fame and fortune courtesy of her celebrity lifestyle, but she put that on hold to entertain troops who had been displaced from their ordinary lives. Miss De Havilland said, "I am happy I did just what I did — taking all my meals with the enlisted men, hearing their stories, talking to them, I had the greatest experience of my life."

Film studios were quite agreeable during the war: they sent stars out on tours to entertain the troops. Under contract with Warner Brothers studio, they barked not when Olivia ventured to the Aleutian Islands to delight the men in the fighting forces, but when Olivia singled out one serviceman to be with, her studio began to stiffen in its stance. During the war, Olivia was enmeshed in a love affair with filmmaker John Huston, who was a member of the military. Miss De Havilland wanted to spend as much time as she could with her lover before he was shipped out, which led to her rejecting a role in the film *Animal Kingdom*. Her studio very much wanted her to star in the film, but Olivia's priorities were those harbored by many women in love during the war: to be with her partner. About rejecting the role in *Animal Kingdom*, Olivia said, "None of us know when our soldier boys are leaving and as long as John is in this country I want to be close to him." Warner Brothers, although upset that Olivia had passed on a role they had assigned her, allowed her to stay with her loved one while he was still stateside — but the stance didn't last.

Olivia made the picture *Government Girl* with the express interest of showing American women how to dress on a tight budget. Not one outfit worn in the film was gaudy and expensive, for she cast aside the lavish frills in an effort to show gals that glamour could be attained on a trim wartime budget. But *Government Girl* was simply one wartime assignment Olivia agreed to while she rejected more offers. Warner Brothers grew tired of Miss De Havilland's rejection of roles so she could be with John Huston, so they chose to take her to court. As a contract player, Warner Brothers felt they weren't getting what they paid for from Olivia, who remained at home with her soldier and away from the studios. The court hearing was a messy affair, but most Americans were behind Olivia who wanted only to be near her soldier before he was shipped out. Her loyalty to her soldier in time of war was deemed admirable and she won the case. Warner Brothers wanted her to spread her loyalty evenly, from soldier to studio, but the actress who Alice Pardoe West called "very gracious by nature," found it difficult to divide an inner commodity, and placed the bulk upon her fighting man.

After Huston was shipped out, Olivia went back on the road to entertain troops. Her initial tour was a resounding success, but she didn't have good fortune on her other tours. Shortly after New Year's 1944, Olivia, who was engaged in a tour of military hospitals, contracted influenza and was admitted to Brooke General Hospital at Fort Sam Houston. Bedridden for a time in an Army infirmary, Olivia, who came out to brush a smile or two on some enfeebled troops, had to be laid-up for a spell. Upset that she was forced to halt her duties, Olivia was grateful to the military hospital staff and the many supporters who came to visit her. She said, "I came out to cheer up the boys and here they are cheering me up." She contracted influenza in 1944, but the final year of the war, Miss De Havilland had a worse malady to contend with. She lined up a tour of the South Pacific in 1945, but her health suffered when she was afflicted with tropical fever. Returned home, Olivia recovered from her ailment while America rejoiced, celebrating the end of the war.

# ★ MARLENE DIETRICH ★

The United States had quite a predicament during World War II, directly created by one of the nation's more boast-worthy selling features: the melting pot culture. Always a nation that has prided itself on giving individuals the wherewithal to achieve success, regardless their stature in their home country, questions began to arise during the war era as to the allegiance of immigrants. Many Americans, not born in this country, had come to our shores from Germany, Italy, and Japan — lands that had become hostile to the American way of life. The melting pot was not melting nationalities, mixing them together in order to create a collective American identity, but was highlighting the differences in individual's origins. More than one aspiring soldier, of Italian or other enemy descent, was refused the opportunity to enlist in the service because Uncle Sam was uncertain of the young man's allegiances. Immigrants during the war had to show where their allegiances lied, and many did just that by taking up arms against their motherland. Marlene Dietrich, German born and raised, gained American citizenship before the war in the 1930s, but there was no denying where her loyalties rested. She became a hero of America, but in her praiseworthy patriotism to her new country, she was deemed a traitor by the vile head of Germany: Adolf Hitler.

Marlene's life was one of tragedy. While growing up in Germany, Marlene's stepfather, who she held dear, was killed during World War I, as were a number of other male family members. A teenager at the time of the First World War, young Marlene had developed into a striking beauty in a nation that had lost many eligible suitors to war. With many of the men in her life taken from her, Marlene had, like many young women of the time, few prospects of an ideal husband, so she set out to fend for herself. Success wasn't instant, but for the sexy, uninhibited blonde, it came in short order. The willowy La Dietrich turned her attention toward acting and began to work among the German thespian ranks. An early star of German films, Marlene had the desire to venture to the world's largest stage, Hollywood, where stardom in every developed portion of the globe could be secured. The opportunity arose when famous filmmaker Josef von Sternberg spotted her performance in cabaret and put her in his film *The Blue Angel* — an instant star-maker for Marlene. Josef von Sternberg escorted her directly to Hollywood as his muse and lover.

Marlene's popularity soared in Hollywood during the 1930s. One of the top earners in the film industry, regardless of gender, La Dietrich was regarded as one of the greatest actresses of the decade. However, when the decade prepared to close, Marlene's roles were of lesser caliber and her star had begun to dim. Many of her films during the late 1930s were lavish, but despite the glitz and glamour, the films were often panned by critics and not well received by audiences. But an occupational renaissance came in 1939 when her role opposite James Stewart in *Destry Rides Again* helped reshape her career. By this time, however, the world was in turmoil and much of the hostilities perpetuated occurred in her native land. As an American citizen of German ancestry, Marlene was scrutinized by many who were suspicious of her as an enemy, simply based on her heritage. Miss Dietrich put those malicious rumors to rest by publicly speaking out against the machinations of Adolf Hitler, and when the United States entered the fighting, she further established her status as a patriotic American by engaging herself wholeheartedly in the war effort.

The selling of war bonds was a constant endeavor for the folks in Hollywood who used their celebrity status to attract crowds. Many actors and actresses toured the nation on war-bond rallies, but it was Marlene Dietrich who made the war-bond junket a popular assignment for celebrities. Early in 1942, newspapers across the nation lauded Marlene for her unrivalled accumulation of wealth for the war effort. Few people beat the drum louder for the war-bond circuit than La Dietrich. She won recognition in the nation's first year in the involvement of the war as the leading seller of war bonds. For her success as a war bond promoter, Marlene was awarded a special citation from the treasury department. So impressed by her work, the treasury department asked Marlene to visit Portsmouth, Ohio, to present a certificate of outstanding participation in war bond purchases.

Her war-bond tour took her to such locales as Portsmouth, Akron, and the California Shipbuilding Company close to her Los Angeles home. The war demanded a sacrifice of time from individuals, and Marlene spent her hours on the war-bond circuit in constant motion. At the shipbuilding company, La Dietrich made three appearances at the plant — one for each shift — to award the workers the treasury department's "T Flag," which meant that ninety percent of the factory's workers put ten percent of their paycheck into war bonds. Marlene made her first appearance at the plant at four-in-the-morning, then returned at noon, and rounded out her day by staying on at the factory until eight at night to shake hands with the late shift. Many of her visits were as demanding as the trek to the shipyard — Marlene forfeit her entire day to place a smile on the faces of hundreds of folks, but she had to get creative on other tours. When she visited Akron, Ohio, early in the war effort, she was informed that little was planned for the war-bond rally. La Dietrich sprang into action. She went to the local university and handpicked twenty of the loveliest coeds she could corral and seated them in a few Army jeeps that were at her disposal. The ladies proceeded to drive their military conveyances up and down the streets of Akron, and beat the drum for the sale of war bonds.

The selling of war bonds was a noble endeavor, but Marlene wanted to be amongst the fighting men — to share in their experiences. In the spring of 1942, she invited a group of soldiers to her California mansion for entertainment. She lined up photographers to preserve the evening in pictures. The soldiers were grateful, for they were allowed to unwind in surroundings that resembled not barracks or training fields, and, most

*Marlene Dietrich.* COURTESY OF MOVIEMARKET.COM

importantly, their hostess was the famous Marlene Dietrich. One soldier, a Guardsman from Missouri named Ron Perryman, was a little hesitant to have his picture taken with the blonde torpedo because he had a gal waiting for him back home in the Midwest. The night was all done in good fun — a lighthearted evening that allowed the men to relax — but Perryman felt that if his girl saw him in a photograph with Marlene, she wouldn't think that her beau was terribly lonely.

Marlene found entertaining the troops to her liking, and she quickly setup a USO tour to visit military bases. She had just turned forty at the outset of America's involvement in the war and had reestablished herself as a heavy-hitter in the film industry, but the nation needed more from its people than ever before, and Marlene answered the call. Shortly after she held the party for servicemen at her abode, Marlene packed her bag and went east. She entertained troops at Fort Meade in the spring of 1942. Although the boys were happy enough to have a dame in their presence, Marlene put on shows for the chaps: she packed her favorite saw, which she used for the sake of melodies and not lumberjacking. She unclasped the latches on her saw's case at several stateside bases, but La Dietrich was eager to venture overseas to her native Europe, and visit the boys in hostile regions. Many of her closest friends urged her to reconsider, afraid that, given her German heritage, she would be a prime target for the Gestapo. Jimmie Fidler summed up her friends' fears when he wrote, "if Miss Dietrich were captured, she would pay a price far greater than the Hitlerites would exact from an American-born girl doing the same work."

Marlene took the advice of others but heeded it not, for the starlet wanted to support the boys, and, most importantly, unseat an evil that had corrupted her beloved Germany. Marlene agreed to record propaganda broadcasts that were transmitted in German, which made her one of Hitler's prime targets. As a German-born girl raised in Deutschland during World War I, Marlene was deemed by Hitler to be a traitor and one of the Nazi's greatest threats. While she was overseas, La Dietrich tried desperately to locate family members, for she knew that the Nazis would seek the blood of Dietrich in earnest. The Nazis accused Marlene of sabotage for her propaganda broadcasts, and her mother, who operated a watch-making firm, had her business seized by the Gestapo for harboring Jewish refugees. Near the close of the war, when Marlene was able to be escorted through Berlin, she searched for her family, and located a sister who was housed in a concentration camp at Belsen.

With worries concerning her family, Marlene kept her mind preoccupied with entertaining the troops. She visited hostile regions where soldiers never expected a Hollywood celebrity to visit. The fact that the enemy was in close proximity to the bases she visited didn't deter Marlene. Wherever the boys were, Marlene went. She visited and entertained troops at Belgium, Czechoslovakia, France, Iceland, and Luxembourg among other locales. Many a celebrity would have been put off by bullets whizzing overhead or bombers deploying their explosive hardware to the ground below, but not Marlene. She was there, near the frontlines with the boys, and the boys worshiped her for her devotion. Before many American soldiers went off to the frontlines, the last woman they saw was Marlene. She understood the significance of her role, the most important role she played in her life, and accepted the duties of a farewell maiden with praiseworthy dedication. She would give farewell kisses to troops before they entered battle and had only one stipulation when it came to osculating: the removal of helmets. When Marlene first began pecking soldiers goodbye, the brim of their helmets would connect with her forehead, and after many such meetings, a bruise was left on her profile. Rather than abandon the role of kissing troops farewell, La Dietrich decreed that the boys had to lose their lids before they received a smooch from her lips.

For their beloved Miss Dietrich, the men of the armed forces would do anything. She braved hostilities when she traveled to war areas to entertain troops before they marched for the frontlines or parachuted into combat. As eager as Marlene was to entertain them, the soldiers were just as eager to assist her. A long way from the leisurely life she had led in Hollywood, Marlene mentioned how she liked pineapple custard pie to a mess sergeant with the Fifth Army in Italy. The sergeant, Claren "Curly" Thompson, made a special dessert for Marlene and surprised her with her favorite after dinner treat. Sergeant Thompson said, "I sure would like to bake a pie for Miss Dietrich every day, especially if I had the opportunity to present it personally." But since she was typically the only woman around, to keep Marlene to one's self was an impossible endeavor. When she was invited to a close-of-the-war party by General Omar Bradley at Bad Wildungern, she danced with countless officers who butted in on her lively stepping. Scribe Robert Meyer wrote, "Nobody could dance with Dietrich more than a couple of steps without having somebody cut in. There hasn't been so much rank-pulling since the Yanks hit the beaches. A lieutenant didn't have a chance."

In 1944, Marlene wowed soldiers at the AAF camp at Labrador. That same year, she watched a firefight near the frontlines at Algiers with hundreds of soldiers who surrounded their heroic femme protectively. The heroes of war — those valiant men who placed their lives in danger to secure liberty — had at their side a darling celebrity, one whose demeanor and style was larger than life but whose devotion to the cause of justice mirrored their own. It meant a great deal to the men of the fighting forces that a member of the fairer sex, especially one of fortune who could do as she saw fit, surrendered a life of luxury and placed herself in the same hazards they were thrust in. She willingly gave up the highlife, glitz, and pomp of Hollywood, where all seemed to shine with an untarnished splendor, for the dirt and filth of the battlefields. Although it was her style, Marlene even traded the sequins and form-fitting dresses for the uniform of Uncle Sam's fighting forces. Hollywood had touted Marlene as one of — if not *the* most — tawdry of their many tawdry lasses, but the excessively ornamental lifestyle of a film industry dame was unsuitable, vulgar beyond words, in the midst of a world at war. While many socialites spent the war years partying like they had before the fighting, La Dietrich traded her lavish Los Angeles mansion for the makeshift barracks and crude tents of the armed forces. The world was not the showman's delight, all bright lights and spectacle, and Marlene Dietrich, who had become accustomed to such ostentatious endeavors, stepped down from the lofty regions of gold and fallacious grace and earned the praise of Americans for her wartime deeds.

## ★ ELLEN DREW ★

Hectic was the life of men during World War II. Those of age were expected to take up arms and fight for their country — many refused to wait for a call from Uncle Sam and enlisted, adhering to their sense of national duty. Young men of eighteen years of age and older, filed into the ranks of the armed forces, surrendering the life they had led during peacetime for the existence of a soldier during war. Unmarried men were initially pursued by Uncle Sam in the draft — family men were given deferment at the outset of the war. But many husbands and fathers knew their nation needed them and they joined the colors regardless. The world needed a hefty fighting force of able-bodied men to subdue foreign evils, which disrupted families and forced many women into the role of single mother. But there were women who also felt a sense of duty — felt obligated to serve their country in some capacity. Many ladies served as military nurses and thousands joined the WACS, but there were others, who donned not a military uniform yet lent support the best they could. Ellen Drew, as the wife of a serviceman, followed her fighter pilot husband to his England base where she witnessed the ravaged streets of a wartime Britain.

Ellen Drew is best remembered today as a horror film icon, one of the first "scream queens," who starred in many fright films during and after the war. But when the war broke out, Miss Drew had yet to establish herself as a genre favorite and worked in various capacities, exuding her natural charm in dramas. A beautiful, alluring actress, Ellen's trademark was her magnetic smile: a grin so bewitching it could coax a little more

*Ellen Drew.*

brightness from the sun. A delicate beauty, Ellen possessed all the finer qualities that make the female gender the fairer sex. But her beauty went beyond the physical, for Miss Drew was more than window-dressing and was regarded by many in the film industry as a swell, level-headed woman worthy of admiration. Ida Jean Kain, who wrote beauty tips for the papers, said of Ellen, "she is one of the most upstanding, beautifully poised actresses on the screen, and an excellent example for my teenagers." Celebrities typically fail in regard to setting examples for youngsters, but Miss Drew was an expert model — not just for pin-up purposes.

Ellen Drew wasn't a pin-up girl at the outset of the war. She had a more demanding role than standing in high heels and thrusting out her caboose for the boys with cameras. As a war bride, Ellen wanted desperately to be with her husband, and her desire to remain by his side did not vanish when he received orders to England. Even with scripts in her lap — for filmmakers wanted Ellen in their pictures — she cast the screenplays aside and ventured overseas with her fighter pilot betrothed. She surrendered the lucrative existence of a first-rate film star for the taxing lifestyle of a soldier's wife. But she had no regrets. Her husband was doing his bit for liberty and she was right there with him, in foreign lands. While her husband flew missions, Ellen did what she could to assist the residents of a ravaged Britain. She visited a London suburb named Bermondsey to sell war bonds, but when she saw the destruction wrought by the bombings, she opted not to solicit money from the folks but helped them in their effort to clean up the streets.

Married to Hollywood producer Sy Bartlett, who willfully left his studio desk and accepted the rank of Major in Uncle Sam's ranks, Ellen's husband was not an idle, paper-pushing officer. On the contrary, Major Bartlett was one of the first American pilots sent to England to assist in the war effort. The day after a secret mission, Major Bartlett and his wife were visited by some newspapers boys looking for the inside dope on Sy's latest assignment. When the reporters began to hound the Major, Ellen didn't know what to make of their unusual interest since her husband kept her in the dark regarding his mission as well. She learned, via the interview with the scribes, that her husband was the first American pilot to drop bombs on Berlin. Admiration for her husband quickly shifted to fear. Ellen said, "When I discovered he had been the first American to drop a bomb on Berlin I was so proud of him I could have wept. But, oh my, how I worried after that — every time he was out of my sight." Ever the proud wife, Ellen was excited by her husband's heroic deeds but couldn't mask her discomfort. One of the newspaper boys there for the interview detected her anxiety, and wrote, "When interviewed in London tonight, Bartlett had a fine audience in his wife, Ellen Drew, famed as a motion picture actress. She looked more exhausted than the Major."

The couple lived together in England for some time during the war, husband engaged in military duties and wife supporting him and the cause. When Major Bartlett was out flying, Ellen refused to sit around the house worrying every moment, and she decided to visit military camps to entertain the troops. There wasn't a base near London that Ellen didn't visit. She would bounce from one camp to another, doing whatever was necessary to build morale among a group of people whose morale had been trampled. But the lifestyle, if not admirable, was certainly taxing on Miss Drew, and wasn't ideal for a wife. Although she was able to see her husband upon occasion, the occasions were usually short, for the Major was kept in constant engagement with his duties as a flier. They agreed that it would be best if Ellen returned home so both husband and wife could work. Miss Drew knew there were many ladies eager to do what she did — follow their husbands to their overseas camps — but she advised against it when she returned stateside. Ellen said, "It is better to stay home — stay put. The greatest love you can show your fighting men is to let them know you are where they always expect you to be — home and keeping the home fires burning."

Ellen understood the hardship of war, for she experienced it firsthand. She came to the realization that a member of the armed forces, whether he is a soldier or a fighter pilot, had to focus on winning the war. The family, of great interest to him, was a distraction if it was uprooted and transplanted in a hostile, foreign setting. Not only did Major Bartlett have to be concerned with his well-being, but he also worried about the welfare of his wife, who had followed him to a land closer to the enemy. They agreed that it would be in both their best interests if Ellen returned to Hollywood and focused on her film career. She left London, albeit a bit begrudgingly, and made her way back to California during the middle of the war. Although she was home, she worried no less for her husband. While shooting the film *The Imposter*, Ellen's heart skipped a beat when she learned that her husband had been hospitalized overseas. Had she remained in London, she could have been by his side — help nurse him back to health — but relief was found when she was informed that his admission to the infirmary was not due to injuries sustained in battle, but a bout with an illness.

Back stateside, Ellen found ways to keep herself busy that other starlets had engaged themselves in while she was overseas with her husband. The pin-up craze was in full-swing and Ellen lent her stunning figure to the trade. She once posed in a cheesecake trio with famed pin-up girl Betty Grable and actress Susan Hayward; the ladies were gathered together in their bathing suits and were asked to stand on their tiptoes — the famous cheesecake posture that accentuated the legs. She posed for a solo shot, flashing that trademark full Drew smile, which had her seated on a diving board at a pool atop a large, inflatable seahorse. Although she went for the cheesecake, Miss Drew was eager to do more for the war effort than pose for photographs that fighting men devoured. She jumped into the war-bond circuit and breathed new life into the popular endeavor.

Ellen joined the war-bond circuit and traveled with wounded soldiers to various cities and towns in the United States. She requested the presence of returned combat veterans and former POWs to travel with her, so folks across America could hear their stories and congratulate the boys firsthand for their heroism. In 1945, she toured with such combat veterans as Marine sergeant Kenneth Mize and Army sergeant Robert Howe. She also extended an invite to female war brides and relatives of soldiers. On her bond junket to Syracuse, Ellen invited the members of the Bataan Relief Organization to join her at the Victory Garden for her bond tour. The organization was comprised mostly of women like her, who had loved ones serving in the Armed Forces. She may have headlined the bond tour, but Ellen Drew wanted to spotlight the heroes, both those engaged in the fighting and those supporting the troops, rather than promote her latest film or elevate her status in show business. Ida Jean Kain claimed that Ellen was an "excellent example for her teenagers," and her character set an example that should still be followed.

## ★ ANN DVORAK ★

Many pin-up girls during World War II found it difficult to manage their time. If they weren't photographed in a studio, they were on a film set shooting a movie, or down at the Hollywood Canteen dancing with the servicemen and playing hostess to the boys in uniform. When they were away from Los Angeles, they were engaged in war-bond junkets or military camp entertainment tours. Very few pin-ups had the luxury of idle hours. But one pin-up, the comely Ann Dvorak, had less time to look appealing for the cameras than others. She was not hotfooting it from studio to canteen during the war, dolling herself up for the troops, but was among them in some of the most war-ravaged areas in England. Ann, who was the wife of a British officer, left Hollywood during the war and followed her husband to his native land to lend support in the war effort. England was not Dvorak's homeland, for the sleepy-eyed brunette was a New York gal, but the devoted wife bid adieu to the stage and promenade of Tinseltown, and substituted it with the hard work and toil of the Women's Land Army.

Before the war, Dvorak and husband Leslie Fenton — an actor turned director — were a Hollywood power couple. Ann had worked in some of the more popular films of the time such as the original *Scarface* opposite

*Ann Dvorak.*

Paul Muni, and her handsome husband had gravitated from costarring parts to leading man roles. The talented couple seemed destined to be heavy-hitters in the film industry, but the ever opinionated Dvorak occasionally ran afoul with her studio. Never one to hold back her wishes and desires, Ann had a rebellious streak that failed to endear her to the executives who handed her paychecks. Because of her brash demeanor, Dvorak's name was passed over more than once for a choice role, which in turn was handed to an actress of lesser talent because she was more amiable than La Dvorak. Due to her temerity, Ann, who had been on the doorstep of stardom, never became an elite actress on par with peers such as Bette Davis and Jean Harlow.

Despite her inability to achieve stardom, Dvorak was a well-respected actress and worked steadily in the film industry. Late in the 1930s, her husband shifted gears and abandoned acting to focus his efforts behind the camera as director. The husband and wife duo were established film players late in the decade, but when the war broke out overseas, Fenton, a native Britain, felt it his duty to return home and assist in the war effort. Able to land a commission with the British military, Lieutenant Fenton became a commander of a torpedo boat. While Fenton was engaged in military maneuvers, his wife, the beautiful brunette from New York, followed him to his homeland and helped build morale among the ravaged residents of England. Ann assisted the British in many capacities, first as an actress who made propaganda films and then as an ambulance driver. Like her husband, Ann earned a lieutenancy, given her in the ambulance corps, which enabled her to patrol the streets during the Blitz.

Dvorak had a front row seat to hostilities and destruction while she patrolled an ambulance through war ravaged England. The devastation was horrendous, but England wasn't Ann's homeland. Despite her foreigner status in Britain, Dvorak accepted any role that was needed and left the ambulance corps to join the depleted, and necessary, Women's Land Army. As a member of this outfit, the former film starlet, who spent the 1930s acting and enjoying the highlife of Tinseltown, was engaged in the occupations of a common laborer. Miss Dvorak would wake in the morning, and she would prepare for the day not by applying makeup and studying a script but by grasping a garden hoe and water pail, to plow and irrigate fields. With many British men engaged in the war, ladies were needed to fill out the ranks of farmers, and Ann answered the call.

During the war, Miss Dvorak toiled with little reprieve, but she was able to pursue her traditional occupation on occasion. The war department used her in several propaganda pieces and she acted some for morale-building purposes at the bomb-blitzed Denham Studios. But acting in England during World War II was a far cry from plying her craft in the setting of Hollywood. The typical film star would carry to the studio all that was necessary for play acting, but Ann, while making her way to Denham Studios, had a gas mask tucked under one arm. The dark-haired actress had to tote the mask from lodging to work every day for fear that the enemy would discharge a chemical weapon that would require the donning of the headgear. But the exposure to chemical attacks wasn't the loan fear for a war-era thespian. While working at Denham Studios one day, Dvorak had a brush with death. She said, "The most terrifying experience came when an unexploded time bomb dropped in on us right smack on the set one day. We tip-toed carefully out of the studio, and it wasn't until days later that a demolition crew took care of the matter and we could go back to work."

As an American woman overseas, Ann saw many contrasts between the females of America and the folks of Britain. Never one to muzzle her thoughts and beliefs, Ann made many friends in the ambulance corps among her fellow female drivers. Despite the friendship, she was dismayed by their feelings toward their husbands off to war. They, just like soldier's brides in America, typically wrote letters to their husbands and looked forward to the day in which they would be reunited. However, what shocked Ann were the feelings the British women had when the reunion with their husbands finally came. When she learned that her husband was coming home, Ann told her ambulance corps friends about his impending arrival and how she planned to welcome her husband back, but was taken aback by their casual regard. Ann said, "When I knew Leslie was coming home on leave I spent hours prettying up for him, hunting out my most attractive clothes. The English girls in the ambulance corps couldn't understand me. 'Why bother when you're married to him,' they'd say." The British girls Ann worked with knew they had their men baited on the hook and were flabbergasted by Dvorak's desire to enchant her hooked husband. In the mind of many gals, the reward for coming home from war was a wife, but to Dvorak, the reward should be made to sparkle and not tarnish, thus enchanting her hero by bestowing upon him all her beauty.

When Leslie Fenton was wounded in action in 1943, the couple prepared to head back to Hollywood and return to their former life as actress and director. But Ann Dvorak, who studios found demanding, off-putting at times, and a rebellious upstart, was a woman of character who understood better than most that the world at war needed sacrifices from decent people. When she was slated to return to the States, she received a letter from an English acting troupe that entertained soldiers in Britain, which requested her presence as a replacement for their ill lead in the play *The Eve of St. Mark*. Although Dvorak wanted desperately to return home, when she heard that the show, which was put on for the benefit of troops, would close if a replacement wasn't found, she decided to act. She had just spent three years in a war ravaged country that wasn't her home and had made preparations to return stateside, but felt it her duty to keep the show going. The show, which was performed nightly and was free of charge for the troops, was doomed to be dropped for the duration, but the selfless Dvorak personally saw that the show would go on by forfeiting a trip home to give one final salute to the troops of England.

When Ann and husband returned to Hollywood from England, newspapermen beat down their door to land interviews with the film industry heroes. Dvorak was regarded as a hero like few women during the war for her work driving ambulances and tending to crops. The ink pushers knew who they were talking to: an opinionated, brash woman of spunk and vinegar who never felt the need to censor her attitudes and beliefs. She had spent three plus years in England, worked in various necessary capacities, and acted a little on the side, so the scribes wanted to hear her views. Her story was a unique one. The papers wanted to relay her wartime experiences and find out her feelings regarding women at war. When one scribe asked Ann about the roles women could play during war, he received a forward response from the unflinching actress. Miss Dvorak felt that since men were subject to the military draft, women should be subjected to a draft too. She felt that if a woman didn't volunteer for war work, she should be subjected to the draft like a man — drafted into the military or war plants. Dvorak said, "American women don't seem to realize that they're needed. I've heard all kinds of excuses."

It was certainly bothersome for Dvorak to listen as dames espoused their own exemptions to war work, since she was engaged in work on foreign soil. She followed her husband when he returned home to fight for his country and helped protect a country that wasn't her homeland. After she returned home, writer Erskine Johnson asked Ann if she thought more American women should follow her example. Dvorak answered, "It's a tremendous question depending for its answer on the individuals. If two people are strong, facing adverse conditions strengthens them — brings them closer. But suppose they aren't strong enough. Would it not be better for her to stay at home? A man wants to know his home is there waiting for him when he's through fighting." Although Dvorak supported her husband to limits that made most females cringe, her betrothed failed to return the favor. Less than two years after their return to Hollywood, Dvorak filed for divorce on grounds of desertion.

## ★ DALE EVANS ★

When a person thinks of singing cowboys, images of Gene Autry, Tex Ritter, and Roy Rogers serenading in the saddle come to mind. These crooning cowpokes sang pasture ditties atop their preferred steeds, speaking of, in melodic fashion, simple days, county fairs, and bonny lasses. One of the more esteemed ladies of musical oaters was Dale Evans. A fixture in westerns during the 1940s, Miss Evans was a pretty songbird who held more than one tune with the famous singing cowboy Roy Rogers. The two often paired in films and after World War II they were married. Later, Dale and her husband starred in the television series titled after the husband: *The Roy Rogers Show*. But before Dale hit it big in Hollywood, she was your typical American working girl, earning her paycheck as a stenographer in a Texas law firm.

Born and raised in Texas, the sweet-voiced Miss Evans was a child bride, married off before her fifteenth birthday. Such unions, where the spouses have yet to study the world and their surroundings, typically fail to develop a strong rooted structure, which is what happened to Dale. The lovely Lone Star lady decided to earn a living on her own and took an assignment in a Fort Worth law firm as a stenographer. The work kept her occupied, but a lark had always resided in the girl's throat, and she would often croon in the office while she pounded away on the keyboard. Her boss thoroughly enjoyed the sound of her voice and when he needed a jingle to be broadcast via the radio to promote his business, he asked his little stenographer to sing the tune. Ever eager to sing, Dale agreed, and her voice became an instant hit. Folks in Fort Worth wanted to know the name of the dame with the heavenly voice on the radio. A little radio advertisement enabled Dale to closet the keyboard and pursue a career as a crooner.

With a soothing voice and pleasing beauty, Dale found that Hollywood was an ideal avenue for her talents. The western genre, always a popular field, became Dale's regular arena as she made numerous pictures during the 1940s — most of which were westerns. Given her Texas heritage and background in music, studio bosses had a hot commodity for their rhythmic rural films in the cute Miss Evans. Before the war, the light-haired actress had become a film starlet and a stalwart in the western genre. But it was her voice, more so than acting talent, which catapulted her to stardom. When the war broke out, men in the armed forces looked to music as an escape from their military training and listened to tunes broadcast on the radio. One of their favorite lady crooners was Dale Evans. Ever the accommodating sort, Miss Evans knew the boys were delighted with her voice, so she took her voice to the boys at various camps.

*Dale Evans.* COURTESY OF MOVIEMARKET.COM

Touring military installations under the auspices of the Hollywood Victory Committee was something Dale relished. She enjoyed the chance to hit the road and soothe the men in the armed forces with her musical numbers. One of the first songbirds to tour the country for the troops, Dale was an immediate hit with the boys. In 1942, Dale was a member of the Edgar Bergen Troupe that performed skits and sang numbers to troops at the encampments. Dale entertained the boys with ballads. On a tour of Marana Airfield, Miss Evans took the stage and dedicated her song *I'm in Love With a Guy From the Sky*, to all the airmen at the base. Her tour of Marana Airfield was one of the first celebrity shows that the cadets had performed for them. They were grateful that Dale took time out from her busy Hollywood schedule to croon them a heavenly love ballad. Colonel Jake Meyers, head of Marana Airfield's basic training school, said, "These men are deeply appreciative. I watched them and it is a treat to see their faces light up. This was their first big show."

Dale traveled extensively during the war. She put on shows at such military bases as Camp Wolters and Camp Berkeley, to name a few. Given the success she enjoyed during these tours, she became a star ticket for service shows. When she was invited to be the featured soloist at the anniversary program held at the US Merchant Marine Cadet School at Coyote Point, she accepted the invite and entertained the cadets with a few of her numbers. Her favorite number was a little love song she created, titled *Won't You Marry Me, Mr. Laramie?* Whenever she would perform this little song, Dale would invite one lucky chap from the audience, latch on to him like a pit-bull does a mailman's leg, and recite the lyrics with a sensual tone. The soldiers in the audience ate the tune up, while the bloke on stage with Dale would typically accept the assignment of Mr. Laramie, and desire to enter into matrimonial bliss with the delightful Texas charmer.

Her ticket was singing for the boys, but Dale was glad to take time out from entertaining the boys to have the boys entertain her. During her travels to various military bases, Dale often took the stage to perform her songs, but when the microphone was unplugged, the southern sensation didn't scurry away to the next base, but stayed and participated in activities. On one base tour Dale visited her native Texas, where she toured the Abilene Airbase, and gave the boys the ditty treatment. Prior to entertaining the crowd, Dale visited the installation's football team. They were in the midst of scrimmage, but when they saw the pretty songstress, the pigskin boys halted their practice and begged Dale to join them on the field. She ventured out on the field and tossed the pigskin with the chaps for a while, which gave the fellows a little feminine reprieve from their tackles and stiff-arms. Shortly after playing with the boys between the lines, Dale took to her natural stage and crooned a few songs for the Abilene airmen.

During the war, men pursued pin-ups who best expressed their ideal of the desirable female, and more than one southern gent adopted Dale as his primary pin-up queen. The singing cowgirl was often photographed in western wear, with a cowboy hat placed atop her curly head of hair. But the Texas charmer took some more traditional cheesecake stills, which showcased her Texas stilts in swimsuits and short skirts. However, it was dolled up as a rodeo pin-up that best suited the lovely Miss Evans. A number of her western-themed pin-ups showed her corralled in a pen, wearing outfits best suited for the set of western epics than cheesecake photo shoots — but the essence of cheesecake was there. Many photographers positioned Dale so that her legs were accentuated, typically by asking her to place one foot on a removed saddle, or prop a leg on a corral fence. Ever accommodating, Dale knew that the soldiers and sailors, those who hailed from her neck of the woods, would appreciate cheesecake of a leggy beauty dressed like the gals back home.

## ★ JINX FALKENBURG ★

During the 1940s, a person couldn't walk by a newsstand, or anywhere that dealt in the sale of magazines, without spotting the comely visage of Jinx Falkenburg. The streamlined brunette was America's top cover girl of the decade — her face graced nearly every periodical published in the nation. With a flawless countenance that seemed the ideal portrait for feminine beauty, Jinx's status as the premier face of modeling went unrivaled. Her beauty was a healthy beauty that overflowed with sporty pulchritude, for the Falkenburg lass was a physical fitness fanatic who participated in professional tennis matches. A fine athlete, Jinx kept her body picture-perfect by never neglecting the strain of exertion. But it was the Jinx facial profile that was plastered on one magazine cover after another. She owned a mane of long, lustrous brown hair and was often photographed with her trademark flowers tucked behind her ears. The flowers highlighted a visage that needed not aesthetic accompaniment, for Jinx alone, minus the perennials, was as pleasing a sight for the eyes as one could hope to encounter. As the ideal face of the 1940s, Miss Falkenburg was a surefire selection as a top pin-up girl.

Beauty is far more difficult to attain than sexiness, for beauty, as the cliché goes, is defined by the eye of the beholder, while sexiness is generally accepted due to the simplicity of crudeness that surrounds the term. Few are the cadre of celebrities whose beauty have been universally accepted, but of this select group, Jinx Falkenburg has been a member for decades. Women of the 1940s knew that Jinx exuded beauty — if they

*Jinx Falkenburg.*

needed reassurance, all they had to do was gather a cart full of magazines and count the number of covers with the Jinx stamp. When a woman is universally credited as being beautiful, other women desire to know the methods by which the beauty attained hers, and, for better use, how she retains her beauty. For if a beauty is born and not formed by outside influences, the tips she passes along are not the inside dope others can learn from, but the good fortune bestowed upon the ravishing dame from birth. Whether Jinx was gifted with the pulchritude touch from the cradle or not was trivial to her, for she was quick to offer the inside information on how to achieve that enchanting flush that graced her heavenly features. Her primary tip was sport. She felt that if women engaged themselves in sport, then they would possess that zesty glow that radiated from her every pore.

Athletics meant a great deal to the Falkenburg clan. Jinx played some professional tennis — she appeared in the tennis championship at Forest Hills. Her kid brother took it a step further and became a tennis phenom after the war, winning Wimbledon late in the 1940s. If Jinx wasn't found returning lobs on the tennis court, she was swatting shuttlecocks in badminton or displaying her dexterity on a ping-pong table. Exercise was the tip that Jinx gave girls to achieve their optimum beauty. Jinx felt that the continuous motion of sport was necessary for the body to retain its alluring properties. By athletic motion, age, which ravages the frame of every person, can be retarded by degrees through the health and buoyancy that physical play possesses. So Jinx urged girls across America to involve themselves in sport, no matter how simplistic the game. Championing table tennis during inclement weather days, Miss Falkenburg said, "Ping-pong is an excellent indoor exercise, and not at all a sissy game if you play it right."

Offering beauty tips is an essential part of being a cover girl, but when the war hit the United States, being a cover girl wasn't all that defined Jinx Falkenburg. Writers picked her brain regarding the essentials of beauty, but the ravishing La Falkenburg felt that her beauty could serve a higher purpose in time of war. As a cover girl, her beauty had established her as a celebrity and she used that status to build morale all over the nation. When the resolve of the American people had been shaken after the bombing of Pearl Harbor, Jinx did all a pretty girl could to help restore the iron constitution the American spirit possessed. Jinx was instrumental in the conception of the "Lips for Liberty" campaign in 1942. The campaign employed a little sensual persuasion to get folks to invest in war bonds, as the buyers of bonds received a kiss from a lovely lady who was engaged in the cause. A resounding success, Lips for Liberty procured a sizable amount of money for the war effort. A big hit in New York City, Jinx attended the rally there and a photograph of her kissing a sallow, bookish professor from Columbia University circulated the nation. A professor of philosophy, Irwin Edman, the lucky chap who planted the kiss on Jinx, forsake Plato and his call to transcend physical desire, and eagerly ushered his lips to meet the delicate mouth of America's number one cover girl. But no one in America could blame him for thumbing his nose at Plato.

Many celebrities hit the bond circuit early in the war and Jinx Falkenburg was one of them. She attended a rally at High Point, North Carolina, with acting stars John Payne and Jane Wyman, where the top war bond buyers could dine with the three celebrities before they entertained the masses. The sale of war bonds was a noble cause that many celebrities engaged in, but Jinx's scope of assisting her country went beyond the average limelight dweller. When she and film actress chum Evelyn Keyes heard that the tomato crop in California would spoil because too many workers had entered the armed forces, the two took action. Noted for their glamour and good looks, Jinx and Evelyn shelved the makeup and donned the wears of the working man. They went to San Fernando Valley and spent a day picking the produce from the vine. The War Manpower Commission had issued the plea for assistance that Jinx and Evelyn heard and after they finished their first day on the job, they went to the radios and used their name recognition to appeal for 500 more pickers. The prospect of plucking produce with two ravishing ladies certainly persuaded more than one gent to employ his hands in the art of tearing tomatoes from the vine.

What Jinx wanted to do beyond all other wartime pursuits was entertain the troops. She wasn't an established actress nor was she a vaudeville entertainer, but what Miss Falkenburg possessed in spades is what every red-blooded American male desired: pulchritude. So Jinx closeted her tomato-picking overalls and packed her grip with supplies that enhance her already otherworldly physical appeal, and went where the boys were. An instant hit on the USO circuit, Jinx did more than just stand on a stage and strike a pose for the boys — she joined them in their training. At Camp Hale, Colorado, Jinx ruck-marched for five miles with a group of troops. During their march, a jeep drove through their formation and La Falkenburg let out a sensual whistle, followed by the cat-call "Yoo-hoo, handsome!" All the marching soldiers around her were flushed, embarrassed that their female guest flirted with the passengers in the jeep. It wasn't the flirting that shocked the troops — it was who Jinx chose to "yoo-hoo" at — Brigadier General Rolfe, commander of Camp Hale. Later that night, Jinx introduced herself to General Rolfe and apologized for the incident on the march. The general felt the apology was unnecessary. Jinx said, "He was very nice about it — told me he would have like to have yoo-hooed back, but was afraid it wouldn't be good for discipline."

Not too long after her wolfish whistling incident, Jinx decided that she would travel to foreign countries to entertain troops. She lined up a USO gig in Mexico in 1943. The stunning cover girl toured military installations south of the border for a time and established herself as a serviceman's icon. With newfound fame, the boys wanted more and more of Jinx, so after her stateside return from the Mexican excursion, Miss Falkenburg landed a radio assignment, which enabled her to relay sporting news to the boys in service five times a week. When she went back out with the boys, Jinx kept her radio gig and often interviewed soldiers for her program. She did all she could for the fighting men. Jinx would visit wounded warriors in hospitals, like the infirmary at Farragut Naval Training Center, and lifted the spirits of men who fell in battle. Although women weren't allowed in battle, they managed to enter battle zones. Jinx, who saw more foreign land than most soldiers, went on USO tours in Mexico, Europe, and the CBI (China-Burma-India) Theater.

In 1944, Jinx led a troupe of entertainers that went to the CBI Theater to entertain troops. An exquisite beauty, Miss Falkenburg, with her long, wavy brown hair, was a fighting man's dream. Very few troops expected, especially in foreign lands, to be graced with the presence of America's most stunning cover girl, but Jinx went where the boys were and they were eternally grateful. Her troupe performed over 160 shows in the CBI Theater and had a brush with the enemy once, when, after completion of their show, a Japanese assault forced them to evacuate. Given her brazen regard to danger, the troops fell for Miss Falkenburg, who in turn fell for them. Before troops would enter into war zones, Jinx would give them a small lock of her hair for good luck. When America's top cover girl returned stateside, her once long, wavy mane of intoxicating brown hair had been shortened due to the petitions soldiers made for her charms made of tresses.

When the calendar flipped from 1944 to 1945, Jinx decided that she would visit the troops in the European Theater, since she graced the boys in the South Pacific with her presence the year prior. A much different experience in Europe, Jinx referred to the zone as the "Luxury Circuit" for USO entertainers. The surroundings, although afflicted with the damages of war, were far more ideal than the muggy, humid atmosphere of the CBI Theater. While in Europe, Jinx was able to meet up with her kid brother and even spent some time with her husband, Lieutenant Colonel Tex McCrary. About touring the European Theater, Jinx said, "Compared to China and Burma this trip is like a prewar vacation on the Riviera, even as bad as the conditions generally are in Italy. We were quartered in beautiful villas in cities such as Florence and Milan and often played in beautiful opera houses."

As alluring as the scenery was in Italy, there were obstacles Jinx and her troupe had to face. The European Theater was a ravaged arena and when entertainers ventured to areas in the theater, their belongings were subject to theft. Many thrifty individuals, looking to make a dishonest buck or five hundred, would rifle through a celebrity's luggage and pilfer anything that might fetch a price. Miss Falkenburg once left her belongings in her quarters during a show and when she returned, she found that all or her dresses had been absconded with. Jinx said, "If the souvenir hunters didn't get them the black market people did. Seems they can sell a dress for $500 over in Italy." But the absence of her dresses was just the beginning, for further inspection revealed that all of her lingerie had been swiped as well. With no undergarments to don, Jinx enlisted the aid of a corporal, hoping he could scrounge up some article of underclothes she could wear in a pinch. Miss Falkenburg said, "I sent a corporal zooming down to the supply department for some GI shorts. He came dashing back with a pair of drawers three times too big. But I wore them anyway."

The troops who weren't fortunate enough to be entertained by Jinx in person had to rely on cheesecake photos to soothe their fix for Falkenburg. There wasn't a short supply of pin-ups circulating that were adorned with the mesmerizing image of Jinx, for countless requests of Falkenburg cheesecake were made by fighting men from Tinian to Tunisia. Although Jinx traveled to war zones on a frequent basis, she found plenty time to pose for cheesecake stills the boys could pin-up on their barracks walls. Numerous poses of Falkenburg were captured by photographers, of which most showcased the beauty with her trademark flowers tucked behind her ears. Soldiers had photos of Jinx sunning by a pool in a bathing suit, or kneeled beside a shed imbibing water from a garden house. She donned the sarong for many shots and cheesecaked with the best of them, flashing some leg and cracking that Falkenburg smile that could warm the constitution of the coolest gent.

As beautiful as Jinx was on the outside, she may have been more beautiful within. During the war, Jinx had an open-door policy at her own home. Few were the nights that Jinx spent alone during the war, for she would always put up travelers in need of a place to stay, allowing soldiers and their gals a place to crash before they separated for the duration. Whenever family members would come to town, Jinx let them stay under her roof. Her brother, who served in the Air Corps, once visited with three cadet chums and Jinx let the fliers have her bedroom, while other visitors slept where they could. About putting up her brother and his battle buddies, Jinx said, "I gave them my bed and tripped over six people before I found the porch swing empty." A selfless, remarkable woman, Jinx Falkenburg sacrificed her comfort to see that others had comfort, if just for a moment. The idol of many fighting men for her actions, Jinx wore the identification bracelet of a flier throughout the war. Although she had given many troops locks of her hair as tokens of good luck, the bracelet given her by the flier had not the same effect. When she learned that the flier was shot down and killed in action, the noble cover girl, generous with her time, her lodging, and her affection, was desolate. But comfort could be found knowing that she brightened the lives of numerous soldiers, some who survived the fighting and those who passed.

## ★ RHONDA FLEMING ★

It has been rumored that Technicolor was adopted by the film industry for the sole purpose of showing the world just how lovely Rhonda Fleming and her flame-red hair were in person. Films were shot in black-and-white early in Miss Fleming's Hollywood experience, but when color was used on a large scale, filmgoers finally got to see Rhonda in all the shades of the color spectrum. The simple shades of the early age of cinema, when the brightest of yellows and sharpness of purples failed to be captured, did not do justice to the extraordinary beauty owned by the ravishing redhead. When Technicolor was introduced, the remarkable beauty who flirted with Robert Mitchum in *Out of the Past*, stunning in black and white, became one of cinema's most intoxicating gems. Films like *Slightly Scarlet*, where Rhonda played the working girl opposite her kleptomaniac sister Arlene Dahl, were written solely to cash in on Miss Fleming's Technicolor radiance.

Before Rhonda was filmed in Technicolor, the world was at war, and Miss Fleming was a young beauty of remarkable appeal looking to crash the gates of Hollywood. Her mother, Effie Graham — a beautiful former stage singer and entertainer — had given up her career to raise her family and tried to help her stunning teenage daughter reach Tinseltown. The bright lights of the film industry weren't far off, for Rhonda had been raised in Los Angeles. When the west coast girl developed into an alluring beauty with an enviable figure, photographs were sent to producers in order to land her an audition. In 1943, with the war well underway, the legendary producer David O. Selznick signed Miss Fleming to a film contract. When a new talent is contracted, publicity departments work

*Rhonda Fleming.* COURTESY OF MOVIEMARKET.COM

overtime in order to build the stock of the newest industry player. There was no better way to promote a new actress during the war than to push her towards the photographer's lens and have her pose for cheesecake stills.

One of the earliest Fleming photos that circulated the nation was war-themed. Rhonda was shown shopping, not wearing the typical pin-up attire of bathing suit and high heels but modest out-on-the-town dress. A quick way to build the stature of a new actress was newspaper promotion, and all Americans applauded celebrities who took care of their servicemen. The war-themed photo of Rhonda wasn't cheesecake at all but more of a publicity shot to help elevate her career. The picture showed Miss Fleming seated in a store, giving the foot care merchandise the once over. She wasn't out inspecting stilettos to place on her feet, but was hunting for foot powder to send in a care package to a gentleman she knew in the infantry. Not only did the photograph show folks that Rhonda was a new, and quite fetching commodity in Hollywood, but it also showcased her thoughtful, caring side, which went a long way during time of war.

In order to build up Miss Fleming's stature among the fighting men, her studio lined up a series of cheesecake stills to be taken. With a statuesque physique that seemed designed for pin-up pictures, Rhonda was a natural fit for cheesecake art. Desirable to an alarming degree, the ravishing redhead was photographed in bathing suits, revealing dresses, and hypnotic poses all for the sake of building morale in America's fighting forces. She may have been an unknown commodity to the many soldiers who owned her pin-ups, but at the height of the war, her star was just beginning to find its spot in the sky. A few minor roles came her way, but with the pin-up push, Rhonda scored a covetable role in an Alfred Hitchcock film — a resident of a mental asylum. An unnamed writer for the INS quipped that her character was a "pin-up girl for the psychopathic ward." She posed for many cheesecake stills, but a straitjacket oomph shot to promote the Hitchcock flick, would have made for an ill-advised pin-up.

Many folks are unaware of the strain placed upon the pin-up girl, who, whether rain or shine, heat or chill, must pose for the camera and pass off fetching. Writer Erskine Johnson once visited Rhonda at a photo shoot, which was shot specifically for the Fourth Air Force's paper *The Clipper*, to get a few quotes and enjoy the scenery no doubt. Johnson wasn't content with the location. He traveled out to Castle Rock, off the coast of Santa Monica, on a day where there was more than a little chill in the air. Posing for the cameras, wearing as little as possible, was Rhonda Fleming, the new Selznick starlet. The atmosphere seemed not to dissuade Miss Fleming from her assignment, as she struck one pose after another in conditions far less than ideal. The ocean was quite spendthrift with its spindrift that day, splashing the photographers and the scantily-clad model with icy water spray. Erskine Johnson found the conditions so uncompromising that he nicknamed Castle Rock "Pneumonia Rock." He lined up an interview with Rhonda the following day, and when he came down with a cold that night, he kept the interview but met Rhonda feeling quite under the weather. He was shocked at how chipper Rhonda was when she greeted him the next morning, writing, "Wearing only a nice smile and a backless, also practically frontless white bathing suit, Miss Fleming posed for the pictures in all that wind and ocean spray and feels fine today."

Many soldiers during the war hadn't seen a film that Rhonda starred in but adopted her as their favorite pin-up nonetheless. Before *The Spiral Staircase* — one of Rhonda's first major film roles — was ready for public viewing, she had been voted "Sea Nymph of the Pacific Fleet." The sailors who bestowed the titled upon the actress cared not that she was a newcomer to Hollywood, whose name had yet to become household, for they desired to give the honor to the most hypnotic beauty who posed for pin-ups, and they found her in Rhonda Fleming. Hitchcock's *Spellbound*, which came in 1944, gave Rhonda her big break, but many men in the armed forces hadn't viewed the mystery at the cinema: they were too busy to engage in idle pursuits. They had, at their disposal, pin-up pictures, many of which were printed for them in the publication *Yank*, which is how many of the fighting men were introduced to the radiant redhead. The soldiers, spellbound by Fleming's enchanting cheesecake stills, were eager to get home and watch the beautiful actress ply her craft on the screen. And when the boys came home, Rhonda wasn't quick to forget the honors the boys handed her.

When the war came to a close and the world could regain a sense of order, many people went about their regular, prewar lives. The actors and actresses in Hollywood returned to work, but Rhonda refused to let the war's end force her into complacency, where personal pursuits that build security for the individual and neglect duty to one's country, reign supreme. Rhonda never forgot the sacrifice made by the men in the fighting forces and continued to visit troops after the war had ended. During Christmas time, after the Japanese had been bombed and Hitler had been defeated, Rhonda kept entertaining troops. She traveled to Salt Lake City and brightened the day of wounded soldiers at Bushnell General Hospital. Severely wounded by battlefield injuries, the troops were glad that a lady like Rhonda, a beautiful young actress whose career was on the rise, was still showing her appreciation for the troops. Much has been written about Rhonda Fleming's unique beauty, such as a cheesecake photographer who claimed that her legs were "worth a 2,000 word essay." This leads one to wonder just how many words a person would have to employ in an essay, simply to do justice to Miss Fleming's sterling character.

## ★ AVA GARDNER ★

Ava Gardner was once bestowed with the misnomer of a nickname in "Angel," for the dark-haired woman was an extraordinary beauty, but fewer actresses in Hollywood history have such a poor reputation as La Gardner. A fixture in tabloids and Hollywood gossip columns before she was ever a star, Ava reached notoriety in America simply on beauty and a mindset that many folks in the film industry described as selfish. During the war, she sojourned into the world of nuptials twice: first with boyish Mickey Rooney and second with big band leader Artie Shaw — her sixteen-month union with Rooney outlasting her twelve month marriage to Shaw. It was written in more than one outlet that Gardner's high-profile marriages were simply a ploy by the North Carolina man-eater to build a name for herself in Hollywood. If it was a ruse for the sake of publicity, it worked. Gardner, who did little by way of acting in Hollywood during the war years, became a star shortly after the fighting with her star-making turn in the crime/thriller *The Killers*. Typically listed in many Top 100 lists of Hollywood beauties, Ava Gardner was a knockout, with a beauty fit for an angel but a temperament ill-suited for a heavenly cherub.

The common story regarding how Ava was discovered by Hollywood concerns her relative's photography studio. When a talent scout walked past the studio and spotted a picture of Ava in the front window, he was so enamored with her beauty that he sought out the cutie and signed her to a film contract, despite her inexperience as an actress. Gardner went west to pursue a career in the field of acting, supported solely on her physical appeal. The raven-haired stunner was quick to find work but it was a vocation that, at first, failed to garner Ava any form of notoriety. The first film she appeared in was produced just prior to America's involvement in the war, but Ava had a limited role. Throughout the war effort, Ava had similar employments in the film industry — no speaking lines, just window-dressing roles as pretty dames in the background. Such an existence was ill-fit for a heavenly beauty such as Ava, so she sought to force the fellows in the film industry to take notice of her.

Ava Gardner's physical attributes were obvious, but her skill as an actress had yet to be tested. When she wasn't standing in the background, looking sharp with nothing to say, Ava was placed before a photographer's lens. The pin-up explosion hit at just the right time for Gardner, who was desperate for attention in Hollywood. When cheesecake stills of the ravishing beauty were circulated, people began to take notice of

*Ava Gardner.* COURTESY OF MOVIEMARKET.COM

Ava. However, the pin-up photos got the ball rolling, so to speak, but the tabloids accelerated the speed. At the time of the war, boyish Mickey Rooney was a film star with the Andy Hardy series of films securing his star status. With Rooney at the height of his career, he and Gardner began a wartime romance that the papers across the country kept strict tabs on. Rooney was the box office sensation, cupiding with some sexy industry newcomer few people knew of. Folks were quick to label Ava — they placed a negative light on the North Carolina cutie — and claimed she was after Mickey simply to get her name in the papers. More than one newspaper scribe ascertained that Ava and Mickey's marriage collapsed at the one year mark because of Ava's ambition for a career in pictures.

While Ava's marriage was on the rocks, her career — or more aptly put, her name — was beginning to rise. She made for a delicious pin-up with her terrific figure and a fresh and bold beauty. By 1943, although she had yet to gain even a modest role in film, men in the military were pinning up her photographs beside established stars like Grable and Landis. In the fall of that year, sailors in the Mediterranean Theater dubbed Ava their "Admiralle," a phonetic pun on a military rank. Glad that the boys were taking notice, and saluting her good looks, the stunning brunette decided to give the Navy boys a proper pulchritudinous how-do-you-do with a special pin-up just for the sailors. Gardner donned the traditional sailor's uniform, slid her curves under the dress of Uncle Sam's watery forces, but added a slight pin-up alteration. She discarded the Navy slacks, shunting the pants aside for the chance to exhibition her legs. Gone were the leg-covering trousers and in their place were substituted a little white miniskirt. The pin-up, as one could imagine, was a favorite among Navy personnel and could be found in the hull of numerous ships.

Although Ava did all she could to make certain her name reached the papers, her studio helped in that regard as well. Pin-up photographs weren't a restricted commodity, resigned for men in the fighting forces alone, but had public appeal and were often found displayed in city newspapers. In order to thrust Ava in the spotlight, her studio handed out cheesecake stills of their hot commodity for publication. A person could flip through the daily ink, peruse the business section, check the stocks, glance over the box scores in the sports pages, and take in a bit of eye candy with a well-positioned pin-up. Photographs of Ava were distributed for mass production in newspapers, which displayed the stunning future star actress in seductive situations. A bikini-clad Gardner was showcased in the *Wisconsin State Journal* with a caption under her pin-up that read, "Any beach at all is improved in appearance when film actress Ava Gardner steps on it." Another mass produced cheesecake still of Ava showed her kneeled on a beach, wearing a two-piece swimming suit described as a "Victory Bikini," holding two dolls dressed as a soldier and sailor.

When the war was in full-swing, stardom was knocking down Ava's door. Servicemen adored her pin-up pictures and studio executives found that the gents in service were eager to see their brunette knockout act on the screen. Although she received as much negative press as she did positive during the war, Ava was an up-and-coming star in the film industry. She did all that she could to secure her star. Near the close of the war, with first husband Mickey Rooney in the military, Ava remarried, accepting the plea for matrimony from big band leader Artie Shaw. There may have been a lull in publicity for Ava after her divorce from Rooney, but it picked up again when she was courting Shaw shortly after her split from Mickey. But the marriage to Shaw would be short-lived as well, and when she finally garnered her star-making role, she was a young woman of exceptional beauty twice divorced. Ava Gardner may have had a poor reputation as an actress with an uncontrollable temper, a revolving door of husbands and an inclination to vices ranging from alcohol to married men, but she was also an elite pin-up who used her physical talents to soothe the homesickness of American men in the service.

## ★ PAULETTE GODDARD ★

The lucky actress is able to land a role that sets her apart, endears her to audiences, and firmly establishes her stardom for future generations. Of all the classic roles for women in film history, Paulette was a finalist for perhaps the most legendary film role for a female in movie history. Meant for one woman, a special talent, the portrayal of Scarlett O'Hara in the epic *Gone With the Wind* required an actress of unrivaled grace, appeal, and theatrical aptitude. Paulette possessed these qualities, but at the time of the rehearsals she was a relative unknown in Hollywood. Her face and figure glistened in the background but she rarely received a close-up. The role that essentially made the career of Vivien Leigh was nearly assigned to Miss Goddard, whose husband at the time — Charlie Chaplin — held more than a little sway in the industry. But the untried beauty was passed on in favor of Leigh and now Vivien, not Paulette, is remembered for giving filmdom its most talked about female performance.

Before the war years, and well before *Gone With the Wind* was in the midst of production, Paulette ventured out to Hollywood to achieve stardom as a film actress. The road to stardom proved a rocky one, for Miss

Goddard was not an overnight sensation who grasped the imagination of the nation shortly after her arrival in Tinseltown, but toiled as a background player for years. Major roles were not extended to Paulette in her first year in Hollywood, or her fourth or fifth: she had to wait and hone her craft. She received an added boost when she married the legendary Charlie Chaplin, for the famous comedian saw to it that his beautiful bride landed a role here and there. After she was passed over for the role of Scarlett O'Hara, good fortune finally found Paulette, who established herself prior to the war in the Bob Hope vehicle *The Cat and the Canary*. Although not of the caliber of the Gable/Leigh epic, Goddard's star was secured with her quality turn opposite the wildly popular Hope. The duo would team up again the following year with the even more successful horror/comedy *The Ghost Breakers*, as the lovely La Goddard found her niche in the comedy genre.

When America entered the war effort after Pearl Harbor was bombed, Paulette and her costar entered the USO scene, which secured Hope's status as one of America's leading actors of the war years. Bob Hope has, over the years, done far more than any Hollywood icon in the business of troop entertainment, but during World War II, Paulette was right there with him — she did not shy away from any assignment. With her marriage to Chaplin over, Paulette had plenty time to devote to the war effort. Between acting assignments, she would attend war-bond rallies and visit the troops at various installations and canteens. So popular was Paulette among the GIs that Royal Crown Cola used her as a spokeswoman during the war. As one of the first star pin-ups, the soft drink company plastered advertisements in newspapers across the nation, which displayed the lovely Miss Goddard seated at a table with servicemen, tilting back a glass of Royal Crown Cola with the boys. One Royal Crown advertisement displayed Paulette singing to a table full of GIs, with a caption under the photograph that read, "Paulette Goddard proves why she's a popular pin-up girl as she sings a catchy number."

Paulette may have lent her image to advertisements, but she did more for the war effort than just strike a pose. Royal Crown Cola used her status as a top-notch pin-up girl to pass along their beverage, but to look good in bathing suits, which Miss Goddard excelled at, was a simpler task than other endeavors she was engaged in. To travel the country and assist in the sale of war bonds and build morale in American fighting forces, was an assignment of greater purpose. She embraced the role of morale-builder and accepted invitations to entertain crowds where she would serve as master of ceremonies at various war-themed events. She toured Delaware County, Pennsylvania, in 1942 and attended the "Salute

Our Heroes" dinner held at the Masonic Temple. Miss Goddard then visited the nearby Sun Shipbuilding and Dry Dock Company, where she praised the workers for their patriotism because they devoted a portion of their salaries to the war effort. At the shipbuilding plant, Paulette handed each worker a miniature American flag as a token of her appreciation for their selfless actions.

*Paulette Goddard.* COURTESY OF MOVIEMARKET.COM

While Paulette applauded the American people for their selflessness, the papers applauded Paulette for various reasons, uppermost her devotion to her country. Prior to the war, Paulette had achieved star status. She put that newfound status to good use by assisting in the war effort. Although she traveled the nation between acting assignments, hosted war-bond rallies, and shook the hands of thousands of Americans at events, her role as a pin-up girl crept its way to the forefront. An ideal beauty with a classy frame, Paulette was one of America's most popular pin-up girls. The *Oakland Tribune* ran an article early in the war effort, surrendering to aesthetic whimsy, which put forth the question as to which Hollywood pin-up had the best figure, Paulette or the shapely blonde Carole Landis. In much the fashion of a prizefighting boxing match, where one pugilist's weight and measurements are compared to his rival, the *Oakland Tribune* compared Goddard and Landis. Listed in the paper were every measurement of the stunning beauties, from the size of their ankles and necks to the width of their waists and busts. The editor simply put forth the question and supplied the statistics for the benefit of an argument.

The physical appeal of Paulette Goddard was obvious — the numerous pin-up pictures taken of her can attest to that — but her general appeal among the American populace may have exceeded her cheesecake allure. She headlined war-bond rallies across the nation, where she netted hundreds of thousands of dollars at such locales as Baker Park in Frederick, Maryland, and the aforementioned Masonic Temple in Delaware County, Pennsylvania. Ever the elegant entertainer, Paulette was a hit on the war-bond circuit among men and women alike. Extremely likable with a down-to-earth charm, Miss Goddard was an ideal seller of war bonds thanks to her far-reaching appeal. About Paulette, writer Rosalind Shaffer said, "A pixie-like lack of inhibitions is the essence of her charm. She meets each person on whatever level they set." It was her agreeable nature that endeared her to Americans during the war effort, for she played not the role of a wartime trumpeter but was simply herself.

With the war in full swing, the typical Hollywood lavish epic seemed out of place for the ravaged areas of the world. Paulette understood this and requested roles that better showcased the modern struggle of a world at war. No longer did audiences accept large-budget epics with grand balls, elegant dresses, and highlife on parade — they craved something more real, easier to grasp. Filmmaking may be an escape from reality, but it also serves as a mirror for society that must, when done right, showcase the human condition including blemishes as well as the desirable. Newer roles for women, unlike those ever offered before, came to actresses during the war. Surrendered were the corsets and sun umbrellas, the white gloves and leisure, and in their place were substituted roles that better represented war torn America. Erskine Johnson wrote about Paulette's change in roles, when he penned, "Goddard deserted milk and orchids recently to play a blood-spattered army nurse on Bataan." Actresses were able, for a change, to showcase their range as thespians and no longer served as window-dressing, where their figures and wardrobe were applauded more than their work.

Paulette playacted throughout the war, but she also took reprieve from the world of fantasy, where lies the acting profession, and embarked on a tour that many celebrities would cringe at the thought of. In 1944, she told her studio that she had made plans to tour the CBI (China-Burma-India) Theater in order to entertain the troops who had been relocated overseas. Her role as an Army nurse inspired her to visit the regions that she visited in fantasy, and her devotion to Uncle Sam's fighting forces spurred her to undertake such an endeavor. Paulette planned a seven-week tour of the CBI Theater with the intent of putting on shows for the boys. Before she left, she requested a fashion designer to create an eye-pleasing ensemble that would set the boys to whistle. She said, "I asked them to concentrate on making the clothes pleasing to soldiers, lightweight and wrinkle-proof." Miss Goddard desired light, wrinkle-proof clothing because, like the troops, she would tote a duffel bag; the closets, with a pole to hang suits and dresses upon, were a luxury that hardly existed on the military circuit. As for pleasing the soldiers with her attire, the troops certainly would have accepted the arrival of Paulette with or without the accompaniment of radiant raiment.

During her seven-week tour of the CBI Theater, Paulette traveled 20,000 miles and entertained soldiers at numerous encampments. A hit in China, even among the Chinese populace, she was given the nickname "Precious Cargo" by the Chinese press. While she visited China, Paulette entertained General Stilwell and his outfit, and then was escorted to Chennault's headquarters. After her tour, she returned stateside and went back to work in the film industry, where she regaled her fellow celluloid players with stories of her travels in the Far East. Living among the soldiers, she understood the sacrifice they made and felt a deep, profound respect for the men in uniform and the lovers they had left behind. Since she was divorced from Charlie Chaplin at the time, Paulette was fortunate enough to have not been separated by the war, but she grasped the strain it placed on couples. When her dear friend Jinx Falkenburg,

America's top cover girl, informed her that her husband was due home after a lengthy stay in Europe with the Armed Forces, Paulette lent the couple her rural guest house so they could celebrate his return in a calm, serene setting.

Paulette Goddard endeared herself to the fighting forces by entertaining them at bases and journeying overseas to put on shows for them in hazardous areas. A sensational performer, who was dubbed "The Streamlined Venus," Paulette was one of the most popular acts on the USO circuit. Adept at comedic timing, thanks to her work with former husband Chaplin and constant costar Bob Hope, Miss Goddard's shows combined playful acts with pulchritude. She found that acting out skits came more natural to her than posing for cheesecake pictures. Miss Goddard may have possessed the ideal image of a pin-up girl, with her pleasing features and ping-girl fuselage, but she worked harder at striking a pose for the cheesecake photographers than she did acting. Paulette said, "When there are pictures to be taken, I try to do it as naturally as possible. Posing can wear you out. If you aren't careful, you get a false smile. You have to think twice to look natural." Natural looking or not, the many soldiers who tacked up her cheesecake stills across the world were thankful for her toil in front of the camera.

## ★ BETTY GRABLE ★

Betty Grable, widely regarded as the pin-up girl nonpareil, became the highest earning star in Hollywood after the war, based almost exclusively on her status as the crowning Miss Cheesecake. A very down-to-earth woman, Betty never viewed herself as a gifted actress. On more than one occasion, Miss Grable would gesture to her legs, and claim that her gams were the reason behind her stardom. As modest as a beauty could be, Betty did not use the war to elevate her status in Hollywood; the desire for pleasing images, of which Betty's photographed figure certainly fit into, catapulted her into the ranks of the Hollywood elite. She may have felt that she couldn't act with the Bette Davises of the world, for her modesty kept her grounded, but she possessed talent in areas that weren't part of her physical assembly. Men adored her pin-up pictures — they tacked them to walls all across the world — but when the fad fell out of favor after the war, when Betty became a big-time earner, she relied on her skill as an actress, which, coupled with her stunning figure, kept the attention of audiences. Miss Grable's legs may have set her apart from other actresses, but she had the acting skill to boot.

Before the war, Betty Grable had been a Hollywood player for slightly over a decade — she toiled in meager roles in less than stellar films. Taken to Hollywood at a tender age, Betty began work in the film industry — on the sly, for her proper age was withheld — at a time when most girls her age were engaged in matriculation. Like most ingénues in Tinseltown, the pretty blonde began her career as a background player but worked her way up the ladder and netted speaking assignments. In the mid-1930s, Betty seemed through with roles that had credits like "first stewardess" and "girl on couch," and began to land supporting gigs. She became a fixture in lighthearted young romantic comedies, often set at college dormitories, starring in fluff like *College Swing* and *Pigskin Parade*. In 1939, her legs were already highly regarded commodities in Hollywood, and she landed a role in the aptly titled *Million Dollar Legs*. Her pins were lauded well before the soldiers pinned up her cheesecake photos at their bases and encampments, and, later in life, her studio even insured her legs with Lloyds of London for one million dollars. For most folks, legs were meant for walking, but to Betty, they were her meal ticket — twin pins that Hollywood felt necessary to protect with an insurance policy.

In the late 1930s, Betty married former child star Jackie Coogan and the two enjoyed success at the end of the decade, but their marriage fell apart just before America's involvement in the war. Her romance with Coogan introduced her to the Hollywood gossip columns, where truth is abandoned for the more juicy tidbits of fictional whimsy writers are apt to concoct. Although her name often swirled on the rumor mill, Betty never did sweeten to the gossip columns. When America entered the war after the bombing at Pearl Harbor, Betty posed for a few pin-up pictures and became a smash hit among servicemen. The pin-up craze would elevate Betty's status in Hollywood, and with the rise in status came the rise in printed exposure. The gossip columns zeroed in on Miss Grable again, as tabloid writers wondered who the divorcee was hand-in-handing with. More perturbed than disgusted by the tabloids, Betty once accepted a guest writing role for columnist Harrison Carroll in which she claimed that she was "suffering from rumor-tism" on account of the excessive publicity in the gossip columns. Stardom, as Betty was quick to learn, had its advantages but perhaps far more disadvantages.

Shortly after America rushed into the war effort, Betty became a symbol for the fighting forces. While many Hollywood stars left the studios to participate in the war bond circuit, Betty set aside the scripts for the wardrobe shuffle of a model. One bathing suit after another was donned by the blonde torpedo, who struck a seductive pose for the cameras to be distributed, in bulk, to the gents in Uncle Sam's armed forces. Although Miss Grable had been exposed to the lifestyle of a celebrity before the war, the public presentation of her swimsuit-clad body expounded upon her celebrity status and made her an idol. She became, seemingly overnight, a pop culture icon. The fellows in the service were the folks most responsible for her rise in popularity, for they appreciated her cheesecake stills. Betty posed because the purpose of building morale among the armed forces was uppermost in her mind. In the spring of 1942, Betty claimed that she received 14,400 fan mail letters a month, of which ninety-one percent came from the pens of servicemen.

By May of 1942, Betty Grable was widely regarded as America's top pin-up girl. She managed her time well, between films, visiting the troops at camps and canteens, and posing for cheesecake stills. Her title as top pin-up girl would be challenged throughout the war, since many starlets saw the effect posing for cheesecake photos had on Betty's burgeoning career. Grable had acted well before the war, but by dolling herself up and sporting the latest nautical fashions, stardom came her way, and other ambitious young women, eager for the fame Betty netted for herself, followed her lead. But in May of 1942, Betty's status as premier pin-up was all but firmly secure. Dee Lowrance wrote, "Betty Grable is fast becoming known around Hollywood as the Pin-up Girl — the star with the most pictures pinned up in the barracks." When other female thespians saw the impact of an act as simple as standing on your tiptoes in a bathing suit had on Betty's career, they went for high heels and bathing numbers but quick. It didn't take long before Grable's corner on the market dwindled and soldiers used their tacks and push pins to display other cuties.

When the pin-up fad hit full swing, Betty's star power was at its height. Soldiers by the truckloads had leggy pin-ups of La Grable tucked in their grips. They waited for orders to their duty assignments, where a proper place to stick a tack through the uppermost point in Betty's cheesecake pictures was on their mind. The majority of Betty's pin-ups centered their attention on her streamlined legs. Asked to slide into bathing suits by photographers, the gents behind the camera positioned Betty in poses that best displayed her legs. Often found in high heels, which gave the legs a few added inches, Betty would flaunt her stellar stilts for the enjoyment of servicemen. Former costar Jack Oakie said, "Having worked with Betty Grable, I know that words can't describe her figure." Betty, like all pin-ups, knew that a streamlined physique was instrumental in the physical arsenal of a pin-up girl, but legs, at least at the outset of the war, were the main focus, and with her enviable pair of pins, Betty knew she would be asked to pose time and again. Many scribes employed plenty ink describing how Betty cared for her legs, but she claimed that their inside dope was non-sense. Miss Grable said, "They used to run long paragraphs about the care I gave my legs. The way I exercised them, the creams I slathered on them, and so on and so forth until I was ready to scream. Actually, I've never done anything about my legs, except use them — for walking and dancing."

*Betty Grable.*

Employment as a pin-up girl gave actresses more exposure than costar-ring in a film. Hundreds of thousands of pin-ups circulated around the globe during the war, which showcased lovely lasses in bathing suits, miniskirts, and other ensembles that gave the boys the come-hither sign. Betty wore two-piece bathing suits, modified sailor uniforms, and form-fitting one-piece numbers for her numerous cheesecake photo shoots. The fellows liked to gander at a gal in her swimming garb, and Miss Grable gladly slid into a bevy of bathing suits to build morale. Betty, eager to assist in the war effort in any capacity, used her figure as a symbol of Americana that troops used as inspiration. A pin-up girl and war bond promoter, Betty did what she could to help America and the allies secure victory, even if all the posing added up to a lot of time peeling and putting on. About her many cheesecake photo shoots, Miss Grable said, "I'd like to have a penny for every one-piece number I've slipped on and off. It would add up to a sum that would buy a very big war bond."

Betty took time out from her schedule posing for pin-up pictures to attend a few war-bond rallies. In the late summer of 1943, Betty partici-pated in the Long Beach war-bond rally with big band leaders Freddie Martin and future husband Harry James. Residents of Long Beach came out to see Betty, listen to some tunes, and then watch an amateur baseball game put on by the war-bond players. The bands of James and Martin went head-to-head in a game of hardball to decide big band bragging rights. After the nine innings were played, an auction was held where numerous items were sold, with the funds going to the war effort. Betty threw in a few items of her own to be auctioned off, including stockings and garters. The big ticket item to be auctioned was the chance to sponsor a Liberty ship launching with Betty.

Selling war bonds and posing for pin-up pictures was a solid way to gain some notoriety for Hollywood ladies during the war, and studios used their actresses rising popularity as cheesecake models to promote their latest pictures. Movie studios knew that male audiences wanted to see their pin-up players in motion since they fawned over their motion-less images, so the studioes took ads out in papers to give the guys what they craved. If the rising production of cheesecake photos wasn't proof enough that fellows wanted to see pin-up girls in motion pictures, the onslaught of fan mail, which came from the servicemen begging studios to place their prime pin-ups in films, was certainly more than enough proof. So studios promoted their newest films using the pin-up status of their actresses as a main drawing card. For Betty's picture *Coney Island*, an advertisement in the paper read, "When it comes to shaking her shoulders (or her legs, or most anything at all) there is only one girl in all Hollywood that can do everything just right! And that, mister, is the gal with those gorgeous gams, Betty Grable!"

Promotion has always been a central ingredient to the rise of thespians in Hollywood, whether it be studio-funded or the typical, more modern version of lewd self-promotion. An actor or actress must have a certain level of arrogance — an ability to sell the self — for to subdue that pivotal component of self-promotion is to hinder oneself in an occupation where image is everything. There have been entertainers capable of stifling their arrogance in order to come off more modest, and those actors have often endeared themselves to audiences over the years. For whatever reason, in-fighting and ruthless behavior sells in Hollywood, where scribes detail fights between celebrities, clawing and biting, accosting and bullying their way to a certain role. But friendships are built in Tinseltown, like other towns in the world, and women, even stunning figures in the cutthroat profession of show business, can assist one another in the field of promotion. After Betty filmed the classic noir *I Wake Up Screaming* with the shapely Carole Landis, gossip columnists fabricated a tale that the two ladies were in the midst of a feud, but nothing could have been further from the truth. The two stunning pin-ups became fast friends during filming and after the movie had finished production, they each went out on military base tours. Betty and Carole showed remarkable respect for one another, as Dee Lowrance detailed in an article she wrote, which claimed, "Carole came back from her camp tours telling studio officials that all the boys love Betty and that she is their favorite pin-up girl. Betty returned from a recent trip through the south with the report that the boys wanted to see Carole more than any other actress in Hollywood."

Although Betty was a war-bond fixture, there were bonds that alluded to Betty and used her star status even when she wasn't there. With her busy schedule, working in films and posing for cheesecake pictures, Betty couldn't be at all the places that desired her presence, but when able, she made certain that war bond buyers could catch a glimpse of her nonetheless. At a war-bond rally in Lumberton, North Carolina, Betty wasn't the rally's headliner nor was she amongst the persons engaged in the entertainment, but folks were lured to the showing of the film *Prelude to War* with a little Betty Grable appetizer. All the patrons who viewed the film and later bought a war bond were given a signed eight-by-ten photograph of La Grable. Granted, the men and women of Lumberton were unable to see the blonde bomber in the flesh, but they were nevertheless given a sampling of Grable for their assistance in the war effort.

Betty liked to reward war bond purchasers with gifts, ranging from autographed photos to her own stockings, but the giver was also lavished with gifts herself. Many soldiers, who fought overseas, would often latch on to some souvenir and mail them to folks back home. Typically, soldiers would send packages to family members, lifting something uncommon from a battlefield to ship back home to little brother or sister, mother or father. But there were other fighting men who sent items home to women they never met — women they gazed upon for hours but never spoke a single word to: pin-up girls. Anne Jeffreys once received a pair of cobra skins from a soldier in the Pacific Theater, which she turned into a bra. Betty didn't sew her own serpent skin brassieres, but she received something a tad more useful from the fellows in the fighting forces. When it was learned that Betty and husband Harry James were expecting a child, the soldiers showed their appreciation for their favorite pin-up girl by sending her things that her child could use. A writer employed by the Central Press penned, "Betty Grable's baby has been receiving bootees, lockets and all kinds of clothing from boys overseas."

At the time Betty was expecting her first child with James, she was filming the motion picture *Pin-Up Girl*. It took little ingenuity to cast Betty in the lead role, but her pregnancy proved to be a distraction and led to a rushed production. The film was a salute to Betty for her wartime role as the ideal symbol of American femininity. Betty showcased her range as an entertainer in *Pin-Up Girl*, singing tunes and dancing to a few songs, while also doing her best in the few dramatic bits in the lighthearted spectacle. But not all her films during the war were a tribute to her status as America's favorite slice of cheesecake. Not every role calls for legs, and Betty, who accepted a role in a period-piece drama, was dressed in flowing gowns with floor-reaching skirts that hid her legs like a tarp covers the infield during a rain delay. Writer John Todd bemoaned, "Putting a bustle on Betty Grable is Hollywood's greatest sacrifice of art to historical accuracy."

Betty Grable's status as a pin-up girl allowed her to make a vehicle written specifically for her role as a cheesecake model. As a pin-up girl, Betty's career skyrocketed and her fame reached heights it never would have had she not taken to the art of cheesecake photography. There have been, over the years — especially during the height of the craze — critics of pin-up girls who fail to see their value and worth. Many critics claimed that returned soldiers would be too obsessed with the image of female perfection found in the form of pin-up girls, that they would refuse to start families with the normal girls they knew back home, wanting only that ideal of form and would boldly refuse those of inferior stock. Such wasn't the case — at least not commonly. There was a tale of Betty Grable ruining one soldier's marriage on account of the grunt's obsession with Betty's pin-up pictures. A private by the name of Webster filed for divorce from his wife because she didn't possess the traits of La Grable. Webster's wife testified that he constantly reminded her of three things, which led to their separation: (1) She didn't look like Betty Grable. (2) Her eyes weren't like Betty Grable's. (3) Her hair wasn't blonde like Betty Grable's.

Although she proved to be an absentee home wrecker, Betty's influence on the men in the fighting forces was not one disruptive but one constructive. By posing for pin-up pictures, Betty built a symbol of wonderment that fighting men could use as inspiration to defeat an evil that gripped the world in a fierce stranglehold. She possessed an ideal figure indeed, one that any woman would have been proud to own, but her image was not one that warped minds, forced them to reject reality, but was used for the purpose of symbolism. Soldiers knew they had little chance of returning from war and falling into the arms of Miss Grable, but they used her image as a symbol of American womanhood, which kept them fighting. For to lose the war, to fall to the enemy, would be to subject purity to the clutches of monsters. As a writer for the *Oakland Tribune* aptly put it, "Miss Grable has become a distinctive, streamlined symbol of our times." And national symbols, those held dear by the multitude, are worth fighting for. The men fought not for Betty Grable, but for what Betty Grable stood for, and by standing for something cherished in the hearts of all fighting men, Miss Grable's influence was one profound.

## ★ JANE GREER ★

To some, it would seem a very difficult task to reinvent oneself, but Miss Greer did exactly that at the end of the war. A ravishing brunette bombshell, Greer called the nation's capital home before her trek to Tinseltown during the war years. Although Howard Hughes receives credit for her discovery, the lithesome lady was a star singer on the Washington night club circuit before Hughes spotted her. As a songbird, Greer crooned under her full name, Betty Jane Greer, which was the handle she packaged up and took with her to Hollywood after she signed a contract with Hughes. However, after some struggles in the film industry, and more publicized struggles in her personal life, Greer decided to abandon her origins in Hollywood and pursue a life on her own terms. She had been a puppet to Hughes and an object of lust for her husband Rudy

Vallee — the famous big band leader — but it was a toxic existence that left her unfulfilled and mentally shaken. She decided to alter her course; she dropped the Betty from her name, left both Vallee and Hughes, and embarked on a career in Hollywood.

When the discoveries of Howard Hughes are mentioned, buxom brunette Jane Russell's name is easily recalled, but Miss Greer was no less an apple to the eccentric millionaire's eye. As a nightclub singer in Washington, D.C., Greer received plenty publicity. In 1942, before Howard Hughes had claimed her many talents as his personal property, Greer was named the "Nation's Capital Glamour Girl of 1942." The night club riffraff found Greer quite easy on the eyes, and with the title of D.C.'s top pulchritude princess of 1942, more folks were introduced to her. However, it was a photo shoot for *Time* magazine that enabled Hughes to size up the capital cutie. With national exposure, the talent scouts of Hollywood, always eager to locate the next classic beauty, took notice of Greer, and Howard Hughes offered her the pen she used to place her name under contract. But Howard Hughes wasn't the only person who was hypnotized by Greer's intoxicating cover shoot for the publication; Rudy Vallee also found her image to his liking.

Howard Hughes devoted most of his time to the war effort, which didn't bode well for the aspiring young actress. Essentially in career limbo, since Hughes was engaged in pursuits of aviation, Greer hooked up with Vallee who wanted her to travel with him and entertain soldiers at military camps. The two hit it off and were soon married. An error in judgment on Greer's part, she accepted the hand of a man who the papers referred to as "The Vagabond Lover." With a roguish outlook on matrimony, Vallee made for a less than ideal husband. The marriage lasted just over a year, and, during the time of their sojourn into the arena of nuptials, the couple were constant tabloid fodder. Gossip columns seemed to run articles on a weekly basis that detailed the marital friction of the band leader and his trophy bride. Greer finally filed for divorce; she claimed that Vallee was impossible to live with. The duo had constant verbal altercations and Greer claimed that Rudy enjoyed belittling her and, above all, correcting her grammar, which was a favorite pastime of the band leader — he would call radio stations whenever he heard an announcer employ poor English. About their constant feuds, Greer said, "We separated and reconciled so many times I lost track. The reconciliations were always nice — for about a week."

As a night club singer, Jane was not unaccustomed to low whistles from crowds. With a beauty possessed by magical ingredients, Greer's eyes had a thaumaturgical quality that aroused admiration in the hearts of many admirers. Hughes was enchanted by her beauty, and Vallee — whose nick-name aptly suited his tastes — was also enthralled with her feminine charms, which made him, for a moment, reconsider his stance as a vagabond lover. She was a lamb on a stage with wolves comprising her audience. The arena was the same, whether she was in Hollywood or crooning in the smoky D.C. night spots. The wolves howled with as much gusto in one location

*Jane Greer.* COURTESY OF MOVIEMARKET.COM

as they did in the other, but Jane had the inside dope on the wolf pack and wasn't ignorant to the mindset of the modern day lothario. She understood the wolfish demeanor of society gents and liked to contrast the wolves of Washington to the wolves of Hollywood. She said, "Those bureaucrats in Washington can howl louder and longer than any Hollywood wolf. Their technique is better, too. Hollywood wolves aren't wolves at all — they just think they are because it is supposed to be fashionable."

Whistles were issued through the lips of many men on account of the beauty and contours of the lovely Jane Greer, but her beauty was viewed mostly in still life. Given that she was a player under contract to Howard Hughes, who was too engrossed in war issues to devote time to his motion picture pursuits, Greer was viewed mostly in photographic captures. Soldiers acquired her pin-ups as their whistles were issued due to how well she looked in a bathing suit, rather than how her hips swayed while she walked in film. She had been in Hollywood for over a year, under contract to Hughes, but hadn't even taken a screen test. Many of her friends pressured her to take Hughes to court so she could be released from his contract and thus able to work, but Jane decided to decline their advice and abandon the notion of a court hearing, instead she opted for a face-to-face chat with Hughes. The talk proved beneficial — Hughes allowed Greer to seek work elsewhere and she quickly landed on with RKO Pictures.

Now that Greer was out from under Hughes's umbrella and had severed the ties of matrimony to Vallee, she was able to chart a course to her own liking. She had posed for numerous pin-ups under the name of Betty Jane Greer, but she chose to discard her first name and work under the handle of Jane Greer. The chaps who delighted in eyeing her pin-up pictures, soaking in the aesthetic images of Jane resting on a surf board in a red and white bikini, or staring enticingly at the camera before a dip in the pool, now could view her in motion. When she joined the ranks of RKO Pictures, she had a design for her career. Gossip column readers knew all about her volatile love life with Vallee, and the brunette stunner wanted roles that placed her in more of an independent light. She had one simple demand for the heads at RKO: all the bad girl roles. She said, "I'm concentrating on getting all the nasty parts RKO has to offer." She would eventually become a star opposite Robert Mitchum in the noir classic *Out of the Past*, playing, what else, a dastardly dame.

# ★ ANNE GWYNNE ★

If you cornered a handful of baseball historians and asked them who the greatest ballplayer in baseball history is, you would probably get differing answers. One might claim Babe Ruth to be the tops, while other experts might say Ted Williams, Ty Cobb, Mays, Mantle, Walter Johnson, or Hank Aaron. The fact of the matter is that there isn't a definitive answer, much like the question of America's top pin-up girl. Although Betty Grable made the film *Pin-Up Girl*, starring as the title character, her status as the nation's top pin-up wasn't firmly established. Grable had plenty competition. Anne Gwynne, although not as popular at the box office as Betty, was nevertheless a celebrated pin-up girl. The star pin-ups posed before the cameras, wearing racy threads, but those cameras were operated by professional image capturers who snapped photographs for distribution to thousands of lads. Anne Gwynne, who also posed for the pros, took pin-up artistry and made it personal, posing for soldiers at the Hollywood Canteen, so they could snap off their own unique shot of her.

*Anne Gwynne.*

Whereas soldiers and sailors by the truckload had the same pin-ups of gals like Grable and her fellow top-flight oomph girls, troops who met Anne Gwynne could tack up a photograph of her that were minus the cheesecake collection of their chums.

Born in Texas and raised in the Midwest, Anne ventured out Hollywood way in the late 1930s and found employment in the film industry a few years before America's involvement in the war. She was a bit player at first, like so many fresh faced girls who relocate to Hollywood with stars in their eyes, before she established herself in "B" pictures. Anne was just about to hit her stride in the movie business when the war was in full swing. Her career was important to her but not nearly as important as the task of building morale among the American fighting forces. A workaholic, Anne would work on movie sets during the day, only to spend her downtime entertaining troops. Gwynne was a fixture at the Hollywood Canteen, where she would dance with troops and don tiny miniskirts and sultry bikinis so the boys, who borrowed a camera that Anne had on hand, could snap off their very own pin-up picture of her. Because of her "for-the-boys" mindset, Anne's name was listed on many polls that tried to answer the question as to who was America's favorite pin-up girl.

Many female celebrities took part in the pin-up girl craze that swept through the armed forces during the war, and many of those ladies also took their pulchritude to the troops. In 1943, Anne went on a USO tour to the east coast where she entertained soldiers at their encampments. Due to her pleasing disposition and eagerness to support the men in the armed forces, Anne was nicknamed "The Down-to-Earth Pin-up Girl." Far more approachable than the common portrait of a female film star, Miss Gwynne wasn't of the vain persuasion, too obsessed with her celebrity to slum around with soldiers at their military bases. She may have been a film star but she possessed not the constitution of the self-absorbed actress. When she received letters from men in the armed forces, Anne would always reply and deliver the chaps a signed pin-up picture, grateful for their devotion. Her amiable makeup endeared her to many servicemen and did not go unnoticed by the newspapermen, who occasionally referred to Anne as "the servicemen's favorite pin-up girl."

When the boys relocated overseas and engaged the enemy in battles and nautical skirmishes, they were disengaged from the USO tours that displayed the occasional pin-up girl. At their disposal were the images — the pin-up pictures. They used these pictures as inspiration to fight onward, not as a symbol of sexism where victory is rewarded by the production of scantily clad dames but by using these images as a guiding light. The pin-up girl would lead them toward victory, so the villains before them would be foiled and unable to ruin the splendor of our nation's beauty. Anne Gwynne was such a symbol of national beauty. The soldier's magazine *Yank*, which displayed a pin-up girl in nearly every issue, could be obtained by servicemen in war zones who didn't have pulchritude in their immediate midst. A big to-do was made of Anne's pin-up in a 1943 issue of *Yank*, her second trip to the soldier magazine's pages, which made her the first doll to be a two-time centerfold for the publication. Erskine Johnson understood why Anne was selected for a second run, "Anne has been selected as the pin-up girl in the current issue of *Yank* for the second time. Get a load of the art on Anne and you'll understand why."

A favorite pastime of the soldiers was bestowing nicknames upon their favorite pin-up girls. Much like the knighting of a celebrity, pin-ups were given titles by military units who adopted certain cheesecake models as their pulchritudinous mascots. Since Anne was a favorite among many servicemen, she was bestowed with a handful of accolades by the boys in the fighting forces. A cavalry unit based at Fort Riley, Kansas, dubbed Anne "The Girl We'd Most Like to Corral," while the boys at Fort Baker got a little more long-winded with their pet name for La Gwynne, bestowing the handle of "Our treasure dish, every jeep's delight, and the symmetrical sensation of us cinema addicts." The girls typically, when informed of the honors the servicemen placed upon them, would take cheesecake photos designed specifically for the unit that made them their special girl.

The fighting men at Fort Baker weren't the only fellows who described Anne as a "symmetrical sensation." Noted for her long, streamlined legs, Anne Gwynne's specialty when it came to posing for cheesecake stills was offering high quality leg art. Often found dressed down in bathing wear, Anne's legs were the central focus of many of her cheesecake photos. Whether she was posed beside a pool in a one-piece bathing suit, or was seated on the ground with her exceptional stems protruding from a miniskirt, her legs always set the boys to whistle. In 1942, when the Retail Clerk's Union sought to honor a pin-up girl with their "Glamour Gams" award, they selected none other than the lady with the gifted landing gear: Anne Gwynne. Shoe salesman Stanley Turner was more than eager to award Anne the title on behalf of his organization.

Men of all walks of life found inspiration in the form of Anne Gwynne, but one man — famed sculptor Yucca Salamunich — used the inspiration of her flawless figure to channel his creativity. Salamunich was disgusted by Axis propagandists who claimed that the American way of life was morally reprehensible and that pin-up art was too decadent for civilized tastes. He used his talents to thumb his nose at the Axis, and he asked Anne to pose for his latest sculpture. Salamunich chose Anne for his work because he thought she possessed the most beautiful figure in Hollywood. Miss Gwynne agreed to pose for Salamunich; the sculptor spent hours in order to capture the stunning Gwynne frame in clay. He sculpted Anne to champion the American female as the ideal figure in the world. He couldn't have chosen a better subject than the streamlined goddess.

Anne Gwynne posed for photographers for cheesecake purposes, sat before a sculptor to duplicate her figure, and agreed to use her pulchritude to sell merchandise. During the war, Anne became the spokeswoman for Hollywood Bread. They used her in print ads, which displayed her figure in newspapers, as a method to hawk their staffs of life. When they used the Anne image, Hollywood Bread didn't employ a close-up of Miss Gwynne's smiling face, joyously grazing on a golden loaf of their produce, but went the pin-up route. They had Anne set her clothes on the chair for her bread-hawking photo shoot, and snapped off a few pictures of her in her undergarments. Taking full advantage of her status as a pin-up girl, they placed atop Anne's locks a soldier's dress hat and ordered her to offer a swift salute. But the adherence to military customs and dress ended there, for below the neck Anne was not enveloped by a khaki coat and slacks, but dressed a little more revealing in bra and panties. The Hollywood Bread advertisement read, "Don't envy pert screen star Anne Gwynne her perfect figure! Start now to retain your youthful slimness the HOLLYWOOD BREAD way!" It was a classic bit of advertising: pretty girl used to sell merchandise — a marketing ploy still used today.

Whether Anne did much swimming during the war meant little to the pin-up hounds, for they were satisfied enough by her swimming-suit-clad cheesecake photos. When writer Erskine Johnson asked Miss Gwynne what she did in her spare time during the war, she replied, "Model bathing suits." And model bathing suits she excelled at. Some of the famous pin-up pictures of the war years were photographs of Anne Gwynne. One of her grandest pin-ups, which university psychology students would dissect in earnest, showed a bikini-clad Anne straddling an explosive projectile, which was positioned with Anne upon it and to appear as if the missile were in flight. Donned in the perfect Uncle Sam outfit, Anne's bikini top was dark blue with white stars littered upon it, while her bikini bottom was striped like the American flag. In her left hand was the famous Uncle Sam lid, while she kept her right hand positioned on the missile for support, and employed her flawless legs on each side of the missile to retain her balance. The pin-up seemed to imply that American womanhood, the ideal pulchritude, was guiding the bombs and torpedoes, sending them direct to the enemy, and offering a wallop that could cripple their resolve. Anne Gwynne, she of exquisite beauty and enviable legs was, without question, an ideal pin-up to represent womanhood.

## ★ RITA HAYWORTH ★

In the case of Rita Hayworth, a sex symbol was not born but made. The daughter of a Spanish dancer who emigrated from Spain to the States, Rita Hayworth (her last name was Cansino before she Anglicized it) had the physicality and voluptuous figure for pictures but too many rough edges for stardom. Her first husband, Edward Judson, was determined to make his shapely wife a star, and the naïve knockout allowed her spouse to control her career. Rita did not come about her beauty naturally, and is often regarded as the first female star to have her features altered via surgery. Her hairline started too low on her forehead — it was decided by Judson and movie executives — so Rita agreed to undergo painful electrolysis to raise her hairline. The procedure paid off, for Rita became one of America's greatest sex symbols of the war era. It was Bob Landry's photograph of her in *Life* magazine, coupled with her star-making film in 1941, *The Strawberry Blonde*, which catapulted Miss Hayworth into the ranks of female superstars.

Rita had worked in Hollywood for the better part of a decade before she attained star status in 1941. As the daughter of professional dancers, Rita was already a master at physical dexterity by the time she signed her first film contract. She used her mastery of managing her limbs to great effect by cutting capers in films with top-male dancing experts. But her background as a dancer did little to advance her career as a legitimate actress. Often viewed as more of a window-dressing actress than a true thespian, Rita's figure and unique beauty charmed filmgoers more than any dramatic scenes she played. Her beauty was responsible for both her rise in the film industry as well as the stagnation that eventually hindered her career. After shooting *Gilda* — unquestionably her most recognizable role — Hayworth's roles never reached the same status, but she continued to work for many more years in an effort to duplicate *Gilda's* success.

Before the world knew Rita Hayworth as the glamorous Gilda, she was an up-and-coming starlet at a time when the world was in turmoil. Hitler was ravaging the European countryside and the Japanese posed a threat to America, which culminated in the bombing of Pearl Harbor.

Prior to the greatest attack on America in the nation's history, Rita had just secured footing in the film industry with her star-making role in *The Strawberry Blonde*. Around that time, men joined the ranks of the military, and these men, who left home to enter the world of the soldier where beauty was nonexistent, needed a fragment of delicacy in their sphere of military operations. Such photographers as Bob Landry understood the soldiers' needs and opted to address it. Landry secured La Hayworth for a photo shoot to be printed in the pages of *Life* magazine. The shapely redheaded sex symbol became a sensation of the fighting boys after the issue of *Life* hit the stands. She was one of the first pin-up girls thanks to her layout for America's top magazine.

Her photo shoot for Landry received a warm reception from the boys in the fighting forces, as the cat-calls and whistles found their way to the ears of Hayworth's studio. When America entered the war effort after Pearl Harbor was bombed, Rita's studio promoted her as "America's Inspiration Girl." The nickname took off, as papers across the nation used the moniker often when describing Rita. When USO tours were lined up for Rita, promoters would often urge folks to see "America's Inspiration Girl" in the flesh. For her part, Rita was happy to go on the USO tours and war-bond-selling junkets. Stardom was new to her and her status as a celebrity attracted crowds wherever she went. She headlined a bond-selling tour that stopped off at Oak Park High School in Illinois, under the auspices of the "Salute to Our Heroes Show." As a multitalented entertainer whose physical charms, some would claim, played second fiddle to her artistry as a dancer, made her a top draw on the war bond circuit. Americans came out to see Rita and, they loosed their purse strings to help their country defeat the Axis.

One of Rita's favorite junkets was the USO "Hullabaloo Tour" that took her to Camp Bowie, where she took part in military training and had a tank named after her. During her visit of Camp Bowie in 1942 under the "Hullabaloo Tour," Miss Hayworth was named an honorary MP and attended the christening of a tank. When the armored conveyance was dubbed the "Rita Hayworth Tank," the titian-haired actress climbed into the turret for a photo-op. Although Rita wasn't allowed to take her namesake for a spin, the soldiers at Camp Bowie were a little more accommodating with other military items. During her camp escort, she was taken to a range where infantrymen were engaged in bayonet training. Rita asked her escort to stop at the range so she could watch the troops employ their blades — they struck and stabbed dummies with their bayonets affixed to the accosting end of their firearms. But the role of spectator fulfilled Rita not, so she asked to borrow a soldier's rifle in order to poke a dummy or two. After she delivered a few quick stabs to the simulated enemy, Rita returned the rifle to its rightful owner and told the troops, "I hope I didn't interrupt any of your games." The soldiers were certainly happy for the pulchritudinous spell that put their training on short-term hiatus.

*Rita Hayworth.* COURTESY OF MOVIEMARKET.COM

Rita worked plenty for the war department the first year of America's involvement in the war, and a beautiful publicist she made for the department too. So appreciative was the war department, they lined up several galas and luncheons for the stunning actress. When she was sent to Hagerstown, folks who purchased a $75 war bond could attend a luncheon with Rita and dine in her company. She worked under the auspices of the "Salute to Our Heroes Show" in 1942 that enabled her to tour various military installations. Although she was engaged in war-bond sales, she was often an absentee seller of bonds. She attended many war-bond gatherings but there were many that simply used her name as a drawing card, such as the one in Syracuse during the fall of 1942. Although she was not in New York at the time, the heads of the bond-selling campaign screened Rita's latest movie, *You Were Never Lovelier*, and enticed people to buy bonds with a free Rita Hayworth signed photograph, distributed at the Onondaga Hotel.

At the time Rita Hayworth's career was at its peak, her personal life had entered a state of distress. Her marriage to Judson had deteriorated and she was rumored to be cupiding around Hollywood with beefcake actor Victor Mature. Her nasty divorce with Judson — an oil magnate — was public fodder given Rita's burgeoning film career, and her romances interested the American populace for the same reason. There were reports that she and Mature had planned to wed, but shortly after Victor joined the Coast Guard, Rita made headlines again when she announced her engagement to arrogant, eccentric filmmaker Orson Welles. Although Rita was an inspiration to thousands of soldiers who fawned over her pin-ups, many young women were informed that Miss Hayworth wasn't an ideal role model given her constant gossip column appearances. Her work with the war department was rightly viewed as admirable, but when gossip columnists claimed she jilted Mature to marry Welles, her status as a role model was questioned.

After she contracted an illness during a USO tour at Corpus Christi Naval Station, coupled with her marriage to Welles, Rita slowed down on the tours. She was admitted for a brief stay at the installation's hospital during the tour, and she dropped ten pounds courtesy her ailment. When she returned to Hollywood, Rita returned to pictures and posed before the cameras for cheesecake purposes again, but she had to put the posing on hold for a time when she became pregnant in 1944. Her pregnancy, as one can imagine, hampered her status as a pin-up girl, but soldiers still had in their possession her early stills taken before the swelling that pregnancy induces. She gave birth to a daughter in 1944, but the celebration of welcoming a new life was replaced by remorse when her mother died shortly after the birth of her daughter. Although Rita became a pin-up girl during the war, her work after the war — most notably her role in *Gilda* — firmly established her as one of Hollywood's leading sex goddesses. She was, simply put, the apex of attraction.

# ★ ROCHELLE HUDSON ★

The motion picture industry has introduced hundreds of beautiful women to the world but perhaps none have matched the delicate radiance of Rochelle Hudson. She began acting professionally in her early teen years and seemed to possess a youthful allurement throughout her career. Her eyes danced with the worldly excitement of an unbridled coquette, flickering with the quality of the stars that have amazed mankind for centuries. The darkest recesses of the human condition, where coldness refuses to relinquish to the warmth of loftier things, could be, by the employ of a simple Rochelle Hudson smile, relieved of its dispirited state and escorted out of the tenebrous spiritual abyss of loathing. To look upon the countenance of Rochelle Hudson was to understand beauty at its purest form. There was nothing gaudy or decadent in the visage of Miss Hudson, but a fairness one would associate with the angels. Her beauty was not showy, her beauty was not base and vulgar, but was ethereal and served many a serviceman well while engaged in battle.

Many pin-up girls used their work posing for cheesecake stills to advance their career, but Rochelle's career was already on stable ground before she donned the bathing suits. The beautiful brunette began work in Hollywood while in her school years. She starred alongside Shirley Temple in *Curly Top* and played the title role opposite the incomparable W.C. Fields in *Poppy*. Miss Hudson did not stand before the photographers with career advancement in mind but for the laudable reason of building morale. Many of her pin-ups focused on her perfect facial structure, for shutterbugs took full advantage of her dancing eyes, captivating smile, and eyebrows women of the era would kill to possess. But Rochelle, who possessed the perfect facial profile, also owned the legs of an oomph girl. Her legs were cast for posterity's sake in 1944 after she was named "The Honorary President of the Perfect Legs Institute of America."

Acting came natural to the lovely Miss Hudson, whose family relocated to the west coast shortly after her birth in the Midwest. As a schoolgirl thespian, Rochelle was the envy of all the children at the learning house, although she had few friends growing up. She was, however, a dear friend to the family of Edgar Rice Burroughs, the famous novelist whose pen created *Tarzan*. Rochelle would often vacation with the Burroughs clan, who were well versed in celebrity given E.R.'s fame as a storyteller. But Rochelle, whose father claimed to be a direct descendent of the man who discovered Hudson Bay, would gain notoriety during the 1930s as a beautiful young actress of unrivalled physical appeal. If good looks weren't

*Rochelle Hudson.*

reason enough to incite envy in the hearts of her fellow schoolgirls, her rise as an actress was quite the catalyst for long leers and cold shoulders.

When America entered the war effort, Rochelle became a war bride, whose husband joined the commissioned officer ranks in the Navy. Her husband, a former film industry executive, attained the rank of lieutenant commander and was stationed in Hawaii for a time. Although Miss Hudson was an actress — perhaps the most beautiful in Hollywood — she wasn't impressed with the limelight, and little was known of her personal life. A woman who enjoyed her privacy, her name was rarely found in the gossip columns and when they were, the inside dope delivered to the public was typically fictional bunkum. In the midst of the war, one of the many knaves of the newspaper, whose occupation it is to regale the populace with spicy tidbits of celebrity's personal lives, claimed that Rochelle was engaged to marry a lieutenant. When word reached Rochelle about this impending marriage, she showed remarkable restraint and shrugged off the incorrect article, for she was already married and had lassoed a man of much higher rank than some gent with a single bar.

When America entered the war effort, Rochelle did her part like most beautiful celebrities, and she assisted in entertaining crowds and troops. There was a popular radio game show titled *Noah Webster Says* that supported the troops during the war. She agreed when the executives of the show asked her to serve as a guest-host for the show. During her broadcast, only servicemen were allowed to appear on the program and the winner of the contest would secure a night on the town with Rochelle. Many actresses were often pressured into dating servicemen and Rochelle, who happened to be married, was asked to serve as escort for the victorious soldier on the broadcast. This wasn't regarded as an open invitation for an illicit affair, coerced by film studios, but a way for soldiers to enjoy the company of a beautiful starlet at night spots before he was shipped overseas.

Marriage kept Rochelle busy during time of war. Many starlets were married to servicemen and followed them to their ports and bases. Most played the role of homemaker during the war, but Miss Hudson's wartime role of wife entailed far more hazards than burning her husband's dress blues while ironing. As a high ranking official in the Navy, her husband was entrusted with pivotal assignments, and given that he and Rochelle both spoke fluent Spanish, they were engaged in missions for Uncle Sam south of the border. Rochelle Hudson did more for her country than any pin-up girl during the war. She stood before photographers in bathing suits, like all other pin-ups, but no other pin-up girl is known to have been engaged in the field of espionage. Rochelle and her husband were tasked with the assignment of traveling to Mexico, posing as a typical vacationing American couple, with the mission of determining if the Germans had any activity south of the border. On their travails, they located a supply of fuel stashed by the Axis, presumably to be used for submarines, and tipped off their superiors about their find. The small fuel depot was never employed thanks to the work of Rochelle and her husband.

In modern times, with Hollywood's influence stretching to every corner of the globe, it seems unlikely that an actress could gain employment as a spy. One of the key requirements in the field of espionage is a low profile, and when one's profile is constantly reproduced on movie screens, the element of secrecy is forfeited. Rochelle, whose name wasn't as well known as Bette Davis or Claudette Colbert, was nevertheless a screen starlet, and one of exceptional beauty. Her enticing physical collection would seem ill-suited for espionage work, but she was successful in the role of spy. She may have been a pin-up girl but she posed for fewer shots in bathing suits than dolls whose wartime pursuits were less essential for the war effort. Rochelle Hudson mastered the art of projecting an intoxicating image, something needed for the role of pin-up girl, but it was in the role of an agent for her country that Miss Hudson is lauded for. Her country is eternally grateful for her devotion and valor as an intelligence gatherer, even if it had an adverse effect on her cheesecake quantity.

# ★ CANDY JONES ★

All things that popular culture entails seem subject to the ebb and flow of fads. Music, clothes, hairstyles, all have changed starkly over time. During the average lifetime of a single man, the styles embraced by society via the influence of popular culture alter, transform, or amend countless times. What was accepted last year by a culture may be passé when the calendar is turned. There once was a time, during World War II to be specific, when models were the image of health and did not bare a resemblance to flesh-toned, shrink-wrapped skeletons. Before the modeling industry embraced inanition, females of the profession were not delicate, narrow-shadow-casting stick figures, but women of contours whose configurations were womanly and not cadaverous. Candy Jones, the statuesque stunner whose bodily structure was full in all the right places, made for the ideal model during the war years. Her tall, well-fed, shapely chassis was made-to-order for the modeling profession during the 1940s, but would be deemed too Amazonian for the gaunt and haggard looking models who populate the modern day runway.

At the outset of America's involvement in the war, Candy Jones was just a teenage girl of unquestioned physical appeal. She had yet to adopt the handle "Candy Jones," which would be bestowed upon her at a later date when she signed a contract with the elite Conover Modeling Agency. Before Harry Conover (the beauty birddog) spotted her, she had entered a beauty pageant with aspirations of participating in the Miss America Pageant. She had just turned sixteen when she entered the pageant and had yet to master the nuances of the circuit, which kept the tall, shapely stunner from winning the crown. Although she was not named Miss America, Jones was spotted by Mr. Conover, who quickly signed the beauty to a contract for his prestigious modeling agency. A rather eccentric individual, Conover liked to christen his ladies with catchy nicknames — he concocted such handles as "Chili" and "Choo-Choo" for his contracted dames — and informed the sexy teenager that her new handle would be Candy Jones.

If man learned how to whistle for the purpose of expressing his admiration for the female form, then that whistle perhaps reached its most voluminous pitch when Candy Jones became a model. The taffy-haired head-turner graced the cover of many of the nation's leading magazines early in the war effort, and due to her exposure as a model, she quickly became the desire of throngs of servicemen. She went the pin-up route and the fighting fellows liked what they saw of the well-proportioned beauty. She was tall, over six feet in height, with long, well-toned legs, a lean midsection, a bosom that tested the durability of her bathing suit tops, and an unblemished face of pure radiance. A NEA service writer described Miss Jones by writing, "she is 128 pounds of wholesome, well-scrubbed, well-fed American girlhood." So admired were her physical charms that Candy was voted the prettiest model at the Banshee's Luncheon by the American Newspaper Publishers Association.

The life of a model may have been as glamorous in Candy Jones's day as it is now, but the profession wasn't a lucrative venture. When a model was photographed, whether it was for a magazine layout or a pin-up photo, the model, as Candy stated, was paid by the length of her posing time. She once joked that her dog Misty, who was often photographed for animal advertisements, earned more as a model than she did. Candy, who was more than just a striking body, supplemented her income as a model with work in the board game industry. Miss Jones assisted in the creation of board games for commercial manufacture, but even this little side endeavor was used as inspiration to pass along more pin-up pictures. In a sexy cheesecake still, Candy was photographed wearing a form fitting top and a skirt that revealed a lot of leg, seated on the floor perusing the pieces of a board game she helped manufacture. The photograph even came with a caption, a personal quote from the intoxicating lips of Candy Jones, which read, "It is sometimes safer and more educational to play games with toys than with boys."

Many of America's most recognizable models were under the employ of the Conover Agency. Candy Jones, as a Conover girl, received plenty exposure and saw her face and figure duplicated one hundred times over in various magazines and papers. The soldiers who adored her pin-ups knew her only as a flawless figure and not as a celebrity like other star pin-ups who acted in motion pictures. All that the boys knew about Candy was that she was sharp-looking and earned her bread by looking pretty for advertisement's sake. But the fighting men were able to learn more about Miss Jones on an intimate level, when she agreed to tour the South Pacific as a member of the traveling group named "Cover Girls Abroad." The patriotic oomph girl packed her suitcase and hit the overseas circuit, where she entertained troops with her pulchritudinous presence.

Hundreds of soldiers in the Pacific region, who had left wives and girlfriends back home, had little feminine comfort at their disposal. What satiated their craving for the female form were the pin-up photos they were able to acquire. Imagine how the fellows felt when they were graced with the likes of shapely Candy Jones, not at their homeland installation but in close proximity to their foxholes. Many pin-ups were referred to as "foxhole warmers," because they kept numerous gents tepid in their uncomfortable earthen fighting positions. Miss Jones, perhaps the shapeliest foxhole warmer of her era, decided that her snapshots weren't enough to combat the chill of the foxhole on those cool nights, so she decided to take the real Candy Jones to the boys in battle. Candy was an instant elixir for the boys overseas. She entertained troops at the camps and soothed the deflated constitutions of battle casualties in field hospitals. Her tour was scheduled at a time that enabled her to be overseas during Christmas, and she did everything in her power to bring a little cheer to the boys, but she felt, that to some, her efforts were in vain. Candy said, "Christmas Eve had been rough. We had carol singing and whipped up a little bit of the spirit of the season and then they brought in some casualties. Somehow, it seemed worse than ever — no matter how many wounded men you might have seen — to see them on Christmas Eve."

While she lived amongst the men and shared in their thoughts and experiences, Candy served as a delicate ear that soldiers could vent their fears and frustrations to. Most soldiers have what is commonly referred to in military lingo as a "battle buddy," someone whose advice is respected — an individual one can confide in — but to speak to a female, the tender sex whose constitution is supposed to harbor sentimentality and understanding, is more appealing to a man than his neighbor's ear. Candy offered her time to the fighting men, listened to their troubles, and offered comfort as they related the activities back home that they could not monitor. She befriended many soldiers and heard more than one tale of an adulterous loved one who a soldier had left back home. Candy wrote a letter to the States, which reprimanded the American woman who refused to wait for the return of her hero. Snippets of this letter were reproduced in the newspapers. Writer Walter Winchell relayed Candy's sentiment, when he penned, "Candy Jones urges us to remind women (who have men in uniform) not to write about parties with other men, whoopee, etc. Candy reports that of 400 men in one group there were 48 divorces — mainly filled by women who got too weary waiting for their heroes to die."

While touring with the "Cover Girls Abroad" troupe, Miss Jones endeared herself to countless soldiers in fighting regions. She would entertain troops on the stage, visit with them in mess halls, and comfort casualties at field hospitals. The war was responsible for numerous casualties, but another culprit was the region itself. Many troops suffered from illnesses they were not properly inoculated for prior to departing the States. Candy Jones became such a casualty. The stunning cover girl contracted the disease eczema while engaged on her USO tour, and when one peruses the symptoms of the malady — which includes discharging lesions — a feeling of repulsion grips the senses. Candy combated the disease but spent the better part of a month in hospitals on Leyte and Morotai. About suffering from the illness, Miss Jones said, "It only had me scared once, when I thought my hair was all going to fall out, but after I lost a little, it stopped falling and everything was all right."

Candy's scare with eczema didn't deflate her lofty impression of her USO tour when she returned home and met with reporters. The taffy-haired beauty felt it her duty to entertain the troops, and the illness, although quite discomforting, did not lead the symmetrical sensation to bare any ill-will towards the tour. After she stepped foot off the ship, she told reporters that the "Cover Girls Abroad" tour did wonders for her skin, because she developed the perfect suntan. About her tour, *Yank* staff writer Al Hine went into modest detail with regards to her occasional plight, penning, "She managed to get involved in two minor earthquakes, to lose the top of her dress on stage, and to spend better than a month in GI hospitals." One of Hine's "earthquakes" was a tremor no soldier would mind, while the other kept a repeat performance from taking place. Candy Jones suffered from the occasional tremor, but she caused countless tremors in the hearts of America's fighting men in the 1940s courtesy of her patriotic posing.

## ★ EVELYN KEYES ★

There are a number of adjectives one might use to describe the lifestyle of Evelyn Keyes, and two of the most fitting might be incendiary and tumultuous. Born deep in the heart of Dixie, Miss Keyes was a southern spitfire who left a trail of broken-hearted lovers in her wake. Late in life, after her film career had stalled, she penned a novel and a biography that flinched not when detailing her many sexual conquests. If one were to judge Evelyn Keyes by the tell-all literature she wrote, or the reviews thereof, an image of a haughty, self-centered dame living to satiate her most carnal desires would spring forth. She married wayward playboys, had affairs with her costars, and left her first husband for a flamboyant director, which forced the man to take his own life. There was fire everywhere Evelyn Keyes walked, but all was not scorched behind her. During the war, there may not have been a more patriotic lady in the film industry than Evelyn Keyes. She was pin-up girl, Red Cross volunteer, and menial laborer. How many dames in modern day Hollywood would leave a film set to pick tomatoes in the California valley? Evelyn Keyes did just that when she heard a plea for help via the radio due to a lack of manpower.

Before Evelyn Keyes and close chum Jinx Falkenburg — both stunning pin-up girls — got their hands red by plucking juicy tomatoes from the vine, Miss Keyes was known to filmgoers as Vivien Leigh's little sister in the epic *Gone With the Wind*. Although Evelyn would go on to star in other films, with top-billing, she will be best remembered for her small role in filmdom's finest venture. But before she worked opposite Leigh and Gable, Evelyn was the property of legendary filmmaker Cecil B. DeMille. Evelyn was introduced to DeMille, who sought a young actress to train, and after interviews with countless dames, Cecil chose to sign Miss Keyes to a contract based on the appearance of her fingers. He informed Evelyn on their initial meeting that she was the first girl with Hollywood ambitions he had seen in ten years that didn't wear fingernail polish. Due to her refusal to apply pigment to her upper unguis, the Atlanta attractor became a contract player for one of Hollywood's grandest talents. But being a DeMille player meant that she was restricted from cheesecake posing and leg art. DeMille found the photography to be crude and kept his actresses from engaging in the practice.

Fortunately for soldiers, who had hundreds of pin-up pictures produced simply for them, when the war hit, Evelyn was no longer under contract to DeMille. Evelyn gained some notoriety before the war with her minor role in *Gone With the Wind*, and when America entered the

*Evelyn Keyes.* COURTESY OF MOVIEMARKET.COM

war effort in the early 1940s, she was quickly becoming a common face in the film industry. But, Miss Keyes often cracked jokes about her inability to gain lasting fame in pictures. She claimed that many filmgoers had trouble recognizing her due to director's constantly asking her to change her hair color for roles. Evelyn might play a blonde in one picture, then her next film she might have dark hair. But through all the alterations to the tincture of her tresses, Evelyn retained that Dixie charm. Dee Lowrance wrote, "There is no other feminine player with the same delicate, almost eerie beauty, with a so rare quality that, for want of a better word, might be given her native Atlanta title — 'gentlewomanly.'"

Her rise in the film industry coincided with the rise of hostilities around the globe. The Second World War was well underway when Evelyn gained a foothold in Hollywood, and the Southern sexpot showed remarkable character by placing her career second so that she could focus on the war effort. She and cover girl Jinx Falkenburg volunteered their time to pluck tomatoes in the San Fernando Valley, and the following day used their celebrity status to lure other volunteers to the vine. But trading her unpolished nails for the green thumb of a gardener wasn't all Evelyn Keyes did for the war effort. She worked tirelessly for the Red Cross during the war, diligently promoting the "V for Victory Book Drive" that collected reading material to be distributed to the troops. About her volunteer work for the Red Cross, Evelyn said, "The Red Cross is such a far-reaching organization and does such wonderful work, that I am only too happy to do anything I can to help in this drive." As the spokesperson for the "V for Victory Book Drive," Evelyn served as the figure for literary donations. The books helped preoccupy soldiers in the downtime of their training.

Her volunteer work with the Red Cross kept her busy, but what Evelyn wanted to do was to visit the troops at their installations. She aligned herself with the USO and toured many stateside military bases. Many entertainers would sing and dance on the stage, or sign autographs for the servicemen, but Evelyn took her USO travels seriously. By parading on the stage in leggy dresses, she felt unfulfilled and desired to do more — to be amongst the soldiers while they trained. She toured Camp Kearns, Utah, with Columbia Studios' publicist Frank Newman, who marveled at Evelyn's exuberance and devotion to the boys in uniform. They witnessed soldiers in gas training, as they tested the effectiveness of their protective masks, but the part of spectator wasn't enough for Evelyn — she grabbed a mask and entered the chamber. Newman said, "You should have seen her at Kearns camp last night. When the warning 'Gas!' was sounded, she put on that gas mask like a professional."

The troops at Camp Kearns fell madly in love with Evelyn who side-stepped not the rigors of military life but embraced it for the boys' sake. She endeared herself more to the enlisted men, who dwelled not in softer quarters and whose paychecks had fewer digits than the fellows with the shiny ornaments on their headgear. When she visited Camp Kearns, she was invited by the commissioned officers to dine in their comfortable quarters, but Evelyn declined the invite and took her meals with the grunts in the mess hall. A photographer snapped off a few shots of Evelyn in the army mess hall, partaking vittles consumed by Uncle Sam's enlisted men, which were published in many of the nation's newspapers. One shot showed Evelyn washing her plate after dinner with a swarm of soldiers flanking her every shank. When asked about her camp tour, Evelyn said, "It is wonderful to visit the boys at the different camps, especially those in the hospitals. If I can help cheer them ever so little, I am very happy."

As a pin-up girl, Evelyn was idolized by many men, but she also served the ladies of America well by passing along beauty secrets. Many pin-up girls were often found in local newspapers, on the women's health page, offering the inside dope on how to cast an enticing reflection. Evelyn was a favorite example of feminine perfection for beauty tip writer Alicia Hart, who said that Evelyn had a "poured-in look" with a "slim waist, firm bosom, flat stomach and well-shaped legs." Due to her refreshing contours, women's health writer Patricia Lindsay used Miss Keyes as her model for her article titled, "Women Must Get Fit and Keep Fit as War Duty." Patricia Lindsay detailed a few exercises women could perform, and she had Evelyn conduct the drills. Lindsay littered her article with a few photographs of Evelyn engaged in the daily dozen. But fitness, face creams, and firmness of figure wasn't the extent of Evelyn's advice; women wanted to know more and pressed beauty tip writers to give them the scoop.

When the pin-up girl craze began, the focus was mainly on leg art, but over time the points of interest tended to rise a little higher on the female anatomy. The film *The Outlaw* — Howard Hughes's little secretive endeavor, which starred the bosomy Jane Russell — was all the rage thanks in part to the much publicized battle with the censors. The censors felt that Jane's blouses failed in the task of concealing her ample breasts, and when the release of the picture was retarded, simply because too much of Jane Russell was filmed, people took a profound interest in the motion picture. Jane Russell became a pin-up sensation even though the film she starred in had yet to hit the theaters, and many of the pin-ups who circulated with the Russell figure made little effort to conceal that the focus of the photographer was on Russell's upper deck. Woman began to wonder just how they could sport an enviable chest, such owned by the full-breasted Russell, and sent inquiries to beauty tip writers. Alicia Hart turned to Evelyn, who claimed to have devised an exercise to increase the bust, without adding weight elsewhere, which Miss Hart reproduced for the benefit of a breast-obsessed readership. The drill was explained, which informed women to "stand erect, elbows at shoulder height, and fingertips of both hands touching. Now, press fingertips together hard — harder, HARDER. Relax, and repeat several times." Evelyn stressed that results would not be immediate.

During the war, Evelyn had far more important things on her mind than offering tips on how ladies could increase their bust size. As a popular pin-up girl she was besieged with fan mail from soldiers stationed across the globe. Cheesecake photos of her in bathing suits, seated under beach umbrellas with her landing gear folded neatly under her backside, adorned the walls of many barracks, both home and abroad. Those soldiers abroad, who leered at the full Evelyn Keyes package, felt a twinge of despair knowing that classy dolls like her were at home, miles away, romancing with gents whose devotion to their country paled in comparison to theirs. When Evelyn received a letter from Charles Kausel, a sergeant in a bomber command at Saipan, she reassured the sergeant and his battle buddies that ladies knew the best of the best were overseas. Kausel's letter read, "Japs don't faze us, but we're frankly panicked at the thought that all the pretty girls are being picked off by the drastically limited number of men at home." Evelyn returned a letter to the forlorn sergeant with reassurance. Her note read, "I think many other girls have the same idea I do. We know that many of the best catches are still overseas, and don't think the girls have forgotten. Rest assured that many of us are going to wait."

The life of Evelyn Keyes is best remembered by film historians as one of turbulence and untapped potential. For whatever reason, her career never did materialize as it seemed destined to. She married men best left unmarried, and she herself was also not the marrying type. (She often told John Huston, one of her former husbands, that she had no desire to have children.) She was a lover — the ideal dream girl for soldiers overseas. The untethered type, Miss Keyes was free to roam, to instill thoughts of amore in the minds of fighting men long separated from the touch of love. Few actresses were more devoted to the men in the service than Evelyn Keyes. She understood her position during the war, as dream girl and pin-up queen, and felt it her duty to give the boys an eye wink and a pick-me-up. Such a class act was Evelyn that when she was invited to attend a ceremony where soldiers were awarded Purple Hearts, she made certain that all the Purple Heart recipients, even those not present, were aware of her gratitude. After the ceremony she went directly to Bushnell Hospital, where the bedridden Purple Heart recipients dwelled, and she greeted each man personally.

## ★ ELYSE KNOX ★

The love that Elyse Knox had for her soldier, former Heisman hero Bob Harmon, was made of the stuff so often missing in today's celebrity lifestyle. Their union seemed a fantasy, for the ex-gridiron great joined the military during the war and Elyse, a stunning beauty at the threshold of film stardom, was pursued by men whose hearts were not as bold as Mr. Harmon's. She married while Bob was fighting overseas, but the wedded state was not ideal, for Miss Knox never surrendered the fantasy of Harmon's return. Elyse couldn't let Harmon's memory slip away, and she kept it fresh in her mind by staying abreast of war news. Her love was a fighter pilot who crash landed in enemy territory, but he fought and made his way back home. Elyse returned to her lover and the two married shortly after her divorce was finalized. Her gown was not the typical bridal dress made of the finer fabrics but one altered from Harmon's parachute — the article that saved his life in the Pacific Theater. The couple had the most uncommon of Hollywood marriages — it lasted over forty years and closed with the passing of Bob Harmon.

Elyse Knox's route to Hollywood was the not altogether uncommon origin in modeling. With a pretty face the camera adored, Elyse took to modeling prior to the war and her face graced the cover of many of the nation's leading magazines. Work as a cover girl is a quick way for a gal to get noticed, and Hollywood birddogs — always on the prowl for the next true beauty — spotted Elyse's cover girl work and felt they found it. The blonde bombshell went out Tinseltown way but couldn't seem to shake her background as a glamour girl model. The pretty face for pictures she possessed, but studio executives weren't sold on her skill as a thespian, so they opted to use her in window-dressing roles and cheesecake situations. Before she became an established film player, Elyse Knox was a favored pin-up girl of the boys in Uncle Sam's khaki. It was by the pen of the fighting men that Elyse Knox gained a foothold in the film industry.

In moving pictures, the southern police are apt to employ bloodhounds to sniff out an escaped convict, but during the war years, soldiers had the bloodhound-like wherewithal to locate the next Hollywood starlet. Hollywood was for the troops full-scale during the war and was quite eager to honor a request from an outfit of servicemen. When Elyse's representatives received letters from a group of bombers based in Africa, they felt their little ex-model was an untapped goldmine. Prior to receiving the letters from the African-based pilots, Elyse was engaged by her studio as a minor player with eye candy roles — nothing that showcased her ability as an actress. However, after the onslaught of letters, they felt they had missed something in their little blonde torpedo who the soldiers found appealing. One letter her studio received read, "Please may we have enough pictures of Elyse Knox to paper the inside of our bomber?" Given that the bombers wanted pin-ups of Elyse and no one else, her representatives cooked up some meatier roles for her so the boys could get a glimpse of their favorite pin-up girl in motion.

Elyse learned a lot during the war, starting out in Hollywood as a cute little ingénue. The beauty was due to become a legitimate actress — free from the bindings of her pretty-face-questionable-acting background and courtesy of her work in the modeling profession — but she had plenty life lessons to learn. Not quite the country rube set rudderless in the big city, Elyse went to work on the film *Hi 'Ya Sailor* as a taxi driver, but had never learned to drive a car. She took lessons on the set and finally became an accomplished enough jalopy jockey to portray one on the big screen. She had lessons behind the wheel, but when it came to homemaking chores, she made things a team effort with two other pin-up girls: Anne Gwynne and Martha O'Driscoll. Given that the times were, as Louella Parsons put it, "maidless," many women of the film industry had to employ their hands for other reasons besides latching onto props and scripts. With the help of the lovely Miss Gwynne and O'Driscoll, Elyse trimmed her chores as the gals assisted one another in common tasks, such as giving each other manicures, taking up hems in their wardrobe, and doing laundry. By employing six hands, the lovely ladies found they could accomplish more, which opened up time to sell war bonds and entertain at the Hollywood Canteen.

Elyse attended a war-bond rally held at Chicago and later visited Charleston, West Virginia, with Hollywood stars Lon Chaney Jr. and Albert Dekker in the same bond-selling capacity. When not engaged in the sale of war bonds, Elyse honed her craft as an actress and posed for photographers with cheesecake intentions. Paul Hesse was a famous Hollywood photographer who found in Elyse his muse. He took the majority of her pin-up photographs during the war, and even though Miss Knox was still in love with Bob Harmon — despite their breakup prior to his military induction — he pursued her and made Elyse his bride. When Hesse was asked about his fair-haired model turned actress, he claimed that Elyse was his "perfect girl," describing not how he felt about Elyse as a person but how he felt about her form. The marriage was doomed from the beginning and when Harmon returned from much turmoil during the war — he had been shot down and spent time behind enemy lines — Hesse lost his perfect figure to a war hero.

*Elyse Knox.*

Elyse followed the actions of the servicemen and was always quick to lend a hand when she was able. An old childhood chum of hers had returned stateside after a tour of duty in Casablanca, and Elyse used her status as a young actress to finagle a party for the chap, complete with Hollywood celebrities. Other soldiers, those she never met, who employed her pin-ups in various corners of the globe, would occasionally make suggestions or write to her with a modest request or two. She once received a package with a return address from the Solomon Islands, and when she opened the box, she found a hula skirt inside with a note underneath it. The note came from the pen of sailors stationed near the islands, and they had one simple request: they wanted photographs of Elyse wearing the skirt. Ever eager to please the troops, Elyse took husband Paul Hesse aside and had him snap off a series of shots of her in the hula skirt. She accommodated the sailors by sending each seaman in the outfit a personally autographed photo of her wearing their gift.

A favorite of the servicemen, Elyse was often cited by military outfits as their honorary pin-up girl. It wasn't uncommon for units to adopt a pin-up mascot — many units went so far as to develop polls in order to vote for the gal they desired to pay tribute to — and Miss Knox would often be informed that she had won a vote. She was named the official sweetheart of the air cadets at Victory Field, Texas. Other accolades bestowed upon Elyse were "Sweetheart of the Ground Crew" at Randolph Field, Texas, "Tent Girl" of the 92nd Evacuation Hospital, and "Honorary Marinette" for the jarheads stationed at Parris Island, South Carolina. The plucky blonde pin-up possessed quite the wallop of pulchritude, and the servicemen saluted her for her cheesecake work by anointing her with various flattering handles.

Despite her work as a pin-up girl, Elyse Knox did not desire to be known in show business as a leg art gal and nothing more. She was grateful for the soldiers enthusiastic support that led to her rise in pictures, but the cheesecake stuff, which served its purpose and advanced her career, didn't serve her well once she became established. Virginia MacPherson echoed the sentiments of many men when she described Elyse by penning, "She is a little blonde gal with big, beautiful eyes that change color and a nice profile all the way down." But the profile was simply the decoration covering the package, which held within the potential of stardom in the field of acting. However, all most people saw was the decoration, and the heart-stopping leg art eventually became quite irksome to the girl with stars in her eyes. She said, "That bathing suit stuff doesn't have anything to do with the kind of actress I want to be." Over time she became a legitimate actress, able to topple the typecast so many models-turned-actress face as pretty decoration. But Miss Knox would later quit acting to start a family with her war-hero husband.

# ★ VERONICA LAKE ★

Trendsetters can recline in the soft seat of vanity and admire their reflection, silently or vocally, and applaud themselves for their influence on American pop culture. There are few things that can elevate the esteem of an individual more than the knowledge that others desire to be like them. Typically, trendsetters concoct a new way to sport an article of clothing, or find a more appealing way to wear their hair, which is how Miss Lake became America's top female trendsetter during the war years. With what was termed a "peek-a-boo hairdo," Veronica Lake, that little blonde stick of dynamite, owned the image that many an American girl longed to duplicate. Girls of the early 1940s stood before their mirrors trying, sometimes in vain, to match their locks with the glamorously golden tresses of La Lake. What set Veronica's hair apart was the peek-a-boo image, which kept her right eye slightly hidden under a wave of honey-colored hair. When Miss Lake debuted the image, boys began to whistle with gusto and girls desired to have those admiring trills directed at them, so they mimicked the peek-a-boo hairdo with the hope that they would absorb a whistle or two.

Born Constance Ockelman, Veronica Lake's mother and stepfather took her out west to secure their stunning gal's space among the stars. When she first began acting, Veronica shortened her first name to Connie and used her stepfather's surname as her stage moniker, but when her career was about to takeoff, the blonde bottle rocket adopted the handle Veronica Lake. Revamping her image came with the new name, for Veronica's peek-a-boo hairdo wasn't a trademark of Constance Ockelman, but the result of attending an audition on what she thought was a bad hair day. Unable to control the curtain-like furl of her hair that concealed her right eye, she felt that she would be directed to the door with a finger of rejection, but the executive holding the audition found the style unique, and more importantly, quite fetching, so he informed Veronica she had the role so long as she kept the peek-a-boo strands in place. By accident was the method Veronica Lake secured her trendsetter status.

When one thinks of pin-up girls, they typically conjure images of leggy gals wearing bathing suits, displaying their gams at a secluded cement pond. When a lass stands at five feet tall, there leaves little room for much leg exhibition, and many sources wondered whether Miss Lake even reached the modest height of five feet. Depending on where you search, Veronica's stature has been listed anywhere from four feet ten inches to five feet two inches. Given her diminutive elevation, Veronica typically wore high heels to appear taller onscreen, or was doubled with truncated actors like her constant leading man Alan Ladd. For the sake of miniature male thespians, many an actress had to ply her trade in a small trench so she wouldn't tower over the leading man, but such a fate never befell little Miss Lake.

Veronica's star-making role came in the film *Sullivan's Travels*, as she gave filmgoers a gander at Hollywood's newest sex symbol. The vest-pocket beauty became an overnight sensation and the girls across the American expanse began to duplicate her hairdo. But with the success that came Veronica's way, many in the film industry labeled her a rebel because she refused to conform to industry standards. Studios felt their female players were ideal escorts and should show high rollers in Tinseltown a good night at the happening night spots, but that jazz failed to suit the opinionated Miss Lake. Married and a mother, Veronica would rather spend an evening at home with her family than bat her eyes at well-dressed wolves in the smoky midnight dives. About studios directing their actresses every hour, arranging dates for publicity sake, Veronica said, "I'm not going to go out and run around to a lot of nightclubs and other party places with a bunch of visiting firemen — just because some studio executive may think that's good business."

What her studio viewed as a rebellious nature was simply Veronica's refusal to wallow in the cheap excess that Hollywood has asked of their players for many decades. Besides arranged dates, Veronica didn't approve of the senseless cheesecake pictures that studios made their ladies engage in. Before the war, when the pin-up girl craze had yet to gain steam on a national level, film studios setup photo shoots for their actresses in order to capture their ladies at numerous angles in numerous stages of undress. Veronica Lake justly found the exercise to be pointless, and refused to pose in bathing suits simply so some well-fed studio big-wig could marvel at how well she fit into a bathing suit. However, when the pin-up girl craze swept the nation during the war, Veronica, who had become one of Hollywood's most mesmerizing starlets, relaxed her stance on the issue of cheesecake stills because it had a purpose — building morale in the American fighting man. There are only a few pin-up poses of Veronica wearing a bathing suit, because she didn't appreciate the long-standing practice studios had of photographing their actresses in bathing gear for their own personal enjoyment. Only when the soldiers and sailors pleaded with Veronica did she don the two-piece for cheesecake purposes.

A hit with American film-going audiences, Veronica Lake was equally appreciated by the men in Uncle Sam's fighting forces. Hollywood churned out an excessive amount of war films during WWII and the

*Veronica Lake.* COURTESY OF MOVIEMARKET.COM

blonde bottle rocket starred in a couple. When she filmed *I Wanted Wings* in Texas, she visited several airfields in the Lone Star State and endeared herself to more than one flyer. The film was shot with the support of southern airfields like Randolph, Kelly, and March Airfields, and Miss Lake was able to visit them all. The cadets had little qualms with puppy-dogging the enchanting Miss Lake's heels, following her splendid figure as she toured the airfields, which enabled her to gather quite a haul of military memorabilia. After she had scorched the earth at the airfields, the incendiary blonde showed her fellow Hollywood players the trinkets the fliers had given her. She had acquired forty-seven sets of wings, seventeen wristlets, and fifteen corps insignias from various airfield cadets.

The girls fell in love with Veronica's hair while the fellows fell hard for her complete package. Although of short stature, Veronica's construction left little room for improvement. The beauty of her countenance possessed a hypnotic quality, whether or not one eye was shielded by her radiant tresses, which lent itself well for roles of seductive leading ladies. Even more enchanting was her dreamlike purr of a voice, reminiscent of a siren's lullaby that no man could resist. Her figure, short as it may have been, was developed in the right areas, which made her physical layout one of remarkable features of peaks and valleys. Although she rarely displayed her corporeal gifts in bathing suit pictures, soldiers nevertheless pinned up pictures of her bewitching likeness wherever there was a wall awaiting a tack. Such walls were constructed in prisoner of war camps as Veronica was the first pin-up girl to receive an autograph request from an American troop held at a Japanese POW camp. A captured Marine sent his request via the International Red Cross, making the lovely little La Lake the first doll to receive a letter from a captured American.

Veronica served the boys well during the war. She agreed to relax her stance on cheesecake pictures to inspire the fighting men, but she was of greater service to America's girls. Wherever a person went during the war there was certain to be a girl or fifty fashioning her locks in the Lake fashion. This created quite a conundrum during the war. Given that a great number of the American male workforce had enlisted in the Armed Forces, ladies were needed to fill the shoes of the newly anointed soldiers and sailors. Labor that had been the employ strictly of men opened their doors to allow women, and many of these gals, like women are apt to, had much longer hair than the previous male tenants of the machinist ranks. When several girls were wounded or left moderately scalped due to their tresses acquaintance with factory machines, a problem only

Veronica Lake could solve had arisen. The War Department asked Miss Lake to tie up her hair for the sake of workplace safety, and photographs were taken of her honoring the war department's request. An article in the *San Antonio Light* detailed the War Department's request, writing, "So many women defense workers wore their hair à la Veronica that the tresses were getting caught in machines and sabotaging the war effort. 'Would Miss Lake kindly change her hairdo?' asked Uncle Sam. And Veronica agreed."

The image of Veronica Lake was everywhere during the war, which led to the mimic-work the girls adhered to regarding the Lake look. The stunning blonde actress had her trademark peek-a-boo hairdo, which elevated her to stardom, but the war meant more than personal vanity, and Veronica was photographed with her hair in pigtails for better workplace management. Alicia Hart claimed that Veronica was the "girl with the most famous hair in the world," and it was a title aptly suited for the diminutive bombshell. Girls duplicated the look, while fellows found the style enticing enough to look at it daily from the pinned-up photographs placed on their barracks wall. Such a popular pin-up was La Lake that the 4th Armored Division bestowed upon her the title of "The Girl We'd Like in the Backseat of a Tank." Her likeness was carried on tanks, ships, aircraft, and motor vehicles, and was painted on the side of planes, all for the sake of morale-building. Her rise as an actress during the war, which secured her fame, kept her from making numerous trips to the photographer's studio for pin-up pictures, but she didn't go for the cheesecake stuff anyway, unless it was for the soldiers.

Another event that limited Veronica's pin-up output was a pregnancy. In the middle of the war, Veronica was expecting a child, and the swollen midsection that maternity causes failed to make an ideal slice of cheesecake. Despite the hold her pregnancy placed on her pin-up pictures, Veronica worked through the incubation period, which proved to have a tragic impact on her life. While working on set, Veronica tripped on a cable and fell violently to the floor. Rushed to the hospital, the impact with the studio floor forced Veronica into early childbirth and she delivered a premature son. But the child lived for only a week. Much has been written about Veronica's battle with alcohol abuse, and the driving stimulant that led her to the bottle was the tragic demise of her son. To cope with such a tragic loss is too much to ask of anyone. Miss Lake found solace in a place where the release of inner demons ushers them outward for but a small time, only enabling them to escort even more demons within.

# ★ HEDY LAMARR ★

There are some women not overly impressed with beauty, who, despite the possession of a countenance other dames would kill for, find little value in a fetching reflection. The stereotype that a beautiful woman serves only an ornamental purpose, because beauty and intelligence are in stark opposition, has been a crutch for many swell-looking dames. Hedy Lamarr, often referred to as the most glamorous actress in cinema history, lived the stereotype but also proved the notion false. The ravishing brunette, who once informed writer Dee Lowrance that being thought of as glamorous scared her, was more than a comely figure, for under her exquisite exterior dwelled an inquisitive mind capable of enviable feats of creativity. Known more as a timeless beauty, Miss Lamarr was also an inventor who, with the assistance of Renaissance man George Antheil, drew up blueprints for a torpedo guidance system that was two decades before its time. The duo earned a patent for their invention but the seeds of their collaboration never bore fruit. Close to twenty years after their initial design, their guidance system was developed with a few added alterations. This endeavor of invention meant more to Hedy Lamarr than her status as filmdom's leading feminine knockout.

Well before Miss Lamarr reached American soil and took Hollywood by storm, she was the elite beauty of European cinema. As a young thespian, she worked under the watchful eye of legendary filmmaker Max Reinhart, and became a worldwide sensation with her provocative turn in the cult classic *Ecstasy*. A very controversial film for its time, *Ecstasy* was a picture that detailed the erotic passions of a married woman, which, in the fashion of late-night cable thrillers, left little to the imagination. Filmed nude in several scenes of the picture, Hedy's exhibition was heavily edited in the motion picture's stateside release. The film made Lamarr an instant hit across the globe and, given her stature as an actress of exceptional beauty, the gates of Hollywood were destined to swing wide. But Hollywood of the 1930s was far more conservative than the loose morals that govern the industry today, and many in the film industry balked at the notion of bringing Hedy Lamarr, and her background with appearing nude in film, to the American audience. But her stardom was not to be denied and she was eventually brought stateside to work in Hollywood for the sake of box office receipts, even though she would remain clothed for the remainder of her career.

Lamarr was quick to gain fame in Hollywood, more so for her beauty than her skill as an actress. Her Hollywood career was more disappointment than success with only a few unforgettable roles such as *Samson and Delilah* and far more roles that fell flat. Hedy is said to have rejected the female lead in the classic *Casablanca*, which made the career of fellow European-born actress Ingrid Bergman, and would have, had she accepted the role, done much to establish her as a legitimate actress. This would have helped to subdue the rants that she was in pictures solely for her exceptional beauty. But Hedy understood the nature of the film industry,

*Hedy Lamarr.*

where actresses had to look glamorous above all, and was reassured over and over that her beauty would keep her in pictures. Dee Lowrance wrote about her beauty, penning, "Long before she made her first picture in America, she was touted as the loveliest creature ever to appear on the screen. She didn't need the touting — her photos proved the point. From the standpoint of perfection of face and form, Hedy fills all bills."

Prior to America's involvement in the war effort, Lamarr and Antheil put their heads together and devised the outline for their torpedo guidance system. The patent was rejected by the Navy, and Hedy relied on her work in the film industry, rather than employ as a designer of mechanical contrivances, to earn her bread. Fortunately for her, the film industry placed a profound emphasis on beauty — an element mastered by the foreign-born actress. Many Hollywood scribes found in Hedy the ideal portrait of feminine perfection, for whenever Tinseltown typists created their short list of Hollywood's most fetching thespians, Hedy typically headlined the roster. Some found her beauty overwhelming, like writer Frederick C. Othman, who couldn't keep his mind on this task of interviewing Miss Lamarr during downtime on a film set. Othman wrote, "I have some vague idea that she was discussing the international situation but that's only a surmise. I don't think I was listening because I was too busy looking, and if you think you can do better, drop around anytime on stage 14 at RKO." The Lamarr Effect was one that made admirers of the apathetic, and rendered them astonished by her high degree of pulchritude.

When America entered the war, the foreign-born Lamarr proved her devotion to her new homeland by engaging in many drumbeating events. She did her bit selling war bonds and was a constant figure at the Hollywood Canteen where she would dance with servicemen and serve as hostess. Actor John Loder, who had worked with Hedy before the war, began to cupid around with the stunning brunette when they reconnected while they entertained at the Hollywood Canteen. The duo palled around aplenty at the Hollywood Canteen and found each other's company to their liking. Such a regular was Hedy at the Hollywood Canteen, film industry writers tended to regale folks with jokes about her residency at the servicemen's dive. One such tale was reproduced in the *Manitowoc Herald-Times*, which read, "It happened at the Hollywood Canteen. A soldier, waiting outside for admittance, asked one of the hostesses if there were any celebrities inside. 'There's Hedy Lamarr,' said the girl. 'Is that all?' asked the soldier. 'Listen,' said the hostess, 'isn't Hedy Lamarr enough for you?' The soldier pushed back his cap and said, 'Listen sister, I could date

Hedy Lamarr, Lana Turner and Rita Hayworth with Ann Sheridan as a chaser.'" Much to the chagrin of the braggadocio, Hedy was taken off the market when she became Mrs. John Loder during the war.

Hedy wore many hats during the war effort. Much was asked of Americans to show their assistance for the war effort by the rationing of goods. Such items that were commonplace prior to the war were now essential for the war effort and thus difficult to get one's hands on. Americans were urged to be more self-reliant — it seemed everyone managed their own little "victory garden," where potatoes, tomatoes, and other small crops were grown — but Hedy opted to purchase a number of chickens in order to operate her own chicken farm. Before she went off to the film set, Hedy would gather the eggs her hens laid. She placed upon her elliptical edibles a unique stamp that marked the eggs as raised by Hedy Lamarr. But Hedy needn't give up her day job for the occupation of egg baron, for she was also engaged as the spokeswoman for Woodbury Complete Beauty Cream. Between acting, egg gathering and stamping, entertaining troops at the Hollywood Canteen, and giving the sales pitch for cosmetics, it seemed Miss Lamarr's itinerary was complete, but she managed to make time for the sale of war bonds.

Having grown up in Europe, the continent most ravaged by the Second World War, Hedy was eager to promote the sale of bonds in order to cease the global hostilities. Hitler needed to be bagged, and Miss Lamarr promoted the sale of war bonds tirelessly. She visited The City of Brotherly Love, where she attended the war-bond luncheon at the Midday Club, and folks willing to purchase $5,000 war bonds were able to take their meal at Hedy's table. On a war bond visit in 1942, Hedy shook hands with every worker at the York Lock and Safe Company. But, offering individuals the hardy hand clasp took second billing to the planting of a kiss on war bond buyers. Many celebrities toured the nation selling war bonds, and when an individual made a large transaction he was often rewarded for his patriotism with an exercise in osculation. The "Lips for Liberty" campaign made the practice of smooching war-bond buyers fashionable, and when Hedy was slated to attend a war-bond rally in Chicago in 1942, a wiseacre businessman named Haffa jested that he might kiss Miss Lamarr if *she* bought a $25,000 war bond.

Hedy Lamarr may have been more successful as a war-bond seller than a pin-up girl. Not one to strut around in bathing suits and have gents snap off a picture or two, Hedy was often photographed in more tasteful poses — typically facial profile shots or waist-up stills. Soldiers didn't seem to mind that Hedy had an aversion for leg art, for they pinned her pictures up regardless; they were intoxicated by her remarkable beauty. During the war, she was one of the most popular dames in show business — her physical appeal admired by throngs of people. She received numerous autograph requests from soldiers and even had a request sent her from Liu Chieh of the Chinese embassy. She was a hit all across the globe, even with the concept of beauty as an eye of the beholder issue, because her beauty was one unquestioned. So popular was Hedy that when soldiers expected her and got another celebrity, they were let down. Once, when Secretary of War Harry Stimson was set to arrive at Newfoundland via plane, he was met by two ecstatic lieutenants whose merriment quickly subsided when Secretary Stimson exited the plane. Noting their long faces, Stimson asked the two junior officers why they bore the appearance of the dejected. He learned, via the disheartened discourse of the lieutenants, that they had been had in a joke, for they were told that they were sent to escort Hedy Lamarr back to base but instead got the less appealing Secretary of War.

# ★ DOROTHY LAMOUR ★

The face and figure of the war-bond drive, the comely Dorothy Lamour seemingly left no acre of America untouched in her mission to raise money for the war effort. Hand selected by Secretary of Treasury Henry Morgenthau to lead the first organized war-bond drive, Miss Lamour ditched her famed sarongs to help in the war effort. She traveled from coast to coast promoting the sale of war bonds, amassing mammoth amounts of currency to be used to defeat the Axis. The papers across the country often referred to the dark-haired dynamo as "The First Lady in Uncle Sam's Bond Selling Campaign." From city to city she would greet throngs of supporters, give them the sales pitch, and then take her tour to the next stop on the map. America has its figures, its symbols of patriotism, such as the bald eagle and the statue of liberty, but one of the nation's grandest figures during the war was the astonishing frame of the country's leading seller of war bonds, the incomparable Dorothy Lamour.

Born in the Louisiana bay city of New Orleans, Dorothy was a starry-eyed girl who sought a career in show business from an early age. Well trained in dance and vocals, Dorothy, who gained early employment as an elevator operator, was able to wave goodbye to the lift and rely on her charms to support her way of life. She established herself as a leading female vocalist with work in bands and on the radio, and given her eastern success as a songbird, the west coast, with its climatic allure and star-making possibilities, was the next stop for La Lamour. Unlike many young beauties who seek stardom in motion pictures, Dorothy's wait was limited, perhaps due to her nonchalance regarding the motion picture industry. She never sought a career in pictures — she trained exclusively for vocals — which enabled her to give a rather relaxed screen test that

*Dorothy Lamour.* COURTESY OF MOVIEMARKET.COM

caught the eye of Hollywood executives. Without formal training as an actress, Dorothy landed a lead role in an exotic picture that catapulted her to stardom courtesy her exceptional, sarong-clad image.

Although less than ten percent of Dorothy's films had her strut around in her trademark sarong, Miss Lamour is best remembered as Hollywood's leading sarong siren. She starred as native princesses, habiting islands with her unique brand of pulchritude, which instilled in the hearts of male leads those feelings of exotic passions with the slightly clad cutie. The sarongs served her well, mostly because she looked dynamite in them, both as an actress and as a pin-up girl. Many Lamour pin-ups for the troops took advantage of her sarong-themed background, as photographers had the dark-haired beauty recline on cots or seated on seashores, showcasing her flawless frame with her long, slender legs protruding from underneath her sarong. Oftentimes, she would employ an exotic flower tucked behind an ear to give her that island girl quality she was constantly asked to deliver in motion pictures.

How Dorothy Lamour found time enough to pose for pin-up purposes is a marvel to her time management. The New Orleans native made several films during the war but was constantly on the go, traveling from state to state on her war-bond junkets. With an itinerary minus an idle hour, Dorothy may have been the most overworked gal in Hollywood. But her southern, down-to-earth upbringing enabled her to soldier through the long hours, lack of rest, train rides, and speeches before crowds. She was always on the move, but everywhere she went folks were grateful for her stop. In many cities, like Augusta, Maine, Dorothy was given a key to the city. On one war-bond junket she was named honorary mayor of Huntington, West Virginia, where the state's Navy named her their first honorary yeomanette. The further Dorothy went with her war-bond drive, the more accolades she piled up.

Adept at giving the war-bond sales pitch, Dorothy has been credited with earning over $300 million for the war effort. When she was first asked by Secretary Morgenthau to lead the war drive, her first northeastern tour was quite fruitful, for she was able to net the War Department over $52 million. She would often take the stage at her war-bond gatherings and regale the crowd with a speech or two about how they could help defeat the evils of the world. She would often tell her gatherings that "there's no need to urge you people to buy bonds until it hurts, because if you do not purchase them, shortly it will hurt." Devoted to the troops, Dorothy knew that many folks at her war-bond gatherings had sons, brothers, and cousins in the service, and she appealed to their sense of familial duty. Miss Lamour would often claim, "I think everyone who is buying war bonds should remember that he is investing in the eyesight, the legs, arms and lives of our boys."

Stages at fairgrounds and platforms at city halls were only a few places where Dorothy would give her bond sales pitch. Oftentimes she wouldn't be elevated on some dais at all, but placed among the working men and women — where she felt right at home. She would typically visit a city and tour their leading manufacturing plants where she would speak to the workers and build morale with her presence. Nicknamed "The Bond Bombshell," Lamour would sell bonds to plant workers, foremen, and bosses, gathering as much for the War Department as folk's modest budgets would allow. Despite the many letters and citations she received from management, commending her for her visits, there were some who felt that Dorothy's presence at plants was counterproductive. An odd shrew named Zelam Monohana, head of the Office Workers' Union, criticized Dorothy by claiming that Miss Lamour "was responsible for the loss of thousands of man hours when she went through war plants and stopped work." Dorothy offered the blowhard an eloquent rebuttal, stating, "The next time Secretary Morgenthau asks me to go on a bond-selling tour I'm going, whether Miss Monohana likes it or not." The union head did not represent the common sentiment of the average American, who looked upon Dorothy's work as admirable — something that a celebrity should be praised for, not subjected to criticism.

Dorothy knew where the best spots were to ply her craft as war-bond saleswoman. Americans had struggled with the Great Depression and not all had deep pockets capable of donating a large amount to the War Department in order to subdue the Axis. On her tour of Charleston, West Virginia, Dorothy made headlines when she averaged $10,000 worth of war bonds sold in a minute. During her visit to the governor's office, Dorothy's first fifteen minutes in the governor's chamber netted her $150,000 in war-bond sales. In order to gather over $30 million worth of war bonds, she had to work not only around the country but also around the clock. On one of her tours, Dorothy said that three hours of sleep was all she could ever get due to the taxing nature of the traveling campaign. But she was merely stating a fact, not making a complaint, for she knew the soldiers faced greater deprivations of sleep while engaged with the enemy. She met with the soldiers whenever possible, and when she had a free hour, which was seldom, she would play hostess at the Hollywood Canteen. The soldiers were grateful for her dedication to her country as bond seller, entertainer, and pin-up girl, so much so that they handed her a bevy of flattering nicknames, from "Miss Wartime America" to the crew of the USS Gudgeon's pet moniker, "The Girl We'd Most Like to Go Down in a Submarine With."

Soldiers and sailors, airmen and Marines are not the only folks who serve their country, for amongst the ranks of civilians can be found those just as patriotic. Dorothy Lamour embodied this concept during World War II. She did not take up arms, but with her dedication to the war effort she saw that there would be arms to take up — the only instruments that can defend liberty and the American way of life. Traveling the nation and meeting Americans in their various settings gave Dorothy a better appreciation for her country. When she returned to Hollywood after her war-bond tour, Dorothy said, "I'd like to write a book and call it 'Salute to America!' That's exactly how I feel about this country. You know, you can sound pretty drippy and silly just mouthing patriotic phrases. I always felt I loved my country but I never really knew how much I can love it — how much it can come to mean to you — until you have gone through one of these nationwide bond-selling tours."

## ★ CAROLE LANDIS ★

Green may not have been the favorite color of any actress during the 1940s, but nearly every dame in Hollywood wore the color when Miss Landis passed by. There wasn't a woman alive who didn't envy Carole Landis her perfect figure, as gals seethed with envy when guys issued admiring whistles at Landis's exquisite hourglass shape. Men in the film industry would bestow upon the shapely blonde one crude nickname after another, which failed to flatter Carole, with monikers like "The Ping Girl" and "The Chest," paying tribute — albeit a lewd tribute — to perhaps the loveliest woman in Hollywood. But the tributes did not impress Carole Landis whose ambition was to be a legitimate actress. She desired focus to be trained on her thespian skills and not her superior chest, and with such terrific work in films like *I Wake Up Screaming* and *Topper Returns*, her star quality was evident. She was a hardworking actress who toiled for a few years in obscurity before her break through role in *One Million B.C.*, which endeared her to filmgoers across the country. But it was thanks to her quality of being a selfless individual that she really found widespread American endearment. She was, during the war years, the unrivalled Queen of the USO, who visited the servicemen wherever they went — territories where soldiers trained as well as hostile regions where bullets flew.

Instant success was not Carole Landis's when first she arrived at Hollywood. She caught the eye of film producers — a regard she never failed at, given her flawless beauty — which enabled her to find work in motion pictures. She typically appeared without a credit in blink-and-you-missed-it parts as background window-dressing. There never was any question with regard to her appearance — she possessed the

*Carole Landis.* COURTESY OF MOVIEMARKET.COM

look and then some to be in pictures — but as a shapely blonde, her skill as an actress was initially questioned. Miss Landis certainly was a woman of unmatched physical charms, with dancing eyes, full bosom, and a quality structure from head to toe. But, for whatever reason, such charms bore the stigma of a lack of talent; the reasoning may have been that a doll with such exquisite dimensions, blessed as she was physically, could not possibly be blessed with intelligence and acting skill as well. The assumption, which may have been true in other regards, proved false in the case of Carole Landis. After several years of toiling in background roles, she achieved a level of stardom with her role in *One Million B.C.*

She captured the attention of film audiences in *One Million B.C.* in much the same way she gained notice among studio executives in Hollywood: via the pulchritude route. A period-piece film that depicted an era in which clothing was at a rudimentary stage, the way her terrific figure strained under her rags drew the admiration of filmgoers — more so than the acting talent she would later display in film noirs and comedies. But at least her delicate foot was in the proverbial door. However, her breakout role coincided with escalating hostilities across the globe, and Carole would soon be engaged in a struggle far more important than the pursuit of a career in motion pictures. A down-to-earth lady, Carole Landis possessed not the constitution of a selfish film starlet, too preoccupied with her own career and the Tinseltown nightlife to take notice of the world around her. If anything, she was the opposite — perhaps too eager to assist others, to make people, strangers even, feel like they were in her heart and prayers. Her actions during World War II were beyond commendable. Miss Landis displayed an attitude of selfless patriotism that words seem wholly inadequate to describe.

When the Americans entered the war effort in late 1941, Carole waited not a split second to get involved. During the 1940s, women were not open to join the ranks of Uncle Sam's fighting forces in the fashion they are today, but there were plenty agencies a woman could gain employment to assist in the war effort. She worked in conjunction with the FBI as a finger printer, inking the distal phalanxes of workers at airplane factories for the sake of national security. Not fulfilled with the assignment, Carole wanted to do more and joined the Aerial Nurse Corps of America and became a member of the Bundles for Bluejackets society. She worked tirelessly for the Bundles for Bluejackets campaign as a storekeeper third class, gathering clothes and sewing kits for soldiers. Of higher rank in the Aerial Nurse Corps of America, Carole was the commander of the First Division with assignments in the instruction of the proper folding and application of bandages.

Carole Landis was not the type of woman to allow others to dictate her actions. Studios preferred dames they could tether, agreeable actresses who would do their bidding, ranging from studio arranged dates to public appearances, and during the war many studios urged their stars to participate in the sale of war bonds. But Miss Landis was a patriot in need of no prodding. Her work with Bundles for Bluejackets and the Aerial Nurse Corps of America proved her devotion to defeating the Axis, but the determined blonde wanted more than an auxiliary role. To lend support in the comfort of her homeland, while many American men were engaged in battle overseas, was a proposition that Miss Landis viewed as unacceptable. She was quite vocal in her ambition to travel to where the boys were, which endeared her to the chaps in the Armed Forces. By the spring of 1942, Carole had established herself as one of the military's preferred pin-ups. She claimed that ninety percent of her fan mail came from the boys in service. Her patriotism was one of the attractions that made servicemen swoon, but Dee Lowrance explained the other, penning "Take one lovely figure, add a saucy smile and top it off with blonde hair — and you have a perfect recipe for the kind of girl servicemen love. Carole Landis has all these ingredients, which explains why she is such a hit on the foxhole circuit."

There certainly wasn't a more appealing foxhole warmer than the gal who actually visited the foxholes, the "Morale Booster" Carole Landis. Discontented with her work in the Aerial Nurse Corps of America, Carole lined up an overseas USO tour of the British Isles, and she persuaded Kay Francis, Mitzi Mayfair, and funny-girl Martha Raye to join her. The comely quartet was initially slated to spend about a month touring the installations on the British Isles, but their itinerary was altered when they met with the boys. The impact they had on the troops, most of whom hadn't seen an American woman since they left for service, pulled at the heart strings of the four ladies, so they decided to extend their stay. One lonely soldier had a lasting impact on Carole, who spotted the forlorn trooper near the mail depot. When she asked him what troubled him, he informed Carole that he had heard nothing from back home. The look of the soldier saddened her, as he asked the lovely actress if he could possibly read one of her letters. Carole said that the soldier claimed, "I'd like to pretend that it's to me."

To befriend Carole Landis was certainly the goal of many soldiers who crossed her path, and the amiable actress was always willing to lend her time to the servicemen. She struck a close bond with a fighter pilot named

Johnny McKee, as the two displaced Americans bemoaned the fact that a person couldn't get their hands on a fresh egg in England. Given Carole's status as a celebrity, she was able to finagle a dozen eggs from a group of British soldiers and promptly contacted Lieutenant McKee to share in her spoils. The pilot desired to dine with Miss Landis, but first he had a mission. He promised Carole that once he returned they could consume the delicacy they had pined for. Carole patiently waited for Lt. McKee's return, but it didn't come that evening. She learned that he had been shot down and feared the worst for her friend, but Lt. McKee had been rescued by the French Underground, who escorted him back to England. He eventually made it back to England and Carole. About Lt. McKee's ordeal, Carole said, "No wonder he set a record for escaping and getting back to London. All the time, he said, he was thinking about those eggs."

What was to be a four week tour of the British Isles, turned into a five-month journey of the European Theater. The ladies saw how much their visit meant to the troops in England, so they amended their initial plans and decided to visit the servicemen stationed in Africa as well. By expanding the scope of their visit, the four ladies of liberty forfeited their stateside Christmas plans and spent the holiday season overseas with the troops. Such a sacrifice by four female civilians did not go unnoticed by the men in service. They became more than just a group of American girls — their image transformed from entertainers to symbols of American womanhood. They represented all the goodness left behind in America, and Carole Landis understood that the soldiers needed her there, amongst them, serving as a beacon who brightened all the darkness, all the mayhem of war, which showed them that not all was violence — not all was in vain. She was not an actress, removed from her lofty setting where lavish leisure was the order of the day, but the bodily representation of decency. Carole said that the boys didn't want to hear stories about Hollywood, the glitz and glamour, the zesty nightlife, the parties, and swell times. They asked her not to regale them with stories of Tinseltown during the holiday season, requesting only that she sing them *White Christmas*. To the soldiers engaged in war, absent the touch of goodness, Carole Landis signified all they were fighting for.

During her five month trip, Carole and her comrades averaged five shows a day. They experienced hardships the like modern day stars could never fathom, for they simulated not the agonies of war but dwelt among them — shared in the experience. Many times Carole's performances were interrupted by the resounding noise of a low-flying plane or, worse yet, the blitz of enemy mortars. More than once, Carole had to seek protection in trenches and foxholes, where she was shielded by the men she came to entertain. The times were tough on Carole and her three companions, but never a complaint was issued from their delicate lips. Miss Landis understood the hardships of the soldier, and complaining about the absent frivolities most Americans take for granted would have been an ill-conceived gesture. She told reporters, after her return stateside, that all she could manage in Africa was two hot baths her entire stay. About her tour of the Dark Continent, Carole said, "We wore turbans and snoods and tried to camouflage the whole affair of knowing how filthy we were — but it was pretty uncomfortable."

Carole returned to the comfort of American soil early in 1943 after her five month USO tour. One would imagine that she'd make a direct trip to Hollywood, where she could return to the lifestyle she had left behind, but she decided to take a solo journey to stateside military bases. One of the first camps she visited upon her stateside return was the Greenville Army Airfield. When she first arrived, a soldier removed a dollar bill from his pocket to have Carole autograph it — a common practice of servicemen during the war — which prompted Carole to dig into her purse and display a signed bill of currency she had brought back from the war regions. She told the soldier, "Look what I have — Eisenhower!" At Greenville she was met with the warmest of receptions, for the papers across the nation kept strict tabs on her doings overseas. She was, given that she chose to venture to war, America's unrivalled morale booster. The troops lavished her with praise, gave her a tour of the installation, took photographs with her in the hangar, and dined with her at their mess hall. Taken aback by Carole's selection of food, she merrily devoured a plate full of Army beans, much to the shock of the soldiers at the base. She told them that the military messes overseas had so few beans.

Miss Landis never complained about her USO tour of the battle regions, even if it wasn't conducive to the pampering that beauty seems to require. She felt it was the grandest endeavor she was ever engaged in and viewed her return to the film industry, where she had several movies in the works, as a lifestyle woefully inadequate during time of war. To keep herself grounded while she shot films, Carole would often attend canteens and dance with servicemen or visit hospitals where wounded soldiers were housed. But people in the film industry saw in Carole a lack of enthusiasm on film sets and knew not from whence it came. Scribe Erskine Johnson spoke with Carole and learned why she had a less-than-thrilled view of her return to Hollywood. Johnson wrote, "After you've flown over battle zones in bombers, crouched in foxholes — once for an hour and forty minutes — while all hell was breaking loose over your head, motion pictures must seem rather unimportant." To Miss Landis, who had worked hard to become an actress, the occupation of acting, where make-believe is the day's order, failed to satiate her desire to serve her country.

What helped Carole through the inadequacy she felt after her return to the States was her work on the book *Four Jills in a Jeep*, which detailed her travels overseas. The story was one of profound interest and her studio felt that they should adapt her wartime biography to the screen. And so the motion picture *Four Jills in a Jeep* was conceived. Many in the industry bloviated that the picture was nothing more than a vanity piece for the shapely star, but Carole made it known that she would rather return to the troops than work on the film. American audiences had fallen in love with Bob Hope and Joe E. Brown, two comedians who traveled all over the globe entertaining troops in war zones (Brown's son was killed in action), and the lady they adored above all others was Miss Landis for mirroring their selfless, patriotic spirit. This spirit shone through in the film, not as a bit of acting or as an engagement for vanity's sake but as the real-life experiences of a woman who sacrificed so much for her country. Before *Four Jills in a Jeep* hit the big screen, Miss Landis said, "You can't put patriotism into words. You can put it in a trench, or a factory. But no one who has ever seen how starved the boys are for the sight and sound of an American girl could rest until she was back doing her ludicrously little to make them happy, to make their lives easier. I've got to go back — and I'm going back as soon as they'll let me. A girl's got to live with herself and I couldn't if I stayed at home right now."

With her tour of the European Theater in the books, Carole decided she should treat the boys with her unique brand of pulchritudinous entertainment in the Pacific Theater. When she heard that comedian Jack Benny was slated to tour the Pacific Islands, Carole jumped at the chance to join the funnyman. Their initial stop was Australia and from there they began a trip to the islands, but Carole, who had battled through pain, discomfort, and hazards in both Europe and Africa, contracted an illness unique to the region and had to be sent home to convalesce. When her tour was cut short, writer George Sampas quipped that the soldiers in the European Theater got Carole while the boys in the Pacific got rubber-faced comedian Joe E. Brown. But the cancellation of her tour distressed Carole, who found it a letdown and no laughing matter. She felt she had disappointed the boys, but agreed to an unusual request to soothe their unbridled desire for the Carole Landis Experience. Miss Landis agreed to sigh over the airwaves so those soldiers who missed her on her travails could get the amorous shudders akin to those experienced by the gents who saw Carole in the flesh.

No pin-up exemplified the all-encompassing role of the cheesecake model more than Carole Landis. It is true, her pin-up production didn't match the output of other wartime cheesecake models, but the servicemen did not mind, given there was a chance they might see Miss Landis in the flesh at one of her USO tours. The woman who brought plenty sunshine to a world darkened by war died young, just a few years after the great battle had concluded. A remarkable woman, who felt it her duty to comfort the tired and the battle weary, was found dead the morning after Independence Day 1948. The servicemen she met lost their wartime angel at the age of 29. She understood better than any woman who ever entertained the troops, better than any woman who posed for a pin-up picture, just what she meant to the boys in service. About her work as a morale-builder during the war, Carole Landis said, "You know, while you stand up there entertaining that most of the time you're not you, Carole Landis, but a symbol to the boys around — a bit of a wife, a sweetheart, a sister, a mother. You're just an American girl to an American boy, lonely for the feel of home." Miss Landis gave the men in service that feel of home. She didn't have to, but that noble heart in her breast, which pulsated with the sense of national pride, of selfless behavior, was one we should all aspire to duplicate.

## ★ JOAN LESLIE ★

Born in the Motor City during the mid-1920s, Joan's family relocated to Los Angeles in order to cash in on the cute appeal she and her sisters possessed. Before she had reached her teen years, Joan appeared in motion pictures under her birth name of Joan Brodel. In the mid to late 1930s, the young Miss Leslie appeared in a few films but typically in unaccredited roles. Only when the budding of womanhood reached Joan did her career take off. She adopted the stage name of Joan Leslie when she landed the second female lead role in the Humphrey Bogart film *High Sierra* with Ida Lupino. The picture was widely regarded as Bogie's breakout role and was also the movie that introduced American audiences to one of Hollywood's newest radiant roses. The film that elevated her career hit the show houses in 1941, and America's entrance in the war late that year helped keep Joan Leslie in the spotlight. The fair-haired beauty became one of America's favorite young actresses with her work in war-themed pictures and reels produced by the Emergency Relief Fund.

Some people are born actors. Joan's family had a bit of the thespian ambition that propelled the lovely redhead to hours on the boards at tender ages; Joan made her acting debut at the age of two. When the family relocated to the west coast, Joan was able to pursue work in the motion picture industry with her sisters. Joan was the only Brodel daughter to eventually gain stardom in the film industry, but during the war

*Joan Leslie.* COURTESY OF MOVIEMARKET.COM

years, the young beauty had to juggle stardom with education. Most of her matriculation came on movie sets. When she received her high school diploma, she knew so few of her classmates because her book learning was not conducted in the typical classroom setting with fellow teenagers, but on a film set where few kids dwelled. She was still a high-school-aged teenager when she became an overnight hit with her work opposite the legendary Humphrey Bogart.

It wasn't long after *High Sierra* hit the theaters when the Japanese bombed Pearl Harbor, which propelled the United States into the Second World War. Not yet a high school graduate at the outset of America's involvement in the war, Joan nevertheless became the youthful face and figure for wartime America. Not only was Joan a budding star with work opposite Bogie and Lupino under her belt, but Miss Leslie was approached to star in a film developed by the Emergency Relief Fund titled *This is the Army*, which turned over all its proceeds to the American Red Cross. The motion picture did not line the pockets of the elite Hollywood producers, nor did it bestow upon Joan the wherewithal to secure the typical lavish Tinseltown lifestyle, for the film's earnings went directly to provide aid for servicemen and their families. Dedicated to securing victory, Joan starred in the venture not as means to promote herself, but as a way to educate Americans on life during war.

During the 1940s, Joan did a lot for the war effort. A rather busy girl, Miss Leslie had to focus not only on her film work but also her studies, yet these two important aspects of her life were often pushed aside to help support the troops. Joan toured aplenty on war-bond drives, and she was a common face at the Hollywood Canteen where soldiers were allowed to unwind and rub elbows with the stars of the film industry. Time management was a task for Joan who, late in the war effort, divided her time between work, troop entertainment, and college preparation exam studies. There must have been times when Joan felt pulled from every direction, but most Americans made sacrifices, so the doll didn't have to struggle alone. The war froze lives, forbade folks to pursue their personal goals, and in more tragic cases, the war ended lives, which put something as minor as halted dreams into perspective.

As one of Hollywood's youngest starlets, the strawberry blonde was a favorite among the young gents just mustered into the service. Her studio was aware that *High Sierra* forced filmgoers to take notice of their latest unveiled beauty, and they set up more than one pin-up photo shoot for further unveiling. During the war, it seemed that every newly designed bathing suit made its way to Miss Leslie's wardrobe to be worn for cheesecake stills that soldiers could acquire. A pin-up fixture, the delicate beauty of Joan Leslie impressed upon the servicemen an image of the girl-next-door they had waiting for them back home. Photographed wearing bathing suits no end, Joan was positioned by pools, seated on towels soaking up the sun's rays, and leaning on poolside ladders. Her bathing-suit-clad image was toted from one military installation to the next, in the possession of young fighting men in need of an ideal portrait of blossoming American womanhood.

As in all walks of life, there are rubes roaming the dust roads, and Warner Studios (Joan's bosses) received an unusual letter to be forwarded to Miss Leslie in 1945: the final year of hostilities. Joan had spent count-less hours climbing in and out of bathing suits and posing for pin-up purposes, which enabled her to have a rather sizable amount of cheesecake stills to her credit. But not everyone understood the reasoning behind pin-up art. A soldier stationed at Colorado was so miffed by all the pho-tographs he saw of Joan Leslie modeling bathing suits that he decided to inquire whether her vocation had changed. When Warner Studios received the letter, they couldn't believe that a man could be so thick-headed — especially one in the service who had been exposed to pin-up art — to not understand the concept of morale-boosting via swimsuit packaged pulchritude. Erskine Johnson wrote, "Psychologists at Warner Brothers are desperately trying to figure out what's wrong with a sergeant at Fort Logan, Colorado, who wrote Joan Leslie wanting to know why the studio sent out so many pictures of her in bathing suits."

Most folks in the military understood why Joan posed in bathing suits and were want to show their appreciation to the beautiful young starlet. After the close of the war, when the USS New York returned stateside and docked at San Pedro after its service in Japanese waters, Joan's presence was requested by the sailors on board who desired to pay tribute to their favorite pin-up girl. The captain of the ship, Grayson B. Carter, crowned Joan "Queen of the USS New York," after its return home. The crowning ceremony was followed by the screening of her movie, *Rhapsody in Blue*, to every sailor on board.

But there was one soldier in particular who credited Joan with his recovery from a serious war injury. Army Staff Sergeant Don Saucke was shot down over France and spent weeks convalescing in various overseas military hospitals. The fight to regain his strength was grueling, but the determined sergeant persevered. He wrote Joan a personal letter that informed Miss Leslie that hearing her voice in the film *Rhapsody in Blue*, singing songs for the film's soundtrack, inspired him to fight his way back to health. Touched by the sergeant's letter, Joan was so moved by the inspiration her film role had on the wounded veteran that she promised to sing to him at the Hollywood Bowl. She proved that the promise wasn't a flimsy commitment to be forgotten shortly after its issuance, for when Sergeant Saucke returned stateside, Joan kept her promise and performed a private solo just for the returned hero.

## ★ MARILYN MAXWELL ★

Marvel Marilyn Maxwell was born a farmer's daughter in Clarinda, Iowa, but after she substituted the cornfields and cow pastures for the charisma and crowning good times of Hollywood, she dropped her first name and adopted her middle as her stage name. The curvy blonde farm girl got her start on the USO circuit and gained a level of fame entertaining the troops as eye candy in Bob Hope's skits. Known to sport tight-fitting sweaters, which accentuated an ample bust in need of little accentuation, Miss Maxwell would often croon love ballads to the soldiers in attendance. The soldiers, captivated by Marilyn's voice as well as the strain on her sweaters, were always a rapt audience and were left awestruck and glassy-eyed by the sultry songs Miss Maxwell sang for them.

Raised very much the rural dove, Marilyn took voice lessons at an early age and developed an extraordinary singing voice. It was her voice, coupled with her marvelous looks, which carried her through the bumps of the world of celebrity. The film industry was not Marilyn's ambition. She had trained as a singer and landed a gig with the top-flight Buddy Rogers Band, but Mr. Rogers was married to a well-known Hollywood player: Mary Pickford. Mary — at one time the highest earning female performer in Hollywood — encouraged Miss Maxwell to give acting a try. Marilyn took the advice of the legendary Miss Pickford and surrendered her role as a vocalist in a big band for a shot at fame in the motion picture business. When Marilyn took her initial screen test for film studios, the war was well underway, and she had agreed to tour military bases under the auspices of the USO. While on tour, she was informed that MGM had been thoroughly impressed with her screen test and wanted her to sign on with their company.

Possessing pulchritude in spades did not hurt Marilyn in regard to entering the ranks of Hollywood film players. A stunning beauty with curves that induced more than one whistle, Miss Maxwell had her appeal factor substantiated on the USO tours. It took little for the buxom blonde to set the servicemen to swoon, for once she set her delicate feet on a stage, the whistles rose in both volume and quantity. After her tour with the USO, the aspiring actress made her way to Hollywood to begin a career in pictures. One of the first films she worked on was the Lucille Ball vehicle, *DuBarry Was a Lady*. The film boasted the alluring talents of a bevy of background beauties, of which Marilyn was one, and a photo shoot was set up for the lovely lasses whose talent had as yet gone untapped. Twelve

*Marilyn Maxwell.*

dames were dressed up as showgirls for the lavish musical with monthly themes, and Marilyn's month was that of February. Her outfit consisted of a red velvet gown which employed Valentine's Day as the February distinction. Artists on set constructed the pinnacle of beauty and chose certain parts of the twelve gals' anatomy to build the perfect woman; they chose Marilyn's ankles as the best of the crop. Of her ankles, the three artists said, "Marilyn's ankles are trim, slim, patrician and above all, exciting!"

When she became a studio player, Marilyn did not let stardom go to her head but remained grounded and returned to the USO tours. Although she was on the cusp of a lucrative acting career, she understood that the war effort was of greater importance and lined up a return trip to the military bases. In 1943, she entertained with a troupe headlined by actor Spencer Tracy that toured bases in what would eventually become the uppermost state in the union. She was able to tour the Aleutian Islands, along the coast of Alaska, before she ventured to more hostile regions near Guadalcanal on the Solomon Islands. Wherever she went, the breathtaking beauty was a hit with the troops. She distributed pin-up pictures when she had them to give, and quickly became a sensation with the servicemen who placed a premium on thumbtacks so they could display their favorite USO doll. A pin-up of Marilyn was produced in the *Long Beach Independent* with a caption beside it that read, "The Army, Navy, Marines have openly stated from the Aleutians to the Solomons, including North Africa and Sicily, that Marilyn Maxwell is a blonde they'll pin up anytime."

A top pin-up girl during the war, Marilyn's cheesecake stills were slightly different from the bathing suit photographs that littered military walls. Many of Miss Maxwell's pin-up photos showcased her exceptional form in lavish shoulder-baring dresses or tight-fitting sweaters, although she was known to pose beside a pool or two like other pin-ups. Oftentimes the dresses she wore for the photographers were leg revealing gowns that showcased her streamlined landing gear. For all the pulchritude that the stunning Miss Maxwell possessed, she was best known to wartime America as a USO entertainer. She devoted herself to the soldiers, touring overseas bases, singing on stages, and performing the occasional skit, but the beauty's heart matched the golden tincture of her hair. In 1945, when the war was at its end, Marilyn kept the boys in her heart and volunteered to tour military hospitals. She visited Camp Davis and other installations on a tour of infirmaries to lift the spirits of our wounded heroes. At the military hospital on Davis, Marilyn sang songs for the injured troops and chatted with them at their bedsides. About the impression she made on the war casualties, Dorothea Tomlinson Love wrote, "Miss Maxwell is graceful and willowy, and possesses a figure that makes the women green with envy and the men pink with admiration; and as one soldier aptly expressed it: 'She not only raises the morale, but the blood pressure.'"

# ★ MARIE McDONALD ★

There have been many women throughout history who have journeyed to Hollywood in search of an acting career, however, the failed attempts greatly outweigh the successes. In an industry that places a profound emphasis on physical appeal, an aspiring actress is better served by pulchritude than acting skill. Hollywood never fails to unearth a new pretty face but oftentimes projects the image of an aversion to thespians with actual skill in the craft of playacting. Marie "The Body" McDonald was an actress who relied chiefly on her physical charms during her foray in the film industry. Although she worked in Hollywood for a number of years, Marie never did establish herself as a legitimate actress with a breakout role. But she tried. She tried so hard that her life became a train wreck, staging outlandish stunts, engaging in illicit affairs, and indulging in illegal drugs all as a method to achieve stardom. It never came for the stunning pin-up who died in her forties courtesy a drug overdose.

Marie McDonald was born with show business in her veins. Her mother was a former Ziegfeld Girl and her grandmother a Viennese opera star, and young Marie was trained, from an early age, to follow in their footsteps. Shapely young women find employment in the modeling industry easy to procure, and The Body began work as a teenager in the field of physical exhibition. The comely cutie, despite her enviable contours, was initially assigned the chores of a hand model, but when she suffered the Curse of the Star of India she became a full body model. As a hand model, Marie was once asked to handle The Star of India for a photo shoot, but shortly after handling the world's largest sapphire, Marie broke a finger. The digit mended slightly crooked, which put an end to Marie's days as an exclusive hand model. The Star of India came with its own personal stigma, as the legend goes, that whosoever disturbs the sapphire shall have evil visited upon them. Fortunately for Marie, the evil visited upon her for laying hands on the great sapphire left her with a finger a tab bit askew — nothing too vile.

With her days as a hand model over, Marie utilized her full assemblage in the modeling business. Her exceptional looks attracted the attention of Tinseltown talent scouts, and she made her way out to Hollywood to test her skills as an actress. At the time she signed her first studio contract, the

United States had just entered the Second World War. With the pin-up girl craze at its infancy, Marie delved into the art and became a sensation in the cheesecake corners. She had modeled for magazines and print ads before the war, but only when she started with the leg art did Marie's career take off. A delight with the servicemen, Marie's studio took notice of the fact that the men in Uncle Sam's fighting forces had adopted her as one of

*Marie McDonald.*

their favorite pin-up girls, and they began to assign roles in film for Marie with a bit more substance than background eye candy. Her first major role came in the Anne Baxter vehicle *Guest in the House*, in which Marie played, what else, a model. A scribe for the *Laredo Times* was impressed with Marie's acting, as he penned, "For a Miss Cheesecake who has been allowed to display only her legs and other charms, it was all pretty nice."

Marie wanted to be a legitimate actress but was regarded around Hollywood circles as the stunning blonde with an equally stunning figure. It was on a studio set, and not via the servicemen, that Marie became known as "The Body." Always one to accept the spotlight, for nothing cheered her more than to see her name in print, Marie didn't mind the moniker — she embraced it wholeheartedly. When the newspapermen began referring to Marie as "The Body," folks wanted to know the origin of the alias — whether it was a name bestowed upon her by a producer or a cameraman who found her fetching. Marie didn't know exactly who christened her "The Body," but she knew the exact moment it happened. While shooting a movie, Marie was seated on a stool at a film set, when some admiring gent sallied by and spotted her seated on the backless pedestal. The flushed fellow exclaimed, "Wow! Who's the body?"

Many women admired the structure of Marie McDonald and wanted to possess the frame of the dame who the papers commonly referred to as "The Body." Born with her appeal, which came courtesy her bloodline, Marie wasn't the type to be found sending volley after volley on the tennis court, or stepping out on the track, but had one simple fitness routine she adhered to; she informed women's health writer Ida Jean Kain that the extent of her physical fitness routine was a few exercises on a stretching bar. Kain ran with McDonald's inside dope. Ida Jean produced a photograph of Marie in one of her articles that stressed the importance of the stretching bar. She wrote, "There isn't any better exercise for filling out the chest, putting dimples over the collarbones and toning the muscles that support the bust than exercising on a stretching bar." To prove her point, Ida pointed to the snapshot of the shapely Marie and informed her readers that the stretching bar, and the stretching bar alone, was the only instrument that Marie devoted any time to in order to maintain her shape. Kain pointed to Marie's bust, which she listed at thirty-seven inches, as proof positive that the stretching bar was ideal for ladies looking to enhance the size of their chest.

Much of Marie's body was the delight of the servicemen who employed tacks to pin up her cheesecake stills. One of the top leg art models of the war, Marie was photographed no end by the boys behind the lens. The leggy cheesecake model was asked by the Navy to christen the plane

*March of Dimes* at the Glenn L. Martin Plant in Baltimore. To the boys in uniform, Marie was a snappy pair of legs who they fawned over not at small ceremonies but on photographs and in soldier magazines. The most famous soldier's magazine of the time was *Yank*, which did the boys a service in every issue by printing a pin-up photo. One such issue displayed a pin-up of Marie in which she was uncomfortably positioned so that only one streamlined leg was visible in the photograph. The soldiers were rarely picky when it came to pin-ups, but T-5 Ivan Kepmer was more than a little irked by Marie's one-leg photo shoot. He wrote into *Yank*, saying, "I'm a guy who whistles just as loud as the next GI when viewing a swell dame — either in the flesh or on paper — and your pin-up picture of Marie McDonald is no exception. But where the hell is her other leg?" The magazine received enough complaints in the vein of Kepmer's that Marie decided to have the photo shoot redone. When the next McDonald pin-up was distributed, Marie informed the boys that she didn't care for the earlier photo shoot either. She claimed that the position she posed in gave her leg a rigid, uncomfortable appearance.

## ★ ANN MILLER ★

What was simply an activity designed to strengthen her legs after suffering from a childhood illness, became an occupation and film trademark of the bubbly brunette. Annie Miller, the lithe-bodied Tinseltown Tapper, took her rehabilitation exercise as a tot and turned it into a career. Annie danced in films with the likes of Fred Astaire, scatter-stepping with her magic feet and keeping time with Hollywood's most famous dancers. Miss Miller danced her way to fame, first in pictures and later on Broadway. Her dancing feet made her a star, but during the war years, Miller was a favorite of the servicemen for her enthusiastic devotion to the boys in uniform. Ann never hesitated to visit the fighting men at their training posts. A popular pin-up girl, Annie even injected a little creativity into the enterprise of leg art and cheesecake stills.

Annie's father wanted a son so badly he imagined that he could deliver a boy via willpower. However, when his child was delivered, the gender was not to his liking, and since he had an affinity for the name Johnnie, he bestowed the handle on his little girl — so she was known as Johnnie Collier. But Annie's folks separated when she was but a little girl and her mother took her out west, where she signed little Miss Miller up for tap dancing lessons in order to regain strength she lost courtesy an illness. The lessons paid off, for Miss Miller became a dancing sensation in her early teens. Talent scouts took notice of the lass who was light on her feet, and when she was approached to sign a film contract, the child dancer was forced to lie about her age. Executives thought she was under the age of eighteen and demanded she produce a birth certificate, to which she did — albeit one fraudulent. She was able to slide her way through the doors of Hollywood with a slight application of flimflam artistry.

Before the war, Miss Miller had established herself as a coming star in Hollywood with her exceptional dancing skill and approachability. Not only could the sunny gal dance with her legs but her inviting eyes danced with an unrivaled degree of likability. Quick to establish herself as a fan favorite, Miss Miller was a hit with the gents in military service. Shortly before the bombing on Pearl Harbor, Annie had been named as a unit mascot for a searchlight battery based out of Albuquerque, New Mexico. The unit dubbed themselves "The Annie Millers," and was one of the first outfits to be sent overseas to engage the enemy at Bataan. A staunch supporter of the military, Annie kept strict tabs on her boys and was brokenhearted when she learned they had been captured by the Japanese and marched to a prisoner of war camp. As their unit mascot, Annie tried desperately to get the gents a collection of personal pin-up pictures, but feared the Japanese would not allow them to have the stills.

During the war years, Annie wasn't at a loss for things to keep herself busy. As a promising young entertainer with a glowing face the camera adored, Miss Miller was a cinch for motion pictures. Her career as an actress was about to spike, but she managed to make plenty time for the troops, who she would visit at bases and dance with at canteens. The famous young tap dancer spent so much time at nearby Camp Roberts that many people thought the delicate dancer had been drafted by Uncle Sam. But Annie Miller didn't visit the troops as a mandatory service for her country — far from it — but by an adherence to sense of duty and loyalty to the boys in the military. She understood that the servicemen led hectic lives and she did everything in her power to make a few of those hours a little less frenetic. When filming the war-era flick *Reveille with Beverly*, Annie got in the up-with-the-bugle's-blare spirit of the military and began her day at four a.m. sharp. The boys in service adored her for her spunky attitude and devotion to their well-being.

One of Miss Miller's favorite wartime hobbies was visiting the servicemen at their encampments and taking part in military training. Not the dainty type who sits from a safe distance and watches the grunts simulate war, Annie longed to be amongst the troops, firing rifles beside them. In 1942, she went on a military base tour and visited such training grounds as Camp Shelby, Mississippi, where she was able to massage her desire to grasp a firearm and send a few rounds down range. At a Camp Shelby firing range, Annie watched the soldiers zero their weapons but couldn't neglect that itch to take up a firing hole and squeeze a trigger herself. Much to her delight, when she asked if she could fire off a round or ten, the overseers at the firing range agreed and set her up on a firing

*Ann Miller.* COURTESY OF MOVIEMARKET.COM

line. Although she had a brush with illness, Annie gushed about her trip to Camp Shelby, telling a beat writer, "At Shelby in Mississippi I came down with something they called the Shelby Cough from dust I got in my throat on the range. I shot a machine gun there and got some bulls-eyes."

Annie Miller embraced her role as a pin-up girl. Many of her pin-up photo shoots were geared toward her career as a tap dancer, as she was commonly photographed in a dancing stance wearing, what else, leg-revealing clothing. With a streamlined figure and a pair of out-of-this-world legs, Annie was a soldier's delight — pinned up on barracks walls from post to post. Always for the troops, Annie wanted to add some ingenuity to the pin-up enterprise, and once had a pin-up puzzle of herself made for the troops. When soldiers requested a pin-up picture of her, Annie would sometimes ship the requester her specially made pin-up puzzle, but the plan wasn't always perfect. Annie once received a letter from a soldier who tried to piece the pretty pin-up girl together, but ran into a snag. His letter said, "I got your photo but one of your parts is missing."

In the winter of 1944–1945, Ann was the first Hollywood entertainer known to line-up a tour of military hospitals for the upcoming 1945 year to lift the spirits of wounded veterans. Never one to push aside a soldier eager to dance, Miss Miller dedicated herself to building morale among America's fighting men — those able-bodied and otherwise. Although many of the gents she visited at military hospitals were unable to cut a rug with Miss Miller, Annie nevertheless showed the men a good time. Tagging along with Annie was a small band that would play tunes to which Ann would sing and dance to. She invited Nancy Barnes, an accordion player whose husband was held at a prisoner of war camp, to keep the lady's mind off her personal struggles. A big-hearted woman, Annie looked out for the troops and kept heartbroken friends preoccupied by engaging them in activities they thrived at. Although tap-dancing will forever be Annie Miller's legacy, what she did for the troops, her desire to uplift countless spirits, was a legacy any decent person would be satisfied with.

## ★ DOLORES MORAN ★

Based solely on pin-up production, it seemed that Dolores Moran would have a better career in the film industry than fellow young starlet Lauren Bacall. The dynamic duo starred opposite the ever suave Humphrey Bogart in the classic flick *To Have and Have Not*, with each blonde raising the temperature on set. A bigger hit with the soldiers, given her ample stock of cheesecake stills, Miss Moran seemed poised for stardom, but it was Bacall and not Moran who became a cinema legend. Both women set the screen ablaze in the film by seducing Bogie, with neither woman clearly outshining the other in the department of acting. Bacall was just a novice at the time, and in certain spots in the movie it showed, while the stunning Dolores Moran, who had worked in lesser roles before filming the picture, displayed a more poised screen presence. Despite her sizzling screen work, Dolores Moran never did achieve the level of stardom that seemed destined her, and is best remembered as the other dame who gave Bogie the doll-eyes in the classic picture that was Bogart and Bacall's initial teaming.

When Dolores Moran first made her way out Hollywood, she was but a teenager with a woman's appearance. Shapely and beautiful, Miss Moran signed her first studio contract at the tender age of sixteen. Given her older-than-her-years look, Dolores was able to handle roles that were removed from the juvenile set, and didn't have to wallow in lesser films that detailed campus life and late night jitterbugging. Her origin in the film industry coincided with the advent of World War II, which, given her penchant to pose for cheesecake purposes, enabled her to transition from a bit player to costarring roles. When the teenager first started in Hollywood she, like so many beautiful ingénues, struggled to make a name for herself with minor roles, but when she began to adorn the lockers of servicemen, Dolores shucked the label of pretty backdrop filler and adopted the status of legitimate actress. Although only in her upper teens at the start of the war, Dolores had a woman's shape, which forced writer Dee Lowrance to gush, "You'd never guess that Dolores is only 16 to look at her. She seems several years older. Poised, sure of herself, and tall for her age, Dolores Moran is one of the most stunning-looking blondes to hit Hollywood in some time." Judging by the numerous pin-up pictures soldiers had secured in their vicinities, they echoed the sentiment of Lowrance.

Studio's publicity departments left no avenue unexplored when the endeavor of promoting a newly signed sensation was assigned. Oftentimes a pretty young actress, even those who had been in Hollywood some time, was pressured to haunt the night clubs simply to be seen with the swell-dressed wolves of Tinseltown. Simply by catting about with the noted tomcat celebrities, studios imagined their young dames would get their names in the gossip columns, which would cause a sense of curiosity as to who so-and-so was cupiding about with. The arrangement of dates was Hollywood's favorite ploy before the war — and even so during the war years — but the advent of pin-up artwork enabled the gals to get exposure without feeling like they were a side of beef to be auctioned off to the wealthiest bidder. Of course, to pose for cameramen wearing skimpy bathing suits could make a gal feel much the same, but at least she wasn't employed as a target for Cupid's arrow. She was not thrust into the arms of some vagabond playboy but positioned before a lens to have her stunning figure mass produced to an audience of captivated gents

*Dolores Moran.*

in need of inspiration. But even the cheesecake route failed to garner a gal the proper publicity, which is what happened to Dolores early in her film career. When a sexy, full page pin-up of the blonde bombshell was produced in *Pic Magazine*, the editors of the publication fouled up and listed her name as "Dolores Jordan."

By any name, Dolores Moran was an intoxicating beauty who captured the imagination of numerous soldiers who searched for inspiration while they fought on foreign soil. Many military outfits dubbed Dolores their special girl — the embodiment of female perfection that served as the unit's mascot of stirring pulchritude. The "Flying Tigers," based in China, dubbed Dolores their "Tiger Girl," while the fellows of the 884th Ordnance Depot adopted Miss Moran as their inspirational girl. Private James Fagan of the 884th, a noted artist among his unit, was engaged to paint a portrait of the "Post War Dream Girl," and he used Dolores as his model. So thought of was Dolores among a group of Marines, that they named her their "Pins-Up Girl," to which Dee Lowrance explained the meaning of the nickname. Lowrance wrote, "She's the gal with the most beautiful pins — and pins, in some lingos, mean limbs, in case you've forgotten."

As the inspiration for countless soldiers, Dolores received a few odd requests from the boys in service. A corporal stationed overseas named Casey Moore, whose only mode of entertainment was a radio, wrote Dolores a letter begging her to fulfill a wish of his. His desire was a modest request but one that would seem inadequate to soothe that yearning for aesthetic delights. He asked Miss Moran to go on the radio for one full minute and "stand perfectly still, wearing a tight sweater." Other requests that came Dolores's way were less unusual, concerned with a soldier's morale. She and fellow pretty actresses Lynne Baggett and Joan Winfield were asked to seek out the loneliest soldier in service and give him a tour of Hollywood. The gals found their man in Corporal Robert Wilson of Titusville, Pennsylvania, whose name littered the nation's papers as the "loneliest man in the armed forces." The attractive trio escorted Wilson about Hollywood. They took the soldier to the night spots and the film sets where he was introduced to Humphrey Bogart, Jack Benny, and Joan Leslie. After a night on the town with Dolores and Company, Corporal Wilson would have to surrender his comfortless title to another gent.

As one of America's leading pin-up girls, Miss Moran's photographed figure was public domain. Seen pinned up on walls and posed in newspapers, Dolores was an accepted symbol of female beauty. Many women's health writers would detail the methods that starlets used to retain their radiant glow, and Lois Leeds, one of the top beauty tip scribes of the war era, turned to the stunning Miss Moran to give girls the inside wire. Many gals would explain how they applied makeup or the exercises they performed to keep their figure, but Dolores's beauty tip was a simple piece of knowledge one could employ with little strain — on either the body or the pocketbook. Dolores explained her beauty tip by informing Leeds's readers to, "Pour a whole glass of common table salt in your bath water. Relax. Rub down — and feel refreshed. It's as simple as that."

A common assignment for pin-up girls was passing on beauty tips, but they had other assignments beyond inspiring the boys, and helping the girls look more appealing. They were often used as models of proper wartime behavior: ladies who did the right thing, or passed along the sacrificial ideas the nation needed to secure victory. With the rationing of numerous goods, pin-up girls were employed to urge folks to be frugal. Dolores was once asked to model a dress made of paper to express to ladies that fabrics had to be rationed — one can only imagine the rustling her attire would make when she took her seat. The paper apparel that Miss Moran was asked to model employed flounces fastened with Scotch tape. By wearing the paper dress, ladies could secure added benefits they could not attain when shopping for other clothes. The paper dress cost all of fifty cents and laundry was not an option, because when the dress was soiled it could simply be thrown out with the rest of the garbage. Of course, the paper garment didn't catch on, but Dolores was game enough to model the unusual attire.

With a figure that seemed designed for bathing suit wear, Dolores Moran was an ideal model for leg art. The blonde pin-up girl was asked to urge girls to wear paper dresses and fix their hair in pigtails to get around the wartime shortage of bobby pins, but it was her ample supply of pulchritude, and not her employ as a spokesgirl, that secured her status as a favorite cheesecake model. When the two tasks of looking good and passing along information were combined, the pin-up girl had reached perhaps the apex of her powers. In order to stress public pool safety, Dolores was photographed wearing a lifeguard's swimsuit in a pin-up photograph titled "Defense Girl." But it was at the Ottumwa Naval Air Station in Iowa where Dolores's status as a pin-up girl was used to full effect. In order to remind cadet fliers to secure themselves fully in their harness, a pin-up of Dolores was plastered in their training area with a quote from her, that read, "I tighten my shoulder straps — do you?" There could be a better way to urge fliers to properly employ their safety harness, for a beautiful girl can be, at times, a little distracting, but a pin-up girl is attention-getting, and her message may have been absorbed by a few cadets.

Dolores Moran's radiant beauty was refreshing to a world at war, where all the majesty and fairness of the human experience seemed cast into darkness. But there were beacons of grace whose allurement, even amongst the tumult of war, could not be denied. The men engaged in the fight, who witnessed hardship and repellence, sought out images to combat the repulsion of the battlefield, where beauty was absent and filth had command. They found the pinnacle of beauty in the figure of woman. As one of the world's leading pin-up girls, Dolores Moran helped many men trudge through the field of despair, for they knew by exiting the bloody fields of battle, they could live to gather a glimpse of their idol once more. Her acting career may not have taken off like that of her early costar Lauren Bacall, but Miss Moran's legacy as a war-era inspiration girl is a legacy that puts many thespians to shame.

# ★ MARTHA O'DRISCOLL ★

Despite a rather fleeting career in the film industry, Miss O'Driscoll enjoyed a prolific career in several film genres. Regarded as more of a "B" actress, Martha's most recognizable role may just be her work in the horror realm, screaming as vampires and werewolves gave chase in the solid fright fest *House of Dracula*. But Martha would marry a wealthy businessman and settle into the role of wife and mother, saying her goodbyes to the film industry for the life of domesticated bliss. Yet before Martha became mother and housewife, she was recipient of whistles from throngs of servicemen who held the image of the stunning blonde dear to their hearts. More than an actress and pin-up girl, during the war Martha was a symbol of female virtue and duty, who did more than was asked of her to see that the morale of the servicemen never flagged or failed. Their morale may have declined from time to time, vigor slackened by the monotony of war, but upon an O'Driscoll greeting, the spirits were renewed and the collective morale rose to higher levels. One of the true dolls of the fighting men, Martha O'Driscoll was a lady whose devotion to the troops was awe-inspiring.

Whether a female thespian in Hollywood is a good actress or not is an issue to be decided by the individual viewer. One filmgoer may enjoy the work of an actress but another filmgoer may find the actress in question, grating and unworthy of a career in the film industry. One cannot impress all comers, but Martha O'Driscoll employed a snappy bit of dramatizing upon her initial visit to Hollywood that no critic could possibly scoff at. Just thirteen years old at the time, the fresh-faced teen was able to convince studio executives that she was eighteen, in order to begin work in the motion picture industry.

Given her early arrival on the film scene, Martha was an established actress by the time America entered World War II. She became a common headliner of war-bond tours. A great number of Hollywood stars appeared in war-bond tours, traveling the nation in order to raise funds for the war effort. Although Miss O'Driscoll did her bit of traveling too, she also found that folks in Hollywood could open their wallets for the war effort. With chum Frances Gifford — a fellow pin-up girl — the two Tinseltown attractors beat the pavement of Wilshire Boulevard, where they sold war bonds to the high rollers of the film industry. In order to promote one of her films, Martha ventured to South Carolina with costar Paulette Goddard on a war-bond tour/film promotion junket. The two beauties attended a ball at Charleston, where they raised interest in the motion picture *Reap the Wild Wind* by dancing with servicemen. There were plenty of civilian males haunting the ball, but the two actresses spent the entire night on their feet, dancing with sailors and soldiers before they accepted the hand of a man minus a uniform.

Martha's acting career was at its height during the war years, and due to her popularity she was a frequent request for cheesecake photography. The typical pin-up girl attire was a bathing suit, whether it be a two-piece or a one-piece made little difference, just so long as it accentuated the stimulating curves of female. However, there were some bathing suits, not too aesthetically pleasing, that pin-up girls were asked to wear for a photo shoot and Martha slid into one that didn't quite catch on. The gamer that she was, Martha donned an unsightly camouflage swimsuit for a pin-up picture, which was reproduced by the Associated Press and displayed in many of the nation's leading papers. The AP writer thought the swimsuit an eyesore, but not the lovely lass in it. He wrote that the suit may have been unappealing but at least "none of [Martha's] charms are concealed." Like a baseball fanatic would claim, Walter Johnson didn't throw a shutout every start, and Martha didn't don exceptional attire every time she posed before a camera. There is no such thing as perfection.

Miss O'Driscoll's for-the-troops mindset never wavered during the war. Not only was she a prolific pin-up model and seller of war bonds but she was also a traveling entertainer who visited the troops at many installations. In the fall of 1943, after cadets had just completed their training at Minter Field, they were shocked when the stunning Martha O'Driscoll made an unannounced visit to their graduation ceremony. The fliers who had spent months in the act of training, absent the company of delicate dames, were able to spend the evening of their graduation dancing with Martha. But it was with the soldiers overseas, and those returning from hostile regions, that Martha made her greatest impact.

In 1944, Martha agreed to attend a USO tour headlined by noted lady-killer Errol Flynn. Their troupe visited the upper regions of North America and entertained troops at Alaska and on the Aleutian Islands.

*Martha O'Driscoll.*

The sailors on the Aleutians fell in love with Martha and bestowed upon her the title "The Girl We'd Like to Dunk Our Doughnuts With." Soldiers were apt to create absurd titles for the pin-up girls they adored, and Martha's was one of the most unusual, but she was more commonly referred to by the boys in Alaska as "Miss Fearless." How she came about that moniker is an interesting story, which took place during a show Martha headlined. While performing at Attu, the westernmost island in the Aleutian chain, Japanese planes interrupted her performance, but the stoic blonde remained on stage while any other performer would have sought shelter. One soldier in the audience gushed, "Martha didn't even flinch. She didn't even look afraid!" Her stage performance, in which she looked the devil in the eye and stood her ground, earned her the catchy nickname "Miss Fearless" among the troops on the Aleutians.

Her trip to Alaska, and the brush with danger when Japanese planes circled over their camp at Attu, endeared her to troops across the globe. She did not cower in the face of adversity but thrived in it, which made her the ideal pin-up girl. Those of a lesser constitution would have fled the region after the Japanese circled overhead, but Martha wasn't your typical entertainer. She understood this and even had to make apologies for it. That instance at Attu, which earned her the flattering nickname, was one of disappointment on Miss O'Driscoll's part. After the danger had cleared, Martha felt a pang of regret — she wanted the adrenaline that kept her on the stage to be justified. Martha said, "The truth is that I was a little disappointed. That sounds terrible, I know. But I knew how exciting things would be if those planes dropped some bombs. And then they turned out just to be reconnaissance planes, after all. Of course, you're going to have to forgive me for saying I was disappointed. Knowing the harm that bombs do, I have no right to say any such thing — but it is the truth."

War presents to those engaged in it many hardships, where the mind must be devoted to the task of defeating the enemy, but there are times, when removed from the battlefields, when soldiers desire relaxation — a reprieve from the struggle. While she toured the Aleutian Islands, Martha helped the chaps unwind by performing skits, as well as singing and dancing with them. The troops were grateful to be in the presence of a beautiful woman, if even but for the briefest of moments, and applauded Martha for her selflessness. On one trip, a pilot who ferried Martha from one island to another invited her to serve as his co-pilot. The task of flying the plane was his, but he engaged Martha as a navigator of sorts, whose task was to communicate with towers in order to acquire landing instructions. The man in the tower hadn't heard a woman's voice in a long time and the last place he imagined a delicate discourse was via a plane's radio. Martha told the story, saying, "I really upset a lot of radio towers by asking for instructions. Not only had they not heard a woman's voice for years, but they certainly weren't expecting a female voice from an Army plane. One radio tower refused to believe his ears — he radioed back demanding the name of the pilot!"

Gags were commonplace in the military in order to keep the mood light, but only when the mood needed an adjustment. There were times for tricks, times for jokes, but only when removed from the battlefield and the training environment. Troops would employ anything at their disposal to use in a rhubarb, which meant the pin-up girls, when they visited military bases, were asked to assist in a gag at times. When Martha toured a submarine, she was asked by a group of sailors to help them pull one over on their mate, who spent the night on guard duty and was fast asleep in his bunk. His sailor chums asked Martha to wake the sleeping sailor up, to which Martha agreed. She told the story, saying, "I went over and touched him. He stirred a little but didn't wake up. I poked him a little harder. He opened one eye then and looked at me — then he closed the eye, only to open it again in a sort of sleepy double-take. 'I'm dreaming,' he announced. No you're not, I said. So the next thing he did was to ask: 'What perfume is that?' I said, *Shocking*. He grinned at me and then said, 'It sure is!' You should have heard all the sailors howling with laughter. I thought it would bulge out the sides of the submarine."

Assisting troops in a little lighthearted play was amusing for Martha, who enjoyed being amongst the troops and keeping the mood light. But the task of building morale, the primary role of the pin-up girl, was one Miss O'Driscoll did not take lightly. She did not shy away from the more tedious, heart-wrenching chores of the pin-up, for not all the gatherings that Martha found herself in were fun and games with the servicemen. By visiting wounded troops in military hospitals, Martha handled the ultimate pin-up girl task of uplifting the spirits of men who had their lives altered by the war. She knew what the men needed to hear and issued the valuable discourse with sincerity. Homesick soldiers abroad were one of Martha's favorite targets, for she wanted to lift the spirits of the weary and wounded. She reassured the gents that America was a land lacking masculinity, for all the greatest men the nation had to offer were overseas, fighting for liberty. About lifting the spirits of homesick troops, Martha said, "We used to tell them things hadn't changed much, except that we miss all of them such a lot. And they seem to like to feel that it was a bit of a man-less world back here, that the fact they were away had made a great difference — as indeed it has. Who would want to tell them otherwise?"

Soldiers overseas spend countless hours dreaming of that reunion with their loved ones — to step foot off their ship or aircraft and enter into the embrace of those they hold dear. But for every soldier there isn't a tender embrace or a loved one waiting with arms outstretched. To return home to a cold world, where life fails to produce the warmth of love's caress, holds as little appeal as the hostile regions they had just departed. When a soldier returns home to muted fanfare, where folks respect not their sacrifice, one questions whether their homeland is a home at all. Martha O'Driscoll understood the sacrifices soldiers made and was eager to show her gratitude to returning troops. When veterans of the 36th Division of Texas returned home after duty in the Anzio Beachhead Operation, they were met by family, loved ones, and pin-up girl Martha O'Driscoll. Many of the soldiers were injured veterans, wounded on foreign battlefields, who thought the world's beauty had been quenched, but those who felt that way were proven otherwise when Martha O'Driscoll embraced them upon their return. A hug and a kiss from a family member is a tender gesture of those happy for your return, while to be welcomed home by a pin-up girl like Martha O'Driscoll, is reassurance that all you had done was not in vain. Martha O'Driscoll was, without question, an extraordinary beauty, but her beauty reached well beyond the physical. To state that America needs more ladies like Martha O'Driscoll is a statement that should not be met with an adverse reply.

## ★ DONNA REED ★

Donna Reed was widely regarded as America's favorite farm girl during World War II. The beauty from Iowa had just become an overnight sensation in Hollywood at the outset of the war with a star-making role opposite Mickey Rooney in one of his popular *Andy Hardy* films. At the end of the war, Miss Reed starred opposite war hero Jimmy Stewart in the classic *It's a Wonderful Life* — her most recognizable film role. But it was her long-running sitcom, *The Donna Reed Show*, that the former Iowa farm girl is best remembered for. The fair-haired Midwesterner had a lengthy career in both film and television, and she was an enigmatic woman who supported the Second World War but was a loud voice of opposition during the Vietnam War. Perhaps just a follower of Hollywood trends, Miss Reed was, nevertheless, one of America's favorite actresses and the ideal girl-next-door pin-up for the troops during WWII.

Born a farmer's daughter in small-town Iowa, Donna had harbored dreams of an acting career from early childhood. After she graduated high school, the former local beauty queen took her down-home appeal out west and enrolled in classes in Los Angeles. By placing herself in close proximity to the film industry, young Donna hoped to get noticed by talent scouts in search of pretty faces. Fortunately for her, Donna

*Donna Reed.* COURTESY OF MOVIEMARKET.COM

possessed the ideal countenance for films, and she was quickly spotted and used in minor roles her first few pictures. But stardom was not long in the making for Miss Reed. After she starred opposite Mickey Rooney, a teen heartthrob during the war years, Donna's star was established. The war years had a unique impact on the film industry and many pictures during the early to mid-1940s were war-themed. Given her girl-next-door image, Donna was widely regarded as the ideal actress to play soldiers' sweethearts due to her wholesome, Iowa farm-girl background.

When a group of soldiers were polled by newspapermen regarding the pin-up girl they'd most like to come home to, the *Port Arthur News* published the final tally which displayed Donna as the winner. Although not as shapely as Carole Landis or Jane Russell, or as stunningly beautiful as Hedy Lamarr or Gene Tierney, Donna Reed was a pretty girl with a fine figure — not the unattainable goddess the other ladies were — which made her title as the "Girl We'd Most Like to Come Home To" reasonable. She exuded that breezy, Midwestern gal personality, the type not above milking a cow or helping plow a field, which endeared her to many troops. The war signaled the end of the pampered era, where women's chief task was to look pretty, and by engaging in manual labor with a removal from the pampered, cloistered existence of earlier times, women developed a more independent collective spirit. War plants were alive with the toil of female hands, and Donna represented the American girl who had few qualms with rolling her sleeves up and getting a tad dirty. This representation coupled with her feminine charms, made girls like her the ideal catch for soldiers in postwar America.

The pin-up girl craze swept into its fold nearly every actress in Hollywood. Many up-and-coming actresses gladly posed for cheesecake art as a way to further their career, but the main reason girls posed was to show support for the troops. Preferred attire for pin-up girls was the bathing suit, but many photographers were asked by an actress's studio to take advantage of the dame's film history and personal background. Donna did don a number of bathing suits for cheesecake purposes, but her most notable spread was a farm-themed pin-up shoot, which paid homage to her homestead upbringing. Shortly after Christmas 1943, the *San Antonio Light* printed a full-page series of Donna Reed's on-the-farm cheesecake spread, which quickened the pace of many readers' hearts in the Texas city. Donna wore short pants on the farm, which showcased her cowgirl gams in various positions, and she partook in hacienda hand tasks ranging from milking a cow, plowing a field, and giving folks some leg art by leaning against a tractor. The paper poked fun at the layout by printing a poem to go along with Miss Reed's cheesecake spread, which read: "Can she bake a cherry pie, Billy Boy, Billy Boy? Can she bake a cherry pie, charming Billy? She can bake a cherry pie, quick as a cat can wink an eye."

The pin-up girl had many tasks, more so than uplifting the morale of troops, and Donna shook off not a one. Asked to pass along beauty tips, Donna had a surefire hot steer for the gals of the war plants. Many gals on the job had to use gloves to protect their hands from the hazards of machinery, which were not well-suited for the glamorous glow and dainty appearance gal's grabbers are want to possess. Donna informed war plants workers that they should attend to their hands before work in order to keep them feminine in appearance. She stressed applying hand lotion before sliding on the work gloves, saying "Your hands will have only nice things to say if you'll give them the old cream-and-glove treatment." The pin-up girl was, above all, the ideal female — one both physically appealing as well as socially aiding. It was her task to guide the young ladies of America, to show them how to be that ideal American girl, and it was a task Donna Reed did not shirk from during World War II.

## ★ GINGER ROGERS ★

Much ink has been expended extolling the gams of the girl from St. Louis, Miss Betty Grable — and for good reason — but the dancing doll born on the opposite side of Missouri possessed a pair of pins that put many to shame. The most streamlined of Hollywood's many streamlined pin-ups of World War II, Ginger Rogers, the dancing queen of 1930's Hollywood, owned a toned body the likes of which could make an Olympian blush. Remembered fondly today as one of Hollywood's all-time dancing standouts, Miss Rogers's dancing regimen allowed her to maintain an exceptional frame. By stepping with Fred Astaire and other lucky gents in a number of movies, Ginger displayed an athletic grace that had few rivals among the cheesecake cuties of her era. With a body in constant motion, Ginger, who also excelled on the tennis court, was able to retain a lean, trim, yet clearly feminine figure. When it came to legs, the landing gear Ginger used to gambol with Mr. Astaire was second to none.

Work as a pin-up girl enabled many aspiring actresses to gain notoriety in the movie industry, for the exposure allowed their stagnant careers to gain traction when the servicemen whistled at their captured likeness. The gents in the armed forces wanted to see these stunning gals in motion.

They constantly wrote letters to film studios imploring them to hand so-and-so a role in their latest motion picture. Dozens of girls in the 1940s started out this way, but Miss Rogers wasn't one of them. Ginger made her way out Hollywood in the late 1920s and had become an established actress well before the Second World War. Before the bombs whistled through the air and arms were taken up to defend liberty, Ginger had

*Ginger Rogers.*

danced with Fred Astaire in several picture shows. It can be argued that Ginger made Astaire's career, for the fancy-footed dancer was a virtual unknown until he teamed with the already established Rogers. The two starred together in ten motion pictures and were to dancing what Abbott and Costello were to comedy.

Not only was Ginger Rogers an established star by the beginning of the war, she was one of Hollywood's highest earners — man or woman. When a list of the highest paid American entertainers was published in 1941, Ginger rested near the top of the roll call, edging out fellow legends like Bing Crosby and Clark Gable. By 1940, she had become an American institution — the face and figure of Tinseltown song-and-dance flicks. Despite her immense popularity, which has a habit of making an individual vain and self-serving, Ginger Rogers was one of the first Hollywood notables to engage herself in the war-bond drive. The stunning actress traveled across the nation to build funds for the war effort, not just by giving an empty speech here and there but through leading by example. On many war-bond tours, Ginger would auction off her own belongings — earrings, bracelets, handkerchiefs, gloves and her dancing shoes. At a war-bond rally held at Tucson in 1942, Ginger auctioned off a kiss for $1,000 in war bonds.

Ginger was devoted to her country and was proud of her work in films glorifying the American girl. An ideal model for young women to pattern themselves after, Miss Rogers surrendered many hours during the war to assist in the war-bond drive. The selfless, flag-waving Rogers was a devoted seller of war bonds, and she would refuse interviews to scribes looking for Hollywood scoops while on her tours. Her mission was to sell war bonds to help the men in service — not offer up details about Tinseltown nightlife or inside dope on her latest pictures. When she sold war bonds it was a role she delved into wholeheartedly. On a tour in El Paso, Texas, a newspaperman inquired on her newest film, to which she replied, "Sorry, I'm here to talk about bonds. I'm on this tour to sell bonds — my personal life doesn't count." It seems impossible to imagine a modern day actress declining an invitation to rattle on no end about herself, but in the Hollywood of World War II, even the biggest stars like Ginger Rogers put the war first.

On many bond junkets, Ginger was introduced to soldiers who she would often chat and dance with. It was certainly a dream come true for many of Uncle Sam's fighting men to cut a rug with Hollywood's most famed dancer, but many of the troops that Miss Rogers met on her war-bond tours were unable to dance. During a trip to honor a west coast war plant, Ginger met a wounded Marine Corps private, and a photograph circulated the nation that showed Ginger inspecting the many wounds the soldier received at Guadalcanal. The pin-up girl's primary function was to look appealing, but she had other roles more important than aesthetic imagery, which endeared her to the nation, such as lifting the spirits of wounded soldiers with a greeting. Although Ginger had legs that Lois Leeds described as making "women sigh with envy," it was her demeanor and her accessibility as a starlet that truly endeared her to the troops.

The collection of pin-up pictures taken during the war was one difficult to count. Ramsay Ames, the B-movie girl, claimed to have posed for close to 1,000 cheesecake photos, and Miss Rogers didn't seem too far behind. The leggy, fair-haired dancer was made to order for leg art, given her otherworldly gams, and many of her pin-up pictures took full advantage of her streamlined lower anatomy. One photo shoot that sent the boys to the moon had Ginger dressed in a revealing polka-dot ensemble that displayed her toned midriff. The skirt, of which there was limited fabric, exposed close to the entirety of the Rogers gams, and given the employ of high heeled shoes, her already extraordinary legs were rendered even more so with the added lift. There were a few poses that Ginger took in this attire, which had what appeared to be a half-buried bass drum of monstrous proportions, which only Paul Bunyan could play, nestled in the vicinity of the streamlined goddess to rest her flawless figure upon. She was, as any cheesecake admirer would agree, assembled quite exquisitely.

Physical assemblage, of which enviable contours is necessary in the arena of cheesecake photography, was not all Ginger Rogers brought to the table. A gifted dancer, quality thespian, and down-to-earth, patriotic lady, Ginger Rogers was the prototype for the all-American girl. Her status as the ideal American girl irked a few dames during the war years who thought Miss Rogers was a bit too sensual for proper girls to emulate. What specifically turned off her critics was her walk. Mary Davis, a beauty dramatics coach, thought Ginger's walk a tad on the erotic side — not nearly conservative enough for girls to adopt. Davis felt that Ginger's hips swung too much as she walked, but Miss Rogers had plenty more supporters than detractors. When the head of Warner Brothers' makeup department, Pete Westmore, heard of Davis's criticism, he defended Ginger and the sensual way she swayed as she took it on the heel and toe. Westmore said, "Show me a producer, or any man, that wouldn't willingly wait outside any window to catch a glimpse of Ginger swinging her hips." Among the many servicemen who adored her pin-up pictures, Westmore had plenty gents to second his sentiments.

# ★ JANE RUSSELL ★

If pretty pin-ups like Jeanne Crain and Rochelle Hudson represented the girl-next-door, then Jane Russell was the embodiment of lust. With her voluptuous figure, man-eating mannerisms, and come-hither stare, Jane Russell was the gal you secretly pursued while you invited more reserved girls home to meet your mother. Respectable young men were not expected to cavort about with lusty dames reminiscent of La Russell, but the entire tawdry bit was just an act — a method to jolt young men into the theaters to watch her perform. Jane Russell had the ideal shape — full in the right areas — and a sultry persona that suited the typecast of a loose woman. But she was an uncommon woman in Hollywood, who fought to save her marriage to football star Bob Waterfield, while many dames of the era were quick to loosen the marital ties. She excelled as a man-eater onscreen, and given her remarkable dimensions, any man would harbor little reservations of being consumed by Jane. She was, for countless soldiers overseas and far from home, the image that kept them warm — kept them yearning for a return to the States. The sexpot bit may have been an act for filmgoers, but it served Jane well in an industry that prefers its decadence layered.

Born to a serviceman and a mother with a background in theater, the Russell clan made its rounds before settling in sunny California. With four siblings, all boys, Jane and her mother were surrounded by a sea of testosterone, but when her father passed away, Jane had to help support the family and sought employ in the clerical field. But the shapely brunette, whose mother had dabbled in the arena of acting, desired to pursue an occupation in that line of work. It came her way when she met the famous film producer Howard Hughes, who, like any red-blooded American male, was initially impressed with Jane's feminine charms. When Jane signed a contract with Hughes, little did she know that the world of entertainment would have to wait years before she would grace the screen with her sensational presence. She signed on the dotted line with Hughes at the time World War II was hot, and Hughes, who put country above making pictures, essentially let Jane wait in the corner, refusing to loan her out to other producers, while he dabbled in the aircraft manufacturing trade. However, Jane's hiatus from acting did not force her career to stagnate, not in the least, but catapulted her into stardom when Hughes's picture *The Outlaw* — Jane's first film — was deadlocked in a battle with censors.

Censorship of the war era did not allow anything controversial in films — especially the display of the female form. Even the thought of a bare female torso on film was uncouth. Hedy Lamarr had created quite a global stir when she appeared nude in the European piece *Ecstasy* before the war, but when she ventured to Hollywood, her charms were kept concealed. The Hays Office, responsible for policing Hollywood producers, was the champion of public decency and halted the distribution of *The Outlaw*. The film was completed early in the war years but was not released to the masses until after the end of the war because of Hughes's battle with the Hays Office. The censors felt that a bit too much of Jane was revealed in the film, for her raggedy outfits struggled to conceal her ample breasts. But conceal them they did — barely. A writer for the *Oakland Tribune* quipped, "Jane Russell is the worst thing that has happened to the Hays Office since Mae West."

The struggle Howard Hughes had with the Hays Office did nothing but give *The Outlaw* unparalleled promotion. Constantly in the papers at the time, filmgoers wondered why the Hays Office had frozen the distribution of the film, and when they got a look at Jane Russell — the newly discovered star of the picture — the interest intensified. Jane became an overnight media sensation despite the fact that she had yet to appear in a film. Even worse, her initial project had been held up, which further built the anticipation to see the shapely brunette onscreen. People became Jane Russell mad during the 1940s and had nothing but billboards, newspaper photos, and cheesecake stills to satiate their thirst for Jane. Howard Hughes took full advantage of the battle with the censors and sent Jane out to numerous events, including entertaining the troops, to further promote his stalled picture. Jane took to the traveling circuit because Hughes was preoccupied with wartime endeavors, which kept him from working in films, and his reluctance to loan out his sexy new find kept Jane from building on her acting résumé. When the Navy asked Jane to help in their recruitment campaign, they used the slogan "Join the Navy and see Jane Russell," as a pun concerning her shelved first motion picture.

With her film halted, there was a campaign to redefine decency. Was the showcasing of a female's form indecent, or was it merely an artistic expression? The question was banded about freely, with learned mouth pieces offering their two cents and the average Joe tossing in his pair of pennies as well. Such actresses as the buxom Marie Wilson were outspoken supporters of the display of female charms in films, while others felt that charms, whether they be of the female or male variety, were best left behind closed doors. Soldiers, who had been told from day one that they were fighting for liberty and womanhood, had much to say on the public discourse. When there were complaints that Jane's pin-ups inspired by *The Outlaw* were too provocative for public viewing, a pair of sergeants, employed as writers for *Yank* magazine, joined the debate, saying, "After looking at the photo every day since publication, we see nothing objectionable about it. We've been told many times we're fighting for liberty and womanhood, so why in the hell can't we see a little of

*Jane Russell.*

the latter?" With discourse much in the same vein as the two sergeants, the censors relented and allowed *The Outlaw* wide distribution, but only after the war had concluded.

During the war, while the Hays Office reviewed the case of *The Outlaw*, Jane had married Robert Waterfield, her high school sweetheart, and she had more important issues than a battle with censorship. The gridiron standout joined the military and Jane became a war bride. Hughes kept his sexy actress busy with film promotion to help keep her mind off the struggles of being a soldier's wife. Jane was seen everywhere — with the notable exception of theaters — as she lent her name to many campaigns to assist the war effort. When the War Department adopted the slogan "A Slip of the Lip May Sink a Ship," to inform Americans to be weary of the information you give others, Miss Russell was used as the body to promote the campaign. Pictures of Jane carrying a sign with the slogan written upon it were distributed to troops and workers at war plants and shipyards. The more Jane was seen, the more people wanted to see her in *The Outlaw*, which further boosted interest in the stalled picture.

A favorite of the troops, Jane Russell was widely regarded as the number one pin-up girl in the world during the war, regardless the methods of press agents who handed the label to their contract players. Even though they had never seen her act, troops everywhere adopted Jane as their unit mascot. Exuding pulchritude in every pin-up picture she took, soldiers lavished Miss Russell with flattering nicknames and often adopted her as a rallying symbol. A group of cadets at the Long Beach Naval Reserve Aviation Base named Jane their "Keep 'em Flying Girl," while a section of fliers at the Stockton Army Air Corps Advanced Flying School took the praise of Jane a step further. The Stockton fliers painted Jane's shapely likeness on the outside of their planes and gave themselves the nickname of "Russell's Raiders." Overseas, troops noticed a pair of mountaintops, equal height and scraping the heavens, and in order to use them as a landmark, christened the duo "Russsell's Peaks," as an homage to her boundless bosom.

The soldiers used Jane's likeness with an abandon rarely seen when admiring an individual is concerned. Pin-up pictures of Jane were scattered in every direction, one was even found in a Nazi officer's quarters after the Allies seized the German hold, proving that although warped ideologically, their admiration for pleasing images was not underdeveloped. Although Jane went the bathing suit route like most other pin-ups, many of Miss Russell's cheesecake stills were promotional captures of *The*

*Outlaw*. Photographs of Jane reclining on a stack of hay, or laying out under the cover of a barn, were her predominate pin-up poses. Provocative to the tenth power, Jane's *Outlaw* inspired pin-ups gave notice to film-goers as to why the distribution of the film had hit a snag. The majority of the pin-ups of the war era were often coined "leg art," but when it came to Jane's *Outlaw* themed stills, there was less an emphasis on gams and more on mams. Her physical assets were clearly on display, as the rural rags Hughes's wardrobe department issued Jane barely succeeded in the task of concealing her breasts. These sensuous pin-ups gave rise to Russell's career even though folks had little knowledge as to the depth of her thespian skills.

When Jane began her promotional tour visiting military bases, different pin-up pictures were taken of her — more typical of the cheesecake circulation. The busty brunette was posed at various military installations where photographers would take photographs of her leaning on airplanes and standing atop an Army vehicle wearing a low-cut top. About having her picture taken at military bases, Jane said, "I posed with planes and tanks. I posed aboard ships and draped over huge guns. Someone once said that if all the pictures taken of Jane Russell were laid out end to end, they'd reach around the world. I wouldn't doubt it." Due to the soldiers' infatuation with Jane, her pin-ups had to be rationed — kept for the servicemen. Men could stomach rationing to a certain extent, but the rationing of Jane Russell pin-up pictures was too much for a group of war-plant workers based in Ogden, Utah. One of the workers wrote a letter to the *Ogden Standard* which read, "Because so many soldiers wrote for her picture, do you suppose if we asked right nice, five of us war workers could get a picture of Jane Russell to pin up over our bunks?" Soldiers may have had first dibs on cheesecake, but the gents who assisted in the war wanted to get their mitts on Russell's stunning likeness as well.

World War II was a time of trial for the American people, who were asked to sacrifice many luxuries in order to support the troops. Victory could be had if Americans did their part and allowed the War Department to hold a monopoly on many goods. Some unpatriotic Americans — of which every generation has many — were disinclined to allow the armed forces to employ goods before them, so pin-ups like Jane were asked to help the less sacrificial understand that the military was of greater importance during time of war. Many fabrics that were used in women's clothing had to be employed to help in the war effort, such as the construction of parachutes. Jane was employed to show women how they could get extra mileage out of their hosiery as well as other beauty tricks. But there was a time during the war when Jane felt in need of a few tips herself. When her husband was sent to his southern installation, Jane moved with him and had to settle into small quarters while her husband trained. A major hardship for anyone, not to mention a young actress on the cusp of stardom, Jane accepted the war-era role and persevered. About being an Army bride, Jane said, "I shared a furnished room with a gang of cockroaches and sold bonds for $15 a week. That room cost ten bucks a week, so I had five bucks to eat on and pay for my bus trips out to camp to see Robert. But it was lots more fun than fighting with women's clubs. And I could wear all the high-necked dresses I wanted to."

Today, the name of Betty Grable is commonly offered when the discussion of most popular World War II pin-ups are concerned, as the blonde bomber is widely regarded as the number one WWII era pin-up girl. But during the war, Miss Grable had plenty competition for the title, and many writers felt that Jane was the top choice of the boys, not Grable. NEA Staff Correspondent Marguerite Young claimed that Jane was the top pin-up girl, accusing press agents of wrongfully lauding their contract players as the top cheesecake model when all signs pointed to La Russell. A poll was conducted on the University of California Berkeley campus in 1943, which urged students to vote for their favorite pin-up girl, and Jane won in a landslide. Jane polled 1,029 votes while Betty Grable came in a distant second with just 42. Scribe Erskine Johnson referred to Jane as "Hollywood's Number One Oomph Girl," which was a term employed to describe pin-up girls.

Many arguments go unresolved, and when the task of anointing a lady as an era's top pin-up girl is undertaken, one must understand that the title is given under a cloud of bias. Beauty is not to be defined by the collective but a personal pursuit, for a man might view Jane Russell as the premier pin-up while his neighbor would cast a vote for Betty Grable or Gene Tierney. To label one woman as the most famous pin-up girl of a generation is a boast issued idly. If we were to decide the popularity of pin-ups by the amount of cheesecake pictures taken, then the forgotten B-film actress Ramsay Ames might be regarded as the war generation's top pin-up. Regardless the futility of the gesture, many outlets attempted to lay to rest the question of who was the top pin-up girl of the war, and *Yank* felt they did just that when they offered a little playful jocularity on the issue. In a July, 1943 issue, *Yank* printed this little piece concerning the desire of soldiers: "Now that us soldiers overseas are allowed to select the contents of our packages from home, here are three types of gift boxes that we would like to receive: One Lana Turner and one case of Scotch. One Rita Hayworth and one case of Scotch. One Scotch and one case of Jane Russells."

Beauty may be an issue reserved for the eye of the beholder, but many eyes during the war years beheld in Jane Russell the ideal image of female perfection. Dee Lowrance described Jane by writing, "Jane is a dream. Forms such as hers have set men gasping for centuries. Her face is truly beautiful — with slumberous, heavy-lidded eyes, suggestive of tropic moons and amorous promises and a mouth to match. She photographs like a million." Other critics, equally enamored with the Russell figure, employed less flowery lyricism and tended to the side of crudeness when describing La Russell. With one glance at Jane it was obvious what attracted the attention of most admirers, and her ample assets were exactly what pin-up photographer George Hurrell was looking for. The shutterbug said, "The first requirement of my idea of a top-flight beauty is bumps. More than curves, bumps. But in the right places of course — really rounded bosoms."

When admirers of the female form boast about their areas of attraction, vulgarity tends to abdicate dominance over a modest exaltation of aesthetic images. George Hurrell found in Jane his ideal pin-up girl, but his discovery wasn't the allurement of Jane Russell, but an attraction for a sizable, well-formed bust. To judge a woman's worth by her beauty and shape is a narrow-minded judgment of an individual's merits, but has, nevertheless, been a scale in place for centuries. Some women have fought against this scale to a certain degree of futility, for all persons, regardless their gender, long to be admired. This concept gave understanding to the rise of the pin-up girl during World War II, for the gents in service were able to employ their visual faculty when gazing upon the image of a swell-looking dame. By gazing upon a pleasing image, like the cleavage-exhibiting pin-ups of Jane Russell, soldiers were able to tote beauty along, captured on a slip of film paper, for inspiration. Jane failed not to understand what her pin-up pictures meant to the boys in service, and regarded her work posing for cheesecake stills not as a demeaning exercise where women are viewed as objects of lust and little more, but as symbols of rightness — the representation of a world where beauty still exists, thus rendering an exercise in war a sojourn into an area of unreality. Jane and her fellow pin-ups were, for the fighting men, the bodily representation of hope. About being a pin-up girl, Miss Russell said, "A pin-up reputation is a very flattering thing, and I am happy if some of my pictures have helped brighten a few moments for our boys fighting overseas."

# ★ SHEILA RYAN ★

Every individual who has followed films for a modest amount of time has that one actress, or typically more, who they feel has gone underappreciated in the film industry. After watching the thespian in question perform on the screen, they wonder why she has yet to garner star status when actresses of far inferior talent thrive in A-list material. She exudes acting talent and a solid screen presence, which should be the envy of all actresses, but, for whatever reason, she is known but to a small pocket of loyal fans. Although Sheila Ryan worked in a large number of films, and delved in the medium of television in the 1950s, she is one of Hollywood's most exceptional talents among the full roster of forgotten thespians from Hollywood's Golden Era. Whether she worked in the western genre or costarred in film noirs, the camera seemed to seek out Miss Ryan, for the lens, at times, has a tendency to promote talent that directors fail to recognize. Such was the career of Sheila Ryan. Forgotten to but a few fans that admired her work, and who found in her performances a level of skill that dwarfed the talents of more established actresses.

Born in the Midwest, Sheila Ryan's calling was in the field of acting, and by the late 1930s, the lovely brunette had made her first appearance in a motion picture. Her first screen performance came in the final year of the 1930s, but she would build a prolific body of work the following decade. Not one to be typecast, or pigeon-holed into one film genre, Sheila bounced from westerns to comedies to thrillers and never missed a beat. Whether she was walking down the dusty trails in westerns, or standing bold with a iron-willed demeanor in film noirs, Sheila Ryan seemed in her element — the mark of a quality actress. But the lovely lass's introduction to the film industry coincided with escalating hostilities across the globe, and the Midwestern beauty showed her dedication to her country when she became one of the first actresses to delve into the Red Cross cause as a volunteer worker.

Sheila had just landed credited roles by the outset of the war — the ambition of all aspiring actresses — but her personal gratification seemed less fulfilling given the turmoil that gripped the nation after the bombing of Pearl Harbor. She had just reached her dream of becoming an actress, but Miss Ryan knew that her newly attained dream might be fleeting. Europe was consumed under a cloud of smoke created by the Nazis, and the solace of the American shores had been compromised by the Japanese. The waters along the West Coast, once alive with the bustle of folks at play, was now, during the early war years, a sea of insecurity that needed to be guarded. Boats began to patrol the Pacific Ocean, as sailors under Uncle Sam's employ safeguarded the waters in their PT boats. Fear had gripped America, and Americans were eager to subdue their fears by engaging in endeavors to assist the servicemen. Sheila did not sit idle while others prepared, for she entered the Red Cross and became such

*Sheila Ryan.*

an expert at first aid administration that she was asked to instruct classes. Other actresses like Myrna Loy and Ida Lupino followed Sheila's lead and became instructors for the Red Cross with her.

A woman of remarkable down-to-earth beauty, Sheila Ryan seemed a natural fit for pin-up pictures. Work in conjuncture with the Red Cross satisfied Sheila, who was not content to spend the war years in the isolated bubble of the leisure-seekers that were Hollywood's most vain. Most Americans felt they had a duty to protect their country, to defend their way of life from foreign evils, and even those persons not allowed to fight on the frontlines — the female sex — sought to assist nevertheless. Women of extraordinary fairness, whose physical charms bore the mark of the radiant, could easily support the troops by posing for pin-up pictures. Sheila, who spent the early part of the war years teaching ladies how to aid the injured, went the bathing suit route and exhibited her exquisite Irish-stock brand of pulchritude via the cheesecake circuit. A pin-up of Miss Ryan was mass produced in the nation's leading newspaper on St. Patrick's Day (chosen due to her Irish heritage), which boasted a caption that described Sheila as "Irish as the Blarney Stone."

Soldiers devoured the pin-up pictures that their favorite celebrity beauties produced, but not all people were as quick to admire a bathing-suit-clad dame as the men in the armed forces. When the pin-up craze was at full swing, a beauty judge based in Chicago proclaimed that glamour was nonexistent in a bathing suit. Given the bevy of beauties that posed for pin-up pictures in the nautical attire, there were many exhibits at hand for those who opposed this notion. One such voice of opposition was Ivan Kahn, Hollywood talent scout, who produced a pin-up picture of Sheila as proof that glamour could be found in bathing suits. Kahn said, "One picture is equivalent to ten thousand words. Take this one of Sheila Ryan and let the public decide." Kahn's pin-up of Miss Ryan was displayed in the *San Mateo Times* as evidence that glamour was not unacquainted with bathing threads. Sheila, displayed in a two-piece bathing suit, was enough to sway any person to Kahn's line of thought.

Sheila Ryan had all the features that soldiers desired. With her exuberant eyes remindful of those playful hours where the heart transmitted its tender caresses through the application of a simple coquettish stare, Miss Ryan was a delight for the servicemen removed from the tender embrace of a woman's love. With her delicate smile and sylph-like features, there was something about Sheila Ryan's appeal that seemed too graceful, perhaps supernatural, for this industrial world of ours. Although simply a girl from Kansas, as fair as the soothing sea breeze, Sheila's beauty seemed to embody something otherworldly, something too unique to be classified, perhaps of a dryadic origin, which captivated her admirers. When a pin-up of Sheila was published in the *Kennebec Journal*, which displayed the breathtaking beauty skipping along a beach, wearing a flattering bathing suit, a writer referred to her as "The Spirit of Something or Other," for her appeal had to have been of a spiritual nature. It was as if some higher power deposited Sheila on the seashore for mankind to marvel.

Sheila understood what her beauty meant, to both the soldiers and the ladies of America who longed to duplicate her nymph-like allurement. Many women would write their local newspapers and request some inside dope on how to become more beautiful, and many gals longed for that radiant glow that was Miss Ryan's. When Sheila was asked to pass along some beauty tips, she offered pointers that gals could employ in the water. She explained that baths were not just for cleansing, and that one temperature, the most comfortable, was not the only one that could be beneficial. She said, "Because there are two kinds of baths that yield beauty dividends far and above the obvious benefits that you expect from them, it's smart in these war-tense times to know what's what." She went on to explain that a hot bath would steam out deep-seated dirt while a bath filled with body temperature water would assist in relaxation, and enable a gal to get that much needed beauty sleep.

While Miss Ryan gave the occasional tip to the ladies she, as a pin-up girl, inspired the boys in Uncle Sam's fighting forces. The building of morale was a chief characteristic of cheesecake stills, but what uplifted the gents more was greeting a gal in person. A busy gal during the war years, Sheila worked steadily in motion pictures, volunteered for the Red Cross, offered beauty tips, and posed for pin-up pictures. But all these endeavors failed to reach the level of fulfillment that came from visiting wounded troops returned home from the war. With actress K.T. Stevens, Sheila toured military hospitals in southwestern United States for two weeks, as the two classy gals spent fourteen days cheering up men injured by the hazards of war. As one of the most beautiful pin-ups of World War II, Sheila Ryan's appeal was unquestioned but it was an appeal that went beyond the physical. A woman dedicated to her country and fellow countrymen, Sheila led the way early in the war — she showed Hollywood actresses that they could be useful during time of war, by assisting the Red Cross. She was pin-up girl, first aid instructor and actress, but most importantly, she was a remarkable woman who served as the ideal role model for America's girls.

# ★ GINNY SIMMS ★

Ginny Simms was the pin-up girl of the radio waves. One of the top songbirds in the world during World War II, Ginny's elegant voice endeared her to throngs of fans, but her tireless work for the war effort endeared her to many more. Miss Simms sang ballads for the servicemen, but more importantly she gave them a voice by inviting soldiers on her radio program *Johnny Presents*. Hosting a radio program designed specifically for the servicemen, Ginny became the idol of numerous fighting men scattered across the globe, who were able to keep tabs on the doings back home, almost exclusively from the lovely lips of Miss Simms. She, perhaps more so than any celebrity, was the symbol of home, for not only were her pin-up pictures plastered on walls overseas but the radio relayed her heavenly voice daily to the troops starved for a little Americana. Ginny was able to satiate the yearning the boys had for an American gal's voice, and due to her dedication to the servicemen, few celebrities were as highly thought of as Ginny Simms.

As a young girl, Virginia Simms was trained on the piano, but it was her voice that escorted her to stardom. Big-band leader Kay Kyser discovered Ginny and brought her into the fold of his little orchestra. By serving as the lead voice of the Kay Kyser Band, Ginny Simms established herself as a ranking star among the leading songstresses in America. In the years directly before the war, Kay Kyser was one of the top big band leaders in the nation and displayed his talents in various mediums — including film. Ginny appeared in a handful of motion pictures that served as Kay Kyser vehicles, but just before the outset of the war, Ginny decided to strike out on her own. An instant hit as a solo vocalist, Ginny became one of the top recording stars of the early 1940s, which she parlayed into her own radio program. American radio audiences could tune in to Miss Simms on her program, as well as hear her voice crooning tunes from time to time.

When the war broke out, Ginny was quick to use her position as a leading radio personality to help in the war effort. She developed the program *Johnny Presents* which was designed for the entertainment of servicemen. On the program, Ginny would typically invite soldiers to engage in patriotic repartee with her, all for the amusement of the gents in the armed forces. But the show wasn't all playful whimsy, for Ginny would occasionally interview a wounded veteran on her program. On one of her earliest programs, Ginny invited a Greek soldier on air who was one of just 27 survivors of the once 1,200 member Greek Royal Air

Force. Ginny helped the man tell his heroic, tragic tale by relaying his words via the airwaves, but she kept the man's identity secret for he feared that his family members, held as prisoners of war, would be executed after hearing his story.

Americans knew that Ginny was devoted to the men in the armed forces and sometimes made requests of her in order to be reunited with their loved ones. Miss Simms would do everything in her power to assist those persons who had loved ones injured in battlefields, and when she received a letter from a wounded Marine's fiancée, who desperately wanted to hear her loved one's voice, Ginny located the Marine at his military hospital and used her radio program as a way to reconnect the troop with his worried gal. The Marine in question, Edward J. Stanton, was invited on Ginny's radio program so that Stanton's future bride and distraught mother could finally hear his voice. Stanton was severely wounded in battle at Guadalcanal and his family had not the wherewithal to visit him, until Ginny stepped in and allowed the Marine a chance to tell his family he was safe and recuperating. Due to this selfless action, Ginny was named an honorary sergeant in the United States Marine Corps. For her patriotic actions, Ginny was honored with Kay Kyser and legendary actor Lionel Barrymore as the three civilians who had done the most to boost morale among the boys overseas via the radio.

Ginny's work in the medium of radio during the war was the purpose for her status as a top-flight pin-up girl. The pretty dark-haired songbird was noted for the soft, lilting love ballads she would sing the servicemen. The gents in the Armed Forces showed their appreciation by making her one of the more heavily pinned-up pin-up girls of the war era. While stationed overseas with few avenues of entertainment, the boys relied heavily on the radio, and Miss Simms was the voice most responsible for delivering those tender caresses from back home. She was not yet an actress and was rarely seen in theaters, and as a radio transmits the voice and not images, her likeness was captured almost exclusively on her album covers and publicity material. But the lovely singer possessed a countenance that radiated goodwill, and those men in the armed forces, who were exposed daily to horrors, used her pin-up pictures as a method to capture fairness and keep it secure. When Ginny invited Major Sanford Greenwald on her program, he informed her just how popular she was as a pin-up girl among the fighting men stationed overseas. The Major said, "I've seen your pictures pinned up in tents all over North Africa, but there are a lot of new tents now, over in Sicily, and I'm sure you're going to have requests for a lot more."

By 1944, Ginny had invited over 500 combat veterans on *Johnny Presents* as a way for the heroes to tell their stories. Her popularity was clearly at its apex. Ginny was said to be the first celebrity to have a Flying Fortress named in her honor. Given her burgeoning stardom, Ginny worked in other show business mediums she had neglected before. She tried her hand at acting, starring with Abbott and Costello in one of their better pictures, *Hit the Ice*. When a soldier named Daniel Moadush won a war bond contest by selling over $200,000 worth of bonds, he asked Ginny to give him a tour of Hollywood as a reward for winning the contest. Ginny escorted the sergeant around Tinseltown. She took him on her radio show and introduced the sergeant to film stars Greer Garson, Walter Pidgeon, and Lana Turner on their film sets. Ginny was named the official pin-up girl of the Potter Battery Boys, a defense battalion stationed overseas in the hostile South Pacific. Wherever one turned during the war years, there was certain to be a reference to Ginny Simms.

When the war was in its final stages, many celebrities went about their work in typical prewar fashion. They had done their bit for the war effort and returned to life as usual in Hollywood, but such a transition back to normalcy wasn't the route for Ginny Simms. Her career had reached its height during the war years, thanks in large part to her devotion to the servicemen, and when the bombs were silent, Ginny refused to bottle up her appreciation for the boys in the Armed Forces. Given that the men in the armed forces boosted her career, Ginny felt a sense of duty to the returning servicemen who saw to her rise as a celebrity. Always the selfless patriot, Ginny founded an organization titled "Lest We Forget," that provided entertainment for hospitalized servicemen. Even after the exit of the battlefields, Ginny Simms remained devoted to the men in the armed forces. She was, to many servicemen overseas, the voice of home during the war, and she retained that status after the dust of battle had cleared.

## ★ PENNY SINGLETON ★

There are some actors who excel in a certain role that their mastery of a given character becomes a typecast. In more recent years, Jason Alexander, who performed in the famous sitcom *Seinfeld*, so mastered the role of excitable sad-sack George Costanza, that he developed a typecast in which roles of emotional losers were sent his direction. Typecasts can be flattering, for your skill as a thespian is not questioned in a certain avenue, but many actors prefer to open other avenues. Many prefer to have avenues unimpeded by the stigma of excelling in one role and one role alone. Penny Singleton, the pert blonde of motion picture fame, suffered the same fate as Mister Alexander, for she garnered distinction in the comedy genre with the title role in the cartoon-strip-turned-film-series *Blondie*. Miss Singleton would star in close to thirty installments of the long-running comic strip, mastering the role of the good-intentioned, empty-headed blonde housewife that was the strip's central character.

*Penny Singleton.* COURTESY OF MOVIEMARKET.COM

Born to be an entertainer, Penny Singleton — who adopted the stage name due to her ample collection of copper one-cent pieces — entertained as a child in plays before she established herself in the motion picture industry. Originally a brunette, Penny bleached her tresses for the role of Blondie and retained the light-haired look throughout her career. She first appeared as Blondie before the war in 1938 and made her final Blondie Bumstead representation in 1950. So expert at portraying the simple-minded blonde housewife was Penny, that she developed a reputation among filmgoers as being equal to Mrs. Bumstead in real life. But nothing could have been further from the truth. An intelligent woman and entrepreneur, Penny's onscreen persona was in stark contrast to her personal life. Scribe Bob Thomas once penned, "Although they are commonly identified together, Penny Singleton certainly is not as dumb as Blondie. She is a shrewd businesswoman and operator of a couple of enterprises."

Penny employed her entrepreneurial spirit during the war years. Married to an officer in the Marine Corps, Penny saw firsthand the state of disrepair that military uniforms are want to possess when troops leave the training field. With numerous obstacles, a soldier's uniform can get snagged on a foreign object, ripped and torn, and in need of mending, but training rarely left a soldier ample time to put the needle and thread to good use. So Penny took matters into her own hands and created what she called "The Sew and Sew Club," that altered and repaired uniforms for servicemen free of charge. To assist her in this endeavor, Penny enlisted the help of Hollywood personalities who took to the sewing machine in their off hours. The woman who Lois Leeds referred to as the "Number One American Blonde," Penny used her status as a film star to promote her side alterations endeavor, with hands lent by several of Hollywood's leadings female stars.

While Penny suffered from a film typecast, she could also be considered a typecast pin-up girl. Married to a captain in the Marine Corps, her husband's fellow jarheads adopted Penny was their official pin-up girl. Although Penny had pin-ups displayed in various camps, it was amongst the Marines where the bulk of Miss Singleton's cheesecake stills were found. During the war many actresses received a bevy of fan mail from servicemen and a great deal of Penny's war-era correspondence came from the pens of Marines. The Marines adored Penny and reassured her, in many of their fan letters, that they didn't accept the dumb blonde stigma that the role of Blondie presented her. One of her husband's Marine Corps chums visited their ranch near the close of the war, and Penny gave the combat veteran a tour of the hacienda on one of their tractors. Penny thought herself a skillful driver, but her methods of maneuvering a vehicle could be defined as reckless, and the Marine buddy of her husband's grew alarmed at the way in which Penny cut corners a tad too sharp. He told the fair-haired actress, "Lady, either let your husband drive this thing or let me off. I've been all over the South Pacific but I've never had an experience like this."

Penny Singleton was for the war effort and so was her onscreen persona Blondie Bumstead. In 1942, Penny starred in an installment of the comic strip that paid tribute to the servicemen, titled *Blondie For Victory*. In the film, Blondie did her bit for the war effort and brought women together in an effort to show their collective support by organizing "The Housewives of America" association. She and Arthur Lake, her onscreen partner who starred as Dagwood, were invited to the Douglas Aircraft Plant based at Long Beach, California, as a show of appreciation for their wartime support of the troops. The film duo christened a pair of C-47 transport carriers "Blondie" and "Dagwood." While Penny supported the troops with her nonprofit alterations business and the occasional pin-up picture, Blondie helped out by giving women tips on wartime lifestyle. Constantly in beauty magazines giving the inside dope on hair care, Penny's onscreen persona of Blondie had the radiant, honey-colored hair look that gals longed to have. A solid wartime role model, Penny and Blondie, the offscreen actress and her onscreen persona, helped ease the struggles of a world at war.

## ★ ALEXIS SMITH ★

Some women seem to be genetically engineered to serve as cheesecake models. In our modern times there are professionals, doctors by calling, who can alter the appearance of an individual through plastic surgery, thus transforming an average image into one worthy of pin-up status. Typically, these alterations are done to the face, figure, or both areas of interest, shaping what once was viewed as an imperfection into an asset. However, the main area of interest for a model who poses for leg art is, as one would imagine, gams. Wherein lies a conundrum for both the aspiring model and the sawbones, for to extend the legs is a task less simple than the accentuation of the bust of the truncation of the nose. One is either born with amazing legs or not, and Alexis Smith came with landing gear that made a dull room erupt in whistles upon the sight of her streamlined physique.

Leggy Alexis Smith was born north of the border, and given her maple leaf origin, she was a favorite pin-up girl of the Canadian military. But it wasn't just the friends from the cold north that adored Alexis. The actress, more so than most other women of her trade, exuded a level of sex appeal that ignited the very film that captured her likeness. She possessed an incendiary appearance, one that exploded with pulchritude, which earned her the nickname "The Dynamite Girl" upon her Hollywood arrival. Her studio milked her sexpot appearance and seemed to resign every seductress role that came down the pike for Miss Smith. But Alexis never was impressed with the "Dynamite Girl" handle her bosses bestowed upon her. Like most striking beauties, she knew she was beautiful and needed no catchy moniker to cement the notion. She wanted to be regarded foremost as an actress — whether the filmgoers thought of her as sexy was their own estimation.

When a young starlet first made her way to the studio-controlled Hollywood of the 1930s and 1940s, her management would often thrust her towards the newspaper gossip pages just so folks could read about their new rising star. It was a common practice of studios to arrange dates for their young female stars, or order them to haunt popular night spots for the sole purpose of public exposure, but such a setup wasn't to Alexis Smith's liking. She was an aspiring actress, not a social butterfly with an inclination to decadence and social shindigs. The studio arranged dates, and these night club mandates irked Alexis who wanted to act — not play Sally Socialite. Alexis wanted to hone her craft, to work with acting coaches so she might be better prepared for her screen roles. She said, "I always figured that a reputation for hard work around the studio would be worth a hundred 'how-do-you-dos' in a night club." She proved her point in 1943 when all her hard work paid off: she landed on the list of box office's "Top Ten Stars of Tomorrow." Although she was listed in the tenth and final spot, such notables as William Bendix (number 1), Anne Baxter, Van Johnson, Gene Kelly, and Gig Young finished ahead of her.

One of the most likable beauties in the film industry during time of war, Alexis didn't have that diva complex — a sour reputation around the industry as a vain dame who is nothing but crooked nails to work with. She was an amiable, dedicated actress who treated people respectfully and worked hard to become a solid actress. Despite her hard work, her studio, who had from day one viewed Alexis as little more than window-dressing, teamed her with self-absorbed playboy actor Errol Flynn in a handful of pictures. Although often found in lead female roles opposite the likes of Flynn, the movies were Errol Flynn vehicles and Miss Smith served as a pretty dish for the aesthetic appetite. Only on rare occasions was Alexis allowed to showcase her skill as an actress, for she was regarded as a pretty face and little more, until she proved she could act. Alexis had the proper temperament to become a legitimate actress. She was dedicated to becoming a quality thespian and refrained from many vice-like

*Alexis Smith.* COURTESY OF MOVIEMARKET.COM

endeavors in order to become the star she desired. Alexis claimed that her major vice was gnawing on green onions.

Alexis made an ideal role model for young women, even if her studio tried to promote the seductress image. A ravishing, level-headed beauty, her name was not often wrought with scandal like so many actresses of the time. Lauded by many in the motion picture industry for her dedication to her craft, Miss Smith channeled that dedication to the war effort. Regarded as one of Hollywood's most intoxicating beauties, Alexis was a common exhibit for the women's health and beauty writers of the day. A photograph of Alexis sporting an unusual coiffure circulated the nation's papers during the height of the war. The new style was dubbed a "victory hairdo" which twisted Alexis's tresses to give her hair the image that three letter Vs were interwoven in the coiffure. The hairstyle, although patriotic, was a tad abnormal and thankfully didn't catch on, despite her efforts. Aside from modeling unusual hairstyles, Alexis was also asked to offer beauty tips and she had an exercise for the eyes that she passed along to the ladies. In order to add sparkle to your eyes, Alexis suggested that a girl should "roll them around in their sockets 20 or 30 times without moving your head. Then close them for a minute, open and focus your vision on one corner of the room, then the other."

The exposure of Hollywood beauty tips was a primary assignment for pin-up girls, but their main duty was building morale among the troops. By posing for the boys in cheesecake positions, pin-up girls became the inspiration of fighting men stationed across the globe. At the outset of the war, cheesecake art was primarily leg art, and when it came to legs, Alexis Smith was in a class by herself. The bulk of her pin-up pictures focused on her legs, which were typically displayed as they plunged hypnotically from the base of a dress or negligee. Often found photographed in prone positions, Miss Smith's legs were crossed, bent, extended, and seductively positioned for the boys in uniform. A writer for the *Arizona Independent Republic* admired Alexis's gams, when he penned, "She posed for literally thousands of pictures and became the crown princess of leg art, the cheesecake queen par excellence." Although not distributed under an official ceremony, the stunning beauty was widely considered the leggiest lovely in Hollywood.

## ★ ANN SOTHERN ★

Ann Sothern sure knew how to make the soldiers fall in love with her. The self-deprecating type who never viewed herself as much of an actress, despite evidence to the contrary, Ann was a demure gal who cheered up the boys by modest displays of support at their installations. A common face on the military camp tour scene, Ann was also known to haunt the west coast canteens, which allowed her to meet and greet numerous gents in the armed forces. Always humble around the boys, Ann never strutted around like a tawdry, full-of-herself starlet, but met the fellows on the level. She never ditched glamour when she visited the boys, for that was what the boys wanted, but she refrained from acting the priggish star, which served the armed forces admirably. A favorite pin-up girl during the war, Miss Sothern was cherished by the fellows in the fighting forces for her accessibility. Easy to approach, Ann was photographed no end amongst the troops — a little slice of glamour amongst a congregation of camouflage-coated admirers.

A firmly established star by World War II, Ann Sothern, like fellow pin-up starlet Penny Singleton, was known primarily for her film alter-ego "Maisie." Ann made a number of Maisie movies in the late 1930s and 1940s, and American filmgoers couldn't get enough of Ann in her signature role. And like Penny Singleton's *Blondie*, Miss Sothern's Maisie helped out in the war effort too. Maisie took a job in a war plant, which

*Ann Sothern.*

was the plot of her outing titled *Swing Shift Maisie*. Hollywood was all-in for the troops during the war, as many films made during the early to mid-1940s were war themed. A number of Hollywood personalities went on war-bond tours and even starred in short war bond videos. Ann appeared as her film alter ego Maisie in a war-bond short to promote the sale of war bonds. Maisie was first introduced to audiences in 1939 and she lasted through the 1940s. There were rumors in the early 1950s that Ann was slated to star in a television series based on her famous character, but the show failed to materialize.

Part of Ann Sothern's wide-reaching charm was her every-woman personality. She may have traveled through this life with a pinch more pulchritude than your average gal, but Ann was just another easy-going lady, and in an industry noted for its larger-than-life characters and inflated egos, she made for quite the breath of fresh air. The outdoorsy type, the mirror and makeup weren't Ann's best friends — she preferred the fishing rod. Many a morn Ann could be spotted on the waters off the California coast — one of her favorite spots to engage in the piscatorial arts was nearby Catalina Island — casting her hook in the cool Pacific waters. She gained a level of fame outside the acting profession when she hooked a large fish near Catalina Island that weighed as much as a stout linebacker. Whenever she entertained friends or acquaintances at home, she was sure to steer them towards her den where she displayed a plaque she cherished as much as a typical actress might covet an Oscar. The plaque proclaimed that Ann caught the heaviest swordfish ever by a female, with the weight of the fish listed on the monument at 259 pounds.

When America entered the war effort, life was hectic for all persons, but none were more affected than the young men who were of draft age. Unlike later wars, many of America's young men volunteered for the armed forces — they didn't wait for Uncle Sam to call their draft number. When the men were mustered off to service, their civilian lives were put on hold for the duration. Ann understood the sacrifice they made and felt it her duty to assist those who had answered the call. A neighbor friend of hers was inducted into the military in 1942, and he looked for a safe place to keep some of his personal effects. Unable to locate a desired storage space, Ann informed the fellow that he could keep some of his belongings in her house. Due to her generous nature, Ann's house became cluttered, as she accepted to store her friend's piano in her sitting room right beside her own piano. Since the men were asked to make sacrifices for their country, Ann was inclined to sacrifice a little luxury for the fellows serving their country.

Ann underwent a nasty divorce proceeding at the outset of the war before she remarried actor Robert Sterling. Their honeymoon was short-lived, for Sterling had entered the armed forces and was sent to an airbase in Texas. Ann continued in Hollywood, where she made pictures and played hostess at the various west coast canteens, but when the chance to tour military bases arose, she was quick to secure her place on the bus. She had one modest demand — any woman in her place would have issued the same request — that their first stop on the tour would be the Texas base where her husband was stationed. She was able to reunite with her husband, who was attending flight school at the time of her visit, but her tour was designed for troop entertainment — not the entertainment of one troop — and Ann had to bid adieu to her beau. While engaged on the camp tour, Ann was a hit with the servicemen due to her approachability. Rather than josh about with the officers in their cushy quarters, Ann hung out with the enlisted in their themes hall, where she pitched back colas with the boys. A photograph of her in the mess hall, whipping up milk shakes for the boys at the Salt Lake Army Airbase, was printed in every leading newspaper in the nation. She was the star the boys kicked back malts with, and to show their appreciation, they made her a popular pin-up girl.

Many Hollywood personalities did their bit for the war effort, and they should be commended for their devotion to their country. Ann Sothern, when she worked on films, also made it a habit to learn something from her film roles that could assist others in that most trying of times. When she agreed to play a military nurse for a film role, Ann wanted to do the part justice and enrolled in a Red Cross first aid class. She studied nursing not just for the role she agreed to play but also to secure a useful trade during time of war. A glamour girl, all that glitz and appeal never went to her head, for she remained grounded, even into her elder years. Miss Sothern never viewed herself as much of an actress, but with a bevy of film credits to her name, she must have done something right for producers to keep hiring her and filmgoers to keep viewing her. Perhaps it was her every-woman image that kept her from realizing the depth of her skill as a thespian. Writer Hubbard Keavy once wrote about Ann, that "She doesn't speak of herself as a glamour girl with any feeling of high self-esteem or inflated ego. Just matter of factly, as another girl might say she is a nurse or a schoolteacher." It's easy to find fault in the person who boasts of their accomplishments, while people like Ann, who have many boast-worthy accomplishments but fail to trumpet them, are those to be admired most.

# ★ BARBARA STANWYCK ★

Should you happen upon a list of Hollywood's greatest actresses, whether concocted by a professional critic or a Johnny-come-lately, and Barbara Stanwyck rests neither in the first nor the second spot, then discard the register for its erroneous categorizing. Widely regarded as the ideal actress, for her exceptional screen presence and adaptability to any role, Miss Stanwyck was a powerful performer the likes of which are no longer seen in Hollywood. Whatever the role, good girl or bad, Barbara Stanwyck was more than convincing in the part, for she seemed to adopt the mental constitution of the characters she played and breathed life into a fictional entity with remarkable conviction. She mastered the cold-hearted murderess in *Double Indemnity*, the stout-hearted ranch woman in *The Furies*, and the iron-hearted matriarch in her television series *Big Valley*. A unique talent, Miss Stanwyck started in the film industry in the 1920s and remained in the wide-ranging medium of camera-captured show business until her death. A class act, both onscreen and off, Barbara Stanwyck's legend in Hollywood is firmly secured.

Barbara's childhood was met with tragedy and abandonment. When she was four years of age, her mother died in an accident, while her father, beset with grief and desirous of combating it alone, left Barbara and her siblings. Parentless, and dwelling in the uncompromising surroundings of Brooklyn, New York, young Miss Stanwyck (whose birth name was Ruby Stevens) was brought up by her eldest sister as an orphan. Raised not in the lap of luxury but within the thunder of a harsh reality, she sought to rid herself of any future storms, not by the hand of the feeble who answers the call of discontinuation but by the hand of the strong who desire to attain security through hard work. Young and beautiful, when Barbara came of age, she pursued a path towards show business, and trampled the pavement in search of employ as a model or dancer. She found work in both arenas but her true desire was to make it in motion pictures — a rather newborn medium when she was in her upper teens. She ventured out to California in the 1920s and landed her first film role in 1927. Her star rose quickly, for the radiant beauty captured the attention of filmgoers with her captivating looks and remarkable acting skill. During World War II, Barbara was listed as the highest earning actress in all of Hollywood.

Individuals in the film industry lauded Miss Stanwyck for her charm, for she was, unquestionably, an elite film star — perhaps the best female thespian the screen had ever displayed — but her constitution was one of remarkable grace. She conducted herself in a businesslike manner and was known to take her work very seriously, but to also show an even-tempered mindset when she worked. She demanded a great deal of herself and expected the same from others, but she was very agreeable to persons on set, and she treated individuals on equal footing. She earned the nickname "Queen" among professionals in the film industry due to her ladylike, almost aristocratic deportment. A woman of exceptional grace,

*Barbara Stanwyck.* COURTESY OF MOVIEMARKET.COM

Miss Stanwyck was neither the type to live life blithely nor work in like manner, but the dedicated type who conceived expectations for herself and desired to live up to the image of what she deemed ideal. With her sense of pride and dignity, the glamorous actress would certainly scoff at the t-shirt-and-jeans-clad girls who cavort about in modern times, absent of even an inkling of glamour. In 1942, Margaret McKay wrote of the self-respecting starlet: "Barbara Stanwyck is Hollywood's best tailored femme." McKay meant not to criticize Miss Stanwyck, for pride oftentimes has a negative connotation. Miss Stanwyck was not possessed of what the French call *amour-propre*, but she held herself with a keen sense of dignity.

"The Queen" was one of Hollywood's top stars during the outset of World War II. Miss Stanwyck had starred in a number of pictures throughout the 1930s and was, to many filmgoers, the premier actress of Tinseltown. With the war on, Barbara understood that her profession came second to the critical task of safeguarding the country. Although the assignment of protecting the country was an occupation for the service-men, civilians were expected to lend a hand in support. Many film stars entertained the troops at various camps or toured in war-bond drives. Filmmakers and actors had the important assignment of creating a realm of fantasy that Americans could enter to escape — if only for an hour and a half — the harsh realities of war. But a greater respect was earned by the actors when they visited troops or engaged themselves in an auxiliary position for the war effort. When Miss Stanwyck finished shooting a film early in the war effort, her studio set up a vacation for her, but Barbara refused the week of idleness and instead requested to be sent on a war-bond tour. She ventured to such locales as Vancouver where a kiss from her lips bought a $50,000 war bond. By willfully refusing vacation time, Barbara showed the American people just how patriotic folks in the film industry could be, and that the stereotypical Hollywood larger-than-life, selfish personality was uncouth during time of war.

When the pin-up girl craze erupted early in the war years, Miss Stanwyck saw it as an outlet for lovely women to show their dedication to the troops. Although regarded as a stately woman, unwilling to perform tasks beneath her, "The Queen" saw nothing demeaning in the engage-ment of posing for cheesecake pictures, and gladly donned the bathing suits to build morale among the men of the fighting forces. Barbara was photographed seated on beaches, perched on rock formations, and — in her most unique pin-up — positioned in the driver's seat of a steam roller. The streamlined actress donned a skimpy two-piece bathing suit and was asked to ascend a steam roller in the flattering nautical attire. She made for quite the display, combining pulchritude with the lassitude of occupational exertion, as if to claim that sexy women have a worth far greater than pleasing the optical faculties of men. With women entering the workforce like never before, the pin-up of Barbara guiding the heavy machinery made a statement that dames, even sharp-looking ones, could carry a bit of the burden.

During the war years, Barbara married the younger actor Robert Taylor, which helped to alleviate the pain of a volatile previous marriage. An up-and-coming actor in Hollywood, Taylor was also made of the patriotic stuff that comprised Miss Stanwyck's inner makeup, and he joined the Armed Forces. Taylor joined the officer's ranks in the Navy's Air Transport Command, leaving Barbara home with her son. The role of a military bride was a demoralizing one for Barbara who, with a history of abandonment, felt isolated and alone with Robert Taylor's absence. She tried to combat the loneliness by immersing herself in work, but it didn't seem to soothe that sense of futility that gripped her. What made her realize that her situation was not uncommon, and that her sense of loneliness paled in comparison to others, was a trip she made to a military hospital. After she toured the infirmary on a morale-building junket for the troops, the assignment also boosted the morale of Miss Stanwyck, who felt her current position was far more ideal than the men she had just visited. About her hospital visit and previous bout of despair, Barbara said, "When Bob left for the service, a great loneliness engulfed me. True, I had my son and my work, but a great void was there. I had only to visit the men in hospitals and hear their stories of longing for loved ones to make me forget my martyrdom."

The pin-up girl craze was not accepted by all, for critics asked individuals to adhere to their moral compass and question whether the tawdry display of the female form was demeaning. Many of the people who disapproved of cheesecake pictures found the entire enterprise of exhibiting scantily-clad girls lewd. They could not, however, disregard that the elements which reeked of debasement, debauchery, and decadence were saleable, and these critics viewed pin-up girl artwork as among the list of decadent things. What pin-up girl pictures asked of society was to analyze good taste, and to analyze whether or not these enticing photographs fell into the category of obscene items. Many felt they did, and they championed the removal of leg art everywhere, while the supporters, whose rank outnumbered the critics, saw not debasement in marveling the female form but an appreciation for the pleasure that their pleasing images instilled. In the arena of burlesque, where strippers before the war era would typically hand out photographs of themselves in limited threads, there was the germ of decadence. But, their calling was the stimulation of paying customers, eager to gaze at sights unseen, and not the morale-boosting that typified pin-up artwork. Barbara Stanwyck had a brief encounter with the world of burlesque during the war.

Miss Stanwyck agreed to play the female lead in a film titled *Ball of Fire*, which engaged the streamlined starlet in the role of a burlesque stripper. Her role was based on the real life exploits of burlesque star Betty Rowland, whose profession was detailed in the film produced by Samuel Goldwyn Inc. Goldwyn knew not what he was getting into — he funded the film based solely on the interest Americans had in burlesque — for the producer knew nothing whatsoever about the scene. When he took in a Betty Rowland act, just to satisfy his curiosity, he was appalled by her show and made alterations to the script. Betty Rowland was not pleased. When she saw the finished product, which displayed a conservative Barbara Stanwyck striptease, Betty was livid. She conceded that Stanwyck had the moves down, but that her striptease was not a "ball of fire," as the film proclaimed, but "a hunk of ice," because Barbara didn't even unhook her bra in the scene. Rowland felt that such a lukewarm striptease would give people a false impression of the burlesque industry — that it didn't deliver in the full showcasing of the female form — and opted to sue Goldwyn for $50,000. Whether or not the realm of burlesque is indeed lewd is a personal judgment, but Miss Stanwyck, the ever graceful and dignified Queen of Hollywood, simply simulated interest in burlesque while she delved wholeheartedly into the morale-building enterprise of pin-up art.

Barbara Stanwyck's signature role came during the war years when she redefined the film industry with her phenomenal portrayal of a devious dame in the classic *Double Indemnity*. Her role as a murder mastermind reshaped the scope of filmmaking, and numerous film noirs that came after the Billy Wilder epic boasted the cold, calculating femme fatale who Stanwyck mastered. But despite her ruthless onscreen persona, Barbara Stanwyck was the ideal doll offscreen, whose acquaintance with glamour was a connection never severed. A classic statesman, Barbara was devoted to her country and those fellows whose task it was to defend it. She was, before the war, first and foremost and actress, but when the war broke out she became a patriot above all else. Lois Leeds wrote, "Barbara Stanwyck is first an American woman! Then a glamorous, top-ranking screen star. She is an amazing example of energy. She winds up studio schedules with visits to servicemen in the hospitals. She carries on handwritten correspondence with a hundred servicemen." A class act in every way, Barbara

Stanwyck may be remembered today as one of the greatest female stars Hollywood has ever known, but her status among the Hollywood legends is a lesser distinction than the one she secured as a devoted patriot.

# ★ GENE TIERNEY ★

To many film historians who have poured over countless movies from the silent era to today, there has never been a lovelier woman captured on the silver screen than Gene Tierney. Cameras attained their reason for existence whenever their lenses were focused on Miss Tierney, for a beauty as unique as hers was meant to be honored for all time. She was not of the sexpot mold, nor was she typecast as a courtly beauty, because Gene's appeal did not reek of the baseness associated with a sexpot or the self-admiration of an aristocratic dame. Her beauty was more heavenly, something ethereal that seemed wholly out of place in this world of disorder and discord. She possessed an angelic beauty that captivated the screen — took attention from her fellow actors and the set pieces — and rendered all within close proximity to her as entities unseen. A timeless beauty never fades, even when the rays of modern beauty shine bright, for what is today's beauty, what is regarded as appealing at the current hour, is subject to the tides of social interpretation and can be swept away. But a beauty that is timeless moves not with the sudden rise and fall of popular taste, but remains fixed, to be cherished and admired always.

Born to a well-to-do family in New England, the lovely Miss Tierney grew up in the lap of luxury. The old cliché that the world is a stage was not ill-suited when applied to Gene, for the breathtaking brunette had the means to pursue her dreams. As a teenager, she traveled to Europe for finishing school, then returned home, and pursued a career in acting. Ever the daddy's-little-girl, Gene was the apple of her old man's eye, and when she was spotted by the famous film producer Darryl Zanuck, she and her father developed a partnership that consolidated her earnings. When Gene became a star, her newly found wealth was too tempting for her father, who had squandered the family fortune, and he then blew through Gene's rising wealth in short order. Miss Tierney's fairytale life began to crumble at that juncture. Unable to trust the man she had admired all her life, Gene sought to secure her own footing in this world and planned to create for herself the perfect family — the one she thought she had descended from. But as the Second World War approached, Gene, who pursued this dream of domestic bliss, had it ruptured by the sharp edges of reality.

Gene appeared in her first motion picture in 1940, a biopic on Jesse James's brother Frank. Her screen appeal was evident from the start. She didn't have to wallow for a few years in background roles — she began her career in Hollywood with credited spots in features. She became a star in 1941 due to her ravishing beauty and burgeoning film career. She had bit roles in films like *Hudson's Bay* and the classic comedy *Tobacco Road* as a barefoot country succubus, before she landed her first starring role in the film *Belle Starr*. Cast as the title character, the film is long forgotten but Gene's unquestioned appeal was cemented thanks to the film. After Miss Tierney wowed audiences with her remarkable work and sex appeal in *The Shanghai Gesture*, Gene was constantly referred to in newspapers as "The Most Beautiful Woman in Hollywood," a title aptly suited for the stunning actress. But right when Miss Tierney's star had been secured, America entered the global conflict and there were soon things more important to the average American than idle pursuits like film viewing. For Gene, the war made her take notice of the important things in life, and acting, although a passion, was not instrumental in her pursuit of happiness. She wanted the security of family and thought she found it with wardrobe consultant Oleg Cassini.

Oleg Cassini designed the lavish costumes that fit the streamlined Gene Tierney flawlessly in her film *Shanghai Gesture*. Gene married Oleg in 1941 when they were in the midst of rising film careers — Gene in front of the camera and Oleg behind it. Gene was quickly becoming a fan favorite, and in 1942 she claimed to receive on average 11,000 fan letters a month. Many of the letters — close to ninety percent — came from the pens of servicemen, who were left astounded by Gene's unearthly beauty. In order to satiate their desire for more Gene, because they couldn't view motion pictures on the rifle range or the training grounds, they asked for signed photographs, and Gene obliged. With a streamlined figure that looked flawless in any attire, the bathing suit pictures were a hit among the servicemen who devoured her cheesecake stills. She was a hit among the servicemen who pinned up her pin-up pictures anywhere they could secure a thumbtack.

In many newspapers, Miss Tierney was considered the top young female star in Hollywood in 1942. Clearly, the heavy stack of fan letters gave credence to the boast, but some individuals wanted to substantiate the appeal of actresses and developed polls to acquire a better grasp on the wants and desires of the average man. Bill Le Baron, a Hollywood executive, conducted his own personal survey among servicemen in 1942, to settle the dispute on the world's most famous pin-up girl. Le Baron polled nothing but servicemen, his questionnaires were sent to various camps, both stateside and overseas, and relayed his findings in the spring. Le Baron said, "In our camps in Iceland — Gene Tierney seems to be far and away the top favorite. But in general, almost any pretty girl is highly diverting to the boys in camp." A diversion in the form of Gene Tierney was one willingly accepted, but her presence played the muse's notes

*Gene Tierney.* COURTESY OF MOVIEMARKET.COM

for a bored soldier stationed in England. Gene received a letter from a flyer across the pond, who occupied his sleepless hours on guard duty by writing stage plays for her. Gene was flattered by the attention lavished her, but the brunette bombshell gave up her career in films when she and husband Cassini expected their first child.

Oleg Cassini, who was born in France but whose family was pushed out of their native land after World War I, became a US citizen prior to the war and showed his devotion to his new homeland by enlisting in the military. Sent to Fort Riley, Kansas, Gene said her goodbyes to Hollywood and followed Oleg to the Army base to engage in her most coveted role of wife and mother. The expectant mother was unlike other Army wives — her Hollywood background was uncommon among the ranks of stay-at-home military wives — and requests were constantly put forth to entertain gatherings and sign autographs. Eager to assist in the war effort — what little a pregnant woman could do to lend support, Gene was ready to perform — she agreed to appear for an autograph signing. After the signing, Gene became ill and was diagnosed with German measles — she contracted the disease from a female servicewoman who had eloped from her hospital quarantine in order to meet her favorite screen star. The fan's show of admiration had a lasting, negative impact on Miss Tierney, whose child suffered through Gene's bout with the disease and was born retarded. Devastated that her child was born handicapped, Gene's dream of building the perfect family seemed unattainable with a daughter whose many needs she could not handle on her own. The child had to be sent to a special hospital, which left Gene distraught, and served as the catalyst to the breakdowns she would have in later life. This troublesome chapter in her life led to her much publicized stints at mental institutions where she received electroshock therapy.

Gene returned to Hollywood in the middle of the war to occupy her time with work. To act was a way of removing herself from the despair that had gripped her initial trial of motherhood. If she hadn't firmly established herself as a ranking star in the film industry prior to her Fort Riley sojourn, she most certainly did afterwards. In 1944, Gene starred as the title character in the film noir classic *Laura*. One of the finest pictures ever made, Gene gives what is regarded as her finest performance as the troubled advertising executive thought murdered. Given the recent turmoil in her personal life, Gene exuded a new worldly, hard-bitten aura in the picture, discarding the bright-eyed nymph image she possessed before the war. She had been the ideal personage of Hebe, the goddess of youth and spring, but like the battle that raged around the globe, the gaiety of youthfulness had begun to mature, as naiveté was shucked for understanding. Miss Tierney was the perfect representation of the world's wartime change, adapting, as she did in her private life, from unforeseen distress.

Despite the stress in her private life, Gene was as popular as ever. Her beauty could not be ignored. She was named Hollywood's best dressed woman in 1945. Captivating as never before, Miss Tierney parlayed her star-making role in *Laura* into several covetable roles that required superior acting. Never had a lovelier woman been more scornful in film than Gene's exceptional portrayal of a woman warped by love in the classic *Leave Her to Heaven*. As gorgeous as she was in *Laura*, the boys who pinned up her bathing suit pictures on barracks walls got a gander of Gene in her nautical wear in live motion. Playing a selfish vixen not opposed to murder, Gene excels in one of the creepiest moments in film history when she allows her brother-in-law, a young man attempting to regain his leg strength after a crippling disease, to drown in a lake. She hesitates before she makes a valiant display of trying to save his life by peeling down to her form-fitting swimsuit and jumping in for the no-chance rescue. Due to her exceptional look in the film, columnist Hedda Hopper gushed about Gene, when she penned, "She is undoubtedly one of the best lens subjects in the industry today. She has graciousness and much personal charm, and a complexion of flawless beauty."

It was Gene's flawless beauty, which she exhibited in films and cheesecake pictures, that gals across America desired to emulate. Many girls copied the famous peek-a-boo hairdo of the stunning Veronica Lake, but the ladies wanted the angelic complexion, that goddess-like appeal, that radiated from the countenance of Miss Tierney. Many of the leading beauty tips writers of the day understood Gene's influence on beauty and sought out her advice. Gene stressed that beauty was not showy — that showiness often tended to gaudiness — saying, "Don't be conspicuous. Conspicuous makeup, color, line, detail and combinations violate the rules of good taste. The well-dressed woman looks just right for the occasion — blends into the moment." Another tip she gave the girls was to be weary of old, accepted beauty rules. The one she particularly abhorred was that hair shouldn't be washed too often. She said, "The trouble with most lackluster hair is that it doesn't get marched to the wash basin often enough and the shampoo isn't as thoroughgoing as it might be." Given her extraordinary physical appeal, girls took the tips of Gene and tossed the old rules of beauty to the ditch.

When the war came to a close, Gene was one of the top-ranking female stars in all of Hollywood. Although she possessed a beauty out of this world, she was a down-to-earth American girl who always wanted to lend a hand. When America cheered in their triumph over the Axis, Gene attended the Navy Day celebration in New York. The heavy-hearted actress, who viewed pictures of the ravaged regions of Europe she had studied at as a teenager, wanted to tour the old country and make films there to restore the damaged morale of the European people. Films of the war era held a higher meaning than just entertainment, and Gene desired to use the medium as a way to rebuild fallen morale. She did much to build morale during the war, acting in films, posing for cheesecake art, and making public appearances, but the loveliest girl who film ever knew, had trouble balancing her own morale. A mental breakdown came, followed by the administering of electroshock therapy. The gal who helped America through its most trying time suffered from trials that ravaged her delicate frame.

# ★ AUDREY TOTTER ★

To say that girls chase the bad boy is to recite an old cliché, but when it came to bad girls of film noir flicks of the 1940s and 1950s, every gent set them in their sights. No actress better personified the bad girl of gritty noir cinema than Audrey Totter. She was remarkable as a flighty heiress in *The Unsuspected*. She raised eyebrows with her cameo as a convertible driving floozy in *The Postman Always Rings Twice*. And she masterly portrayed the cold-hearted, manipulative, succubus in the terrific B noir *Tension*. So good was Audrey at being bad that when she landed a role as a good girl, such as her poignant performance as a boxer's devoted bride in *The Set-up*, she seemed extracted from her element and placed in the eye of the hurricane, removed from her typical surroundings of chaos and fury that swirl around the calmness of the storm's center. When once classified as a volatile, bad-girl character actress, like any typecast, it becomes difficult to shuck the label, for audiences expect their villains to be villainous and their heroes heroic, no matter the picture. But Audrey Totter was capable of playing the good girl — she just wore the bad girl role quite fittingly.

At the start of World War II, Audrey Totter was an unknown commodity in Hollywood. One of the many ladies who benefitted from the exposure of cheesecake stills, Audrey was catapulted into stardom at the end of the war due, in large part, to her posing for pin-up pictures. The fair-haired Miss Totter had aspirations of a career in show business, but to pay the bills she accepted odd jobs when they came. Prior to her Tinseltown discovery, Audrey was a door-to-door saleswoman who canvassed the streets hawking floor wax. She used the experience to her benefit. Audrey said, "I got inside every kind of home and I picked up a lot of new dialects that I thought would come in handy when I started to act." While plying the sales patter, Audrey would often get off-topic and discuss her desire to entertain a career in show business. Gals eager to bask in the spotlight of Hollywood's magnificent rays weren't too highly thought of by every American — which Miss Totter was quick to find out.

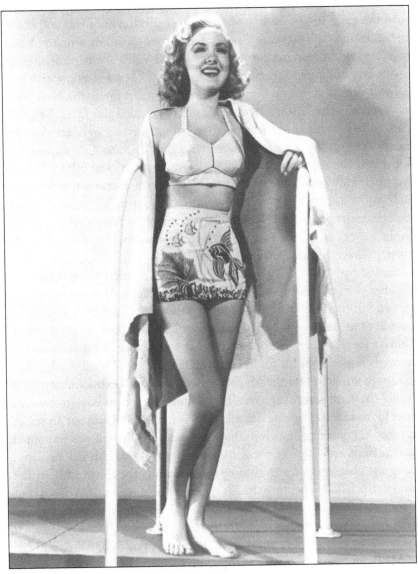

*Audrey Totter.*

An elderly female patron, who treated Audrey respectfully upon initial greeting, ushered the buxom aspiring actress out the door when Audrey let on how desirous she was of entering the film industry. She thought so little of actresses, given their tawdry lifestyle and newspaper scandals, that the old bird sent Audrey out the door quick. Miss Totter said of the incident, "The old gal told me I didn't look like a wicked woman, but she allowed as how you never can tell."

In the early 1940s, Audrey was able to shelve the floor wax and enter the vocation of playacting. A natural at comedy, Audrey employed her traveling saleswoman background to good use when she became a voice actress on radio programs. She became a squawk box sensation with her comedic turn as an Ingrid Bergman impersonator. A hit on the New York radio scene, Miss Totter's Bergman mimicry tickled the funny bone of many folks who inclined their ears to the sound box. Eager to act, Audrey also worked on the stage and toured with the *My Sister Eileen Company*. But it was the medium of radio programming that established Audrey, and when Hollywood talent scouts ventured to the east coast, they found Audrey just as amusing as the many folks she set to hysterics with her vocal dexterity on the east coast. However, when the Tinseltown birddogs set their eyes on Miss Totter, they felt that folks should get a load of her entire package and not just her voice.

Signed by MGM due to her dual capacity for entertaining audiences with her physical appeal as well as her acting talent, Audrey packed her bags and trotted out west during the war years. What attracted the MGM executives to Audrey may have been her radio work, but what secured a contract for the honey-haired doll was her assemblage. Built on the same assembly line responsible for the construction of Jane Russell, Audrey was an instant attraction for the MGM scouts given Jane's extraordinary fame during the early years of the war. They wanted their own buxom thespian since Howard Hughes, Jane Russell's manager, refused to loan out his starlet to other studios. And, much in the same way Jane Russell was promoted, was the manner Miss Totter was displayed by the boys at MGM. Escorted along the cheesecake route, Audrey received quite the showcasing by her studio, which dolled her up in bathing suits for publicity stills to be sent out to soldiers across the world for the sake of whistles. The bathing suit publicity campaign worked, and due to the fan letters received by the servicemen, the heads at MGM nicknamed their chesty new find "The Whiz Kid."

Many photographers who snapped off pictures for the sake of cheesecake purposes could get a little creative, but when it came to full-chested ladies like Audrey and Jane Russell, their focus was obvious. One Totter pin-up that set numerous temperatures to rise, showcased the sexy blonde sitting on the beach, not in the typical bathing suit attire of pin-up art but dressed in white shorts and a striped blouse. Given the pattern of the top, her bust, already stuffed to the gills, was accentuated further, as the studio bosses went the visual route to promote the film *The Sailor Takes a Wife*, which showcased the many talents of Miss Totter. The promo shot for the motion picture filled the pool of eagerness stored in the minds of men, who wanted to drain that pool by spying Audrey on the big screen. The studio heads at MGM also set-up a series of pin-up photographs for Audrey that depicted her as athletic. For a little leg art — a change of pace from the bust exhibiting that dominated the majority of her stills — Audrey was seated on a tennis court, clutching a racket, wearing a tiny pair of short pants. The bigwigs at MGM claimed that Audrey kept her enviable figure by playing two hours of tennis each day.

The promotional endeavor that MGM established for Audrey, attracted the attention of every male whose visual faculties functioned even moderately, but the build-up was initially a letdown, for she was cast in several films as a voiceover actress. Given her background as a radio personality, the sultry-voiced Miss Totter landed a few roles at the outset of her film career in which her voice was the lone print she left on the picture. Dismayed that their favorite pin-up girl was employed as an issuer of utterances and nothing more, soldiers felt that MGM had simply aroused their desire for Miss Totter with the cheesecake build-up, and failed to satisfy it by not displaying her voice as well as body on the big screen. MGM understood her capacity for attraction. They knew her voice could start any motor without employing a twist of the key. John Todd echoed this sentiment when he penned, "Audrey Totter has a voice that's been labeled out of this world. That's where it sends the customers when they hear her — and whistling like a chorus of rocket bombs, at that!" Be that as it may, the soldiers stationed in war zones, who had not a theater on the corner to visit, had her pin-up pictures in their possession and knew not the erotic tones of her feminine tongue. They wanted Audrey, voice and all.

Near the close of the war, Miss Totter was seen in a handful of features, but in minor roles. Her career didn't take off until after the war. During the latter stages of the war, she was mainly regarded as a pin-up girl with acting aspirations. Before she made good as an actress, she had to put in hours posing for publicity stills and cheesecake shots, while also honing her craft as an actress in minor roles. But it helped that Audrey's appearance was attention-getting. Once, when scribe John Todd was dining at a studio cafeteria with a group of actors, Audrey walked up to introduce herself. A collector of all things elephant — Audrey cluttered her abode with elephant trinkets and statues — the day of her introduction to Mr. Todd she wore a blouse that showcased a pair of the ponderous animals. Todd took notice of Audrey's design secondly, only after admiring her filled-out chassis. He wrote, "The front of the blouse was embroidered with two elephants facing each other with upraised trunks, and, believe us, the trunks were really upraised."

With her popularity on the rise, thanks to pin-up pictures, Audrey became an idol to many servicemen who cherished her cheesecake pictures while stationed overseas. A famous flyer of the day, Henry Myers — who gained notoriety for ferrying Roosevelt to Yalta and Eisenhower back to the States — was reported to be Totter-obsessed. He supposedly haunted the Hollywood Canteen, simply to meet Audrey and bestow upon her some treasures he had obtained during the war. Myers wanted to lavish his pin-up goddess with jewelry he acquired while serving in Paris. Myers certainly was carried with the tide of the pin-up craze, which began as a display for leg art, but thanks to bosomy ladies like Audrey Totter and Jane Russell, the focus on gams shifted to mams. Audrey, whose physical attributes were the recipient of envy from dames and praise from gents, became one of the top pin-up girls at the close of the war. A photograph printed of her in the *Salt Lake Tribune* echoed the change in course that pin-up pictures had taken, with a focus north of the equator rather than the stilts that carried a gal. She was referred to in the paper as "Postwar Pin-Up Girl # 1."

## ★ LANA TURNER ★

Lana Turner could expertly paint a person's face red, no matter the individual's sex, for the capacity to make men and women blush was unique to the bleach-blonde sexpot. Lana made the boys red with desire, an ardor almost impossible to contain, while the gals blushed due to the scandalous, tawdry lifestyle the starlet led. If Lana had to use a separate finger for each wedding band given her, then she would have had to employ both hands to adorn all the matrimonial rings she was offered. She had a rolodex full of lovers' numbers and a bedroom door that seemed set to rotate at all times. Although she had the shape and image guys craved, she was the untethered type, who couldn't resist batting her eyes at the wolf who issued an admiring whistle. Seven husbands she had and countless lovers. There may not have been a single parent who would have accepted Lana Turner as their daughter's role model, but the sultry starlet had all her chips in it for the boys. She loved the boys and the boys loved her. So admiring of Lana were the fellows in the armed forces that they made Lana, despite her constant ignominious exploits in the newspapers, one the nation's leading pin-up girls.

Born in Idaho but raised in California after the death of her father, the story goes that Lana was discovered by a talent scout while skipping

*Lana Turner.* COURTESY OF MOVIEMARKET.COM

school, sipping a cola when she should have been studying. The story has been questioned, but whether it is factual or not, it certainly fits with the image that Lana Turner painted for herself. In the late 1930s, Lana was spotted by a Hollywood birddog — imbibing a cola or not — and was signed to a contract based solely on her physical appeal. The sexy young woman had always desired a life in the film industry and was quick to apply ink to the contract placed before her. From the very outset of her career, Lana was Hollywood's number one "sweater girl." Around the time of World War II, the sweater look caught on and was adopted by many girls who felt the tops flattered their chests, and Lana Turner was the reigning queen of sweater girls. Her first film role she was propped up on a barstool at a dinner table, wearing a tight skirt with an even tighter sweater, which earned her the nickname around Hollywood as "The Sweater Girl." Another famous Turner nickname would be "The Nightclub Queen," which she developed early in the war effort.

Many studios, in order to promote a pretty young actress they had just signed, would often arrange dates for them so they could be seen out on the town with some Hollywood hunk. When reporters spotted the beefcake hand-in-handing with a fresh, unknown piece of cheesecake, the scribes would expend a bit of ink writing about the new stunner that so-and-so was seen with the previous night. Lana seemed made-to-order for this lifestyle. The nightclub scene suited Lana like water does a school of fish, which earned her yet another sultry nickname to go along with her sweater girl moniker. She loved the night scene, the playboy-hopping, the self-exhibiting that came with the club atmosphere, but she also wanted to be regarded as a legitimate actress and not just some light-haired floozy who batted her eyes into a film role. Lana said, "For a beginner, glamour is swell. It gets her more attention. But I've had the buildup for years. It's time the public knew that I could do something besides go to night clubs."

The boys in the military cared not whether Lana Turner could turn in a performance worthy of an Oscar nomination — their chief concern was that of pleasing the senses. The sexy actress certainly was pleasing on the eyes, which made her one of America's favorite pin-up girls. The boys loved their sweater girl despite all the tabloid trash written about her. Grateful for their devotion, Lana posed for a series of pin-up pictures for the boys, typically ensconcing herself in furs or sporting a lacy bit of nighttime wear that showcased plenty flesh. Due to her output of cheesecake stills, Alicia Hart referred to Lana as "the number one pin-up girl of servicemen all over the world." But in 1943, Lana, who had her many romances detailed in newspapers across the country, married and expected a child. The encroachment of motherhood, as one could imagine, put a halt on her pin-up production, and Lana handed the baton to other cheesecake favorites. When soldiers at Fort McClellan, Alabama voted for their "Bivouac Girl," Lana came in second to the girl best representative of the pin-up craze: Betty Grable.

# ★ MARTHA VICKERS ★

Born Martha MacVicar, the sultry actress who would become Martha Vickers was in the same lofty league when it came to leg art as the more famous Betty Grable and Ginger Rogers. Betty Grable's legs were photographed at a greater frequency than Mount Rushmore on a bustling day of summertime tourism, and Ginger kept her exceptional pins in top order by dancing the day away with Fred Astaire. Martha posed for numerous pin-up pictures that emphasized her enviable legs too, and many soldiers saw in her streamlined form the ideal female assemblage. Although not as well known today as Ginger and Betty, Martha Vickers was a premier pin-up girl. The leggy lass's most notable screen performance was as Lauren Bacall's sultry little sister in *The Big Sleep*. Miss Vickers displayed some tantalizing skin wearing the briefest of shorts in the noir classic. Martha's career never did takeoff like many critics had envisioned, but she left cinema one of its most sensual nymphet roles opposite the power couple of Bogart and Bacall in *The Big Sleep*.

At the time America entered the fighting during World War II, Martha had yet to make a name for herself in Hollywood. When she first stepped foot on Los Angeles soil, the sultry brunette retained her surname, and refused to adopt a more snappy stage moniker. While still a teenager, Martha landed her first acting gig, albeit a minor one, in the B horror flick *Frankenstein Meets the Wolf Man*. Other small roles came her way in 1943 in forgettable films like *Captive Wild Women* and *Hi'ya, Sailor*. In 1944 the roles remained minor. Martha became known more for her model work during the latter stages of the war than her turn as an actress. But it was in the arena of modeling that enabled her to gain secure footing in the film industry. When folks took notice of her plucky, youthful beauty, the girl who changed her last name to Vickers had suddenly become a hot commodity. Barracks walls were adorned with her sensuous, leggy photographs, which made a return to acting imminent.

Martha MacVicar redefined herself in 1944. After she toiled for a couple years with minor film roles, she shifted gears, adopted a new last name, and began posing for modeling purposes. Although the cheesecake pictures soldiers devoured were her bread and butter, Martha was better known to civilians for her modeling of non-nautical garments. She became one of America's most popular models late in the war effort by donning threads ladies could wear while living on frugal budgets. An entire page of the *Southtown Economist* displayed nothing but Miss Vickers modeling everything from travel suits to hourglass hats. She became famous

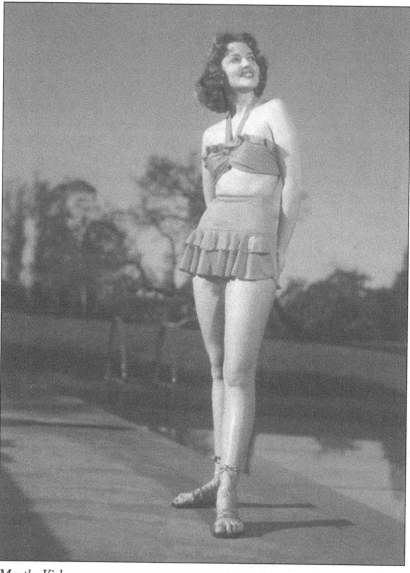

*Martha Vickers.* COURTESY OF MOVIEMARKET.COM

as a model when she and fellow stunner Pat Clark were engaged by the Army to model nurse's uniforms. The military was in dire need of nursing professionals, but many dames felt the uniforms were unflattering, so the Army employed Martha and Pat, two lovely ladies who could make a strategically sliced turnip sack look appealing on their frames, in order to reassure girls that nurse's uniforms too could look fetching. The ploy worked and gals joined the nursing corps.

Martha Vickers enjoyed a slight surge in popularity as a model and pin-up girl, but her fame as a cheesecake poser reached its fever pitch when Halloween hit. A series of alluring pin-up pictures of Martha circulated that showed her engaged in numerous witch-like activities — such as stewing a cauldron full of ol' crone's brew — dressed in witch's attire with a little pin-up twist added to the proceedings. Although donned in black threads and a large, pointy hat, Martha's leggings were rather revealing, which made her the most fetching broomstick driver who man had ever set eyes on. Those Halloween inspired pin-up pictures enabled Martha to make a return trip to the film industry. Warner Brothers signed Martha to a contract, then referred to their newest contract player not as a pin-up girl, but as a "nail-up girl," since no one would ever want to remove her cheesecake stills from the wall. Jack Warner, the head of the studio, went overboard with his praise of Martha, likening her to a more physically appealing version of screen superstar Bette Davis.

The Halloween pin-up pictures secured Martha a studio contract, but the lovely lady also posed for cheesecake pictures during other holidays. On July 4th, 1945, Martha was featured in numerous newspapers across the nation with an Independence Day themed pin-up picture. Per usual, Martha was attired in a leggy red, white, and blue costume that couldn't have fit Betty Grable any better. For the picture, Martha clasped the American flag in her delicate paws and waved it proudly. Things were beginning to look up for Martha, as they were for the nation in general in 1945, as she returned to the film industry with a freshly signed contract with Warner Brothers. The boys who pinned up — or nailed up — her cheesecake photos — returned home from the war to spy their sexy leg model on the big screen opposite Bogart and Bacall in the film noir classic *The Big Sleep*. When the boys got a load of Martha in motion, wearing that erotic little pair of shorts she sported so enticingly, they understood the glamour gal whose captured image they fawned over during time of war, would be a sturdy symbol of all the beauty they fought to protect.

# ★ FRANCES VORNE ★

Many of the top pin-up girls during World War II were celebrities who entertained patrons with playacting, singing, or dancing — sometimes all of the above combined. Soldiers secured racy photographs on their barracks walls of lovely ladies who they had viewed at the theater, watched on the big screen, or listened to on the radio. Other top pin-ups were burlesque queens like Ann Corio and Sherry Britton, while pretty models like Madelon Mason and Candy Jones achieved a level of stardom they never would have, had the pin-up girl craze not materialized. But there were other girls, more modest than the social butterflies that populated Hollywood and the stripteasers who tantalized audiences in the burlesque circuit. Frances Vorne, affectionately known as "The Shape," was such a gal. Her fifteen minutes of fame came during the war years. The stunning beauty never entertained a career in acting, and was, after the end of the war, all but forgotten to a populace who applauded their former war-era pin-up girls on the movie screen.

Frances was a New York model just starting out in the profession, and she was not among the stable of the famous Conover Girls who were all the rage during the war years. The Conover models all had snappy nicknames, like Dusty, Candy, and Chili, while Miss Vorne, with the mundane handle of Frances, seemed too old-fashioned for the flighty gals that made up the Conover ranks. Despite her down-to-earth mindset, Frances Vorne was regarded by many soldiers as the pin-up girl with the best assemblage, which earned her the nickname of "The Shape." It all started with a simple photo shoot under the direction of *Life* magazine's shutterbug Michael Levelle. The spread of Miss Vorne made both the lady posing for the pictures, as well as the gent taking them, hot commodities in 1944. Vorne quickly established herself as one of America's top ranking pin-up girls when fellows in the armed forces got their mitts on the famous mag.

With her overnight entry into stardom, Frances was pursued by Hollywood talent scouts. She was awarded a movie contract based solely on the spread she posed for in front of Levelle's lens. Both she and Levelle were handed film contracts, but many of Frances's friends felt that she wasn't suited for the bright lights of Hollywood. Not made of the tawdry stuff that comprised the constitutions of film starlets like Lana Turner and Ava Gardner, the lovely Miss Vorne was a simple girl of values, even if her physical attributes put the aforementioned film starlets to shame. Her friends described Frances as a modest gal who never imbibed alcohol, never haunted the night clubs, and had an aversion to staying out late. Given Hollywood's obsession for steering young gals to the popular night hangouts, where wolves whistle after taking a snort from the fire-water, it should come as no little shock that the conservative Miss Vorne did not make a name for herself in movies, despite the requisite awe-inspiring anatomy. She may not have shined on the silver screen, but few dolls shined brighter on the pin-up circuit.

Countless soldiers pinned up Frances's most famous pin-up still, which exhibited the breathtaking beauty with a silken garment wrapped around her fuselage. The garment was specially altered; a bathing suit modified from a captured Nazi's parachute. Not only was the pin-up Frances's personal favorite, but it was one of the most sought after pin-up photographs of the war years. What was once an instrument to slow down the descent of a Nazi paratrooper, became a body-hugging bathing suit that did much to alter the blood pressure of many soldiers. Due to her parachute bathing suit, and the enchanting manner in which her flawless body filled out the ensemble, Miss Vorne was so widely regarded by the men in service that she was listed in the *Reno Evening Gazette* as "Pin-up Girl of the Year" for 1944.

A morale-builder for millions of soldiers, Frances Vorne became one of the nation's leading swimsuit models. Her enviable figure was reproduced a hundred times over, displayed in flattering bathing suits, enticing girls to buy certain swimsuits, while coaxing admiring glances from the boys. Writer Dorothy Roe thought that designers had done all they could to bathing suits during the war years. They had become more revealing, could be purchased in one piece or two, and left little to the imagination. In an article Roe penned, she said, "They've gone about as far as they can go in the brevity of 1945 sun and surf fashions. Bare midriffs, strapless bras, brief shorts and sarongs are the order of the day." To drive home her point, Roe used a photograph of Frances modeling a one-piece bathing suit that had a strategically placed opening which showcased a bare Vorne midriff.

Small bathing suits didn't bother the boys in service. Frances, whether she modeled a Nazi parachute or donned a more traditional nautical wrap, was the inspiration soldiers needed to keep their morale healthy. When the troops decided they would have a little fun with their Japanese enemies, they decided to employ "The Shape" to stick one to the Japanese. Numerous pin-ups of Frances were requested. The soldiers' intent was to dump a series of Vorne pin-up pictures behind enemy lines, where the Japanese could snatch them up and marvel at an American girl's frame, with a little wisecrack written on the reverse side. Flyers in the Pacific Theater desired to write on each pin-up, "Eat your hearts out, you monkeys — here's what we are fighting for!" They could have picked no better pin-up girl than Frances Vorne to drive home that message.

## ★ CHILI WILLIAMS ★

Harry Conover, the eccentric founder of the famous Conover Modeling Agency, liked to corral pretty young dames and quarter them in his stable of pulchritudinous players. Once in his stable, Conover would take the alluring young lass and redefine her. He would take a girl like Marian Sorenson, a voluptuous fair-haired beauty from Minnesota, and reshape the dame into a breathing mannequin that exuded exceptional appeal. Young Marian, after she had been lassoed by the beauty birddog, was given the alias Chili Williams, for Conover felt the name was more fitting for a stunning poser than the common phonebook tag of Marian Sorenson. The sexy blonde became Chili Williams and was regarded as the premier model in America by several outlets during the war years. One of those outlets was the men in service. When a pin-up of her was displayed in their favorite magazine, *Yank*, wearing a polka dot bikini, Miss Williams became the idol of servicemen everywhere. From that moment on, Chili would often be referred to as "The Polka Dot Girl."

One of Harry Conover's favorite games was the bestowing of names. He wasn't content with christening his dog Rover or his cat Boots, for the naming of the family pet was one that children undertook. Conover preferred things on a grand scale, and to perform the mundane task of naming critters, which everyone was capable of doing, seemed beneath him, so he opted to rename people. As the founder of a modeling agency, numerous dames would enter his office door eager to earn a paycheck based principally on their physical charms. When these charms impressed Conover, he would offer the dame a contract and then proceed to toss aliases at her until one stuck. When Marian Sorenson entered his office, Conover wasted little time in offering the Minnesota man-eater a contract and a new name. Harry Conover said about renaming Marian, "My wife suggested the name Chili. I kept it in mind for some time before giving it to a model. Then this girl came in and she just seemed to have that spicy sparkle that made me think the name fitted her."

The stunning blonde became a sensation during the war years. Her face and figure were seen everywhere. In 1943, she set a record for the number of times a model graced the pages of *Life* magazine in a month: three times. But the height of her popularity did not come from a photo shoot for the famous magazine but for a simple polka dot bikini shot that was distributed in an issue of *Yank*, the soldier's magazine. The racy pin-up captured the attention of troops everywhere and, before long, walls across every military installation were covered with the polka-dot-clad Chili Williams. One writer quipped that the bikini Chili wore looked like a "bra and diaper swimsuit," but the boys found it quite fetching. She became known from that moment on as "The Polka Dot Girl." The picture not only made a star out of Chili but also Harry Krainin, the photographer who snapped the shot. Chili's signature attire became the polka dot from then after, but when she tried to buy the bikini off Krainin — who spent $1.87 on the suit — he refused to part with it, believing he could sell it for a more significant price as a piece of memorabilia.

Many pin-up girls, from Betty Grable to Gene Tierney, were listed in various papers as the nation's number one pin-up girl, but the title, whenever thrust upon one of the gals, was simply an idle boast. A writer for the *Massillon Evening Independent* reasoned that Chili was the nation's top pin-up girl, when Miss Williams told reporters that she had received over 40,000 requests for autographed pictures of her wearing a polka dot bikini by men in service in the short span of three months. Given the staggering amount of requests by the boys in the armed forces, the scribe reasoned that Chili had to be the undisputed pin-up queen. But the popularity came at a price. With so many requests for autographed, polka-dot-bikini-clad pin-ups, Chili calculated that it would take somewhere in the neighborhood of $2,000 in stamps and envelopes to honor the many inquiries. She had a quick remedy for the situation — since she couldn't afford to send out so many pictures, she would visit the troops in the Pacific Theater. Chili packed in haste and when she showed up on her first military grandstand, the boys wondered where her polka pot bikini was kept. She had forgotten to pack her signature polka dot attire and had to have some spotted threads shipped to her in order to appease the servicemen.

Although Chili Williams was not a movie star, she was a popular figure among the servicemen. Entertainer Jack Carson claimed that Miss Williams was just as popular among the men in the armed forces as film starlet Betty Grable. With her popularity on the rise, Chili was pulled in many directions, asked to sign autographs here and wave to troops there. Radio personality Milo Boulton saw the impression she made on the troops, and asked her to be a guest on his popular program *We, the People*, just so servicemen could hear her voice. The popular Conover cover girl was asked to visit Hollywood and entertain a career in pictures, a medium she dabbled in briefly, but all her roles were minor, decoration spots and had little influence on the pictures at all. The film *Having Wonderful Crime* cashed in on Chili's polka-dot popularity, as she appeared briefly in the film, credited as "Blonde in Polka Dots."

Given Chili's popularity among the nation's boys, girls traipsed down the same avenue they did when Veronica Lake made the whistles fill the air. Numerous gals mimicked Lake's famous peek-a-boo hairdo, and when Chili became a mammoth American sex symbol, girls began to mimic her hair. Easier to mirror than Lake's cascading tresses, Chili's popular style was to employ a headband, which she used to pull back her hair to highlight her flawless facial features. Veronica Lake had the peek-a-boo hairdo while the press coined Williams's headband approach "The Chaplet." Girls imagined that they could pull the Chili trick on the boys and thus receive a whistle or two meant for the Minnesota manne-quin. But there was more to it than just a unique way of wearing the hair. Chili had other qualities, enhanced to an alarming degree, which heated the temperature of many a man. Labeled a man-eater, Chili was once interviewed by scribe Erskine Johnson, who felt it his duty to mankind to relay the spicy lifestyle choices made by the blonde bomber. Erskine Johnson wrote, "She doesn't like clothes. 'I run around the house in as little as possible.' Sometimes, Chili admitted, she doesn't wear anything at all."

Chili Williams may have been a popular pin-up and an enticing dish to awestruck men everywhere, but she was regarded as a poor example for the young women of America. Wanton to an alarming degree, Chili was a common face in the Hollywood nightlife scene, cupiding about with numerous Hollywood bachelors, as well as men removed from the market. A huge scandal rocked Chili's career during the war years which led to a nasty divorce hearing between famous photographer Earl Moran and his wife. The nation's papers kept strict tabs on the Moran divorce proceedings, and when Mrs. Moran offered her reason for divorce, people began to look at Chili a little disapprovingly. Mrs. Moran claimed to have made an unannounced visit to her husband's studio, where she found Chili Williams in the raw and her husband stripped down to his under-shorts. Since her shutterbug husband didn't typically work with his pants off, Mrs. Moran opted to sever the matrimonial ties. The scandal didn't harm Chili much, for her status as a preferred pin-up girl did not waver, but it further gave credence to the many critics who felt celebrity wasn't befitting a lady. Lady or not, Chili Williams gave the servicemen what they wanted during time of war, and their Polka Dot Girl, despite her shortcomings, was one of the nation's leading builders of morale.

# ★ ESTHER WILLIAMS ★

Sometimes our dreams are dashed by influences beyond our control. While in high school, Esther Williams found her sanctuary in the swimming pool and spent so much time in the water that she developed into quite the competent swimmer. So good was Miss Williams in the act of natation that she was considered a favorite to qualify for the 1940 Olympics. However, with a world at war, the Olympics were not held that year and the stunning aquatic star was kept from competing on the world's greatest athletic stage. Four years later, still the battlefields sang with the report of rifle fire and mortars, thus restricting Esther from ever competing in the Olympics. Although she seemed destined to compete in the world's grandest showcase of athletic talent, Esther never did get the chance to perform in the Olympics, nevertheless, she earned a name for herself on the world's stage as a film starlet. Destiny had other designs for Esther Williams. Denied her chance in the epic competition, Esther instead achieved fame in the motion picture business.

As sharp as she was beautiful, young Esther Williams studied psychology in college, and she devoted hours to swimming. But when the Olympics was axed due to the evils of the Axis, the champion swimmer sought employment to occupy the time she should have been engaged in Olympic competition. The girl who would become known as "America's Mermaid," found employment in the water as the star of San Francisco's World's Fair Aquacade. Due in large part to her appeal as the lead of the Aquacade, Esther was given a studio contract and became a promising young star with her turn in the film *Andy Hardy's Double Life*, which starred war-era teen idol Mickey Rooney. The film did wonders for Esther's career. She found that her denial of a trial at the Olympic Games had not restricted her from achieving success.

Esther shined opposite Rooney in the campy *Andy Hardy* vehicle, but it was her work posing for photographs in bathing suits that truly elevated her career. Many of her swimsuit-clad stills became cheesecake fodder for the boys in service, and Esther quickly became a pin-up delight for the servicemen. A great many of Hollywood actresses went the cheesecake route during the war, posing for photographs as a way to build morale among the fighting men, but many of the dames felt uncomfortable posing in skimpy bathing suits. They had sported dresses of great elegance in films, but for the cheesecake stills soldiers needed, more skin was required, which forced shutterbugs to populate their models' wardrobes with nautical numbers. Posing in swimming wear was not a chore for Esther, whose second home was the swimming pool. Dressed in form-fitting bathing suits for leg art, Miss Williams's level of comfort in bathing suits made her the ideal bathing suit pin-up girl. It didn't hurt that the California cutie was also breathtaking. William C. Payette claimed Esther was a premier pin-up girl, when he wrote, "Miss Williams has about the nicest figure we can think of."

*Esther Williams.* COURTESY OF MOVIEMARKET.COM

If the *Andy Hardy* vehicle set her career up, then her role in *Bathing Beauty* secured her star status. It isn't too often that a film star has a genre created specifically for them, but that is what happened to Esther. Her acting was limited, but the lady was a phenomenal entertainer who could carry a tune, so her studio decided to erect a new genre designed for Miss Williams: the nautical musical. These films were lavish, with oodles of dough invested in order to secure the picture's spectacle status, which served as vehicles for Esther's swimming talent and remarkable physical appeal. So enchanting was Esther in *Bathing Beauty* that movie houses had to be on the alert for light-fingered gents. When the show hit the theaters, a young man made headlines when he stole five reels of *Bathing Beauty* from his local theater. At the hearing, the love struck gent told the judge, "Esther Williams is the most gorgeous creature I have ever seen. Since I could not have her, I made up my mind to get the film." The judge, not as impressed with the man's actions as the thief was with Esther's beauty, fined the fellow for his theft.

Around the time *Bathing Beauty* was filmed, the "Swim For Health" campaign got underway. To the heads responsible for the campaign, Esther Williams was a no-brainer to serve as the face and voice of the pitch. The lovely brunette swimming queen was the portrait of health with her physical, streamlined physique and buoyant radiance. So highly was her beauty regarded that many newspapers commonly referred to Miss Williams as "America's Dream Girl." Hollywood writer Bob Thomas most certainly agreed with the alias. When he visited a film set for the purpose of interviewing Esther, she agreed to give the scribe a swimming lesson. The pen-in-hand man had trouble focusing on both the lesson and his interview, saying, "If I had trouble concentrating, it might have been because of her vermillion, form-fitting bathing suit."

The allure that Esther Williams exuded stretched beyond the Knights of the Ink in Tinseltown and larcenists of film reels, and knitted its way to the boys in the armed forces. The enchanting mermaid was named the official pin-up girl of the 668th Tank Battalion, and had a bomber named after her with a life-sized portrait serving as nose art on the flying "Esther W." An article in the *Salt Lake Tribune* referred to Miss Williams as "Number One Pin-up Girl." They reasoned that since she graced the cover of more magazines than most models, the title was hers. Her appeal was of the obvious variety, for the ravishing brunette was typically photographed in her fuselage fitting swimsuits, which made for the ideal piece of cheese-cake soldiers liked to pin up. From the stateside bases to the makeshift quarters overseas, Esther Williams's bathing-suit-clad photographs were seen everywhere. Jimmie Fidler quipped, "A man doesn't need a telescope to recognize Esther Williams as a heavenly body." She was an ethereal beauty placed on earth but her inner beauty was just as inspiring.

All in for the boys, Esther Williams made her rounds touring bases where she uplifted hundreds of soldiers. It is easy for a lady to peacock about, to have the guys admire the way she fills out her get-up, but Esther Williams wasn't at all made of the show-'em-what-I've-got stuff. With a heart made of pure gold, Esther preferred visiting the wounded warriors to uplift the downtrodden esteem of courageous young men. She entertained for the USO aplenty, and she spent many hours dancing as hostess at the Hollywood Canteen, but nothing was more important than putting a smile on the face of a soldier who had returned home physically impaired. Once, Esther was informed that she was to take part in a swimming race against a group of soldiers, which she eagerly anticipated, but when the soldiers were wheeled to the pool by doctors and nurses, because their bodies had been ravaged during the war, Esther felt a sharp pain and didn't want to enter the water with these wounded warriors. But when the wounded troops entered the water and showed Esther how well they could still swim, their prodding for her to join them in a little race spurred her to enter the water. She was afraid that she would show the boys up by swimming circles around them, but that was all they wanted — to share the pool with the heavenly bathing beauty. She entered the water — the boys got their wish.

## ★ MARIE WILSON ★

Before there was Marilyn Monroe or Loni Anderson, Marie Wilson was Hollywood's number one buxom blonde character actress. Typically cast in dimwitted roles, Marie was instrumental in constructing the dumb-blonde stereotype. Best remembered today for her work as the well-intentioned yet constant muck-up in the *My Friend Irma* series, Miss Wilson set the mold for countless bosomy blonde retreads who further added to the unflattering stereotype. But Marie had an edge on the ditzy, fair-haired actresses who came after her: a little something called likability. The doe-eyed blonde exuded an innocent quality, flashing her bright, radiant eyes that didn't seem brushed with the tainted colors of a decadent society. Her Irma was always well-intentioned, but her best laid plans did nothing more than light the fuse on the stick of disaster. While there most certainly were blonde dames who behaved like Marie's screen persona, the real Marie Wilson wasn't one of them. Off camera she was an intelligent dame, and during the war years, a staunch supporter of the troops who entertained the fighting men in a way that only the bosomy, batty-eyed blonde could.

Marie began work in Hollywood before the war years — her film career was launched in the 1930s with a little help from an enchanted director. When she first entertained a career in acting, she caught the eye

*Marie Wilson. courtesy of moviemarket.com*

of director Nick Grinde who helped further her career. During the mid to late 1930s, Marie had established herself as a solid character actress in the comedy genre, but by the time America entered the war effort, Marie's film career had stalled. Miss Wilson spent more time in theater on west coast vaudeville-like skits around the time Pearl Harbor was bombed. She seemed best suited for stage work due to her exceptional improvisation abilities. Once, while working with funnyman Jack Carson, Marie played an assistant to Carson's magician role. The act required Carson to cut Marie in half, but there wasn't a good line written for Marie, so she improvised. After getting sawed in half, Marie gushed, "This is the first time I've ever lost my head over an actor."

Marie, with her voluptuous figure, was an early favorite as a pin-up girl for the men in service. She wasn't the bashful type. Open with her views and feelings on social concerns, Marie went to bat for cheesecake stills early in the war effort, and she tried to make the photographs a bit racier. In 1942, Marie was slated to star in a film that detailed the life of showgirls, but the picture was axed due to concerns on the censor's behalf. To save the film, Marie took it on the heel and toe to the Hollywood police commissioner's office. The censors put the kibosh on the film because they reasoned too many scantily clad dames cavorted about in the picture. Miss Wilson defended the film; Marie claimed that it was under production for enjoyment by the men in the armed forces. She felt that the vocation of a stripteaser was an art, and pleaded her case with the commissioner, saying, "It is an art. It even has a name: ecdysiast, from the Greek, meaning to peel or unfold." Not impressed with Marie's verbal defense, the bosomy blonde actress felt she could sway the commissioner by means more corporeal. She peeled down to her black lace lingerie ensemble in front of the commissioner, and asked the gent, "Our boys are fighting for American womanhood — why can't they see what they're fighting for?" Marie went prepared to the commissioner's office, toting a sign that read: "Home Morale Needs Ecdysiasts and They Got Me Covered."

Marie was the type of woman who knew where her assets lied. She was regarded as one of the chestiest actresses of her day, and she would often flaunt her admirable torso by wearing tight-fitting sweaters for cheesecake pictures. She never missed an opportunity for the boys to gush at her curves, whether that display of encomium came via the cheesecake route or in the flesh at her camp tours. A magnet for male whistles, the ample-chested actress was a cheesecake hit with her cleavage-baring pictures in swimwear or midnight attire. The sweaters were also a favorite of Marie's, and when she was signed on to star in the motion picture *You*

*Can't Ration Love*, the wardrobe department littered Marie's closet with sweaters. The bevy of contour displaying sweaters forced a critic to quip, "Sweater scenes of Marie Wilson in *You Can't Ration Love* will make men wish they could ration Marie." But Marie didn't want to be rationed, to have her portions allotted to admirers on a fixed basis, and desired to supply plenty Wilson charms by way of the cheesecake circuit.

On the Fourth of July, 1944, Marie posed for a cheesecake picture with the lovely Laraine Day. The two gals were outfitted in ensembles that represented the American flag, with a heavy dose of the red, white, and blue. Marie, far more full-figured than Miss Day, was displayed in a tight sweater that was striped in the three shades that comprised the Stars and Stripes. Pin-up pictures were commonly referred to as "leg art," but when it came to gals like Marie, the emphasis rested a little higher on the female assemblage. Hollywood had known Mae West, whose chest inspired soldiers to refer to their life preservers aboard their ships, as "Mae Wests," but the common portrait of the prewar actress was of the lithe-bodied mold, represented by such classic actresses as Katharine Hepburn and Ingrid Bergman. Marie, on the other hand, represented a healthier image of the American girl — one whose figure was filled out in the proper places. Scribe Virginia MacPherson wrote, "Lucky for Miss Wilson she was just a youngster during the flat-chested period of the '20s. In the sweater girl days of '44 she tops 'em all."

In the middle of the war, Marie agreed to tour with Ken Murray's "Blackouts," an outfit reminiscent of the old New York vaudeville scene. While under the tutelage of Murray, Miss Wilson entertained the boys at their various camps, showcasing, much to their delight, her physical charms. The striptease, as one can imagine, was a popular art amongst the soldiers, but the endeavor had a more conservative approach than the soldiers, sailors, and Marines are used to nowadays. While working with Murray's "Blackouts," Marie would give an impromptu striptease that tickled the boy's funny bone, as well as raised the blood pressure. During the skit, Murray, who served as emcee, would invite Marie on stage and proceed through a list of rationed goods that she would have to surrender for the war effort. All these rationed goods were articles of Marie's clothing. She had to surrender her shoes for Russian relief and when Murray told Marie that she had to ration her wool, she removed her skirt for use in Army uniforms. When Murray informed Marie that silk was needed to construct parachutes, she discarded her blouse. There the doe-eyed, undressed Miss Wilson would stand, on center stage wearing just a stitch here and there, to the thunderous applause of the men in the audience.

Ken Murray's "Blackouts" were a huge hit amongst the soldiers — the biggest reason for their success was Marie. During one of her most famous skits, Marie would stand on stage, dressed in the thinnest of slips, and jokingly bemoan her plight of receiving so little attention where she worked most. With a mirror as a prop on stage, Marie would gaze at her reflection while she applied makeup, but would lament the futile gesture of painting her face so men would notice her countenance. She would say, "I spend hours and hours putting on my makeup. It takes only a second to get into my clothes. But nobody ever looks at my face. I can't imagine why." As an encore, Marie would take the stage on the final skit, in a dress that barely succeeded in its task of concealing her breasts. She would take a few bows, with the dress struggling to contain her full chest, while the troops rewarded her with a steady dose of applause. After her final bow, Marie would return backstage, dress intact — but barely so — which would make Murray the emcee toss his cigar in disgust. He would playfully berate the audience, and yell, "Whyn'cha keep clappin'? One more bow woulda done it, you suckers!"

# NOTES

## Chapter 1: The Origin of the Pin-up Girl

Homer. *The Iliad.* Trans. Fagles, Robert. New York: Penguin Classics, 1998.

Euripides. *The Trojan Women and Other Plays.* Trans. Morwood, James. New York: Oxford U., 2009.

Tacitus. *Agricola and Germania.* Trans. Mattingly, Harold. New York: Penguin Classics, 2010.

Information on inventor Joseph Nicephore Niepce, noted for producing the first photographic image, was viewed at *inventors.about.com/od/pstartinventions/a/stilphotography.htm.* Written by Mary Bellis, the article details the history of photography with mention made to the famous inventor.

Author Reid Stewart Austin has published books on both Alberto Vargas and George Petty, the two most famous pin-up artists in America. A good biography on Vargas, which also displays some of his terrific work, is Austin, Reid S. *Alberto Vargas: Works From the Max Vargas Collection.* New York: Bulfinch, 2006.

Artist Raphael Kirchner was a painter whose work was typically reproduced in postcard format. A small biography of Kirchner can be found at *firstworldwar.com.*

The website arthistoryarchive.com gives a biographical sketch of pin-up artist Charles Dana Gibson.

At *arthistoryarchive.com/arthistory/pinupart,* the term "pin-up" was claimed to have been first used in 1941. The *Oxford English Dictionary* supports this claim.

C.E. Chidester's quote appeared in the *Massillon Evening Independent,* December 9, 1943.

For accounts by a vaudeville veteran, one should pick up the enjoyable read: Gilbert, Douglas. *American Vaudeville: Its Life and Times.* Mineola, NY: Dover, 1963.

Accounts on the life of former New York Giants skipper are best read from his autobiography, McGraw, John. *My Thirty Years in Baseball.* New York: Bison Books, 1995.

Wood Soanes's interview with Lynn Bari was printed in the *Oakland Tribune,* February 5, 1942.

DeMille/Keyes article in *Salt Lake Tribune,* January 25, 1942.

Veronica Lake, *Ogden Standard,* May 3, 1942.

Alexis Smith, *Arizona Independent Republic,* May 24, 1942.

Audrey Totter, *Middlesboro Daily News,* April 7, 1945.

The article on Constance Dowling, *Rhinelander Daily News*, July 2, 1943, gives an in-depth account of her start in show business and her fears regarding the reputation of showgirls.

Joan Caulfield, *The Independent Record*, November 2, 1945.

## Chapter 2: The Rise of the Pin-Up Girl

For a collection of nose art images, see Valant, Gary. *Vintage Aircraft Nose Art*. Minneapolis, Zenith Press, 2002.

The informative website imdb.com details the career of every actor and actress, from silent films to today's CGI extravaganzas. There, a person can read biographies of Hollywood personalities where, oftentimes, the military service of actors is listed.

Sheila Ryan and Myrna Loy's Red Cross work was detailed in *Uniontown Evening Standard*, May 5, 1942.

Much of Carole Landis's early support roles were detailed in an article printed in *The Racine Journal Times*, April 10, 1942.

One of the best attacks on censorship came from comedienne Marie Wilson. Her comical brush with the Hays Office was printed in *The Joplin Globe*, October 14, 1942.

Jane Russell, *Oakland Tribune*, September 6, 1942.

In her autobiography, Russell, Jane. *Jane Russell: An Autobiography*. New York: Franklin Watts Inc., 1985. She describes Howard Hughes's fight with censorship and how she felt about the media circus that surrounded *The Outlaw*, her first motion picture.

Marlene Dietrich, *UP*, August 11, 1942.

Dorothy Lamour, *Arizona Republic*, February 14, 1943.

Paulette Goddard, *Chester Times*, September 29, 1942.

Ginger Rogers, *Tucson Daily Citizen*, September 28, 1942. This article shows a humility from Miss Rogers — one quite admirable.

Greer Garson, *Charleston Daily Mail*, September 5, 1942.

Frances Gifford, *Fitchburg Sentinel*, November 18, 1942.

Dee Lowrance's article on the bevy of new starlets unveiled by Hollywood was printed in *Montana Standard*, August 16, 1942.

The story concerning Jinx Falkenburg and Evelyn Keyes picking tomatoes was printed by, *UP*, September 21, 1942.

The *Laredo Times*, May 9, 1943, displayed an article on the selfless actions of Joan Bennett — her furnishing of servicemen's canteens.

Carole Landis, *Racine Journal Times*, April 10, 1942.

Dorothy Kilgallen lauded Eve Whitney's wartime occupation in her column which appeared in *Mansfield News Journal*, February 12, 1942.

Vera Zorina, *Titusville Herald*, June 11, 1942.

Olivia De Havilland, *Winnipeg Free Press*, July 22, 1943.

Vivian Austin, *Havre Daily News*, August 10, 1945.

Michèle Morgan, *Zanesville Signal*, June 27, 1943.

The remarkable story of Ann Dvorak's admirable character was printed in the *Wisconsin State Journal*, August 6, 1943. One of the most opinionated and patriotic women in the annals of civilization, Miss Dvorak was a unique celebrity.

Dee Lowrance's tug-at-the-heart-strings article concerning Lucille Ball and Desi Arnaz was printed in *Arizona Independent Republic*, August 29, 1943.

Pin-ups like Betty Grable were often depicted on movie posters that were printed in newspapers, as advertisements took advantage of a starlet's popularity as a cheesecake girl. Movie posters would showcase the legs of Ginger Rogers, the heavenly leer of Gene Tierney and the ample bust of Jane Russell simply as enticement to see a motion picture.

Deanna Durbin, *Vidette-Messenger*, July 25, 1942.

With rationing in full swing, lavish productions were criticized by people who felt Hollywood should feel the constraints of rationing. Erskine Johnson wrote an article about this sentiment, which appeared in the *Joplin Herald*, February 18, 1944, after viewing for review the war nurse biopic *So Proudly We Hail*.

Jimmie Fidler's vehement criticism of Hollywood's "Down to Earth Movement" was printed in the *Salt Lake Tribune*, April 15, 1942.

Marie McDonald, *Montana Standard*, July 19, 1942.

Martha Holliday, *Joplin Globe*, February 17, 1945.

Lorraine Miller, *Ogden Standard*, October 9, 1944.

In order to combat envy of professional pin-up girls, writer E.V. Durling urged American girls to do what some British gals decided to do: send pin-up pictures of themselves to their serviceman. Durling's plea was printed in the *Delta Democrat-Times*, May 5, 1945.

Virginia Cruzon's "beautiful eyes" photograph was printed in the *Mexia Weekly-Herald*, October 1, 1943.

Marlene Dietrich's rebuttal on the value of legs was printed in the *Oakland Tribune*, February 22, 1942.

Hal McAlpin, *Wisconsin State Journal*, January 9, 1944.

Evelyn Keyes's breast-enhancing exercise was relayed through the papers courtesy women's beauty writer Alicia Hart. Hart's column appeared in the *Cumberland Evening Times*, September 9, 1943.

Evelyn Ankers, *Manitowoc Herald-Times*, February 17, 1945.

## Chapter 3: *The Role of the Pin-Up Girl*

The lamentations of a soldier from the Navajo tribe, Harry Yazzi, were published in the *Gallup Independent*, July 25, 1944. Homesick for Native American girls, Yazzi urged his tribe to select a pin-up girl and send him a photograph of her.

Pin-up portraits brought soldiers good luck, like Staff Sergeant Harry Blake, who painted a leggy pose of his wife on his leather jacket. He said the jacket brought him good fortune on his raids in the ETO.

Lynne Baggett, *Winnipeg Free Press*, March 8, 1944.

Jane Randolph, *Arizona Independent Republic*, July 19, 1942.

An article in the *Laredo Times*, May 9, 1943, went into detail describing the work Joan Bennett did for the troops. She took initiative and saw to the construction of military canteens without prompting from outside sources.

Deanna Durbin, *Zanesville Signal*, November 28, 1943.

Marjorie Woodworth, *Pampa News*, October 6, 1942.

Ida Lupino/Myrna Loy, *Massillon Evening Independent*, February 14, 1942.

The heroine of the many *Blondie* features, taken from the pages of the comic strips, Miss Penny Singleton, established her unique alterations business for troops, which was detailed in the *Soda Springs Sun*, August 19, 1943.

Marlene Dietrich, *Joplin Globe*, November 1, 1944.

Martha O'Driscoll, *The Big Spring Daily Herald*, April 14, 1944.

Rochelle Hudson was a guest host on the radio program *Noah Webster Says*. Her appearance on the program was mentioned in the *Lima News*, August 10, 1943.

Betty Rhodes, *Wisconsin State Journal*, August 8, 1944.

Ginny Simms, *Long Beach Independent*, January 5, 1943.

The touching story as to how Ginny Simms assisted a Marine battle veteran in reconnecting with his fiancée was printed in the *San Antonio Express*, May 4, 1943.

Lynne Carver, *Del Rio News-Herald*, September 8, 1943.

Jinx Falkenburg's work for the "Lips for Liberty" campaign was printed in nearly every newspaper of the day. An AP photograph showed Jinx prepping for a kiss with an over-eager professor who bought a war bond from the famous cover girl.

Barbara Stanwyck, *Ogden Standard*, November 1, 1942.

Cindy Garner, *Big Spring Daily Herald*, June 27, 1944.

The story as to how Gale Storm broke into motion pictures, and how she came about her unique stage name, was printed in the *Dunkirk Evening Observer*, October 22, 1945. Her bond rally held at Galveston, Texas was detailed in that city's paper, the *Galveston Daily News*, September 10, 1943.

The USO tour headlined by Ellen Drew, in which she opted to travel with war heroes rather than fellow Hollywood personalities, was written about in the *Syracuse Herald*, June 28, 1945.

Jeanne Crain, *Tipton Tribune*, July 29, 1944.

The deeds of actors during World War II can be found by visiting their respective pages at the website imdb.com.

Anne Baxter met with General Omar Bradley when her studio okayed her wish to promote her films at wounded soldier hospitals instead of theaters. The story that detailed this experience was printed in the *Winnipeg Free Press*, September 13, 1945.

Ingrid Bergman discusses, with sharp frankness, her extramarital affairs in her autobiography: Bergman, Ingrid. *My Story*. New York: Warner Books, 1993.

The scandalous affair that gained notoriety for Chili Williams was written about in the *Port Arthur News*, June 14, 1944.

Ann Sothern, *Salt Lake Tribune*, August 11, 1943.

Lenore Aubert, *Waterloo Daily Courier*, October 4, 1942

A terrific small biography of the eccentric Maria Montez was printed in the *Arizona Independent Republic*, August 16, 1942, that informed the public on how the Latin sexpot entered show business and her bizarre antics once there.

Jane Russell's quote, found in the *Tipton Tribune*, June 2, 1945.

Paulette Goddard, *Arizona Independent Republic*, June 21, 1942.

The quip about "pins" issued by a soldier from Monett, Missouri was printed in the *Massillon Evening Independent*, December 26, 1944.

An amusing yarn written by Robert Myers, who interviewed Evelyn Ankers at her Hollywood home, was printed in the *Manitowoc Herald-Times*, February 17, 1945. Miss Ankers informed Myers that she journeyed to the backyard nude every morning, before the sun rose, and rolled around in the fresh dew. This trick maintained her rosy complexion, and the information forced a few amusing quips from the male scribe.

Jane Randolph/Lois Leeds, *Charleston Gazette*, March 11, 1942.

Selene Mahri, *Maryville Daily Forum*, March 3, 1943.

Angela Greene, *Wisconsin State Journal*, September 10, 1944.

Newspapers across the country displayed pin-up pictures of Elaine Riley on her war department crusade to urge women to save their kitchen fats. The stunning brunette had a photograph printed in the *Ruston Daily Leader*, February 16, 1944, that showed her operating a large anti-aircraft gun.

Barbara Bates/Jean Trent, *Reno Evening Gazette*, July 11, 1945.

Penny Edwards, *Wisconsin State Journal*, April 12, 1945.

The unusual dress Dolores Moran modeled, which was made of paper, was described in the *Daily Inter Lake*, June 15, 1943. To promote the dress and make it appear economically appealing, the newspaper stated that it cost all of fifty cents and "can be thrown away when soiled."

Maris Wrixon, *Port Arthur News*, May 25, 1943.

The interview with screen actor Louis Hayward, husband of Ida Lupino, was printed in the *Titusville Herald*, March 12, 1945. A Marine during the war, Hayward was in a minority when he viewed pin-up art as destructive.

Joan Leslie, *Helena Independent*, August 17, 1943.

The vast work Evelyn Keyes performed for the Red Cross was detailed in the *Ogden Standard*, March 11, 1943.

Candy Jones, *Yank*, October 12, 1945.

Betty Hutton, *Salt Lake Tribune*, September 26, 1943.

Linda Darnell's wartime endeavors were listed in the *Uniontown Evening Standard*, May 5, 1942.

## Chapter 4: The Soldiers and the Pin-Up Girl.

The anti-pin-up rant espoused by Dorothy Dix was printed in the *Danville Bee*, May 1, 1945

Although girls felt they couldn't hold a candle to the pin-up girls when it came to acquiring the affections of servicemen, deployed scribe Ernie Pyle put their minds at ease. Among the fighting in Europe, Pyle wrote a column when the concept of pin-up art warping the minds of men was put forth by critics of the art. Pyle's words were printed in the *Montana Standard*, February 2, 1944.

The story of war hero Don Saucke, who was shot down in the ETO, and who corresponded with Joan Leslie while he convalesced in a military hospital, was printed in the *Titusville Herald*, September 28, 1945.

Joan Bennett, *Salt Lake Tribune*, July 22, 1942.

Anne Gwynne's unique Canteen endeavor — she would let soldiers take their very own pin-up photographs of her, striking a pose they desired — was told in the *Paris News*, April 17, 1944.

The story courtesy Harold Weislocher, the author's uncle, was told this writer upon a visit with the gentleman in the Spring of 2012.

Rita Hayworth, *Port Arthur News*, September 2, 1942.

Ginny Simms, *Oakland Tribune*, January 16, 1944.

Brenda Joyce, *Bismarck Tribune*, February 3, 1942.

Confusion was not uncommon given the soldier's desire to nickname their aircraft after starlets. The amusing tale about Marguerite Chapman and her stand-in was printed in the *Coshocton Tribune*, November 21, 1943.

Ann Miller, *Yank*, August 5, 1942.

A list of "Girl Who..." nicknames was published in an issue of the *Arizona Independent Republic*, April 30, 1944.

Dee Lowrance's *Leave Us Phrase It* article was issued by the Associated Press and was published in many leading papers.

Lynne Baggett, *Winnipeg Free Press*, March 8, 1944.

Daun Kennedy, *Huntingdon Daily News*, January 5, 1944.

Betty Rhodes, *Long Beach Independent*, October 7, 1943.

Clare Wagner/Marjorie Woodworth, *Winnipeg Free Press*, July 29, 1943.

While stationed in Italy, scribe Ernie Pyle witnessed plenty action of servicemen, to include their downtime diversions. When he visited a mechanic's headquarters, he was impressed with their pin-up collection and wrote an article about it. His article was printed in the *Montana Standard*, February 2, 1944.

Jinx Falkenburg, *Bradford Era*, May 3, 1944.

Elaine Shepard, *San Antonio Light*, July 8, 1942.

Veronica Lake, *Havre Daily News*, November 6, 1942.

Gene Tierney, *Salt Lake Tribune*, May 24, 1942.

Elyse Knox, *Delphos Daily Herald*, December 22, 1943.

Photographs of Anne Jeffreys wearing her "co-bra" were reprinted in many of the nation's leading newspapers. The former Powers Model used the gift she received from a soldier for inspiration to be employed in a cheesecake photo shoot.

Dee Lowrance's article on how Linda Darnell finally broke through in Hollywood was printed in the *Arizona Independent Republic*, October 31, 1943.

Wood Soanes/Yvonne De Carlo, *Oakland Tribune*, February 21, 1945.

Elyse Knox, *Arizona Independent Republic*, January 16, 1944.

The Book Drive that Evelyn Keyes diligently supported was detailed in the *Portsmouth Herald*, February 24, 1942. Her Purple Heart ceremony, as well as the extension she made upon it, were printed in the *Ogden Standard*, March 12, 1943.

The assignment Dolores Moran spearheaded — lifting the spirits of the most forlorn soldier — was discussed in length in an article that appeared in the soldier's hometown paper, the *Titusville Herald*, December 27, 1944.

Rita Hayworth, *Port Arthur News*, September 2, 1942.

Joan Blondell, *Kingsport News*, May 29, 1943.

Martha O'Driscoll, *Bakersfield Californian*, August 28, 1943.

Dale Evans's songs were discussed in print in an edition of the *Tucson Daily Citizen*, December 9, 1942, in which she dedicated the tune *I'm In Love With a Guy in the Sky* to airmen. The song she wrote specifically to entertain troops, *Won't You Marry Me, Mr. Laramie?* was discussed in the *Montana Standard*, May 24, 1942.

Gale Robbins, *Yank*, March 10, 1944.

Shirley Ross, *Lubbock Morning Avalanche*, December 14, 1943.

Ginny Simms, *Kingsport News,* August 8, 1943.

Rochelle Hudson, *Lima News*, August 10, 1943.

Ann Sheridan's quote about the USO was printed in an edition of the *San Antonio Light*, April 2, 1944. A top pin-up girl early in the war effort, Miss Sheridan's stock plummeted among the servicemen when she cancelled, without explanation, an overseas USO tour she had lined up. Media outlets criticized Ann for skirting her USO promise.

The comedic striptease act Joan Blondell performed was detailed in the *Kingsport News*, May 29, 1943, while Marie Wilson's act was described in amusing detail in the *Waterloo Daily Courier*, June 28, 1944.

The stories of Ellen Drew and Ann Dvorak are tales of great personal sacrifice the likes of which will never again come out of Hollywood. The life Ellen Drew led during the war was best depicted in an edition of the *Waterloo Daily Courier*, June 20, 1943. In detail, her wartime life was discussed as she traveled to England to be near her bomber pilot husband. Ann Dvorak, an American married to a British film executive, went to her husband's homeland and braved death every day. Erskine Johnson wrote an admiring article about Ann that was printed in the *Laredo Times*, October 31, 1943, which detailed her wartime experiences.

Carole Landis's experiences in the war were sensationalized by Hollywood, by the production of the motion picture *Four Jills in a Jeep*, but her story was one worthy of praise. In an edition of the *Kingsport Times*, March 23, 1943, her tour of Europe was discussed, while the *Arizona Independent Republic*, August 1, 1943, discussed in great detail her tour of northern Africa.

Jinx Falkenburg, *Neosho Daily Democrat*, December 18, 1944.

Candy Jones, *Yank*, October 12, 1945.

A Must have for any library, especially lovers of cinema, Marlene Dietrich's biography, Dietrich, Marlene. *Marlene*. New York: Avon Books, 1990, is a delight from start to finish. She devotes plenty pages to her experiences during the war, making this biography a terrific companion for military history buffs as well.

Martha O'Driscoll, *Arizona Independent Republic*, March 12, 1944.

Lois Collier, *Aiken Standard and Review*, July 18, 1945.

Esther Williams, *Salt Lake Tribune*, February 11, 1945.

Bonita Granville, *Piqua Daily Call*, March 7, 1944.

Ginny Simms's support of wounded soldiers endeavor, the "Lest We Forget" campaign, was described in an edition of the *Delphos Daily Herald*, May 31, 1944.

Rhonda Fleming, *Salt Lake Tribune*, December 28, 1945.

June Vincent, *Wisconsin State Journal*, December 13, 1943.

The interview with General Mark W. Clark's wife was printed in the *Danville Bee*, May 3, 1944.

Rochelle Hudson's false scoop was reported in the *Wisconsin State Journal*, October 10, 1945, but her hand was soon to be free shortly after the war when she filed for divorce from her former Navy officer husband. He was a carouser who held illicit parties while Miss Hudson was away working on films.

Rita Daigle, *Lowell Sun*, July 25, 1944.

The unusual "love insurance" policy that entangled film starlet Janet Blair was detailed in the *Montana Standard*, March 28, 1943.

Martha O'Driscoll, *Arizona Independent Republic*, March 12, 1944.

Evelyn Keyes, *Huntingdon Daily News*, August 28, 1945.

Barbara Stanwyck, *Charleston Gazette*, July 24, 1944.

Carole Landis's touching quote was listed in an edition of the *Arizona Independent Republic*, August 1, 1943.

## Chapter 5: The Height of the Pin-Up Girl

Many actresses detested the studio's practice of setting up photo shoots for the purpose of stocking their acting portfolio. This was a common practice in Hollywood, as actresses were photographed in various wardrobes, to include bathing suits and undergarments, which, it was reasoned, gave executives a better gauge on what genres they would look best in. If an actress looked sharp in a bathing suit, she could be assured of a role in which she would don nautical attire. Other actresses looked their best in period piece dresses and thus were used in films that told stories whose plot centered on older generations. Veronica Lake was one actress who despised the practice of these needless photo shoots — as well as many other studio designs that had become commonplace — and she wasn't afraid to voice her displeasure. An article printed in the *Ogden Standard*, May 3, 1942, relayed Miss Lake's disgust for her studio's long-held, sexist practices.

Lizabeth Scott, *NEA*, October 24, 1945.

Jeanne Crain, *Racine Journal*, April 20, 1942.

The unusual and amusing, in a way, story on the Hoboes of America, was printed in the *Troy Record*, May 12, 1945.

Brown & Bigelow, *Twin Falls Times News*, December 18, 1945.

Ramsay Ames, *Ogden Standard-Examiner*, February 12, 1945.

Russell, Jane. *Jane Russell: An Autobiography*. New York: Franklin Watts, 1985.

Susan Hayward, *Alton Evening Telegraph*, November 4, 1943.

Irene Manning, *Fitchburg Sentinel*, December 17, 1943.

Rita Hayworth, *Syracuse Herald Journal*, November 11, 1942.

The trials Lynn Bari had at reaching her level of film fame were discussed in a candid interview that was printed in the *Montana Standard*, May 10, 1942.

Conflicting reports were given as to how Yvonne De Carlo was able to gain her studio contract. It was written that a relative of hers, who served in the military, urged his unit chums to name her their official pin-up girl to draw attention to his cousin. Another scoop, printed in the *Salt Lake Tribune*, August 19, 1945, claimed that a photograph of her was sent into a contest to find the star of the motion picture *Salome* — a role in which Miss De Carlo won. The two stories have also meshed, as Roslaind Shaffer, in the *Salt Lake Tribune* article, claimed that her cousin's military outfit sent in the photograph of Yvonne to the contest.

Nan Wynn, *Waterloo Daily Courier*, February 16, 1943.

Audrey Totter, *Bakersfield Californian*, June 13, 1945.

Marilyn Maxwell, *Bradford Era*, October 12, 1943.

Linda Christian, *Wisconsin State Journal*, May 24, 1946.

The method Jane Nigh's studio took to setup her star was written about in an edition of the *Zanesville Recorder*, October 27, 1944. The story of her discovery was printed in the *San Antonio Light*, April 8, 1944.

Jane Randolph's background information took up an entire page in the *Arizona Independent Republic*, July 19, 1942.

An edition of the *San Antonio Light*, December 26, 1943, had a page devoted to Donna Reed, which displayed several pin-up photographs of her at work on the farm.

Ramsay Ames, *Laredo Times*, December 28, 1943.

Candy Jones, Conover model, *NEA*, March 28, 1942.

The Chili Williams scandal was covered in the nation's leading newspapers. Her story is not uncommon, but given her status as a top pin-up girl, the newspapers ate up the affair. Her affair with married photographer Earl Moran was detailed best in an edition of the *Port Arthur News*, June 14, 1944.

While Dusty Anderson's Marine captain husband was stationed in China, she served him divorce papers so she could marry Jean Negulesco — flamboyant European filmmaker. This scoop made headlines in an edition of the *Syracuse Herald-Journal*, September 29, 1945.

Lucille Bremer, *Titonka Topic*, September 7, 1944.

Lizabeth Scott, *Salt Lake Tribune*, August 26, 1945.

Pin-up artist Alberto Vargas waxed poetic about Hazel Brooks's legs, which enabled the beauty to land a studio contract. In an edition of the *Moberly Monitor*, November 3, 1942, Vargas described Hazel's legs by saying, "Her legs are lithesome, with fragile ankles, length, satin skin texture and enticing line."

Lorraine Miller, *Muscatine Journal*, August 4, 1944.

Gloria Nord, *Fitchburg Sentinel*, April 19, 1944.

Ann Corio, *Coshocton Tribune*, May 23, 1943.

Marie McDonald, *Laredo Times*, June 29, 1944.

Gloria Grahame, *Salamanca Republican Press*, November 1, 1944.

Adele Jergens, *INS*, September 13, 1944.

Marjorie Riordan, *Wisconsin State Journal*, November 11, 1943.

The trials Michèle Morgan experienced during the war years — trying to locate her family in war ravaged Europe — was told in an edition of the *Racine Journal Times*, February 27, 1943. Jimmie Fidler wrote about June Duprez's like struggles, which was printed in the *Uniontown Evening Standard*, March 9, 1942.

## *Chapter 6: The Effect of the Pin-Up Girl*

Dorothy Kilgallen, who kept strict tabs on the high-life of New York City during the war years, had a dream for pin-up art after the war. A rather eccentric woman with a proclivity for whimsy, Kilgallen's favorite pin-up girl was her chum Sherry Britton — striptease artist at the famous Leon & Eddie's Nightclub. Her dream was to erect a museum of World War II popular culture, which she translated through her paper, the *Lowell Sun*, March 21, 1945.

Elm, *Hutchinson News-Herald*, February 14, 1945.

Ruth Millett, *Statesville Daily Record*, February 20, 1945.

Mary Ann Hyde, *Montana Standard*, November 19, 1942.

Elyse Knox, *Waterloo Daily Courier*, May 4, 1944.

The glamorous Gene Tierney issued her warning about bad taste to beauty writer Hedda Hopper, whose article was printed in many leading papers, to include the *West Bend Journal*, May 24, 1945.

Mary Davis's casting of stones at Ginger Rogers for swinging her hips when she walked, as well as Westmore's words of support, were printed in the *Burlington Daily Times*, July 7, 1945.

Jinx Falkenburg, *Dunkirk Evening Observer*, May 11, 1945.

Ruth Millett, *Twin Falls News Times*, March 18, 1945.

Supporter of the "matchstick image," where feminine charms were pushed down and not exhibited, socialite Lilly Dache complained heartily about pin-up art's influence on fashion. Her voice was relayed via the *Indiana Evening Gazette*, October 2, 1945, which printed her words after her state-side return from Paris.

Audrey Totter, *Salt Lake Tribune*, April 1, 1945.

John Todd wrote a rather lengthy piece on actress Audrey Totter when she was just starting out in Hollywood. The enamored scribe wrote some about her personal life — her collection of elephant trinkets — which he used as an opening to make a quip about her healthy bust. Todd's smitten words were printed in the *Hammond Times*, October 10, 1945.

The ill-advised exercise Anne Baxter adopted to gain a few inches in height was covered in the *Big Spring Daily Herald*, November 8, 1943.

Evelyn Keyes/Alicia Hart, *Cumberland Evening Times*, September 9, 1943.

Veda Ann Borg, *Joplin Globe*, June 14, 1943.

The Divorce by Betty Grable story, *Oakland Tribune*, July 14, 1942.

Brown & Bigelow's calendar research was covered in an edition of the *Twin Falls Times News*, December 18, 1945.

Alice Stone Blackwell, *Lowell Sun*, September 15, 1943.

## Chapter 7: The Top Pin-Up Girls of World War II

Ramsay Ames, *Big Spring Daily Herald*, July 1, 1943; *Salt Lake* Tribune, December 12, 1943; *Laredo Times*, December 28, 1943; *Arizona Independent Republic*, January 16, 1944; *Salt Lake Tribune*, January 30, 1944; *London Stars and Stripes*, July 24, 1944; *Ogden Standard-Examiner*, February 12, 1945.

Evelyn Ankers, *Oakland Tribune*, April 29, 1942; *Charleston Daily Mail*, September 6, 1942; *Oakland Tribune*, November 8, 1942; *Salamanca Republican Press*, December 9, 1942; *Arizona Independent Republic*, March 19, 1944; *Manitowoc Herald-Times*, February 17, 1945.

Vivian Austin, imdb.com; *Wisconsin Rapids Daily Tribune*, June 30, 1943; *Hagerstown Daily Mail*, December 9, 1943; *Port Arthur News*, June 18, 1944; *Associated Press*, July 5, 1944; *Middletown Times Herald*, February 15, 1945; *Havre Daily News*, August 19, 1945.

Lucille Ball, *NEA*, August 8, 1943; *Arizona Independent Republic*, August 29, 1943; *Chester Times*, January 24, 1944; *Massillon Evening Independent*, February 5, 1945; *Salt Lake Tribune*, May 6, 1945.

Lynn Bari, imdb.com; *Oakland Tribune*, February 5, 1942; *Montana Standard*, May 10, 1942; *Hutchinson News-Herald*, August 30, 1942; *Nevada State Journal*, February 10, 1943.

Anne Baxter, *Wisconsin State Journal*, July 24, 1942; *Montana Standard*, July 26, 1942; *Waterloo Daily Courier*, August 2, 1943; *Big Spring Daily Herald*, November 8, 1943; *The Capital*, January 29, 1944; *Winnipeg Free Press*, September 13, 1945; *NEA*, September 20, 1945.

Joan Bennett, imdb.com; *Salt Lake Tribune*, July 22, 1942; *Laredo Times*, May 9, 1943; *Valley Morning Star*, December 16, 1944; *Havre Daily News*, December 14, 1945.

Ingrid Bergman, imdb.com; Bergman, Ingrid. *My Story*. New York: Warner Books, 1993; *Waterloo Daily Courier*, March 21, 1943; *Associated Press*, October 21, 1943; *Arizona Independent Republic*, April 30, 1944.

Janet Blair, *Oakland Tribune*, March 29, 1942; *Arizona Independent Republic*, June 30, 1942; *Montana Standard*, March 28, 1943; *Laredo Times*, April 15, 1943; *Altoona Mirror*, November 20, 1944; *Altoona Mirror*, December 1, 1944.

Joan Blondell, imdb.com; *Racine Journal Times*, October 9, 1942; *Kingsport News*, May 29, 1943.

Leslie Brooks, *Charleston Gazette*, January 17, 1943; *Fitchburg Sentinel*, May 19, 1943; *Salt Lake Tribune*, January 9, 1944; *Frederick News*, April 29, 1944; *Wisconsin State Journal*, May 5, 1944; *Long Beach Independent*, January 7, 1945.

Marguerite Chapman, *Salt Lake Tribune*, May 9, 1943; *Coshocton Tribune*, November 21, 1943; *Yank*, January 28, 1944; *Delta Democrat Times*, January 31, 1944; *Laredo Times*, April 26, 1945.

Ann Corio, *Port Arthur News*, March 23, 1943; *Coshocton Tribune*, May 23, 1943; *San Antonio Light*, June 6, 1943; *Lima News*, September 29, 1943; *Winnipeg Free Press*, March 24, 1944.

Jeanne Crain, *Racine Journal*, April 20, 1942; *Yank*, December 10, 1943; *Tipton Tribune*, July 29, 1944; *Arizona Independent Republic*, July 30, 1944; *Berkeley Daily Gazette*, January 1, 1945.

Linda Darnell, *Ogden Standard*, January 24, 1942; *Waterloo Daily Courier*, April 15, 1942; *Uniontown Evening Standard*, May 5, 1942; *Winnipeg Free Press*, November 20, 1942; *Big Spring Daily Herald*, December 13, 1942; *Yuma Daily Sun*, December 29, 1942; *Arizona Independent Republic*, October 31, 1943; *Oakland Tribune*, June 22, 1945; *The Morning Herald*, July 26, 1945; *Paris News*, November 9, 1945.

Yvonne De Carlo, *Dunkirk Evening Observer*, October 27, 1944; *Oakland Tribune*, February 21, 1945; *Associated Press*, May 13, 1945; *Massillon Evening Report*, June 9, 1945; *Salt Lake Tribune*, August 19, 1945; *Stars & Stripes London*, October 13, 1945.

Gloria De Haven, *Havre Daily News*, September 16, 1943; *Laredo Times*, July 30, 1944; *Joplin Globe*, September 22, 1944; *Massillon Evening Independent*, June 14, 1945; *Joplin Globe*, September 13, 1945.

Olivia De Havilland, *Salt Lake Tribune*, April 9, 1942; *Waterloo Daily Courier*, March 29, 1943; *Winnipeg Free Press*, July 22, 1943; *Ogden Standard*, September 6, 1943; *Cumberland Times*, November 7, 1943; *Paris News*, January 4, 1944; *Waterloo Daily Courier*, May 21, 1944; *Associated Press*, May 14, 1945.

Marlene Dietrich, Dietrich, Marlene. *Marlene*. New York: Avon Books, 1990; *Ogden Standard*, June 11, 1942; *Van Wert Times*, June 20, 1942; *Portsmouth Times*, June 25, 1942; *Mason City Globe*, March 11, 1943; *Nevada State Journal*, April 14, 1944; *Paris News*, June 12, 1944; *Joplin Globe*, November 1, 1944; *Joplin Globe*, January 30, 1945; *Waukesha Freeman*, May 14, 1945; *Twin Falls Telegram*, July 19, 1945.

Ellen Drew, *Charleston Gazette*, March 29, 1943; *Waterloo Daily Courier*, June 20, 1943; *Port Arthur News*, November 7, 1943; *Syracuse Herald*, June 28, 1945; *Wisconsin State Journal*, November 6, 1945.

Ann Dvorak, *Wisconsin State Journal*, August 6, 1943; *Benton Harbor News-Palladium*, October 14, 1943; *Laredo Times*, October 31, 1943; *Bradford Era*, July 24, 1944; *Winnipeg Free Press*, March 23, 1945; *Council Bluffs Nonpareil*, October 25, 1945.

Dale Evans, *Montana Standard*, May 24, 1942; *Tucson Daily Citizen*, December 9, 1942; *San Mateo Times*, August 23, 1943; *Abilene Reporter*, November 14, 1943; *Avalanche-Journal*, May 28, 1944.

Jinx Falkenburg, *Havre Daily News*, February 2, 1942; *Ogden Standard*, May 14, 1942; *High Point Enterprise*, September 13, 1942; *Lima News*, January 24, 1943; *Lowell Sun*, May 13, 1943; *Fitchburg Sentinel*, October 2, 1943; *Salt Lake Tribune*, October 26, 1943; *Lowell Sun*, November 12, 1943; *Bradford Era*, May 3, 1944; *Twin Falls Telegram*, June 22, 1944; *Neosho Daily Democrat*, December 18, 1944; *Dunkirk Evening Observer*, May 11, 1945; *Cumberland Evening Times*, August 6, 1945; *Winnipeg Free Press*, August 22, 1945.

Rhonda Fleming, *Hamilton Daily News*, September 25, 1943; *Lock Haven Express*, October 9, 1943; *Bradford Era*, December 25, 1943; *Waterloo Daily Courier*, February 6, 1944; *Tipton Tribune*, July 17, 1944; *Miami Daily News*, March 20, 1945; *Salt Lake Tribune*, December 28, 1945.

Ava Gardner, imdb.com; *Wisconsin State Journal*, June 29, 1943; *Wisconsin State Journal*, November 4, 1943.

Paulette Goddard, *Arizona Independent Republic*, June 21, 1942; *Chester Times*, September 29, 1942; *Alton Telegraph*, September 9, 1943; *Salt Lake Tribune*, October 31, 1943; *Joplin Herald*, February 18, 1944; *Burlington Daily Times*, April 12, 1944; *Waterloo Daily Courier*, May 14, 1944; *Port Arthur News*, August 10, 1944; *Salt Lake Tribune*, November 1, 1945.

Betty Grable, *Montana Standard*, May 24, 1942; *Uniontown Evening Standard*, June 27, 1942; *Oakland Tribune*, July 14, 1942; *Winnipeg Free Press*, August 25, 1942; *Zanesville Signal*, July 25, 1943; *Robesonian*, July 27, 1943; *Abilene Reporter*, September 5, 1943; *Long Beach Independent*, September 19, 1943; *Bradford Era*, May 3, 1944; *Oakland Tribune*, June 4, 1944; *Tipton Tribune*, December 19, 1945.

Jane Greer, *Lowell Sun*, August 20, 1943; *Waterloo Daily Courier*, April 24, 1944; *Winnipeg Free Press*, June 11, 1945; *Frederick Post*, June 27, 1945; *Nevada State Journal*, August 28, 1945.

Anne Gwynne, *Cumberland Evening Times*, January 8, 1942; *Wisconsin State Journal*, July 14, 1943; *Avalanche-Journal*, December 5, 1943; *Frederick News*, December 21, 1943; *Wisconsin State Journal*, January 10, 1944; *Paris News*, April 17, 1944; *Northwest Arkansas Times*, June 3, 1944; *Hayward Review*, July 26, 1945.

Rita Hayworth, imdb.com, *Hagerstown Daily Mail*, August 27, 1942; *Port Arthur News*, September 2, 1942; *Oak Park Oak Leaves*, September 17, 1942; *Syracuse Herald-Journal*, November 11, 1942; *Benton Harbor News-Palladium*, December 29, 1942.

Rochelle Hudson, ERBzine.com; *Lima News*, August 10, 1943; *Dunkirk Evening Observer*, August 4, 1944; *Wisconsin State Journal*, October 10, 1945; *Nevada State Journal*, November 2, 1945.

Candy Jones, *NEA*, March 28, 1942; *Tipton Tribune*, April 30, 1942; *Salt Lake Tribune*, June 9, 1944; *Lowell Sun*, March 12, 1945; *Nevada State Journal*, April 11, 1945; *Yank*, October 12, 1945.

Evelyn Keyes, imdb.com; *Salt Lake Tribune*, January 25, 1942; *Portsmouth Herald*, February 24, 1942; *Charleston Daily Mail*, August 9, 1942; *Ogden Standard*, March 11, 1943; *Fitchburg Sentinel*, May 24, 1943; *Cumberland Evening Times*, September 9, 1943; *Huntingdon Daily News*, August 28, 1945

Elyse Knox, *Lubbock Morning Avalanche*, March 3, 1943; *Port Arthur News*, May 14, 1943; *Salt Lake Tribune*, September 5, 1943; *Charleston Daily Mail*, September 16, 1943; *Lowell Sun*, November 13, 1943; *Delphos Daily Herald*, December 22, 1943; *Arizona Independent Republic*, January 16, 1944; *Waterloo Daily Courier*, May 4, 1944.

Veronica Lake, *Ogden Standard*, May 3, 1942; *Cumberland Times*, August 30, 1942; *Havre Daily News*, November 6, 1942; *NEA*, November 20, 1942; *London Stars & Stripes*, October 23, 1943; *San Antonio Light*, November 14, 1943.

Hedy Lamarr, inventions.org; *Wisconsin State Journal*, August 28, 1942; *Ludington Daily News*, September 1, 1942; *Ogden Standard*, September 21, 1942; *Manitowoc Herald-Times*, December 29, 1942; *Wisconsin State Journal*, August 6, 1943; *Salt Lake Tribune*, September 5, 1943; *Winnipeg Free Press*, August 25, 1944.

Dorothy Lamour, *Daily Kennebec Journal*, September 17, 1942; *Arizona Independent Republic*, February 14, 1943; *Valley Morning Star*, January 7, 1944; *Arizona Independent Republic*, April 30, 1944; *Charleston Gazette*, June 8, 1944.

Carole Landis, imdb.com; *Racine Journal Times*, April 10, 1942; *Arizona Independent Republic*, May 24, 1942; *Kingsport Times*, March 23, 1943; *Delta Democrat*, June 26, 1943; *Arizona Independent Republic*, August 1, 1943; *Lowell Sun*, July 28, 1944; *Wisconsin State Journal*, August 13, 1944.

Joan Leslie, *San Antonio Light*, August 1, 1943; *Helena Independent*, August 17, 1943; *Salt Lake Tribune*, June 24, 1945; *Titusville Herald*, September 28, 1945; *Port Arthur News*, October 7, 1945; *Port Arthur News*, December 2, 1945.

Marilyn Maxwell, *Salt Lake Tribune*, March 7, 1943; *Bradford Era*, October 12, 1943; *Salt Lake Tribune*, October 31, 1943; *Long Beach Independent*, December 21, 1943; *Statesville Daily Record*, June 5, 1945.

Marie McDonald, imdb.com; *Montana Standard*, July 19, 1942; *Arizona Independent Republic*, August 16, 1942; *Laredo Times*, June 29, 1944; *Valley Morning Star*, October 15, 1944; *Yank*, November 24, 1944; *Hagerstown Herald*, January 20, 1945; *Wisconsin State Journal*, May 31, 1945.

Ann Miller, *Big Spring Daily Herald*, April 19, 1942; *Yank*, August 5, 1942; *Salt Lake Tribune*, December 21, 1942; *Big Piney Examiner*, June 8, 1944; *Long Beach Independent*, January 3, 1945.

Dolores Moran, *Arizona Independent Republic*, November 15, 1942; *Annapolis Capital*, April 2, 1943; *Nevada State Journal*, May 15, 1943; *Charleston Gazette*, May 25, 1943; *Daily Inter Lake*, June 15, 1943; *Miami Daily News*, July 26, 1943; *Nevada State Journal*, November 7, 1943; *Carroll Times Herald*, March 28, 1944; *Titusville Herald*, December 27, 1944; *Wisconsin State Journal*, June 2, 1945.

Martha O'Driscoll, *Arizona Independent Republic*, June 21, 1942; *Cumberland Evening Times*, November 4, 1942; *Salt Lake Tribune*, August 8, 1943; *Bakersfield Californian*, August 28, 1943; *Arizona Independent Republic*, March 12, 1944; *Wisconsin State Journal*, March 29, 1944; *Big Spring Daily Herald*, April 14, 1944.

Donna Reed, imdb.com; *Salt Lake Tribune*, March 22, 1942; *San Antonio Light*, December 26, 1943; *Edwardsville Intelligencer*, February 17, 1944; *Port Arthur News*, May 13, 1945.

Ginger Rogers, *El Paso Herald*, September 25, 1942; *Tucson Daily Citizen*, September 28, 1942; *Wisconsin State Journal*, October 14, 1943; *Charleston Gazette*, January 7, 1944; *Salt Lake Tribune*, February 20, 1944; *Burlington Daily Times*, July 7, 1945.

Jane Russell, Russell, Jane. *Jane Russell: An Autobiography*. New York: Franklin Watts, Inc., 1985; *Ogden Standard*, July 13, 1942; *Montana Standard*, August 30, 1942; *Oakland Tribune*, September 6, 1942; *Yank*, July 2, 1943; *Nevada State Journal*, August 21, 1943; *Brownsville Herald*, September 7, 1943; *Winnipeg Free Press*, July 12, 1944; *Tipton Tribune*, June 2, 1945; *Joplin Globe*, June 6, 1945; *Reno Evening Gazette*, August 16, 1945.

Sheila Ryan, *Uniontown Evening Standard*, May 5, 1942; *Fitchburg Sentinel*, January 25, 1944; *Racine Journal Times*, April 3, 1944; *Kennebec Journal*, February 28, 1945; *Associated Press*, March 23, 1945; *San Mateo Times*, April 6, 1945.

Ginny Simms, *Long Beach Independent*, January 5, 1943; *San Antonio Express*, May 4, 1943; *Kingsport News*, August 8, 1943; *Long Beach Independent*, August 8, 1943; *Oakland Tribune*, January 16, 1944; *Salt Lake Tribune*, April 6, 1944; *Delphos Daily Herald*, May 31, 1944; *Mason City Globe*, December 23, 1944.

Penny Singleton, *Havre Daily News*, September 4, 1942; *Abilene Reporter News*, May 23, 1943; *Soda Springs Sun*, August 19, 1943; *Mason City Globe-Gazette*, May 14, 1944; *Coshocton Tribune*, December 17, 1944; *Titusville Herald*, October 31, 1945.

Alexis Smith, *Raleigh Register*, January 19, 1942; *Arizona Independent Republic*, May 24, 1942; *San Antonio Light*, August 2, 1942; *Oakland Tribune*, October 17, 1943; *Edwardsville Intelligencer*, December 2, 1943.

Ann Sothern, *Bradford Era*, February 20, 1942; *Phoenix Arizona Republic*, November 29, 1942; *Salt Lake Tribune*, August 11, 1943; *Pampa News*, May 9, 1944.

Barbara Stanwyck, imdb.com, *Ogden Standard*, January 29, 1942; *Albuquerque Journal*, February 22, 1942; *Oakland Tribune*, June 21, 1942; *Ogden Standard*, November 1, 1942; *Joplin Globe*, May 12, 1943; *Charleston Gazette*, July 24, 1944.

Gene Tierney, imdb.com; *Waterloo Daily Courier*, May 10, 1942; *Salt Lake Tribune*, May 24, 1942; *Port Arthur News*, June 6, 1943; *Waterloo Daily Courier*, March 19, 1944; *West Bend Journal*, May 24, 1945; *Waterloo Daily Courier*, June 10, 1945; *Wisconsin State Journal*, October 28, 1945.

Audrey Totter, *Salt Lake Tribune*, April 1, 1945; *Middlesboro Daily News*, April 17, 1945; *Port Arthur News*, May 13, 1945; *Bakersfield Californian*, June 15, 1945; *Uniontown Morning Herald*, July 6, 1945; *Hammond Times*, October 10, 1945; *Middletown Times Herald*, December 26, 1945.

Lana Turner, *Salt Lake Tribune*, April 15, 1942; *Edwardsville Intelligencer*, June 17, 1943; *Arizona Independent Republic*, July 2, 1943; *Port Arthur News*, October 29, 1944.

Martha Vickers, *Joplin Globe*, October 24, 1944; *Gettysburg Times*, January 31, 1945; *Yuma Daily Sun*, April 3, 1945; *Corsicana Daily Sun*, June 25, 1945; *Southern Economist*, October 28, 1945.

Frances Vorne, *Port Arthur News*, September 6, 1944; *The Capital*, October 9, 1944; *San Mateo Times*, December 12, 1944; *Fitchburg Sentinel*, January 2, 1945; *Reno Evening Gazette*, January 6, 1945.

Chili Williams, *Nevada State Journal*, December 8, 1943; *Waterloo Daily Courier*, December 13, 1943; *San Antonio Express*, December 19, 1943; *Wisconsin State Journal*, March 9, 1944; *Massillon Evening Independent*, April 25, 1944; *Laredo Times*, April 26, 1944; *Port Arthur News*, June 14, 1944; *Joplin Globe*, August 30, 1945.

Esther Williams, *Hammond Times*, December 21, 1942; *Winnipeg Free Press*, July 29, 1943; *Lubbock Morning Avalanche*, December 1, 1944; *Salt Lake Tribune*, February 11, 1945; *Beatrice Daily Sun*, April 27, 1945; *Elyria Chronicle-Telegram*, September 24, 1945,

Marie Wilson, *Joplin Globe*, October 14, 1942; *Joplin Globe*, August 17, 1943; *Joplin Globe*, December 16, 1943; *Waterloo Daily Courier*, June 28, 1944; *Charleston Gazette*, July 4, 1944.

# INDEX